Multi-Party Litigation

Law and Society Series
W. Wesley Pue, General Editor

The Law and Society Series explores law as a socially embedded phenomenon. It is premised on the understanding that the conventional division of law from society creates false dichotomies in thinking, scholarship, educational practice, and social life. Books in the series treat law and society as mutually constitutive and seek to bridge scholarship emerging from interdisciplinary engagement of law with disciplines such as politics, social theory, history, political economy, and gender studies.

A list of the titles in this series appears at the end of this book.

Wayne V. McIntosh and
Cynthia L. Cates

Multi-Party Litigation
The Strategic Context

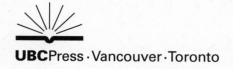

UBCPress · Vancouver · Toronto

15 14 13 12 11 10 09   5 4 3 2 1

Printed in Canada on ancient-forest-free paper (100 percent post-consumer recycled) that is processed chlorine- and acid-free, with vegetable-based inks.

Library and Archives Canada Cataloguing in Publication

Multi-party litigation : the strategic context / Wayne V. McIntosh and Cynthia L. Cates.

(Law and society, 1496-4953)
Includes bibliographical references and index.
ISBN 978-0-7748-1596-3

1. Actions and defenses. 2. Actions and defenses – Political aspects. I. Cates, Cynthia L., 1950- II. Title. III. Series: Law and society series (Vancouver, B.C.)

| K2243.M35 2009 | 347.053 | C2008-906493-3 |

Canadä

UBC Press gratefully acknowledges the financial support for our publishing program of the Government of Canada through the Book Publishing Industry Development Program (BPIDP) and the British Columbia Arts Council.

The authors also wish to acknowledge the support of the Department of Government and Politics at the University of Maryland.

UBC Press
The University of British Columbia
2029 West Mall
Vancouver, BC V6T 1Z2
604-822-5959 / Fax: 604-822-6083
www.ubcpress.ca

Contents

List of Illustrations / vi

Acknowledgments / vii

Introduction / 1

1 Theoretical, Historical, and Legal Underpinnings / 13

2 Mass Torts and Class Action: An Overview of the Contemporary American Landscape / 44

3 The Politics of Tobacco Litigation / 74

4 The Politics of Gun Litigation / 101

5 The Politics of Food Litigation / 123

6 International Developments in the Politics of Litigation / 151

7 Conclusions / 190

Notes / 204

General References / 234

Case References / 255

General Index / 266

Index of Cases / 274

Illustrations

Tables

2.1 State tort reform limitations, 1986-2004 / 65

5.1 Comparison of multi-party litigation characteristics in tobacco, gun, and food cases / 145

Appendices

2.1 Asbestos timeline / 72

3.1 Tobacco litigation timeline / 96

4.1 Gun litigation timeline / 119

5.1 Food litigation timeline / 147

Acknowledgments

We would like to take the opportunity to thank a number of people who helped in a variety of ways as we completed the long task of research and writing associated with this project. First, several outstanding graduate and undergraduate students at the University of Maryland devoted considerable time and effort to retrieving court opinions, accumulating background materials, and double-checking references. Jenny Rosloff, Elizabeth Flamm, Marlaine White, and Mike Evans were extremely helpful with these things and also contributed enthusiasm and ideas in the process. Richard Pacelle read the entire manuscript and offered extensive comments and suggestions that were quite useful to us in making final revisions. We also very much appreciate the outstanding index work done by DeAnna and Jeremy Millett. A number of colleagues offered useful and constructive criticism and suggestions along the way, including two anonymous reviewers, and our respective departmental colleagues have been very supportive throughout.

Multi-Party Litigation

Introduction

Litigation? Is it the most effective response to the sometimes malignant behaviours of corporations, governments, and other large institutions? Or is
litigation itself a cancer spreading through, and even beyond, the body pol-
itic? Is it an even battleground where David has a reasonable chance of defeating Goliath (Jacobson and White 2004)? Or is it more like the Roman
Coliseum where the lion nearly always wins (Galanter 1974)? Is it an effective
method for redressing injustices, punishing wrongdoers, and regulating in
the public interest (Banzhaf 2004)? Or are attempts to create social and political change through the courts merely pursuing a "hollow hope" (Rosenberg
1991)? On the one hand, we are reminded of small heroes battling behemoth
corporations – chemical technician Karen Silkwood (Rashke 2000), paralegal
Erin Brockovich (Grant 2002), and attorney Jan Schlichtmann taking on
Kerr-McGee, Pacific Gas and Electric, and W.R. Grace and Beatrice Foods,
respectively (Harr 1996). While, on the other hand, we shake our heads in
dismay over smokers, junk food addicts, and little old ladies who are ignor-
ant to the fact that coffee is, after all, *supposed* to be hot, frustrated as they
tie up courts and corporations in endless silly lawsuits.[1] In any event, this
public face of litigation – the entertainment – offers a very mixed message.

   This book is about the politics of lawsuits – a form of politics that has become more sophisticated and hard-fought over time, as opportunities have
developed enabling plaintiffs to attack large powerful entities, attempting
to hold them accountable for their increasingly far-reaching actions. To
construct a meaningful court-centred strategy requires an institutional context that not only accommodates such an approach but also holds promising
impact potential. Procedural rules set the parameters for action and are exploitable by those with sufficient resources (an important prerequisite) on
either side of any issue. Although some have been rendered far less accommodating in recent years, the US rules allowing litigation to proceed with
flexible structures for setting attorney fees have long met with criticism as
making the system too available and encouraging entrepreneurial lawyering.

Comparable rules in the United Kingdom, Australia, and Canada have been considered by some critics as being historically too restrictive, although they are evolving in a more accommodating direction. Moreover, judicial authority in the governing regime is a critical component of the litigation context. The US courts were constitutionally designed as a "co-equal" branch of government. One can certainly argue about the true political significance of their decisions, but they have enjoyed a long tenure as acknowledged centres of constitutional authority with the ability to exercise judicial review and to engage significant policy issues. Such elevation of judicial authority is of more recent vintage in other systems. Yet, as constitutional changes have been enacted, we have witnessed the enhanced profiles of their courts. Indeed, charges of excessive "activism" were lodged against the Supreme Court of Canada after the 1982 *Canadian Charter of Rights and Freedoms,* and a similar scenario played out in Australia after 1986 constitutional reforms gave the High Court more independence (see, for example, Dickson 2007).[2] No doubt, the Supreme Court of the United Kingdom will face like challenges when the new justices take to the bench for the first time in 2009 and begin deciding cases.[3]

Among the most challenging cases, for a variety of reasons that we will explore shortly, are those that aggregate claims of similarly situated parties. Such lawsuits may be instigated by one or a few aggrieved individuals such as, for example, Karen Silkwood's father. With increasing frequency, however, the plaintiffs are large groups or whole classes of individuals such as the residents of Hinkley, California, who were made famous by the film *Erin Brockovich* (2000) or the folks of Woburn, Massachusetts, who were immortalized in *A Civil Action* (Harr 1996). Nor is this simply an American phenomenon. Rolah Ann McCabe met an early death at the age of fifty-one after a lifetime of smoking but not before setting off a virtual windstorm after winning the first Australian tort action against the tobacco industry in 2002. In the intervening years, the headlines have only become bigger, as the McCabe case has moved in fits and starts through the judicial hierarchy. Continued by her surviving family members, it has reverberated with revelations of the intentional destruction of internal documents, which have been confirmed by a tobacco company whistle-blower, and has since moved into class action territory. What is more, the defendants – whether tobacco companies, food giants, or pharmaceutical concerns, to name a few – have seized on (and frequently created) their own institutional opportunities.

We begin with the premise that litigation is both a legal and a political enterprise. In form, of course, it is legal – an activity orchestrated by lawyers, administered by judges, and situated in courthouses. In strategy and outcome, it is frequently quite political – campaigns are conducted, pressure is utilized, and wealth is redistributed. Thus, when carried out on a huge scale, all of the potential benefits and liabilities of both law and politics loom very large indeed. With this in mind, we focus on several separate, but related, issues. As a legal venture, litigation was designed to address individual claims brought one at a time and judged on the unique facts of a singular human disagreement. The mass tort utterly alters this simple configuration. Hundreds – even thousands – of complaints are conflated, with one individual's story representing all of the others. And justice, rather than being discretely applied to one, is formulaically distributed among many. As an implement of law then, mass litigation stands as a trade-off between traditional notions of individual due process and more recent drives toward group rights.

The emphasis on groups in turn impels litigation increasingly toward the political. Every political regime produces winners and losers. This is as true of litigation politics as it is of legislative wrangling. Thus, we would expect certain resource and structural advantages to accrue to larger, wealthier, more experienced entities with influence in other political realms. Of course, in order to make politics more advantageous, process participants are always well advised to seek allies. Groups thus coalesce to influence legislatures more effectively. With the global expansion of judicial authority, even in traditionally strong parliamentary systems, we would expect the same to occur in the litigation universe, with like-minded litigators sharing costs and resources. As Ran Hirschl (2004, 1) has observed, "[a]round the globe, in more than eighty countries and in several supranational entities, constitutional reform has transferred an unprecedented amount of power from representative institutions to judiciaries ... An adversarial American-style rights discourse has become a dominant form of political discourse" (also see, for example, Tate and Vallinder 1995; Dickson 2007; Russell and O'Brien 2001).

Finally, we expect (or at least hope) that a political system will produce effective policy, particularly, as the subject matter of this book suggests, regulatory policy. However, such a result is not always the case. Even legislatures, the traditional front-line lawmaking bodies in a republic, sometimes produce bone-headed policies and, not infrequently, due to gridlock or a simple lack of political will, no policy at all. Regulatory bodies, too, can be "captured" by the subjects of regulation, acting more as client agents than as watchdogs. Hence, we consider the effectiveness of collective litigation as a tool for political change, particularly for regulatory change.

A Definitional Digression

Though not exclusively, this book is primarily concerned with large-scale litigation – litigation encompassing many like claims (Hensler 2001, 181). More particularly, we focus on mass torts, a form of large-scale litigation involving personal injury or property damage and "arising out of product use or exposure" (*ibid.*, 182). Because such torts have a way of becoming unwieldy, several devices or forms may be utilized to make them manageable.

In the United States, for example, they may be consolidated under the aegis of a single federal district court for pretrial proceedings in order "to avoid duplication of discovery, to prevent inconsistent pretrial rulings, and to conserve the resources of the parties, their counsel and the judiciary" (Judicial Panel on Multi-District Litigation 2005). Known as multi-district litigations, such mass tort consolidations are generally remanded to their original districts for individualized consideration following the close of pretrial activities.[4] Analogues at the state level include formal consolidation and informal aggregation. In the United Kingdom, aggregation of similar claims, regardless of the usual jurisdictional boundaries, is accomplished with the issuance of a group litigation order. In Canada, cases from disparate venues can be combined as a national class action, and, in Australia, the Federal Court Rules allow judges to consolidate claims within a single jurisdiction that present similar issues.

Perhaps the most well-known and controversial means of managing large-scale litigation is the class action, a form of consolidation in which one individual, or a small group of individuals, sues on behalf of a much larger number of people.[5] Thereafter, all members of the class are bound by the outcome of the litigation, whether at trial or in settlement (Hensler 2001, 182).[6] Such suits, which are far-reaching now, are likely to become even more extensive as the judicialization of politics and economic globalization continue apace. Mattel's recent massive recall of toys made in China with dangerous magnets and coated with lead paint, for example, did not confine itself to worried American parents. Of the 436,000 ill-painted and recalled Sarge cars alone, 186,000 were sitting on store shelves, or being played with in homes, outside the United States. The even larger recall of Polly Pockets, Barbies, and other popular toys containing tiny magnets, included 1.9 million sold in the United Kingdom alone (British Broadcasting Corporation 2007). It does not require great imagination to conjure up notions of litigation on a very broad scale.[7]

Indeed, nowhere is the globalization of risk and retribution more evident than in the rapid rise and fall of Vioxx. In 1998, pharmaceutical giant Merck asked the Food and Drug Administration to approve a new, superior painkiller, one touted as causing fewer stomach problems than existing palliative treatments. Accepting Merck's safety studies, the health watchdog agency approved the drug the following year. Subsequent analyses soon began exhibiting a disturbing link between Vioxx and heart attacks and strokes, some of which were omitted from a report published in the *New England Journal of Medicine,* which later complained of being "hoodwinked" by Merck. Meanwhile, evidence of the problems kept mounting (the journal *Lancet* estimated that 88,000 Americans suffered heart attacks after taking Vioxx, 38,000 of whom died), forcing Merck to recall the drug in 2004 (Prakash and Valentine 2008). The response in the United States was swift and predictable.

The plaintiffs' bar began advertising "on the Internet, the subway, the television, and on city buses encouraging people to join in a class action lawsuit if they had ever taken Vioxx" (Melnick 2008, 762), individuals sued (see, for example, *Merck v. Ernst* 2008),[8] classes formed,[9] and large numbers of cases were consolidated and transferred under a multi-district jurisdiction (*In re: Vioxx Marketing, Sales Practices and Products Liability Litigation* 2007).[10]

Like other "miracle" drugs, however, Vioxx had not merely been marketed in America. By 2005, it had reached a worldwide market estimated at around twenty million users (Deer 2005)! And, with this exposure, came a flurry of litigation. Thus, within days of Merck's decision to withdraw Vioxx from the market, at least ten class actions were filed in four Canadian provinces and in Canada's federal court (Kondro 2004, 1335).[11] In the United Kingdom, a number of law firms recruited clients to bring a claims in England under the country's *Consumer Protection Act* (The Lawyer.com 2005).[12] Other British firms took their cases to US courts, hoping for bigger pay-offs.[13] In Australia, law firms quickly geared up to find clients, some touting alignment "with well-known and leading U.K and American vioxx lawyers" (Vioxx Lawyer Australia 2005). Obviously, the litigation world is getting smaller and smaller.

Litigation as Law and Politics

As Law: Individual Fairness Considerations

As we alluded to briefly at the outset, litigation is first and foremost the centrepiece of the legal system. And, in advanced democracies, the centrepiece of litigation is fairness to the individual. This relationship may be expressed in terms of "due process" as the American, British, and Australian systems do or of "fundamental justice" as in the Canadian system, but, at the very least and however expressed, it stands for basic procedural rights that an individual may expect upon engaging the adjudicative process. The word "individual" is key here, and, indeed, both the US Constitution and the *Canadian Bill of Rights,* for example, speak directly to principles of fairness *individually* administered, and it is also constitutionally implied in Australia.[14] In the United Kingdom, the concept was written into law by a 1368 act of Parliament.[15] Thus, in the traditional model of litigation, an individual argues his case in court with the expectation that a set of facts, distinctive to him, will be fully heard and impartially considered by the court.

Recent comparative judicial scholarship has observed a general movement in democratic systems toward enhanced constitutionalism and judicial empowerment. In Hirschl's (2004, 2) assessment, the motion "reflects these polities' genuine commitment to entrenched, self-binding protection of basic rights and civil liberties in an attempt to safeguard vulnerable groups and individuals from the potential tyranny of political majorities." In many cases, this commitment has involved constitutional revision and formal recognition of something like a bill of rights, often accompanied by reform legislation intended to enhance "access to justice" (also see, for example, Tate and Vallinder 1995; Dickson 2007; Russell and O'Brien 2001; Stone Sweet 2000).[16]

It is the essence of mass litigation – the class action, in particular – however, to meld the individual story with that of many others – often many highly disparate others and often where insistence on the individual case model would leave many entirely without recourse. These issues, as succeeding chapters will reveal, have frequently plagued jurists who are appropriately sensitive to individual rights, derailing many potential class actions in the process.[17] Of course, as we explain subsequently, of the many arguments in favour of mass litigation, political expediency is among the most prominent. Mass torts bring the power of collective action to bear against large institutional entities with the resources to crush individual opponents. Thus, what the individual loses in terms of her singular day in court is presumably ameliorated by her newfound muscle. This is the spirit of group politics.

As Politics
Politics may be many things, but, in the end, it all boils down to a struggle for power. And, of course, litigation works in the same way – it is the quintessential fight well fought. The two – politics and litigation – both involve competition, which is often over very high stakes. And, in both politics and litigation, there are bound to be winners and losers. Legal scholar Lon Fuller (1978, 364) once said that "the distinguishing characteristic of [law] lies in the fact that it confers on the affected party a peculiar form of participation in the decision, that of presenting proofs and reasoned arguments for a decision in his favor ... The results that emerge from adjudication are subject ... to a standard of rationality that is different from that imposed on the results of a [political] exchange." Of course, Fuller was speaking of the end result of litigation – the judicial decision.

Litigation, however, is far more than adjudication. The law governs private relationships, designating sets of officially recognized rights and obligations. To possess a right is more desirable and advantageous than to possess an obligation. For this reason, law is a highly conflictual commodity, and courts are the public arenas in which the conflict can be played out. If one feels wronged by another party, it is his or her decision whether to seek redress. The civil suit is only one option on a varied menu of strategies for doing so. A court is one among an array of points of popular access to government. The division of governmental labour, in terms of dealing with personal and social conflicts and related demands, is a hazy one. Most public agencies are targets for such demands, particularly in the event of serious conflict where the debate is carried from one arena to the next with no true settlement emerging from any. Thus, the more frequently litigation is used as a problem-solving or demand-making instrument, the more openly politicized the courts become. Indeed, much litigation actually represents demand for def-inition of the current meaning of public policies, calling for remedies such as a reaffirmation or change of community norms, cessation or performance of some government or private activity, redistribution of values and resources, recognition of rights and obligations, or adjustment in established balances of power between competing interests. Litigation is thus inevitably a political exercise, requiring each party to marshal available resources and to manipu-late the legal system in order to create strategic advantages and to protect a set of interests *vis-à-vis* the opposition.

The more frequently that courts are involved in problem solving and judges respond with reasoned decisions to such scenarios, the more they will become embroiled in the process of governing and rule making, which is functionally not terribly dissimilar from legislating. This is a role that is familiar to the one played by US judges, but one that their colleagues in most other systems are only recently developing. As Robert Kagan (2001) observes, this scenario augurs well for decentralizing authority and ongoing challenges and opens the door to "adversarial legalism." Moreover, Alec Stone Sweet (2000, 3) theorizes that "the continuous settlement of disputes by a third party dispute resolver will construct, and then manage over time, specific causal linkages between the strategic behavior of individuals and the development of rule systems." Mastery of the rules translates into ad-vantage, and, thus, those with the means to do so will always construct strategies to utilize the process to their benefit (for example, Galanter 1974).

Notwithstanding the soundness of the phrase "the personal is political," group politics inevitably has more force than individual endeavours. Clearly, this is true of legislative and executive politics.[18] And we anticipate the same in the judicial arena. Most probably, Oliver Brown and his young daughter Linda could not have successfully sued the Topeka, Kansas, school district without the strategic and organizational resources of the National Associa-tion for the Advancement of Colored People. Indeed, even before *Brown v. Board of Education* (1954), which refers to interest group litigation during the 1940s and 1950s, Justice Jackson asserted that "[t]his is government by lawsuit ... – the stuff of power politics in America" (Jackson 1941, 287).

Winners and Losers

Politics produces winners and losers. As the history of the many early cases brought by individual smokers against the tobacco industry suggest, we would expect this outcome to be magnified within the judicial system (for example, *Cipollone v. Liggett Group* 1992; *Hodgson v. Imperial Tobacco Ltd.* 1998). Where legislative politics can include compromise and conciliation as well as blunting or masking the benefits and liabilities, full-blown litigation looks more like a zero-sum game. Under the adversarial model of justice, any given trial will result in one winner, one loser, and no one in between. Of course, this scenario, though paradigmatic, is a rarity: "The vast majority of all tort cases are disposed through some form of settlement, with only 3 percent of all tort matters resulting in a jury trial" (National Center for State Courts 2004). Thus, as with legislative politics, we would anticipate compromise of some sort in most litigation politics.

The question then becomes "does litigation produce a different configuration of winners and losers than legislative politics?" As E.E. Schattschneider (1960, 34-35) points out in his commentary on pluralism some four decades ago, "[t]he flaw in the pluralist heaven is that the heavenly chorus sings with a strong upper-class accent." Thus, part of the damning critique of the so-called legislative pressure system is characterized by the old saw that "money talks." Such classic means of political influence peddling, however, are considered unethical – even illegal – when applied to the judiciary. The rules of the judicial process simply prohibit such direct encounters between lobbyists and judges. Thus, if interest groups want to influence the outcomes of legal disputes, they have to find alternative routes of "lobbying" – routes that correspond to the norms of the judiciary. Presumably, these are much more difficult – at least, the rules are far more rigid.

Common wisdom would suggest that these tactics are especially difficult for the most powerful of interests. Hence, those with enormous influence over the overtly political branches of government, political mythology would have it, lose some of their advantages in the courts of law. After all, the mid-century litigation successes of African American interests and the Warren Court era decisions favouring defendants and other disadvantaged groups have fed the notion that courts are particularly amenable to minority interests and unpopular groups. The decision *Mabo v. Queensland (No. 2)* (1992, 42) by the High Court of Australia, which followed a decade of litigation, spoke to different, but similar, political-legal dynamics, finally acknowledging Aboriginal land rights after more than a century of denial (also see Russell 2005). Speaking for the court, Justice Brennan stated firmly that, despite precedent to the contrary, "[a] common law doctrine founded on unjust discrimination in the enjoyment of civil and political rights demands reconsideration."[19]

Moreover, the media, which devote few resources to covering appellate decision making, tend to focus on the occasional high profile, constitutional case. Such cases frequently involve facially non-economic interests such as those involving race, censorship, and abortion. Alternatively, the media would suggest that, groups aside, courts are the places where the little guy can win – and win big – in government. The "McDonald's coffee lady," winner of a supposedly huge amount of money from the burger giant is, today, an American household term.[20] Court statistics, however, tell a very different story. If we look overall at groups in the United States that sponsor litigation – excluding government – we find that commercial interests dominate pressure group activity, at least in the Supreme Court of the United States. In fact, commercial interests sponsor more litigation than all other interests combined (Epstein 1991, 354). Moreover, statistical examinations of *amicus* participants – again, excluding government – similarly suggest commercial domination *(ibid.)*. Thus, the same interests that dominate the pressure system in the legislative and executive branches also dominate the judicial system (see, for example, Rosen 2008).

In fact, quite aside from litigation sponsorship and *amici* participation, one might argue that the powerful tend to "come out ahead" not only in such overtly political fora as the legislature and executive but also in the supposedly apolitical judiciary. This is precisely what Marc Galanter (1974) argues in his classic treatise "Why the 'Haves' Come Out Ahead." Of course, collective litigation, involving hundreds or thousands of "little guys" ("one shotters" in Galanter's terminology) might be expected to even the playing field. Mobilized and united, these plaintiffs might appear to assume the advantages of larger, more powerful entities (Galanter's "repeat players"). However, according to Galanter (1999, 56), this is not necessarily the case:

> We might think of lawyers as crudely divisible into two great congregations: On the one side we have a large Party of Facilitation that helps clients do what they want to do and avoid the costs of what they have done. The great majority of the private bar, along with in-house counsel, belong to this party. On the other side are what we might call the Party of Internalization: a much smaller band of plaintiffs lawyers, public interest lawyers, and government lawyers who spend their days trying to make enterprises internalize the costs they are imposing on third parties (injury victims, consumers, neighbors of waste sites, etc.) ...
>
> The course of [much modern class litigation] should temper our optimism about the eventual outcome. It reveals that the limited material and organizational resources of the Party of Internalization show up in a lack of endurance and susceptibility to opportunistic dealing by those who view themselves as champions of the public interest. This is not because the Party of Internalization is manned by bad people, but because it lacks the organizational sinew for sustained and coordinated strategic struggle that is possessed by its opponents.

There are, in other words, repeat players and REPEAT PLAYERS.

Litigation Coalitions
Legislative politics revolves around coalition building. Interests seeking voice in legislatures are well advised to band together with like-minded groups in pushing for favourable policies or in pushing back against any law that is perceived as harmful. And, of course, once a bill becomes part of the process, the bargaining and alliance formation continues apace. We would expect litigators to engage in similar behaviours – the classic example being the solicitation of *amici* briefs where the more one can solicit the better. Even in moving toward trial (or pretrial settlement), recruiting friends with similar interests may be expected in order to result in economies of scale and demonstrations of political muscle. After all, these are the premises underlying modern multi-party lawsuits, which are often large coalitions of strangers. They are also the reasons that attorneys, representing both plaintiffs and defendants, might seek alliances for the purposes of information allocation, cost sharing, and the like.

Regulatory Effectiveness
A major end of politics is policy, frequently regulatory policy. The *US Code of Federal Regulations* alone contains fifty titles, governing a huge range of activities from homeland security to telecommunications to wildlife and fisheries. The thousands of rules contained within the *US Code* are the result of a complex political process, generally involving legislation, public comment, and executive rule making. Similarly, more than 3,300 statutory orders and regulations, covering an equally comprehensive list of practices, are available for public review at the Department of Justice Canada.[21]

And, then, there is litigation, particularly litigation that is aimed at "forcing ... industr[ies] to take greater responsibility for reducing the amount of damage done by [their] products" (Cook and Ludwig 2002, 68). The question is whether this is an effective, efficient, and cost beneficial means of regulation? Answers to this question vary widely. On the one hand, "[c]onsumer advocates argue that without the threat of such lawsuits, businesses would be free to engage in illegal practices that significantly increase their profits as long as no one individual suffered a substantial loss" (Hensler et al. 2000, 9). Clearly, there is anecdotal evidence to suggest that this possibility may be the case. Thus, upon hearing news of a government warning in March 2004 that "people newly taking antidepressants can become suicidal," one primary care physician reacted by stating: "We're going to continue to use these drugs pretty freely until we start seeing the ads in the newspapers from lawyers saying, 'Have you or your family member been prescribed these drugs? If so, you may have a case.' When the big L word, liability, raises its ugly head, that's when things will really change" (Grady and Harris 2004, A14).

Clearly, not everyone would agree that lawsuits are the best (or even a good) means of regulating. Not surprisingly, the American Tort Reform Association (2002, 14) takes a particularly dim view of the practice, asserting that "[l]egislating public policy in the courtroom violates the 'separation of powers doctrine' – the fundamental rule upon which this country's entire system of government is based." These are strong words indeed! However, even some who would not question the constitutionality of the practice, harbour doubts about its efficacy. Thus, for example, President Bill Clinton's secretary of labor, Robert Reich (1999, 15A), while asserting that "regulating through lawsuits is better than not regulating at all," nonetheless acknowledges that "[r]egulating US industry through lawsuits isn't the most efficient way of doing the job. Judges don't have large expert staffs for research and analyses, which regulatory agencies possess. And when plaintiffs and defendants settle their cases, we can't always be sure the public interest is being served." And Gerald Rosenberg (1991, 343) reminds us that "courts are not all-powerful institutions. They were designed with severe limitations and placed in a political system of divided powers. To ask them to produce significant social reform is to forget their history and ignore their constraints."

Organization

This book addresses all of the issues posited earlier. Chapter 1 presents a history of group-based litigation developments. Here we look to the ancient roots of mass tort actions in Europe as well as to American variations on the theme. Alexis de Tocqueville (1969, 270), of course, wrote that in America "[s]carcely any political question arises ... that is not resolved, sooner or later, into a judicial question." Thus, the idea of group-based litigation would find truly fertile soil in the United States. The modern variant is the class action, and Chapter 2 examines this variation as well as other contemporary manifestations of the politics of litigation. It begins with a summary of litigation aimed at private institutional change – a brief survey of modern legal battles against a wide array of corporations. It also looks at the growing counter attack on plaintiff litigation, from legislative efforts at tort reform and industry-specific liability shields to the increasing use of mandatory arbitration clauses and aggressive public relations campaigns.

In the next three chapters, we move from a telescopic to a microscopic perspective, as we examine, in depth, three categories of litigations. Two of those chapters include the latest data and analysis on tobacco and gun litigation, with special emphasis on litigants' strategic choices. Chapter 5 is devoted to a much newer field of strategic multi-party litigation, the battle for healthful food. Having learned often painful lessons from the tobacco and gun wars, coalitions on both sides of the food wars demonstrate more mature, more modest, and frequently more successful tactics. In Chapter 6, we look beyond the United States to consider developments in Australia,

Canada, and the United Kingdom, where multi-party litigation is increasingly taking hold. In each case, the most significant movements have followed the implementation of constitutional change and the enhancement of judicial independence. Finally, Chapter 7 reconsiders our general themes and speculates on future avenues of inquiry.

1
Theoretical, Historical, and Legal Underpinnings

Class action litigation has received considerable political and press attention in recent years because it has produced some notorious outcomes, involving huge sums of money, affecting major sectors of the economy, and having significant public policy implications. Regardless of the outcomes and despite the procedural complexity (which is usually glossed over and simplified), the group-based claim represents a means by which the scales of power can be recalibrated – at least temporarily. Stephen Yeazell (1987, 10), who has written extensively on the early phenomenon and is considered an authority on its historical roots, asserts that it "creates power." Judge Jack Weinstein (1995, 132), who has overseen a number of major class actions and multi-district consolidations in his federal district court in Brooklyn, says that "the class action actually changes the real power and substantive rights of those whose claims are aggregated." Perhaps.

It certainly is a way to challenge the political and economic power of large entities and possibly to hold them accountable for their actions. It is probably the only feasible way to deal seriously with a series of similar small claims that individually are not worth anyone's time or effort and that rise to a level of real significance only when considered collectively. Moreover, bundling like claims shifts the focus to the conflict itself rather than to any of the specific litigants. However, herein lies part of the rub. It means that collective litigation carries regulatory and public policy implications. And, of course, there are those who argue that such activity lies entirely outside the province of judicial authority. It also involves internal conflicts between group leverage and individual due process rights, corporate and government accountability and just compensation to individuals who have been (or likely will be) harmed, as well as institutional and collective efficiency and individual justice. Bundling claims means that in the very institution of government, constructed precisely to address the stories of individuals, few individual stories will be heard. These issues have bedevilled judges facing aggregated claims in the United States from the earliest of cases, and because we grant such high value to the rights of individuals they are the themes that can be heard in the refrain of the collective litigation song to this day.

We use these themes to organize our analysis. This chapter explores the origins of the group litigation form and traces its development, laying the groundwork for the analysis that follows. The class action is a curious form, often permitting litigation by an ad hoc collection of individuals that is formally recognized as a group only for the purposes of pursuing a common legal complaint against a single powerful defendant or set of defendants.[1] In many cases, the vast majority of individual members are total strangers, and many may be entirely oblivious to the fact that their interests are being represented.

Although the aggregation of activities and effort routinely occurs in our political, economic, and social lives, achieving class status for litigation purposes is clearly something quite different. It represents an exception to the standard model upon which courts generally function, allowing access to individuals who claim an immediate and direct harm (or one that is likely to befall them) – the idea being that it should be each individual's responsibility to decide whether to seek redress and to represent her own interests. Moreover, in a conflict, each participant, in the interest of fairness and justice, must be afforded an opportunity to make an appearance and to interject supporting evidence – to have her "day in court" – an opportunity that is compromised when multiple claims are aggregated into a single one.[2]

These issues, alone, have given pause to any number of serious jurists over the years. And, although as we shall see, good and valid reasons for proceeding in this manner arose very early, providing subsequent courts with precedents that could serve as useful guides in deciding whether to allow litigants to engage the process collectively, a number of related questions continue to arise. What commonalities must be shared by a collection of individuals in order to qualify as a group for the purposes of litigation? Who is acceptable as a representative of the larger collective? In other words, which groupings cross the judicial threshold and which representatives satisfy the presiding judge that they are sufficiently representative? Beyond these questions, issues such as proper notification and the validity of a judgment without proof of notification have long been the subject of judicial consideration.[3] Can the interests of absent parties be represented without their consent and without their input? Should they be allowed to opt out in order to pursue their own individual claims? Must they "opt in" before they can be bound by the outcome, affirmatively allowing others to represent their interests? All of these questions directly relate to our developing conception of due process.

Although not necessarily contradictory, there is a tension that complicates any effort to find solutions to problems that benefit the larger community without sacrificing the interests of individual members. The "takings clause" of the Fifth Amendment to the US Constitution testifies to the existence of this tension as early as the founding era.[4] In addition, the American political-legal system emphasizes individual rights, while, at the same time, recognizing and accommodating a pull toward collective or group interests. James Madison noted this potential incompatibility before the ratification of the Constitution, at once acknowledging the great value of freedom for individuals to follow their own selfish pursuits and the natural divisions of interests that entice people into "factions" (*Federalist* No. 10). French scholar, Alexis de Tocqueville (1969, 513-14), also observed Americans of the 1830s to be keenly aware of their individual self-interests and worried that full-flowered individualism could draw folks so much into themselves that it might be difficult to create a collectivist spirit necessary to nation building. However, he also found a countervailing tendency: "Americans of all ages, all stations in life, and all types of disposition are forever forming associations. There are not only commercial and industrial associations in which all take part, but others of a thousand different types – religious, moral, serious, futile, very general and very limited, immensely large and very minute."

Although individualism and factionalism are long-running political concerns, a consciousness of individual legal rights is a relatively recent phenomenon, generally associated with the judicial development of bill of rights issues in the early twentieth century. Development of civil rights and liberties took off in the 1940s, and the most active era was spearheaded by the Warren Court of the 1960s. Coincidentally, development of individual rights paralleled an official recognition and enhancement of collective litigation during the modern era. The *Federal Rules of Civil Procedure,* and, in particular, *Rule 23,* which specifically delineates the class action, were adopted in 1938, and the 1966 revisions, in effect, allowed for much wider use.[5] Indeed, the 1966 version was produced during an extraordinarily active milieu of civil rights and liberties advocacy, and the panel's deliberations took place with this legal context in full flower and in full view.

Similar coincidental developments have also occurred outside the United States. Indeed, as the movement to adopt principles of the *Universal Declaration of Human Rights* has generated an enhanced focus on individual rights and equality at the national level, constitutional revisions across a range of democratic systems in the late twentieth and early twenty-first centuries have generally empowered courts to enforce them domestically (see Hirschl 2004; Dezalay and Garth 2001).[6] Moreover, such changes seem to presage the easing of restrictions on representative litigation and aggregation of claims. This has certainly been true in Canada, Australia, and the United Kingdom.

The class action form has become easier to invoke. And, while it remains atypical, it has increased in number over the past quarter-century and has been used to engage the courts in a range of highly visible and important legal issues, which has affected a huge swath of the population.[7] Moreover, although virtually all judges are at least familiar with the model, with each petition seeking certification as a class, the courts have had to revisit the questions and somehow rationalize the tension between communally invoked accountability and individually based due process rights. We begin this chapter with some historical background to group-based litigation. We also reflect upon some of the theoretical issues involved in collectivized litigation and then assess a few highly visible examples – tobacco, guns, and food – and extend our analysis to consider recent developments that have formed collectivized litigation in several other political-legal systems, focusing especially on Canada, Australia, and the United Kingdom.

Individual Rights and Group Power

Law and politics are inseparable. Indeed, developing a system of legal rights has inevitable political implications. As Yeazell (1987, 2) notes, "Anglo-American law has proved to be durably, perhaps excessively, individualistic. In numerous contexts it exalts individual choice. From ancient doctrines of property to recent developments in American constitutional law, one finds expressions of the proposition that the individual is the bedrock unit both of social action and of legal thought." Although we organize ourselves into groups for a range of purposes – corporations, labour unions, cities and townships, religions, political parties, interest groups, civic associations, just to name a few – a great deal of effort has been spent to develop the rights and obligations of individuals in relation to collectivities and to the state, itself.[8] Much time and effort was expended throughout the twentieth century to assert and maintain a system of constitutional rights that is understood to accrue to individuals as individuals without regard to identification or association with any particular cluster of others. Thus, rights extend to all regardless of race, nationality, gender, or marital status.

At the same time that we observe this trend toward the creation of the fully right-equipped individual, the US legal system has also accommodated collectivization for a variety of purposes. Thus, the governing regime has chartered cities and townships and allowed groups of business people to incorporate, labour unions and churches to form, and a full range of voluntary organizations to formalize their status.[9] There is a legal process for each of these activities, but it allows a collective to own property, accrue debt, own and distribute assets, among other things – as if it were an individual person under the law. Formal recognition of the group requires compliance with a formal legal process and also implies individual consent. Indeed, one can move freely from one state or locality to another, generally without forfeiting citizenship rights or a legal status conferred in the state of origin.[10] People are not coerced into becoming stockholders of a particular company, and religious affiliation is usually considered a voluntary matter (although entry into some religious groups is not so simple, exit is usually understood to be a matter of choice). Although early organizing efforts were met with significant resistance, labour unions exist by collective choice, and individuals often are granted the ability to opt out if they wish, increasingly so by "right to work" laws. Moreover, the basic family unit, a married couple, is sanctioned by the state, with the understanding that each participant has exercised the choice to join free of coercion,[11] and, similarly, exiting (divorce) has progressively become a less onerous strategy across all states. In all of these situations, the notions of "voluntariness" and consent have grown in importance. Given the value of these concepts to the unfolding of constitutional due process, it should not be surprising that they have also played a significant role in the development of the class action or representative litigation form.

Early Developments in Group Litigation in England

In his research of Anglo-American law, Yeazell (1997) reports that unincorporated groups appeared as litigants in as early as medieval times in British courts. In fact, much of medieval life was group based for social, religious, and agricultural reasons, marked less by individual self-reliance than by mutual dependence. Without formal recognition, the law tended to reflect the realities of life – so suits could be filed by a group representative or filed against a representative in the name of the collective, with all members held accountable by the outcome. Among the earliest examples is a late-twelfth-century case involving Father Martin and his local congregants. In 1199 in the court of the Archbishop of Canterbury, Martin, a parish rector, "brought suit against four of his parishioners – as representatives of the rest – asserting his right to certain parochial fees ... Father Martin was in part insisting that his parishioners carry the bodies of their dead several miles to a place where he could bury them for a customary fee; alternatively, he was benevolently prepared to let them bury their deceased in a nearby chapel graveyard – so long as they remitted to Martin the same customary burial fee as he would have earned had he conducted the service himself" (*Martin, Rector of Barkway v. Parishioners of Nuthamstead* 1199; cited in Yeazell 1997, 688).[12]

   This case not only reflects the natural groupings and way of life prevalent in medieval England, but it also indicates that the law recognized and endorsed "natural" collectives. No doubt born out of necessity and practicality, representative litigation had clear political implications. To file a claim against each member of his flock individually would certainly have cost Martin far more than he would have seen in return. Moreover, allowing him to sue all of his congregants at once, rather than individually, probably saved the court considerable time and resources. Presumably, the interests of any un-named (perhaps unaware) parties were considered aptly represented (albeit indirectly) by those who were clearly identified. At the same time, efficiency of process worked to the advantage of the already more powerful rector as well, providing a mechanism whereby he could impose legal sanction (a death tax) on all of his parishioners in a single action. Thus, such a case outcome would also have public policy consequences. After all, death is universal, and payment of a burial tax to Father Martin to administer the passage from this world to the next (even if he did not perform the ceremony himself) applied equally to all within his parish. Finally, it is significant to note that the case involved a defendant class rather than the now familiar plaintiff class. This was not at all unusual for that era: "Medieval group litigation was not a systematic instrument of oppression. It was not a systematic instrument of anything. One can find about equal numbers of plaintiff and defendant groups, and some of the plaintiff groups seem to be using litigation as a weapon in struggles with social superiors" *(ibid.).*

Raymond Marcin (1974) contends that the first true class action litigation came a century after Father Martin's case. Filed in 1309, *Discart v. Otes* (1914) involved a conflict over payment of royal commissions owed to Sir Otes Grandison, who had been given dominion over the Channel Islands after the Norman Conquest. Since the value of the local currency had fluctuated considerably, Sir Otes demanded payment in the more stable French notes, thereby tripling the tax. A number of his minions filed suit, including Jordan Discart, seeking a judgment that would allow them to pay in the traditional local tender. As there were several cases presenting the same issue, the court consolidated them, in effect creating a plaintiff class, and passed the case to the King's Council for resolution (Marcin 1974, 521-23).[13]

Like its medieval counterpart, the modern class action is based on two distinct efficiency rationales. Indeed, it is a way to overcome a multiple small claim problem for potential plaintiffs. Where an individual claim would not be worth the expense of litigation, plaintiffs can pool their resources and operate with an economy of scale. Likewise, a defendant can consolidate multiple similar claims and cut the costs of legal defence. And, for the court, because each individual claim would present similar legal questions and factual scenarios, it is far more efficient to deal with all of them together rather than individually. Thus, on the one hand, providing a mechanism for consolidating claims encourages litigation that would otherwise likely not go forward, while, on the other hand, it diminishes volume – an interesting contradiction in efficiencies.

Martin and Sir Otes' cases also predate the more modern construction of due process. At some point in the sixteenth century, English judges developed what became known as the "necessary parties" rule, which required that any person with legal interest in a case outcome be included as a named

party, be served notice of the pending litigation, and be afforded the opportunity to make a formal presentation to represent their own individual
interests. Indeed, there was no guarantee that anyone (including the "representatives") would promote any interests other than their own: "Several
reasons were advanced for the rule: complete justice can only be done by
determining the rights of all parties connected with the subject of the suit
or the relief to be granted; multiplicity of suits should be prevented; and,
assurance should be provided that those persons before the court could safely
execute the decree" (Hazard, Gedid, and Sowle 1998, 1858-59; also see Hazard
1961).[14] Among the most troublesome conundrums was the issue of what
to do when there simply were too many parties (on either side of a case) to
identify and join them all realistically. Should they all be bound by the
outcome? One could reason that those who were directly involved effectively
represented the others because of the similarity in their interests.[15] One could
also reason that a principal party should have the benefit of fair notice of
the action and an opportunity to make a presentation during the course of
the proceeding – what has since become fundamental to the concept of due
process. English courts grappled with these problems over the next two
centuries and came to apply the "necessary parties" rule fairly rigidly, which
made it quite difficult to move forward with cases in which there were
multiple parties.[16] Of course, life in those days was very different from that
which we know today. Classes were cohesive. People lived in proximity to
each other and knew one another well. They often worked and worshipped
together. In collective litigation, they were certainly aware of the legal action
and very likely participated in selecting a representative.

Some cases could take decades to resolve. Indeed, Charles Dickens' ninth
novel, *Bleak House,* which he published in 1852, was meant to dramatize
the problems associated with long, drawn-out litigation. The centrepiece of
the story is the fictional case *Jarndyce v. Jarndyce,* which consumes a hapless
family and, ultimately, their entire estate. The saga actually worked as a piece
of popular fiction. It did not work, however, as a fact of legal reality and
called for reform. It ultimately led the courts to consider some representative
litigation under the "bill of peace" form, allowing for assignment of a master
who would be responsible for notifying all of the relevant parties and bringing matters to a close. This design was most often used in creditor cases to
prevent one or a few creditors from gaining unfair advantage over others
who happened to be absent or unaware at the time of the original complaint,
thus draining a common debtor of all resources before the other creditors
had any opportunity to engage the process to demand their fair share (see,
for example, Hazard, Gedid, and Sowle 1998).

Moreover, a bill of peace, in its early forms as developed by the English
chancery courts, generally allowed a plaintiff to join all of the defendants
and whatever series of claims that had been, or would potentially be, filed

into a single action – if there were too many parties for standard practice, if it could be demonstrated that they shared a real interest regarding the question in contention, and if the court were satisfied that the absent group members could be satisfactorily represented by those who had made an appearance (Weinstein 1995, 132; also see Chafee 1932). Unlike the situation today, however, the group had an independent existence that preceded the litigation. As Weinstein (1995, 132) asserts, "the early class action did not empower a scattered mass of individuals who did not know each other and had no bonds except those created by a grievance and the group litigation." In addition, sixteenth- and seventeenth-century group litigation often concerned property issues; generally confirmed existing socio-political status differences; genuinely represented a collective, as opposed to an individual, set of rights such as a death tax or use of a commons area; and usually invoked local norms and customs.

Early Developments in the United States
The necessary parties principle and the bill of peace eventually found their way across the Atlantic. Justice Joseph Story is credited with exerting the greatest influence over the original construction and later unfolding of the American version of class litigation, even if his understanding of the British experience and precedents was less than complete (see, for example, Yeazell 1987, 216-17; Hazard, Gedid, and Sowle 1998, 1878-80).[17] He viewed the bill of peace as a procedure for minimizing unnecessary litigation (which also introduced unnecessary costs to the courts) as well as for managing situations that would otherwise become unwieldy if multiple actions were filed involving a single party. However, he also felt that the necessary parties rule was important to the concept of justice. While riding his circuit in 1820, Story considered an equity case that set the stage for his subsequent articulation of group litigation provisions in his *Commentaries on Equity Jurisprudence* (Story 1836) and *Pleadings* (Story 1838). The controversy, *West v. Randall* (1820), was brought to federal court under diversity jurisdiction by a resident of Massachusetts who claimed that he had been cheated out of a rightful share of his family estate in Rhode Island. This particular case, however, presented no exceptions that the court should consider, and Justice Story found that all interested parties should be named and included in the proceedings before any legal action could go forward.

Nonetheless, focusing on the "necessary parties" aspects of the litigation, and citing an array of English precedents for authority, Story took the opportunity to deliver his understanding of legal theory, which proved to have long-lasting influence. The general rule should be that "all persons materially interested, either as plaintiffs or defendants in the subject matter of the bill ought to be made parties to the suit, however numerous they may be" – the "necessary parties" principle (*West v. Randall* 1820, 721). However, as Story also states, there will likely be situations where rigid application of the rule will result in true injustice to the parties actually before the court: "[W]here the parties are very numerous, and the court perceives, that it will be almost impossible to bring them all before the court; or where the question is of general interest, and a few may sue for the benefit of the whole; or where the parties form a part of a voluntary association for public or private purposes, and may be fairly supposed to represent the rights and interests of the whole; in these and analogous cases, if the bill purports to be not merely in behalf of the plaintiffs, but of all others interested ... the court will proceed to a decree" (*ibid.*, 722).

Not long after *West,* Justice Story had an opportunity to apply this reasoning (*Beatty v. Kurtz* 1829). The conflict arose over a plot of land in what is now in the Georgetown section of Washington, DC. In 1770, two wealthy landowners, Charles Beatty and George F. Hawkins, set aside several pieces of property for public use, deeding three lots for churches (Lutheran, Church of England, and Calvinist Church/Presbyterian) and one for a market house. Soon thereafter, a small group of German Lutherans came together, erecting a small building on their designated plot, which they used intermittently throughout the years as a church and a school, and reserving some of the grounds as a cemetery. The group never incorporated to become an officially sanctioned organization, and the building deteriorated extensively, although they did periodic repairs and had plans to construct something more permanent if they could raise the necessary donations to pay for it. This went on for some fifty years, during which time Georgetown became part of the District of Columbia and demand for property in the nation's new capital city increased. Beatty's son and surviving heir sought to reclaim the parcel, and, under his authorization, a colleague "entered upon the lot and removed some of the tomb stones" and planned to remove all of the graves, to take possession (*ibid.*, 580). A small committee, claiming to represent the interests of all church "members," filed suit in federal court to preserve their rights to the property under the original understanding in the grant, and the court found in their favour (*Kurtz v. Beatty* 1826). Beatty appealed to the Supreme Court of the United States, believing that he had a strong case. After all, a "real" church had never materialized at the designated location, and the loose-knit congregation had used the site for worship only haphazardly. In addition, he challenged the plaintiffs' ability to represent the interests of other unnamed claimants because there never had been an organization of record.

However, the court was not persuaded. Justice Story acknowledged that the church, projected by the elder Beatty's grant, had never gotten fully off the ground, and he observed that

[t]he Lutherans ... have not been able, therefore, to maintain public worship constantly in the house so erected, during the whole period ... But efforts have been constantly made, as far as practicable to keep together a congregation ... The house, however, in consequence of inevitable decay, fell down some time ago ... The Lutherans in Georgetown ... are not and never have been incorporated as a religious society. The congregation was consisted of a voluntary society, acting in its general arrangement by committees and trustees, chosen from time to time by the Lutherans belonging to it. There do not appear to have been any formal records kept of their proceedings; and there have been periods of considerable intermission in their appointment and action. (*Beatty v. Kurtz* 1829, 581-82)

Despite these facts, the justices were clearly taken aback by the younger Beatty's actions in the cemetery – "not ... a mere private trespass; but a public nuisance" (*ibid.*, 584)[18] – and they were not inclined to find in his favour. Indeed, Justice Story delivered the punch line in no uncertain terms. He explained that the land in question "was originally consecrated for a religious purpose; it has become a depository of the dead; and it cannot now be resumed by the heirs of Charles Beatty" (*ibid.*, 527). Nonetheless, the more important long-term issue related to the competency of the plaintiffs to enter their claim in the first instance, and Justice Story seized the moment to declare that they did:

The only difficulty is whether the plaintiffs have shown in themselves a sufficient authority, since it is not evidenced by any formal vote or writing. If it were necessary, to decide the case on this point, we should incline to think that under all the circumstances it might be fairly presumed. But it is not necessary to decide the case on this point; because, we think it one of those cases, in which certain persons, belonging to a voluntary society, and having a common interest, may sue in behalf of themselves and others having the like interest, as part of the same society; for purposes common to all, and beneficial to all. (*ibid.*, 585)

Although this opinion has been cited in some 152 subsequent cases across a wide range of courts, most of the references occurred in the nineteenth century, and they have represented conflicting outcomes.[19] Indeed, the understanding of law that Justice Story articulated in *Beatty* was muddled by relevant sections of his text, the *Equity* treatises, which were published in the following decade (Story 1836; 1838). Geoffrey Hazard, John Gedid, and Stephen Sowle (1998, 1880) note that his thoughts on the issues were far from clear. At one point he is arguing that representative litigation could go forward in the absence of some interested parties when their numbers were so large that it was impractical to join them all (as he suggests in *West*), but, at another point, he is contending, for example, "that a suit to dissolve a voluntary association cannot be maintained by representatives because all members had an 'equal interest to be heard.'" Yeazell (1987, 218) suggests that by the second edition, which appeared two years after the first, "Story seemed even less sure what the question ought to be." Turning his attention to those cases that we would today "describe as group litigation, he did not thus characterize them ... instead of looking for circumstances in which the absentees would be bound, [he] sought ways to proceed without binding or indeed affecting them at all" (*ibid.*, 219).

Multiple parties can be joined by mutual interest or by consent (even if they have different types of claims). Story was prepared to forego requiring that the parties demonstrate a pre-existing "community of interests" that connected them, but he was more concerned about the issue of consent – "the possibility that someone not a party to litigation would be bound by its results. He recognized that it had happened, but found it difficult to come to terms with. By justifying representative litigation as a device to be resorted to only when repetitive litigation would result – and then solely to prevent some vaguely defined injustice – Story assured that such cases would not expand beyond the narrow bounds of a few recognized categories" (*ibid.*, 220). Clearly, this ambivalence regarding how to deal with absent parties was a problem then, and it has plagued judges and justices ever since. For example, three years before Story's death in 1842, the Supreme Court of the United States adopted *Federal Equity Rule 48*, as part of the governing rules of procedure that would remain in effect until 1912.[20] In language reminiscent of Justice Story's *West* opinion some two decades earlier, *Rule 48* allowed group representative suits to go forward, "where the parties on either side are very numerous" and it would not be practicable, without producing excessive delay, to attempt to bring them all before the court.[21] However, also reflecting Story's reticence regarding such litigation, absent parties would not be bound by the outcome of such litigation.

A short twelve years later, the court reached a conclusion that contradicted its own rule. *Smith v. Swormstedt* (1854) arose from a fracture among Methodist Episcopal preachers over the issue of slavery – in particular, the ownership of slaves by ministers. The church, headquartered in Cincinnati, held property and cash in a common "book concern" valued at about $200,000, which had been generated by contributions from the approximately 1,500 southern and 3,800 northern individual clerics out of proceeds from the sales of religious materials on their house-to-house visitations as they fanned out across a number of states. By establishing a common fund, these travelling preachers were able to provide support and promise a small pension for members who were unable to continue to deal with the rigours of itinerant life. At the general conference in 1844, the northern and southern factions acknowledged their irreconcilable differences on the matter of slavery and agreed upon principles of separation, whereby each could vote to go its separate way. Shortly thereafter, the southern group voted to break away as the Methodist Episcopal Church South. A small group, claiming to represent all of the other southern colleagues, filed suit against a similar group representing their northern counterparts to obtain what they considered to be their fair share of the common holdings of the previously united church. For their part, the defendants argued for dismissal on the ground that the plaintiffs had failed to join all interested persons as parties.

Rule 48 notwithstanding, Justice Samuel Nelson, for the court (selectively citing Justice Story as the authority on the question but making no mention whatsoever of *Rule 48*), asserted that "[t]he rule is well established, that where the parties interested are numerous, and the suit is for an object common to them all, some of the body may maintain a bill on behalf of themselves and of the others; and a bill may also be maintained against a portion of a numerous body of defendants, representing a common interest" (*ibid.*, 302). Furthermore, "[f]or convenience, therefore, and to prevent a failure of justice, a court of equity permits a portion of the parties in interest to represent the entire body, and the decree binds all of them the same as if all were before the court" (*ibid.*, 303). The court then considered the merits of the controversy and found that the division of the church was done according to agreed-upon rules and that both sides had valid claims to the pension fund. Thus, "our conclusion is that the complainants and those they represent are entitled to their share of the property in this Book Concern. And the proper decree will be entered to carry this decision into effect" (*ibid.*, 309).[22]

So, while *Rule 48* indicated that absent parties were not to be bound by outcomes, the *Swormstedt* court indicated precisely the opposite. Moreover, as Hazard, Gedid, and Sowle (1998, 1902) state, "[f]rom that point at least until 1912, when the Equity Rules were further revised, Rule 48 and *Swormstedt* coexisted in peaceful contradiction. The courts progressed case by case, almost never referring to both Rule 48 and *Swormstedt* in the same decision and never confronting the inconsistency." According to our own searches, *Rule 48* was cited in twenty-eight federal court opinions between 1853 and 1912 (including four cases decided by the Supreme Court of the United States), while *Swormstedt* was cited in twelve (including five by the high court).[23] Only one case, decided by a US circuit court, refers to both!

American Steel and Wire Co. v. Wire Drawers' and Die Makers' Unions (1898) exemplifies one of the major conflicts of this era – union strikes and the strike-breaking tactics of corporate employers. In this case, the corporation sought an injunction against the striking union members, designating a few leaders as defendant representatives of all of the others, who were left nameless. It posed the question whether all, both named and clearly identified as well as those who were absent but anonymously associated with the specified defendants, be bound by the court's injunction? In the end, the court found that "the chief officers, for purposes of suits, represent a corporation, generally, and they may so represent a voluntary association ... and by aid of the court ... all absent parties not actually served with process [will be] protected by ... the reservation of equity rule 48" (*ibid.*, 606). Thus, a reasonable judge can be counted upon to protect the interests of undesignated parties, the concern raised by Justice Story and voiced in *Rule 48*. Moreover, in the very next paragraph, the court also found the *Swormstedt* logic persuasive, noting that sufficient care had been taken to make sure that the defendants did in fact represent the interests of the others and that "there are sufficient ... members of the unions to defend this suit, and enough to answer all practical purposes of the orders and decrees that may be asked against them ... and the court can see that those mentioned fairly represent the whole" (*ibid.*, 607). Thus, the court found that the workers, present or not, could be bound for the purposes of this litigation by their common interests. Although *Wire Drawers* was a circuit court opinion, it seems to be indicative of a larger shift in judicial thinking. Indeed, the Supreme Court of the United States, "without acknowledging any great change," was subtly preparing at the turn of the twentieth century to discard "the last vestiges of an organization-based concept of group litigation and to have adopted an interest-based model" (Yeazell 1987, 225).

Thus, establishing that an aggregation of parties could be bound together as a community of interests was deemed to be more important than obtaining the affirmative consent of each and every individual member of the now acknowledged group. Converging upon this solution (although not fully embraced by the courts for several decades) was an important step toward allowing litigation to go forward in cases where there had been no formal association among class members but where there was a similar interest. This would be true, for instance, where there were small shareholders who happened to have purchased stock in the same corporation that was engaged in questionable financial dealings to their detriment or, much later, where there were women who independently received faulty breast implants made by the same manufacturer.

The British High Court also seemed to be converging on this understanding. In a frequently quoted opinion at the turn of the century, Lord Macnaghten opined that "[g]iven a common interest and a common grievance, a representative suit was in order if the relief sought was in its nature beneficial to all whom the plaintiff proposed to represent" (*Bedford v. Ellis* 1901). However, the spin given to this precedent less than a decade later took an entirely different approach (*Markt and Co. v. Knight Steamship Co.* 1910). Indeed, *Markt* found that interests among a representative group of litigants must be identical, a criterion that few could meet.[24]

Late Nineteenth and Early Twentieth Centuries

The states have generally followed the lead of the federal courts on questions related to representative litigation, although their rules are often more liberal than those in the federal system. According to Hazard, Gedid, and Sowle (1998) almost all nineteenth-century class litigation in state courts fell into only a few discrete categories – for example, taxpayer suits, creditor litigation, and estate and property transfers.[25] One of the leading cases was *Hale v. Hale* (1893), where the Supreme Court of Illinois was presented with an interesting set of questions. If the court applied the "necessary parties" doctrine, an estate case – such as the one brought by the heirs of Ezekiel Hale, who had died twelve years earlier and whose will divided his vast holdings to a large and growing family in stages over a period of years – could go unresolved indefinitely. Indeed, yet unborn heirs clearly had no opportunity to represent their own interests, but they would nonetheless be bound by the outcome. Taking a common-sense approach, the court reasoned: "Such possible parties can not as a matter of course be brought before the court in person, and it would be highly inconvenient and unjust, that the rights of all parties in being should be required to await the possible birth of new claimants until the possibility of such birth has become extinct. If persons in being are before the court who have the same interest ... and thus give such interests effective protection, the dictates both of convenience and justice require that there should be a complete decree" (*ibid.*, 259).

In taxpayer litigation, the courts generally asked whether there existed a true "community of interests" to decide whether parties should be bound by previously determined outcomes in proceedings to which they had no opportunity to engage (see, for example, *Lightle v. Kirby* [1937] finding that one group of taxpayer claims, antagonistic to a second one, should not be bound by the first outcome). In the most common type of situation, where a single debtor faces claims from multiple creditors, the courts have mandated the consolidation of claims into a single case, based on the theory that the plaintiffs hold an interest in common (for example, *Guffanti v. National Surety Co.* 1909 and, compare, *Schuehle v. Reiman* 1881) (consolidating separate claims against a single debtor filed in different courts). Thus, at the turn of the twentieth century, state judges, like their federal counterparts, were also converging upon a "community of interests" rationale in allowing class litigation to proceed and downplaying the "necessary parties" principle that would present a serious hurdle to such cases.

In 1912, the Supreme Court of the United States issued revised rules of procedure, rewriting *Rule 48* as *Federal Equity Rule 38,* which was essentially the same – except without the language that disallowed binding decrees on absent parties.[26] The ensuing years brought several cases in which the Court substantiated the notion that individuals not bound by incorporation could be considered bound by common interest for the purposes of litigation.[27]

For example, in 1921, in a case involving an internal conflict in a fraternal organization whose leadership had tried to reorganize the group when its financial situation took a downward turn, the Court recognized a collection of litigants as representative of others similarly situated (*Supreme Tribe of Ben-Hur v. Cauble* 1921). Yeazell (1987, 227) reads the *Supreme Tribe of Ben-Hur* opinion as opening the door to a new possibility: "[I]f one took seriously what that case implied about interest representation, then any interest that could find a representative might qualify as a temporary litigative entity."

In the following term, Chief Justice Taft, for the Court in *United Mine Workers v. Coronado Coal* (1922, 385), noted that "at common law an unincorporated association of persons was not recognized as having any other character than a partnership in whatever was done, and it could only sue or be sued in the names of its members, and their liability had to be enforced against each member."[28] Although not incorporated, the United Mine Workers, which had been sued by Coronado Coal, was well organized with an international membership of 450,000. Taft went on to observe that the union's dues "make a very large annual total, and the obligations assumed in traveling expenses, holding of conventions, and general overhead cost, but most of all in strikes, are so heavy that an extensive financial business is carried on, money is borrowed, notes are given to banks, and in every way the union acts as a business entity, distinct from its members. No organized corporation has greater unity of action, and in none is more power centered in the governing executive bodies" (*ibid.*, 385). Moreover, labour unions were recognized by federal and state legislation. Thus, the Court allowed the litigation to go forward. In so doing, as Taft acknowledged, the Court fell in line with recent British precedent in *Taff Vale Co. v. Amalgamated Society of Railway Servants* (1901), a decision that was upheld by the House of Lords.[29] There remained, however, the small issue of paying for legal services. In a class litigation situation, who should pay the legal fees?

Legal Fees
In two unrelated cases decided during the late nineteenth century, the Supreme Court of the United States dealt with this important question and, in so doing, developed the common fund doctrine, which addressed the possibility that members of a plaintiff class, through no effort or expense of their own, might be "unjustly enriched" by successful representatives who shouldered all of the financial risks. In *Trustees v. Greenough* (1881), the Court allowed a bond holder to pay his lawyers' fees from a common trust fund that was preserved as a consequence of the litigation, on the rationale that the litigant and/or lawyer who works for the good of the larger group should receive just compensation from the fund and to prevent the other bondholders from receiving "unjust enrichment" at his expense: "[W]here one of many parties having a common interest in a trust fund, at his own

expense takes proper proceedings to save it from destruction and to restore it to the purposes of the trust, he is entitled to reimbursement, either out of the fund itself, or by proportional contribution from those who accept the benefit of his efforts" (*ibid.,* 532). A few years later, in *Central Railroad and Banking Co. v. Pettus* (1885), Justice Harlan, writing for the Court, expanded the *Greenough* logic, finding that the attorneys who had successfully represented a creditor class action against an insolvent corporate debtor should be eligible for an award beyond what the individual client had already paid in fees. Otherwise, the Court reasoned, class members would benefit from the legal action without paying any of the freight – a classic "free rider" problem.[30]

Greenough and *Pettus* are now considered benchmarks in American law on the issue of the distribution of legal fees in group litigation cases. Although the logic extends beyond class actions, both cases certainly had implications for legal representation in such litigation, and they clearly have the effect of connecting parties according to their interest in a particular legal proceeding and/or outcome even when they are not formally associated. Indeed, one of the most vexing theoretical and practical issues in the development of group or representative litigation has been the question of how and under what circumstances to compensate legal counsel (see, for example, Fiss 2003, 123-26; Erichson 2000b; Misko, Goodrich, and Conte 1996; Resnik, Curtis, and Hensler 1996).

In 1796, the Supreme Court of the United States first articulated the rule that parties should bear their own legal fees rather than extracting payments from the losing side, stating simply: "The general practice of the United States is in opposition to it; and even if that practice were not strictly correct in principle, it is entitled to the respect of the court, till it is changed, or modified, by statute" (*Arcambel v. Wiseman* 1796, 306). Some 180 years later, Justice White succinctly summarized the origin and development of the so-called "American rule" regarding the distribution of legal fees in *Alyeska Pipeline Co. v. Wilderness Society* (1975, 247-57).[31] The British system, as Justice White notes, developed as early as the thirteenth century and comprised the opposite rationale – that losers should pay.[32] Indeed, legal precedent in the United States and the United Kingdom have taken divergent paths on this issue, the result being that British lawyers are more reticent about bringing class actions than are their American counterparts, which, by extension, applies across commonwealth jurisdictions such as Canada, New Zealand, and Australia.

The First Rule 23

In 1938, the procedural rules were revised yet again by an advisory committee appointed by the chief justice. This time, the issue of collective litigation was treated in *Rule 23* of the *Federal Rules of Civil Procedure,* which formally distinguishes three types of class suits: "true" actions, in which class members are clearly bound together structurally and all absent members would be bound by the outcome; "spurious" class suits where the parties have a common interest with no formal structure and absentee parties must agree to be bound; and "hybrid" cases, such as those subsequently addressed by bankruptcy, in which unnamed parties might (but not necessarily) be bound.[33] In addition, upon initiation of the litigation, the representative parties were to choose a category and present arguments to convince the trial judge to accept the *"Rule 23"* status for the claim.[34]

While the tripartite division of class actions seems to have made sense to one of its chief architects, James W. Moore, the effort was probably tainted by the New Deal experiences and heightened concern during this era with "the question of individual consent and collectivization ... in the context of labor legislation" (Yeazell 1987, 231).[35] Indeed, the "true" class category bound already connected parties, while the "spurious" class anticipated prior agreement to be so bound: "The rule strove to resolve both the political belief in individual autonomy and the dimly perceived possibilities of litigative representation" (*ibid.,* 232; also see Kalven and Rosenfield 1941, 702ff). It also diminished considerably the "community of interests" rationale to which the courts had converged, based upon the *Swormstedt* logic, in the last quarter of the nineteenth and first quarter of the twentieth centuries, making it much more difficult to launch a claim in the interest of individuals otherwise disconnected. Such litigation would fall into the "spurious class" category, and any outcome would not be considered binding on absentees unless they "opted in," thereby giving their affirmative consent. Absentees could also intervene after the fact in order to take advantage of a favourable ruling under the principle of *res judicata* ("the thing has been judged"). As Hazard, Gedid, and Sowle (1998, 1938) note, "[p]roperly speaking, a 'spurious' class suit, then, was not really a class suit at all ... it was really no more than a permissive joinder device."

Two years after the adoption of *Rule 23,* the Court heard *Hansberry v. Lee* (1940), a controversy arising from a racially restrictive residential covenant in Chicago. According to the covenant, 95 percent of all neighbourhood homeowners could agree to exclude a particular buyer and thus block a sale or transfer of property. Instead of applying the recently adopted *Rule 23,* the Court relied upon the due process clause of the Fourteenth Amendment to overturn a decision by the Supreme Court of Illinois that found that all absent members of a previously allowed class should be bound by that decision (*Lee v. Hansberry* 1939). The Illinois high court had been a leader in developing class litigation principles, and its opinion, even if complicated by the issue of race discrimination, was indicative of the disagreement among the state judiciary with the recently promulgated federal rules of procedure, particularly on the question of binding absent parties.

The previously designated class in *Hansberry* (1939) came from an earlier case that was, in all likelihood, fraudulent and collusive. In 1933, Olive Ida Burke filed an action on behalf of herself and all others (several hundred white property owners) in a Chicago residential subdivision against four parties who had allegedly violated the terms of the covenant that restricted black families from buying into the neighbourhood. Burke claimed, without producing evidence, that the 95 percent agreement threshold had been reached, and the defendant offered no rebuttal, thus allowing the 95 percent claim to be stipulated as fact. The court issued a decree in 1934 to enforce the covenant, requiring the black families to vacate (see *Burke v. Kleiman* 1934). Five years later, Anna Lee and a number of white neighbours filed a petition to prevent a property transfer to the Hansberry family, who were black, arguing that all parties were bound by the decree resulting from the earlier litigation. The Hansberrys countered that they had not been parties in the *Burke* case and were, thus, not bound by the decree and that the finding of facts in that case had been based on false claims. Moreover, to disallow their challenge to the covenant would amount to a denial of their rights to due process under the Fourteenth Amendment. The state trial court determined that there was no evidence to support the 95 percent claim (indeed, the court found that only 54 percent of the property owners had signed the covenant) and that the earlier litigation was collusive, but it nonetheless deduced that the validity of the *Burke* agreement was *res judicata* and could not be revisited. The Supreme Court of Illinois substantially agreed (*Lee v. Hansberry* 1939), concluding that, because *Burke* was a class suit and because the current parties should be considered members of the class, they were bound by the outcome).[36] The Supreme Court of the United States overturned. Justice Stone, for the Court, reasoned as follows:

> It is one thing to say that some members of a class may represent other members in a litigation where the sole and common interest of the class in the litigation, is either to assert a common right or to challenge an asserted obligation. It is quite another to hold that all those who are free alternatively either to assert rights or to challenge them are of a single class, so that any group merely because it is of the class so constituted, may be deemed adequately to represent any others of the class in litigating their interests in either alternative. Such a selection of representatives for purposes of litigation, whose substantial interests are not necessarily or even probably the same as those whom they are deemed to represent, does not afford that protection to absent parties which due process requires. (*Hansberry v. Lee* 1940, 44-45)

Thus, the *Hansberry* Court did not help to clarify the recently adopted *Rule 23* that had been drafted to address class litigation issues, especially regarding the question of when and under what circumstances decisions should be considered binding on all absent parties. While *Rule 23* suggests that a class can be joined on the basis of common interests (a spurious class), the *Hansberry* Court could not in good conscience bind absentees when the result would be a clear denial of due process rights and generally seems to assume divergence of interests among class members. Indeed, the Court stated flatly that "[i]t is a principle of general application in Anglo-American jurisprudence that one is not bound by a judgment *in personam* in a litigation in which he is not designated as a party" (*ibid.,* 40). Moreover, as Hazard, Gedid, and Sowle (1998, 1946) state, "[t]he Court ... announced a rationale for determining when class suits should be given preclusive effect – only upon adequate representation. It provided little guidance, however, concerning the content of that standard. In particular, it did not indicate what types of procedures were appropriate for ensuring, at the outset of litigation and during its course, that representation would be adequate."

Hansberry is a prototypical example of the kind of class litigation issues that make the format so interesting, yet so difficult, for the courts to resolve. The legal controversy presents internal conflicts between group leverage and individual due process rights, corporate and government accountability, as well as just compensation to individuals who have been injured, institutional and collective efficiency, and individual justice. Moreover, the case implications clearly superseded the principal litigants. The Court had to understand that any outcome would have a far-reaching public policy impact. It has also had an active afterlife. As of August 2008, *Hansberry* had been cited in 1,079 subsequent decisions, twenty-eight by the Supreme Court of the United States (according to *Shepard's Citations*).

As an interesting historical note, the petitioners in this case included the family of Lorraine Hansberry, who went on to publish "A Raisin in the Sun" in 1959. The Hansberrys were represented by Earl B. Dickerson, the first black graduate of the University of Chicago Law School and one of the founders of the National Association for the Advancement of Colored People's (NAACP) Legal Defense and Education Fund in 1939 (see, for example, Kamp 1987; Vose 1959).[37] Thus, *Hansberry* was a pivotal case on a number of counts, and it occurred at a critical point in US legal history. In 1940, the nation was emerging from the depths of the Great Depression, Franklin D. Roosevelt's New Deal was taking shape and ushering in an unprecedented era of regulatory activity, labour unions were growing, civil rights organizations were beginning to realize some genuine success in the courts, to name a few of the major changes that were occurring. It was in this context that Harry Kalven and Maurice Rosenfield (1941) published a provocative piece in the *University of Chicago Law Review* regarding the potential for class litigation under the recently revised *Rule 23*. Indeed, in their view, "[m]odern society seems increasingly to expose men to such group

injuries for which individually they are in a poor position to seek legal redress, either because they do not know enough or because such redress is
disproportionately expensive. If each is left to assert his rights alone if and
when he can, there will at best be a random and fragmentary enforcement,
if there is any at all ... The problem of fashioning an effective and inclusive
group remedy is thus a major one" (*ibid.*, 686).

Their vision perceived class litigation serving a regulatory function similar
to the one performed by the newly created executive agencies under the
developing administrative law regime, with plaintiff attorneys serving as
the equivalent of private attorneys general.[38] Moreover, as they observe,
because there were "many fields in which administrative bodies have not
made an appearance ... private litigation must still police large areas of
modern law and provide the exclusive remedy for many large-scale group
injuries" (*ibid.*, 687). They note that the rules, particularly with respect to
allowing large numbers of claimants with a similar grievance to join together
to seek common relief, had become by 1940 much less onerous than they
once were. Nonetheless, this model is based upon the notion that all interested parties will somehow recognize their commonality and take the necessary steps to bind themselves to a group claim at the initial stages of litigation.
This vision, however, ignores the realities of the world. Indeed, "such spon-
taneity cannot arise because the various parties who have the common interest are isolated, scattered, and utter strangers to each other. Thus while
the necessity for group action through joinder clearly exists, the conditions
for it do not. It may not be enough for society simply to set up courts and
wait for litigants to bring their complaints – they may never come" (*ibid.*,
688). Thus, they find great promise in collective litigation as a means for
holding powerful entities accountable in an increasingly complex world.
They take issue with the "opt in" requirements associated with the "spurious" class category of federal *Rule 23*, offering a forceful argument and
rationale for yet further revision. Nonetheless, this revision would not come
until 1966.[39]

More Recent Developments

In 1974, Justice Douglas, in a case presenting questions regarding notification requirements for a plaintiff class, clearly saw the class action as a political
tool:

> I think in our society that is growing in complexity there are bound to be
> innumerable people in common disasters, calamities, or ventures who would
> go begging for justice without the class action ... Some of these are consum-
> ers whose claims may seem de minimis ... [s]ome may be environmentalists
> ... [o]r the unnamed individual may be only a ratepayer being excessively

charged by a utility, or a homeowner whose assessment is slowly rising beyond his ability to pay.

The class action is one of the few legal remedies the small claimant has
against those who command the status quo. I would strengthen his hand
with the view of creating a system of law that dispenses justice to the lowly
as well as to those liberally endowed with power and wealth. (*Eisen v. Carlisle
and Jacquelin* 1974, 185-86 [Douglas, J., dissenting])

Justice Douglas's view represents a sea change in judicial perspective from
that of the earlier periods. Indeed, it is far more in line with the reasoning
offered by Kalven and Rosenfield (1941) than with the judicial opinion of
their era. Granted, Justice Douglas was inclined to take an expansive view
of the legal process – but he was not alone in expressing this particular
understanding of the purpose of the class action format. Justices Brennan
and Marshall joined him. While these gentlemen were also judicial liberals,
the fact that this viewpoint could be unabashedly articulated at the pinnacle
of US jurisprudence is indicative of how much the world had changed.[40]

The role, purpose, and scale of collective litigation had evolved into something quite different in 1974 than it had been in 1941. Since its adoption
in 1938, *Rule 23* had generated considerable criticism and confusion, particularly surrounding its tripartite division (true, spurious, and hybrid), and
expressions of dissatisfaction with its application were ongoing. In 1960,
Chief Justice Earl Warren appointed an advisory committee to revisit the
rules of civil procedure and, on the basis of their research and recommendations, issued an overhauled version of *Rule 23* in 1966. As we have seen, the
NAACP and its affiliate Legal Defense and Education Fund (LDEF) exploited
the earlier rule's uncertainty to attack racially restrictive residential covenants, beginning with *Hansberry* (1940), which set the stage for *Shelley v.
Kraemer* (1948), and struck down all such restrictions as unconstitutional a
decade later. Indeed, the LDEF, under the able leadership of Thurgood Marshall and Charles Houston, among others, developed a legendary strategy
to launch a full-scale assault on a wide range of racially discriminatory laws
and policies.[41] Although the political branches were largely inaccessible, the
civil rights movement did find the federal courts to be comparatively receptive, and a number of important legal breakthroughs were accomplished
through the class action form.

Group dynamics, anticipated under our foundational theory of politics
and accommodation of group formation within the structure of our governing system have always had considerable political and economic implications.[42] Aggregations of individuals need no special recognition to engage
in social, political, or economic action. Indeed, groups can be spurred into
action spontaneously without any organizational structure or explanation.

Although such group formation is possible, success is certainly not guaranteed. Many years of interest group research tells us that organizational history and strength are critical political assets (for example, Bentley 1908; Truman 1951; Salisbury 1984; Schlozman and Tierney 1986; Walker 1991; Lowery and Gray 1998), and this seems no less true in the courts than in the other political branches (for example, Galanter 1974; Kritzer and Silbey 2003). As we have seen, obtaining judicial approval to litigate as a class with no prior history or structure has been an uphill battle. Moreover, issues of constitutional due process aside, claiming to represent the interests of total strangers without any prior consultation, agreement, or consent could easily be viewed as quite presumptuous.

Yeazell (1987, 241) observes that "although blacks, because of their exclusion from many parts of society, have often been driven into close association, there are not now nor have there ever been local or national groups that encompassed all black persons." Indeed, not only were they oppressed in every possible sense of the word, changing the laws that confirmed the oppression was a long, hard slog. Resistance was met at every turn, including attempts to prevent black citizens from joining forces in groups and organizations to represent their collective interests. One such instance was made part of the official history of the period by the Supreme Court of the United States. In 1958, Justice Harlan, writing for a unanimous Court, stated: "It is beyond debate that freedom to engage in association for the advancement of beliefs and ideas is an inseparable aspect of the 'liberty' assured by the Due Process Clause of the Fourteenth Amendment, which embraces freedom of speech ... Of course, it is immaterial whether the beliefs sought to be advanced by association pertain to political, economic, religious or cultural matters, and state action which may have the effect of curtailing the freedom to associate is subject to the closest scrutiny" (*NAACP v. Alabama* 1958, 460-61).[43] In this case, the NAACP was attempting to protect its members from political harassment, but, more generally, the organization engaged in a concerted effort to utilize the courts to promote a social and political agenda that would not have been possible to pursue as unconnected individuals.[44]

The campaign for civil rights is probably the most familiar and perhaps most studied organized litigation effort of the twentieth century, and, as we have noted, much of the legal strategy was centred on the use of the class action formula. *Brown v. Board of Education* (1954), in fact, represented a consolidation of five separate class actions.[45] The legal challenges orchestrated by the NAACP's LDEF built upon the idea that a collection of individuals with no organizational structure could nonetheless engage in litigation as a group because they shared a set of interests *vis-à-vis* a common defendant with superior political and economic firepower. This is very much the image that Justice Douglas was attempting to convey in his *Eisen* dissent noted earlier.

Success breeds emulation.[46] The *Eisen* controversy saw a group of odd-lot stock traders banding together in collective action against powerful Wall Street brokerage houses on behalf of some 200 million identifiable class members, to press claims of antitrust violations and price-fixing of stock values. Initially filed in 1966, it was the *first* "mother of all classes," which, if approved, would have included virtually all citizens of the United States versus the symbolic chiefs of capitalism.[47] Although it was a bit over the top in terms of scope, it involved the type of controversy that Kalven and Rosenfield (1941) had envisioned as prime candidates for class action status. It was also indicative of the politics of the era. Ralph Nader, quintessential and quixotic advocate for the American consumer, published *Unsafe at Any Speed* in 1965, which helped to launch the public interest movement of this era.[48] Coincidentally, at approximately the same time, concerns about the degradation of the environment, such as air quality (as a result of industrial development and auto emissions), water quality (due to extensive use of pesticides and herbicides, agricultural run-off, and toxic waste seepage), increasing numbers of endangered species and diminishing tracts of undeveloped land, among other issues, led to a full-blown environmental movement. The first major legislation *(National Environmental Policy Act)* became law in 1969, and the Environmental Protection Agency came into being in 1970.[49]

Thus, it was within this volatile context of enhanced awareness of the potentials for using litigation as a political instrument and a regulatory tool – especially by civil rights proponents, environmentalists, and consumer advocates – that the advisory committee, empanelled in 1960 by Chief Justice Warren to revise the procedural rules, conducted their review. In 1966, the Civil Rules Advisory Committee issued its revisions, including an amended class action rule – *Rule 23* – acknowledging that unincorporated groups could constitute a class for litigation purposes and laying out criteria for determining representativeness. At least one of the commission members has noted that the effort was influenced by the times. In a statement submitted to a House subcommittee in 1998 regarding the Civil Rules Advisory Committee's deliberations three decades earlier, member John Frank asserted that "[t]he social setting had a most direct bearing on this rule. Rule 23 was a work in direct parallel to the Civil Rights Act of 1964 and the race relations echo of that decade was always in the committee room. If there was a single, undoubted goal of the committee, the energizing force which motivated the whole rule, it was the firm determination to create a class action system which could deal with civil rights and, explicitly, segregation" (quoted in Hensler et al. 2000, 12).

The new *Rule 23* discarded the old and troublesome tripartite division and anticipated several situations where the class action formula would apply.[50] Due process concerns were also addressed (in section c). In cases where money damages were not an issue, where the petitioner was seeking injunctive relief or equal treatment for all members of the asserted class, commonality of interests could be assumed. Moreover, in cases seeking money damages, reasonable effort was made to notify all individuals identified as class members to alert them to the contours and objectives of the action, the fact that their interests were being represented by someone else, and the fact that they would be bound by any outcome achieved (who should pay the costs associated with such notice was left unaddressed and was one of the primary issues presented in *Eisen*). Under the old rule, class members had to "opt in," a requirement that discouraged class actions. The 1966 version assumed post-notification silence to represent a decision to accept class membership and the self-appointed representation, but it allowed individuals to "opt out" if they wished and to represent their own interests themselves.[51]

The typical kind of money-damage scenario that the advisory committee foresaw found small investors banding together to hold corporate executives accountable, a type of action not likely to move forward at the individual disaggregated level since the costs of litigation would have quickly surpassed any likely award. With regard to torts, the advisory committee specifically counselled that the class action format would not likely be a useful way to proceed: "A 'mass accident' resulting in injuries to numerous persons is ordinarily not appropriate for a class action because of the likelihood that significant questions, not only of damages but of liability and defenses to liability, would be present, affecting the individuals in different ways. In these circumstances an action conducted nominally as a class action would degenerate in practice into multiple lawsuits separately tried."[52]

As US District Judge Jack Weinstein (1995, 135) asserts, "[a]s a judge I have been forced to ignore [my own earlier warning against using class actions] when faced with the practicalities of mass tort litigation. In the earlier 1960s we did not fully understand the implications of mass tort demands on our legal system." While this does seem to have been true, and the advisory committee who revised the class action rules did not anticipate what was to come, there are devices for pursuing large-scale litigation other than the class action, including formal and informal consolidation and multi-district aggregation (which did not exist until 1968, a development discussed further later in this text).[53]

The accepted doctrine for allowing a joinder of similar cases in federal court, which would be the most likely way to combine tort actions against a common defendant, has held since 1939 that claims cannot be aggregated to meet the jurisdictional dollar requirement but that each claim must meet separately the minimum requirement (*Clark v. Paul Gray, Inc.* 1939).[54] In the event of serious disaster, this is not an issue for many victims. However, it runs contradictory to one of the theoretical bases for the class action – that is, to allow small claimants to band together to hold a common defendant accountable. In 1966, when *Rule 23* was issued, the only mass tort actions that had been filed had resulted from airplane crashes (for example, *Van Dusen v. Barrack* 1964) and major highway accidents (for example, *State Farm Fire and Casualty Co. v. Tashire* [1967], which involved a bus/truck collision).

More generally, tort law theory, particularly that dealing with product liability, was moving in a direction that would eventually be conducive to considering claims under the class action formula. If one can calculate risks associated with a given activity or use of a product, then appropriate degrees of liability can theoretically be assigned. However, as social and economic conditions became more complex and the margin for error was rendered infinitesimally small across a range of activities, where an otherwise insignificant act of negligence or minute flaw somewhere along the chain could lead ultimately to disaster, judges gradually acknowledged that risk was becoming nearly impossible to assess. Some activities, such as rocket launch testing (for example, *Smith v. Lockheed Propulsion Co.* 1967) or crop dusting (for example, *Loe v. Lenhardt* 1961), were recognized to be inherently ultrahazardous or abnormally dangerous, and damages to injured parties (who were largely oblivious to the danger) that arose from such activities should be assessed by a strict liability principle.[55] Indeed, the list of such activities was, by 1970, growing longer, and strict liability had gained considerable purchase as a standard in product liability litigation (see, for example, Sayles and Lamden 2001; Friedman 1987; Lieberman 1981). In general, most rules associated with tort liability were loosening significantly, and, by the mid-1970s, the Supreme Court of the United States had begun to ease restrictions on advertising by practising attorneys (for example, *Bates v. State Bar of Arizona* 1977).[56]

Consolidation of tort claims from multiple jurisdictions into a single proceeding found its roots in the same time period. In 1962, Chief Justice Earl Warren established a Coordinating Committee for Multi-District Litigation for the United States District Courts in response to a nationwide tidal wave of antitrust cases against major electrical equipment manufacturers after they were criminally convicted for violating the *Sherman Antitrust Act*.[57] Indeed, in 1961, some 2,000 cases were filed, representing about 25,000 claims, in thirty-six US district courts. To address this challenge piecemeal would be an unending nightmare for the court system. The charge to the coordinating committee was to consolidate and centralize all pretrial proceedings in the interest of efficiency and fairness. The experiment was subsequently considered to have been a grand success – a mere nine cases moved to trial, and only five of those went the full distance to final decision (see, for example, Cahn 1976; McDermott 1973). In addition, the Judicial Panel on Multi-District Litigation (JPML) was given a more permanent status in 1968, and the *Multi-District Litigation Act* was passed through Congress.[58] Under the provisions of the 1968 act, parties could request that the JPML aggregate suits arising out of the same or similar circumstances that were filed in different jurisdictions and transfer them to a single court and judge to deal with all pretrial matters. A court that had been assigned multiple cases from other jurisdictions could not retain jurisdiction after resolving the pretrial issues. Instead, the cases must be returned to the districts where they originated for trial (Galanter 2004, 41). As James Wood (1999, 327) reports, "[i]n spite of this legislative limitation, it became a standing practice for pretrial coordinating courts to transfer cases to themselves for trial." This litigation management device ultimately came before the Supreme Court of the United States thirty years later, in *Lexecon Inc. v. Milberg Weiss Bershad Hynes and Lerach* (1998), which held that such self-transferal is improper and that cases must be returned to the court of origin for trial. This problem (in addition to a range of other issues) was addressed by Congress in 2002, and, under current law, a multi-district litigation (MDL) court can retain jurisdiction for the purposes of a trial.[59]

The number of sets of consolidated MDLs has steadily risen since the 1968 provisions went into effect. The panel packaged and transferred 295 case bundles in 2002, compared to 117 in 1972, with the two largest collections of claims being those associated with asbestos (106,069 cases) and breast implants (27,526) (Galanter 2004, 42-23). By comparison, class action torts estimated to have been filed in US district courts in 1978 numbered fewer than 200, and, by 2002, the figure had nearly reached 600, with the most significant increases occurring after 1998. Although not dramatic, the rise is noticeable, particularly given the nature of the issues involved. As Judge Jack Weinstein (1994, 474-75) asserts,

> [m]ass tort cases and public litigations both implicate serious political and sociological issues. Both are restrained by economic imperatives. Both have strong psychological underpinnings. And both affect larger communities than those encompassed by the litigants before the court. Like many of our great public cases, mass torts often embody disquieting uncertainties about modern society and the individual's relation to our institutions. School desegregation cases involve underlying issues of racial and social prejudice, sexual fantasies, and concern about safety, property values, and power. Prison reform cases raise questions about the role of punishment and theological assumptions about the inherent badness or goodness of humanity. Catastrophes such as the Exxon Valdez oil spill or the New York City World Trade Center bombing of 1993 may seriously affect a town, a state, or an entire country. Many constitutional cases dealing with privacy, sexuality, hate, or abortion require analysis in terms of group psychology or psychiatry and sociology.

Indeed, courts have hosted some of the most momentous issues of each decade since class action *Rule 23* was revised in 1966 and multi-districting became an option in 1968, as judges have faced the tremendous challenge of sorting through the legalities associated with human tragedies on both an individual and social level. As we noted earlier, those who drafted the class action revisions were addressing a legal world dominated by civil rights and consumer issues. And, in fact, civil rights issues far outnumbered all other class actions until the mid-1980s (Galanter 2004, 39). Similarly, those who wrote the MDL provisions thought they were addressing a legal world dominated by corporate-consumer relations. In 1972, antitrust and securities litigation accounted for 48 percent of all MDL consolidations (44 percent in 1977). They could not have known what was on the horizon. Peter Schuck (1986, 945-96), who has written extensively about Agent Orange litigation, places matters nicely within the perspective of the time:

> Imagine that it is the summer of 1969. The term "mass tort" has not yet been coined, although it has been loosely applied to airline crashes, large fires, and other single-event accidents that happen to affect numerous claimants ... Clarence Borel has not yet filed his soon-to-be paradigmatic mass tort action against the manufacturers of asbestos insulation materials. With the blessing of the Food and Drug Administration (FDA), physicians routinely prescribe Diethylstilbestrol (DES) to prevent miscarriages. Agent Orange is widely deemed a miracle defoliant that will save the lives of soldiers and civilians rather than putting them at risk of serious illness or death. The newly-designed Dalkon Shield is being heralded as a safe, effective contraceptive. Bendectin is still considered to be a wonder drug by the FDA and by tens of millions of women suffering from morning sickness. Silicone breast implants have been on the market for only a few years; two decades will elapse before the FDA begins to warn women about them ... Repetitive-strain disorders and electro-magnetic field syndromes are not even a gleam in the eye of the most resourceful and creative plaintiffs' lawyers. Cigarette manufacturers have won the first wave of litigation against them by a "knockout," causing the wave to retreat and discouraging further suits by smokers until the 1980s.

Rules, regulations, laws, and principles have always been adapted by those using the process of litigation to meet the exigencies of their situation and of their era. The rules of procedure regarding collective litigation are no exception. The advisory committee who worked to revise the rules of civil procedure in the mid-1960s, as we have noted, hoped to remedy problems with the old rules and viewed the class action within the contemporary context of civil rights and consumer advocacy. They did not believe, and did not foresee, the class action as an appropriate vehicle for mass torts. They considered the problem presented by "mass accidents" but were careful to build into the rule notification requirements if *Rule 23* were utilized for a collective tort as well as an "opt out" provision to allow individuals to present their own cases on the assumption that personal injuries would be likely to involve idiosyncratic harm that would be masked by a necessarily generalized class action claim. However, modern mass tort situations often present issues of more general concern that transcend the parochial interests of individual plaintiffs. Indeed, there are far-reaching social interests involved when hundreds of thousands of asbestos workers have their lives shortened by disease and whose final days are predictably horrific. Similarly, millions of patients were treated for obesity with a combination pharmaceutical regimen thought to be a miracle appetite suppression drug only to find out too late that they now faced much elevated risk for a series of cardiovascular diseases. True, use of the drug "Fen-Phen" produced scores and scores of individual stories of pain and tragedy. However, marketing and prescribing the drug on such a scale elevates the issues well beyond the individual level.

Even assuming that system efficiency and logistical problems could be overcome, allowing plaintiffs to proceed individually may well produce a collective outcome that most observers would consider to be undesirable – even irresponsible. Indeed, in these and similar cases, a very large number of individual plaintiffs do have compelling stories. If they are independently compensated in the amounts that they truly deserve, at some point the defendants' ability to pay will be challenged, thus making bankruptcy a real possibility. Some might argue that such an outcome is a rich reward for what they perceive to be corporate greed and disregard for human life. However, what of the other victims left entirely uncompensated if bankruptcy occurs with cases pending (or yet to be filed)? In such cases involving multiple tort claims against one or a few defendants, the larger issues are, indeed, similar to those found in bankruptcy proceedings, where consolidation of petitions is the norm and outcomes are binding upon all involved, including those with potential, yet unfiled, claims. Thus, one's calculations are restricted by the limited fund qualities of defendants' resources as well as by the actions of other similarly situated claimants (see, for example, Cramton 1995, 817). One might easily conclude that to reconcile the social and individual interests involved in such cases would require collectivizing the litigation. Yet, of course, this notion shifts the emphasis away from the parties and their respective presentations and places it upon the conflict and its broader implications.

In addition, torts can be very complex, and proving causation, after a lengthy series of transactions of various types and given the latency effect associated with most toxic exposures, can be quite costly. A case-by-case approach is highly inefficient for all concerned, especially considering the redundant expenses that would be devoted to research, discovery, and expert testimony. A collective approach is often an attractive alternative to plaintiffs and defendants alike and especially to courts and judges who will nearly always prefer processing one big case as opposed to thousands of separate ones that present the same or very similar issues. And, as we have noted earlier, by sharing the expenses in collective litigation, plaintiffs (and their attorneys) can avoid the "free rider" problem inherent in single actions, where others similarly situated reap all of the benefits of their effort without contributing anything to the costs associated with preparing and conducting a successful assault.

Although aggregating tort claims in certain situations does have unambiguous advantages, there is significant tension between safeguarding individual rights and achieving individual justice, on the one hand, and promoting collective justice, on the other. It is a tension that has plagued those who have considered these questions in the United States from at least the time that Justice Story initially attempted to address them in the 1820s and 1830s. But they do not end here. Once claims are collected into a single action, all of the incentives seem to encourage settlement. Indeed, trial and adjudication adds significantly to the cost for all participants while offering little promise of finality. For claimants, a settlement has the obvious advantage of bringing matters to a close with some financial compensation (although it is often insufficient, given the personal trauma that they have experienced) and with the knowledge that the defendants have paid dearly for their actions. Their attorneys are guaranteed payment for their considerable investment. Judges can put the entire matter finally (and hopefully) to rest. And defendant corporations can convert uncertain liability to a finite, manageable total, while limiting their exposure to future claims arising from the same set of actions. Presumably, they will also take corrective measures to minimize repeating the offending scenario.

This scenario has given impetus to the quite recent phenomenon of settlement classes, cases filed under *Rule 23* explicitly for the purpose of settlement. As part of the deal, all parties, including any potential class members not yet identified, are bound by the resolution. To achieve this result, the presiding judge must officially approve it. Pre-settlement activities in such cases can consume enormous time and resources on the part of all of the major players, and coming to such terms is no small matter. Nonetheless, in addressing the controversy as a social problem and in carving a solution that has larger policy and regulatory implications, problems of individual justice are sacrificed. Moreover, the settlement, if approved by the court, is binding on all without their input and without their consent, which brings forward the age-old problem. Some have observed that this kind of format may solve the "free rider" issues, but it simultaneously creates a "kidnapped rider" problem (see, for example, Garth 1982).[60] This is precisely the issue presented to the Supreme Court of the United States in two relatively recent cases stemming from the massive tide of asbestos litigation, *Amchem Products v.*

Windsor (1997) and *Ortiz v. Fibreboard Corporation* (1999) (see further discussion in Chapter 2 in this text).

Although the dimensions of the asbestos litigation are unusually huge and the injuries irreversible and far-reaching, the conflict between individual and collective justice embedded within it is a stubborn reality of group action. Such a scenario is particularly true given the historical and contemporary purchasing power of focus on the individual and individual rights in political and legal debate in the United States. When *Rule 23* was revised in 1966 and openly accepted the class action form, some observers were hoping for justice on behalf of the "small claimant," society's "lowly," who had suffered injuries at the hands of "those who command the status quo ... those liberally endowed with power and wealth" (*Eisen v. Carlisle and Jacquelin* 1974, 186 [Douglas J., dissenting]), much like "white knights in shining armor" who would use the class action as a sword to slay the dragons that preyed on the helpless. Others, however, saw the procedure as a "Frankenstein's monster," which, although created with good intentions, would quickly wreak havoc across the system (Miller 1979). Indeed, investigators have noted the persistent effort of networks of "white knights" who have engaged the system on behalf of the many who need protection (for example, Kluger 1976; Tushnet 1987; Schuck 1986). This view of the process is tempered by the observation that in litigation the "haves" usually come out ahead (Galanter 1974; and see, for example, Kritzer and Silbey 2003), because they have the resources to devote to developing winning strategies and to engage in prolonged, multi-tiered efforts, and still further by research that finds the courts to be institutionally too weak to take a lead in fostering social change (for example, Rosenberg 1991).

Characterizations of group litigation, particularly class actions, in the political process and in the popular media tend to be hyperbolic. Indeed, William Haltom and Michael McCann (2004a) thoroughly document and assess the broad scale effort of the corporate community and their political allies to wage a very successful media campaign to portray the tort law system (especially regarding product liability) as facing crisis because of frivolous claims brought by greedy, undeserving individuals represented by unscrupulous and relentless lawyers.[61] However, given the scope of truly significant issues that have been litigated as class actions, and the far-reaching regulatory and policy implications that flow from them, we should probably expect hyperbole. The list of paramount questions that have been placed before the courts in this form is quite impressive, ranging from civil rights, environmental protection, and asbestos-related injuries, as we have noted, to a long list of problems associated with pharmaceutical drugs, medical products, corporate securities and sales issues, and workplace-related injuries. In each instance, the threshold consists of such problems as representativeness of the named parties who have come forward on behalf of all others whose interests they claim to signify and whether care has been taken to protect the rights of unidentified group members. In each case, the court is asked to acknowledge the larger policy repercussions of the challenged activity/product/condition as well as the regulatory implications of solution options and to reconcile inherent tension between the greater good and individual rights and compensation. Judges have dealt with them in different ways, but these issues have accompanied group litigation from the earliest of cases. It is this tension and the challenge of confronting it that we trace in the chapters ahead.

We first assess the full flowering of mass tort litigation in the United States, how it has unfolded as a legal phenomenon in the post-*Rule 23* contemporary era, and the strategies crafted and deployed by either side of the conflict. In Chapter 3, we appraise the development of what became wide-band litigation in the United States against the tobacco industry, and, in Chapter 4, we examine the broad court-centred effort against gun manufacturers. Chapter 5 investigates the use of the class action model in response to problems associated with mass production, distribution, and consumption of food products. Although the United States was relatively late in addressing the problems of group litigation, compared to the United Kingdom, and early American jurists looked across the Atlantic for guidance, the US project diverged from others by the late nineteenth century. Chapter 6 assesses recent developments in group litigation beyond the United States, particularly in the United Kingdom, Canada, and Australia, allowing us to put the US experience in a broader perspective. Finally, Chapter 7 re-addresses the central issues in light of our observations.

2
Mass Torts and Class Action: An Overview of the Contemporary American Landscape

If any subject captures both the possibilities and the problems of modern mass tort litigation in general, and class actions in particular, it is, in Justice Souter's words, "the elephantine mass of asbestos cases" (*Ortiz v. Fibreboard Corp*. 1999, 821). Though of a kind of mythic proportion all of its own, the story of asbestos litigation is also the story of modern mass litigation. It begins with a wrongdoing – a tort. Like many other such cases, the wrong is exacerbated by an attempted corporate cover-up. At some point, a single harmed individual sues the offender. He or she is followed by other aggrieved parties. As news of these events proliferates, masses of filings follow, some in the form of class actions or attempted class actions. Initially, defendants tend to fight back aggressively in court. However, mounting legal fees, actual or feared losses, and potentially damaging publicity increasingly suggest that settlement is preferable to battle. Throughout it all, defendants look for ways to minimize their losses, from seeking protection under Chapter 11 bankruptcy to lobbying legislatures for immunity and, thinking more long term, wholesale tort reform (see, for example, Haltom and McCann 2004a).

Anatomy of a Mass Tort: The Case of Asbestos
The current dimensions of asbestos litigation are nothing short of breathtaking. Since the first serious case was launched in 1966, over 600,000 people have filed claims against some 6,000 companies. As of 2000, $54 billion had already been spent on trials, settlements, and transaction costs. Between 1991 and 2003, Judge Charles Weiner of the federal district for eastern Pennsylvania oversaw more than 105,000 asbestos-related lawsuits (Administrative Office of the US Courts 2003). Estimates of future costs "are all extremely high." All accounts agree that, at best, only about half the final number of claimants have come forward. At worst, only one-fifth of all claimants have filed petitions to date, meaning "500,000 to 2.4 million asbestos claims still may be looming" (O'Malley 2008, 1102). Estimates of the total costs of all claims range from $200-265 billion (Carroll et al. 2002).[1]

Asbestos is a fire resistant mineral that is easily mined and processed. It has a long history, beginning, at least in modern times, with the opening of the first asbestos mine in Québec in 1879 (Brodeur 1985). Named "the mineral of a thousand uses," asbestos production mushroomed through the late nineteenth and into the twentieth century, with industrial and consumer applications numbering well over a thousand (Gee and Greenberg 2001). Nearly as long as the history of the "magic mineral's" widespread use, however, has been the history of its deleterious affects on health: "The earliest account of the health hazard of working with asbestos was provided by Lucy Deane, one of the first Women Inspectors of Factories in the UK. Writing in 1898, Deane included asbestos work as one of the four dusty occupations which came under observation that year, 'on account of their easily demonstrated danger to the health of workers and because of ascertained cases of injury to bronchial tubes and lungs medically attributed to the employment of the sufferer'" (*ibid.*, 2001, 2). In 1906 in France, asbestos was linked to the deaths of fifty textile workers. And, by the 1930s, scientific studies had demonstrated a causal association between the mineral and lung disease, including cancer (Tomatis 2004).

Such news was hardly greeted by industry-wide attempts to redress the problems. On the contrary, Johns-Manville, the largest asbestos manufacturer in the United States, chose to engage in a massive cover-up. According to court documents throughout the 1930s, 40s, and 50s (see, for example, *Johns-Manville Sales Corp. v. Janssens* 1984; *Fischer v. Johns-Manville* 1986), the asbestos manufacturer failed to warn workers about the known risks of its product, including death; pressured researchers to change study results; ordered company physicians to withhold from employees X-ray results that indicated asbestosis; and, when workers did bring compensation claims forward, it entered into a secret settlement, in which the plaintiffs' attorney agreed, among other things, not to bring any more cases against the company (*Johns-Manville Sales Corp. v. Janssens* 1984; *Fischer v. Johns-Manville* 1986). Nor was Johns-Manville alone in its behaviour. Other manufacturers and users of asbestos engaged in similar long-term deceptions (American Association for Justice 2004).

In 1966, the luck of the asbestos industry began to run thin when Claude Tomplait filed suit against Johns-Manville, Fibreboard, Owens Corning Fiberglas, and eight other manufacturers of asbestos-containing insulation products (*Tomplait v. Combustion Engineering, Inc.* 1968). Tomplait lost his case at trial, but his attorney, Ward Stephenson, subsequently sued on behalf of a co-worker, Clarence Borel, who had contracted mesothelioma, the deadliest form of asbestos-induced cancer. A Texas jury awarded damages to Borel's widow. And, in 1973, the trial court decision was upheld on appeal, finding manufacturers of asbestos *strictly liable* to injured workers (*Borel v. Fibreboard Paper Products Corporation* 1973).

The mid-1960s through the early 1970s marked a turning point in asbestos litigation for several other reasons. Groundbreaking research by Irving Selikoff "concluded that up to 80 percent of asbestos insulators were contracting asbestosis after a latency period of 20 years, that the risk of lung cancer for asbestos workers (especially those who smoked) was 90 times greater than expected, and that asbestosis was killing hundreds of asbestos insulators" (United States, House of Representatives 2000). Moreover, during the 1970s, both the Occupational Safety and Health Administration (OSHA) and the Environmental Protection Agency (EPA) moved to regulate asbestos, with the OSHA developing standards for workplace exposure and the EPA deeming it a major industrial hazard and banning its use in insulation (United States, Environmental Protection Agency 1999). Thus, the sprinkling of lawsuits became a litigation tsunami.

At first, there was considerable resistance. Statutes of limitation in many states made it difficult for workers to file suit when their injuries appeared many years – even many decades – after exposure. In other jurisdictions, so-called "one-injury" rules prevented litigants who had sued after contracting asbestosis from later instituting an additional suit when cancer became apparent. And, at first, defendant manufacturers fought back aggressively, invoking a "state-of-the-art" defence – essentially creating a cover that "we just didn't, and couldn't have, known how bad things were prior to the Selikoff studies." The line was successful, defeating a number of claims and discouraging many others (Brodeur 1985, 82).

The solution was the mass tort:

> By the mid-1980s ... plaintiff law firms in areas of heavy asbestos exposure (such as jurisdictions with shipyards or petrochemical facilities) had learned that they could succeed against asbestos defendants by filing large numbers of claims, grouping them together and negotiating with defendants on behalf of the entire group. Often defendants would agree to settle all of the claims that were so grouped, including those claims that were questionable, to reduce their overall costs of litigation. By agreeing to pay questionable smaller-value claims in exchange for also settling stronger and larger-value claims, defendants could also contain their financial risk. Some plaintiffs might receive lower values for claims that were settled as part of a group. But litigating claims en masse lowered the cost and risk per claim for plaintiff law firms. (Carroll et al. 2002, 23)

For their part, defendants responded with a two-fold strategy. On the one hand, as a means of reducing transaction costs, mass settlement was preferred over individual battle. These settlements generally took the form of agreements to pay "large numbers of cases with leading plaintiffs' attorneys' firms" (*ibid.*, 25). On the other hand, as a means of reducing the cost of damages, bankruptcy became the order of the day. Between 1978 and 1993, twenty firms declared bankruptcy (Plevin and Kalish 2002).[2] Even today, asbestos bankruptcy filings continue to occur. Between 2000 and 2003, thirty-four more companies declared bankruptcy, including such giants as W.R. Grace, Bethlehem Steel, and Kaiser Aluminum.[3] All told, by 2004, more than seventy companies had gone bankrupt (Asbestos Alliance 2004).

As litigation mushroomed – by the 1980s, over 20,000 claimants had initiated suits (Carroll et al. 2002, 2) – attempts were made to achieve some kind of global settlement. Such settlement agreements could take several forms, and parties to asbestos litigation tried to achieve two of these forms.[4] Thus, in 1991, federal asbestos cases were transferred to a single judge in a multidistrict litigation procedure (MDL). From the courts' perspective, this procedure was much preferable to allowing the cases to proceed piecemeal in dozens of different forums. The purpose of the MDL transfer was to allow a single judge in a single courtroom to resolve all of the pretrial matters collectively. The consolidation was supposed to achieve a global settlement, but it failed, breaking down under the sheer weight of interests (*ibid.*, 27).

Of course, another option was the class action.[5] In the early 1990s, parties to federal asbestos litigation began settlement proceedings. Represented were twenty defendant companies and thousands of plaintiffs. Defendants, allied through the counsel for the Center for Claims Resolution (CCR), agreed to resolve through separate agreements the claims that had already been filed. The deal maker, then, was a class-creating accord between the CCR and the plaintiffs' representatives. The class was to comprise plaintiffs who had not yet filed lawsuits, including nine identified plaintiffs who would supposedly represent the amorphous grouping of future litigants – potentially millions of individuals. The pact was meant to "preclude nearly all class members from litigating against CCR companies, all claims not filed before January 15, 1993, involving compensation for present and future asbestos-related personal injury or death" (*Amchem Products v. Windsor* 1997, 597-603).

In 1997, the Supreme Court of the United States demurred. The class, asserted the Court, was simply too diverse to be adequately represented by a single settlement, thus running afoul of *Rule 23*. Moreover, the treatment of present versus future claimants was found to be seriously inequitable, with those currently manifesting symptoms potentially reaping far greater damages than so-called "exposure-only" claimants (*ibid.*, 626). Notably, Justice Ginsburg, writing for the six-to-two majority, urged Congress to step into the asbestos quagmire (*ibid.*, 599). In 1999, the Court again rejected an attempt to form a mass class settlement – this time on the part of Fibreboard Corporation and its insurers (*Ortiz v. Fibreboard Corp.* 1999). Again, the Court urged Congress to enter the fray, noting that the asbestos litigation "cries out for a legislative solution" (*ibid.*, 865 [Rehnquist J., concurring]).

The colossal politics of mass litigation are hard to contain. Beginning in board rooms and law offices and trickling, then cascading, into court, they can – as asbestos did – pour into other arenas as well. In the case of asbestos, those other arenas have had no more success at containment than the judicial system. To date, Congress has still not fashioned a politically acceptable framework, despite both judicial and presidential scolding.[6] The last major attempt was sponsored by Senator Arlen Specter (a Republican from Pennsylvania) as well as fourteen fellow Republicans and three Democrats. It involved the introduction of the *Fairness in Asbestos Injury Resolution Act of 2006 (FAIR Act)*,[7] which was an attempt to create a central payment fund out of deposits made by defendant companies and their insurers. The fund, which was to be administered by the Department of Labor, would have compensated present and future claimants based on the severity of injury. Largely backed by corporate and insurance defendants under the umbrella group, the Asbestos Alliance, the bill faced stiff opposition from labour unions and plaintiffs' attorneys. Moreover, many in the defendant community were unhappy with some provisions (Deligiannis 2004). The bill continues to languish. The history of this long and sordid story is presented in Appendix 2.1 at the end of this chapter, and, as we shall see in Chapter 6, although the cases bear different names, the asbestos saga is not appreciably different outside the United States.

Cases in the Contemporary Landscape

As suggested in the previous chapter, the class action, in form if not in name, has an ancient pedigree. Its rise to prominence in modernity is often associated with the battle for civil rights during the mid-twentieth century. Most of the school desegregation cases – including, notably, *Brown v. Board of Education* (1954) – were class actions. Major advances in women's rights sometimes were the result of class litigation (see, for example, *Roe v. Wade* 1973 and *Dothard v. Rawlinson* 1977). The welfare reform movement of the 1970s was, in large part, fuelled by class demands (see, for example, *Rosado v. Wyman* 1970 and *Graham v. Richardson* 1971). Similarly, prison reform efforts were generally launched via class actions (for example, *Wolff v. McDonnell* 1974). The political bases of such suits were plain. They tended to be based on the US Constitution (due process or equal protection claims) or on a particular statute (for instance, the *Civil Rights Act*). And, significantly, the litigants seldom sought money damages but, rather, broad institutional reform of, primarily, government agencies and practices.

Although civil rights and liberties are still pursued via class action, such endeavours have been swamped by the burgeoning wave of the mass tort.[8] Generally initiated by consumers, workers, and shareholders, these class actions seek real money damages. They often involve aggressive class recruitment on the part of law firms. And they are ubiquitous, covering numerous products, pharmaceuticals, and services. This new class action terrain, as noted previously, can be traced to the 1966 revision of *Rule 23*. Under the old provisions, all parties seeking money damages needed to "opt in." The new rules, however, reversed the dynamic, sanctioning the opportunity for individuals to "opt out." A few plaintiffs could now claim to represent huge numbers of people – individuals who would be part of the suit unless they explicitly removed themselves. During the following decade, states revised their own class action rules to match the changes in federal law. Moreover, Congress and state legislatures enacted numerous consumer rights statutes, increasing the grounds on which class actions for money damages could be brought (Hensler et al. 2000, 1). Thus, it was in the era of most intense individual rights development that collective action moved to the fore (Yeazell 1989).

The 1980s witnessed an explosion of massive product liability suits, ushering in the age of the "mass tort." Asbestos and similar litigations swamped both federal and state courts. Plaintiff law firms became more assertive, coordinating their efforts. Judges began certifying mass tort class actions (*ibid.*, 2). In a symposium held to discuss the subject, it was explained that, where "[i]n the 1960s a tort suit involving one hundred common plaintiffs would have been considered exceptional," today thousands are frequently joined in shared actions (Symposium 2003, 151). Since there is no central clearinghouse or national registry of class actions, the number of such suits, particularly at the state level, remains unknown. What is known is that the form covers a wide swath of the economy.

Pharmaceuticals

A major target of class actions over the past thirty years has been the pharmaceutical industry. Most drugs, of course, have side effects. Yet failures to warn of certain side effects and particularly the devastating outcomes have not only led to serious consequences among those who took the drugs but have also inspired a number of large-scale actions. Among the progenitors of the toxic pharmaceutical tort were the alleged teratogens (birth defect-causing drugs), diethylstilbestrol (DES) and Bendectin. Although these lawsuits were very different in configuration and outcome, they set the stage for latter day efforts – one giving some succour to plaintiffs and the other to the defendants.

DES was manufactured from 1937 to 1971. Significantly, the drug was never patented and thus was able to be produced by any pharmaceutical manufacturer that obtained permission from the Food and Drug Administration (FDA) (*Bichler v. Eli Lilly and Company* 1982, 183). Originally used as a treatment for "vaginitis, engorgement of the breasts, excessive menstrual bleeding and symptoms of menopause," the FDA approved its use in 1947 for the prevention of miscarriages (*ibid.*, 183). Over about two decades, millions of women were prescribed DES, which was seen by many physicians "as a possible panacea for pregnancy problems" (*Lyon v. Premo Pharmaceutical Labs, Inc.* 1979, 194). The "cure," unfortunately, was worse than the disease. In 1971, the FDA ordered drug companies to stop "marketing and promoting DES for the purpose of preventing miscarriages, and to warn physicians and the public that the drug should not be used by pregnant women because of the danger to their unborn children." DES, it seems, could result in "cancerous vaginal and cervical growths" in daughters of mothers who had taken the drug during pregnancy (*Sindell v. Abbott Laboratories* 1980, 925).

What made the DES litigation particularly problematic was the fact that most plaintiffs were unable to identify any specific defendant company. After all, the drug had been produced by as many as 148 separate companies and ingested by plaintiffs' mothers twenty to thirty years earlier (*Bichler v. Eli Lilly and Company* 1982, 184). Thus, litigants faced the "problem of the indeterminate defendant" (*In re "Agent Orange" Product Liability Litigation* 1984). Not surprisingly, the major defendants, such as Eli Lilly and Abbott Laboratories – the "deep pockets" of the industry – argued that if specific, individualized injurers could not be identified there could be no case (*Sindell v. Abbott Laboratories* 1980, 926). However, in a major blow to the industry, the Supreme Court of California disagreed, advancing a "market share" theory of liability in the class action:

> [W]e approach the issue of causation from a different perspective: we hold it to be reasonable in the present context to measure the likelihood that any of the defendants supplied the product which allegedly injured plaintiff by the percentage which the DES sold by each of them for the purpose of preventing miscarriage bears to the entire production of the drug sold by all for that purpose. Plaintiff asserts in her briefs that Eli Lilly and Company and five or six other companies produced 90 percent of the DES marketed. If at trial this is established to be the fact, then there is a corresponding likelihood that this comparative handful of producers manufactured the DES which caused plaintiff's injuries, and only a 10 percent likelihood that the offending producer would escape liability. (*ibid.,* 937)

The Court of Appeals of New York followed suit several years later (*Hymowitz v. Eli Lilly* 1989), as did courts in Washington and Wisconsin (Cardinale 2004, 164; but see, for a different result, *Sutowski v. Eli Lilly and Company* 1998).[9]

If the DES cases could be seen as being plaintiff-friendly, the Bendectin cases ultimately favoured defendants or, more precisely, *the* defendant, Merrell Dow.[10] First marketed in 1956, Bendectin was a combination of three ingredients (later two) that were touted as an antidote to morning sickness (Sanders 1992, 317-18). By the late 1960s, the possibility that Bendectin was a teratogen began emerging. And "by the mid-1970s, the FDA had on file over ninety physician reports noting defects among children whose mothers had taken Bendectin" (*ibid.*, 318). Finally, in October 1979, the *National Enquirer* ran a cover story on the drug under the headline: "The New Thalidomide Scandal: Experts Reveal." Significantly, the story had been given to the tabloid by super-attorney Melvin Belli, who was then representing the first of the Bendectin plaintiffs (Green 1996, 134).

The initial Bendectin case was brought by a single family on behalf of its infant son, born with "malformed and missing fingers and a missing pectoral muscle" (*Mekdeci v. Merrell National Laboratories* 1983). Merrell committed enormous resources to its defense. According to Sanders,

> [c]ompared to plaintiffs, defendants generally have a substantial early advantage. Their financial resources are much greater. They can hire counsel who are experienced in the defense of defective pharmaceuticals against personal injury claims and who are well connected to governmental agencies. They have ready access to nearly all the safety data concerning their product. All these advantages inured to Merrell's benefit in the Mekdeci case. The company committed unlimited resources to Bendectin's defense, hiring Lawrence E. Walsh and the firm of Davis Polk and Wardwell as defense counsel. Moreover, after its experiences with Thalidomide and MER/29, Merrell probably had as much experience as any firm in defending prescription drugs in court. (Sanders 1992, 350)

The commitment paid off when the plaintiffs lost in a second trial, a loss that was upheld on appeal (*Mekdeci v. Merrell National Laboratories* 1983). Aside from its size and experience, Merrell benefited during the first case from the history of the litigants themselves. Mrs. Mekdeci, the child's mother, had ingested numerous drugs during her pregnancy. Thus, any link to Bendectin was tenuous. As a result, the plaintiffs' attorneys began mobilizing in search of shared resources and cleaner cases (Sanders 1992, 355). These efforts resulted in thousands of filings, many of which were consolidated for trial.[11] Among these, one of the largest and most significant was a MDL in the southern Ohio district, involving 818 cases (*In re: Richardson-Merrell, Inc. "Bendectin" Products Liability Litigation* 1985). In 1983, Merrell voluntarily pulled Bendectin from the market. And in an effort to avoid further trial, the company offered "the total sum of $120 million for all Bendectin cases, both current and future" (*ibid.*, 1216). As of 1984, it was the third largest settlement proposal of all time, yet the plaintiff lawyers challenged the offer as being "too little and too vague" (Lauter 1984). Moreover, they objected to Judge Rubin's certification of "a 'non-opt out' class for settlement purposes of all persons exposed to Bendectin" (*In re: Bendectin Products Liability Litigation* 1984, 302). Thereafter, hopes of settlement quickly evaporated.

At the heart of the Bendectin trials and appeals that followed was the legitimacy of scientific evidence presented by the plaintiffs. Indeed, Bendectin's greatest contribution to law is its role as progenitor of a major ruling on expert scientific data by the Supreme Court of the United States. At trial, plaintiffs offered three kinds of evidence: test tube and live animal experiments; pharmacological studies of substances known to be teratogens, which allegedly bore chemical structures similar to that of Bendectin; and "the reanalysis, or recalculation, of previously published epidemiological studies" (*Daubert v. Merrell Dow Pharmaceuticals, Inc.* 1993). In 1989, relying on long-established precedent, a US District Court judge in California granted summary judgment in favour of Merrell.[12] "A necessary predicate to the admission of scientific evidence," asserted Judge Gilliam, "is that the principle upon which it is based 'must be sufficiently established to have general acceptance in the field to which it belongs'" (*Daubert v. Merrell Dow Pharmaceuticals, Inc.* 1989 [citing *United States v. Kilgus* 1978, 510]). This being the case,

> [t]he court concluded that petitioners' evidence did not meet this standard. Given the vast body of epidemiological data concerning Bendectin, the court held, expert opinion which is not based on epidemiological evidence is not admissible to establish causation. Thus, the animal-cell studies, live-animal studies, and chemical-structure analyses on which petitioners had relied could not raise by themselves a reasonably disputable jury issue regarding causation. Petitioners' epidemiological analyses, based as they were on recalculations of data in previously published studies that had found no causal link between the drug and birth defects, were ruled to be inadmissible because they had not been published or subjected to peer review. (*Daubert v. Merrell Dow Pharmaceuticals, Inc.* 1993, 583-84)

The Supreme Court of the United States, however, disagreed, ruling that the "general acceptance" test had been superseded by the *Federal Rules of Evidence (FRE)*. On the face a defeat for the defendants, the Court went on to assign a powerful "gatekeeping role" to judges that presumably would keep junk science from diverting juries (*ibid.*, 597). First, judges were to conduct "a preliminary assessment of whether the reasoning or methodology underlying the testimony is scientifically valid and of whether that reasoning or methodology properly can be applied to the facts in issue" (*ibid.*, 592-93). Second, since "[e]xpert evidence can be both powerful and quite misleading," the trial judge may decide whether scientific testimony that is relevant and reliable should nonetheless be excluded as more prejudicial than probative under *Evidence Rule 403* (*ibid.*, 595). Finally, "in the event the trial court concludes that the scintilla of evidence presented supporting a position is insufficient to allow a reasonable juror to conclude that the position more likely than not is true, the court remains free to direct a judgment ... and likewise to grant summary judgment" (*ibid.,* 596). Thus, at least in the case of Bendectin, the facial victory for plaintiffs turned out to be a major win for Merrell when, on reconsideration under the new *Daubert* standard, the Ninth Circuit Court again affirmed the district court's grant of summary judgment (*Daubert v. Merrell Dow Pharmaceuticals, Inc.* 1995). Although cases continued to filter through the courts, by the late 1990s the Bendectin litigation had effectively ended (see *Blum v. Merrell Dow Pharmaceutical, Inc.* 1997). Merrell "never ultimately lost a case" (Kolata 2000, F1).[13]

Today, pharmaceuticals remain a prime target of litigation. Indeed, their products are marketed on the widest scale possible, very often globally. Thus, even minor glitches causing unanticipated reactions among a small percentage of consumers can have severe, even devastating, consequences for large numbers of people and their families. A few of the many examples include the diet drug Fen-Phen, which was found to cause heart and liver damage (*In re: Diet Drugs* 2004);[14] the cholesterol-lowering drug Baycol, which was alleged to cause rhabdomyolysis, a disease that leads to muscle damage, kidney failure, and other injuries (*In re: Baycol Products Liability Litigation* 2004); Paxil and other selective serotonin reuptake inhibitors, which were used in the treatment of a variety of depression and panic disorders and alleged to cause dependency and severe withdrawal symptoms (*In re: Paxil Products Liability Litigation* 2003);[15] the diabetes medication Rezulin, which was charged with causing liver damage (*In re: Rezulin Products Liability Litigation* 2000); the heartburn medication Propulsid, which was linked to heart rhythm abnormalities (*In re: Propulsid Products Liability Litigation* 2000); and, as noted in the introduction to this book, the popular pain medication Vioxx, which had adverse effects on the heart (*In re: Vioxx Products Litigation* 2005).[16]

Medical Products

In addition to pharmaceuticals, a variety of medical products have been the subjects of liability proceedings. Among the earliest was the Dalkon Shield litigation, an example both of the judicial acceptance of the mass tort class action by the 1980s and the increasing sophistication of both the plaintiffs' and defendants' bars. Rights to the Dalkon Shield, an intra-uterine birth control device, were acquired by A.H. Robins Company Incorporated in 1970. Notably, "[p]rior to that time (*i.e.,* the purchase of the Dalkon Shield), Robins had never marketed any kind of a birth control product and had no gynecologist on its medical staff. Nevertheless, Robins did no further testing, readily accepted the figures of the inventor's testing, and aggressively promoted the device to the medical profession and, uniquely for such a device, to the general public" (*In re: A.H. Robins Company, Inc.* 1989, 711). Enormously successful, in just three years 2.2 million Dalkon Shields were sold, generating gross revenue for Robins of over $11 million and a gross profit of $505,499

(*In re: A.H. Robins Company, Inc.* 1988, 557). Simultaneously, however, problems and complaints were surfacing. Users experienced perforated uteruses, pelvic inflammatory disease, and septic abortions, some of which were fatal. As early as 1973, Robins began sending out "Dear Doctor" letters, warning of the risk of abortion. In 1974, the company suspended US sales and, in 1975, foreign sales *(ibid.)*.[17]

Although thousands of women were affected, class action status did not come easily. Despite courts being inundated with lawsuits, early attempts at class certification were notably unsuccessful. The first such attempt was in New York where plaintiffs sought class certification under a state statute modeled after *Rule 23*. In denying class status, courts in this case were clearly concerned that "issues of fact" could only "be resolved on an individual basis" (*Rosenfeld v. A.H. Robins Co., Inc.* 1978, 20). Subsequently, an attempt by a federal district court judge to form a nationwide class was rejected on appeal, with the Ninth Circuit, as late as 1982, apparently rejecting the class action device as a means of resolving product liability generally:

> In products liability actions ... individual issues may outnumber common issues. No single happening or accident occurs to cause similar types of physical harm or property damage. No one set of operative facts establishes liability. No single proximate cause applies equally to each potential class member and each defendant. Furthermore, the alleged tortfeasor's affirmative defenses (such as failure to follow directions, assumption of the risk, contributory negligence, and the statute of limitations) may depend on facts peculiar to each plaintiff's case. (*In re: Northern District of California Dalkon Shield IUD Products Liability Litigation* 1982, 853; also see *In re: Northern District of California Dalkon Shield IUD Products Liability Litigation 1981*)

Indeed, it was not until 1989 that a class was certified for settlement purposes. By this time, Robins had entered into Chapter 11 bankruptcy, greatly reducing its liability and that of its buyer, American Home Products.[18] By the time the Dalkon Shield Claimants Trust was liquidated in 2000, it had paid out nearly $3 billion. However, much of this amount went to claimants who chose, for certainty's sake, the flat sum of a mere $725. Moreover, many who did not select the flat sum option had to wait thirteen years before receiving compensation for serious injuries ("Mass Tort Litigation and Bankruptcy" 2003; Szaller 1999). Approximately half a million prospective claimants were disqualified from proceedings altogether because of inadequate notice (Sobol 1991, 102-3). The struggle to deal with the consequences of this clearly defective product presents a good example of the tension between individual due process and collective rights, frustrating attempts to compensate victims and simultaneously hold a large corporation accountable for its actions.

Since the Dalkon Shield case, actions against other medical product manu-facturers have included: Dow Corning for silicone breast implants (*In re: Silicone Gel Breast Implants Products Liability Litigation* 1992), which were al-leged to cause "connective tissue disease, auto-immune responses, chronic fatigue, muscle pain, joint pain, headaches, and dizziness" (Public Broadcast-ing Service 1999, para. 27); Bayer and other pharmaceuticals for the produc-tion of HIV-tainted blood used by haemophiliacs during the 1980s (*In re: "Factor VIII or IX Concentrate Blood Products" Products Liability Litigation* 1993); Safeskin Corporation and Johnson and Johnson Medical for manufacturing latex gloves that caused allergic reactions among some users (*In re: Latex Gloves Products Liability Litigation* 1997); Pfizer and St. Jude for defective heart valves (*Bowling v. Pfizer, Inc.* 1996; *In re: St. Jude Medical, Inc., Silzone Heart Valves Products Liability Litigation* 2001); and Sulzer for defective hip and knee implants (*In re: Sulzer Orthopedics, Inc., Hip Prosthesis and Knee Prosthesis Products Liability Litigation* 2001).

Environmental Containments

Although asbestos is the colossus of industrial carcinogen litigation, it has certainly not been the only one. Among the most commented upon modern classes is that composed of Vietnam-era veterans exposed to the herbicide Agent Orange. For the American military, one of the great frustrations of the Vietnam War was the dense Asian rainforest that allowed Viet Cong forces to move almost invisibly. As an antidote for a ten-year period from 1961 until 1971, the military sprayed parts of South Vietnam with various chemical herbicides designed to defoliate the countryside. According to a recent study conducted by the Columbia University School of Public Health, about twenty-one million gallons of herbicides were sprayed over the course of the decade (Mydans 2003). Roughly 55 percent of the amount was Agent Orange, which, in turn, was contaminated by TCDD (tetrachlorodibenzo-dioxin) or dioxin. High exposure to dioxin may lead to an increased risk of cancer, heart disease, diabetes, and reproductive and developmental problems (National Institute of Environmental Health Sciences 2002).

By the late 1970s, veterans were already complaining and attempting to seek redress for health problems blamed on Agent Orange (Schuck 1986, 37-57). Although the 800-pound gorilla in the proceedings was the US gov-ernment, defendants were limited to pressing charges against chemical companies, including Monsanto, Dow, Hercules, Diamond Shamrock, T.H. Agriculture and Nutrition, Thompson Chemicals, and Uniroyal.[19] Encom-passing the first certification of a massive toxic exposure class, the Agent Orange litigation was settled for $180 million in exchange for the denial of all liability by defendants (*ibid.*, 165; *In re: "Agent Orange" Product Liability Litigation* 1987).

Among more recent chemical torts has been large-scale litigation aimed at silica products. Silica (silicon dioxide) is a major component of industrial sand and gravel. Overexposure by workers can lead to silicosis, "a disabling, nonreversible and sometimes fatal lung disease" (United States, Department of Labor, Occupational Safety and Health Administration 2008). Significantly for these purposes, silicosis litigation may be responsible for more stringent (and defendant-friendly) screening procedures with potential impacts for a number of contaminant litigations, including asbestos. In 2002, a virtual silicosis epidemic appeared to be occurring in the state of Mississippi. During this year, 10,642 silicosis claims were filed in the state, followed in 2003 and 2004, by an additional 9,837 claims aimed at over 250 corporate defendants. The 2002 filings alone represented "more silicosis claims ... per day in Mississippi courts than had been filed for the entire year only two years earlier." Over the entire three-year period, the new claims were "over five times greater than the total number of silicosis cases one would expect over the same period in the entire United States" (*In re: Silica Products Liability Litigation* 2005, 572). The answer to the puzzling surge in claims, according to Judge Janice Graham Jack, was a "phantom epidemic" *(ibid.)*.

On the basis of fact sheets filed by claimants, the court discovered that a mere twelve doctors had diagnosed in excess of 9,000 plaintiffs with silicosis. Moreover, the doctors who made the diagnoses were not the plaintiffs' regular physicians nor did they work in the same city or state as the plaintiffs. Rather, they were doctors affiliated with several plaintiffs' law firms and mobile X-ray screening companies *(ibid., 580)*. Notably, many of the plaintiffs had also previously been diagnosed with asbestos disease. In short, the plaintiffs had been mass-screened. Judge Jack was not amused. In a strongly worded 249-page decision, she admonished the participating doctors and the plaintiffs' attorneys, asserting: "[I]t is apparent that truth and justice had very little to do with these diagnoses – otherwise more effort would have been devoted to ensuring they were accurate. Instead, these diagnoses were driven by neither health nor justice: they were manufactured for money" *(ibid., 635)*. Although the immediate up-shot of Justice Jack's decision was to send most of the cases back to the originating state courts, the discovery and tenor of the case is expected to have long-term ramifications, particularly with respect to the use of mass screenings to demonstrate injury. Indeed, in the wake of the decision, judges in other states have begun to demand detailed medical records from silicosis and asbestos claimants (Goodwyn 2006).

Other recent chemical torts have included large-scale litigation aimed at manufacturers and distributors of welding rods, the fumes from which are alleged to cause lung cancer, heart disease, skin disease, and manganism, which closely resembles Parkinson's disease (see, for example, *In re: Welding Rod Products Liability Litigation* 2004).

Securities

A mainstay of mass and class lawsuits has been securities litigation and other money-based complaints. As of July 2008, an impressive fifty-two securities case bundles have been transferred to federal district courts as multi-district litigations. In 2007, 166 class actions were filed. Such suits frequently have involved thousands of small investors, along with wealthier shareholders. Among the current crop, several stem from the corporate abuse scandals of the late 1990s and early 2000s, including suits against Enron, Global Crossing, and WorldCom (see generally, Judicial Panel on Multi-District Litigation 2005; 2008).[20] Although the number of such lawsuits is large and has seen recent growth that is attributable to the mortgage crisis and stock market instability, current filings are actually below historical averages. Analysts believe this decrease may be due to one or two theories. On the one hand, many observers contend that there is simply less fraudulent activity occurring that would spark such suits. And, indeed, since the turn-of-the-century corporate scandals, federal enforcement has increased and monitoring by boards and auditors has gotten better. On the other hand, some analysts contend that a strong stock market dampens the tendency to sue. Thus, the increased volatility of the markets brought on by fears of recession, the housing crisis, and soaring fuel costs may augur a future rise in this kind of litigation (Cornerstone Research Group 2008). An additional factor, no doubt, has been the enactment of the *Private Securities Litigation Reform Act of 1995*, which passed despite President Clinton's veto.[21] The law was designed to make it easier for companies to defend themselves against class action suits brought under federal securities laws (see, for example, Grundfest and Perino 1997). Since its passage, the act has been forcefully upheld by the Supreme Court of the United States (see, for example, *Tellabs v. Makor* 2007).

Intellectual Property

Intellectual property disputes, though not currently a large segment of the class or mass litigation universe, may potentially come to be so. On the plaintiff side, disputants would tend to be atypical. For example, a recent litigation against Internet file-swapping sites StreamCast Networks and Grokster featured a plaintiff class of professional songwriters and music publishers (*MGM Studios, Inc. v. Grokster* 2005).[22] The future of intellectual property disagreements may, however, lie more in the creation of defendant classes. After all, *Rule 23* does read that a class may "sue or *be sued*." And as we observed in Chapter 1, early group litigation on both sides of the Atlantic has often involved collective defendants. In either case, outcomes tend to have broader policy implications that do not necessarily accompany litigation of the standard form. An interesting, though ultimately unsuccessful, example is found in *Tilley v. TJX Companies* (2003b). Gerardine (misspelled in case) E. Tilley created, published, and copyrighted "Harbortown Border," a wallpaper design. Allegedly, an importer, Dennis East International, copied the design without permission and "sold home decor items bearing the replica to approximately 557 retailers throughout the United States" *(ibid.)*. The district court certified the retailers as a class and assigned TJX Companies as its representative *(Tilley v. TJX Companies* 2003a). In a holding that was the first of its kind (but, presumably, not the last), the First Circuit Court decertified the class, ruling that "defendant classes generally lie outside the contemplation of Rule 23(b)(2)" *(Tilley v. TJX Companies* 2003b, 50). In all probability, other appeals courts will have the opportunity to address the issue of defendant classes in the future.

Civil and Employment Rights

As noted earlier, the modern class action is grounded in the civil rights movement, and civil rights claims have remained a bastion of the form. A recent example is illustrative. In June 2004, Judge Martin J. Jenkins of the US District Court in San Francisco certified a class in a sex discrimination case against Wal-Mart *(Dukes v. Wal-Mart Stores, Inc.* 2004). Women employees were alleging that they had been paid less than men in comparable positions, despite having higher performance ratings and greater seniority, and that they were receiving fewer promotions to in-store management positions than men. Those who were promoted, they contended, were having to wait longer than their male counterparts to advance. Represented were the 1.6 million women who had worked at Wal-Mart anywhere in the United States since 26 December 1998. The case has the distinction of pitting the largest class ever certified against the largest private employer in the world![23] Notably, Judge Jenkins addressed the individual due process concerns of creating such a massive class:

> While plaintiffs' claim for punitive damages does not preclude certifying this case under Rule 23(b)(2), minimum due process requirements do apply where the monetary relief sought, albeit not "predominant," is nonetheless "substantial." Recognizing the Supreme Court's "growing concerns regarding the certification of mandatory classes when monetary damages are involved," the Molski court[24] held that HN36 "notice and the right to opt-out must be provided to bind absent class members when substantial monetary damages are involved." The Court further indicated that any claim for punitive damages is "substantial." ("Because the statutory damages ... provide for treble [i.e. punitive] damages, the remedy must be considered substantial"); (due process requires provision of notice where Rule 23(b)(2) class seeks monetary damages, while provision of opt-out rights is optional). *(ibid.,* 172-73 [notes omitted])

The Strategic Politics of Mass Torts and Class Actions

As the modern class action has matured, so have participants' strategies for winning or, at least, for losing more modestly. Game plans obviously differ depending on the particulars of any given case and, of course, on whether the contestants are plaintiffs or defendants. However, some general strategic trends may be observed.

The Plaintiffs' Bar

According to the American Association for Justice (AAJ),[25] the largest group representing trial lawyers, plaintiffs are to David as corporate defendants are to Goliath (Jacobson and White 2004). And historically, the corporate bar has had traditionally a considerable advantage over far less resourced and experienced plaintiffs' attorneys (see, for example, Galanter 1974). Nonetheless, over the past several decades, and particularly since the advent of easy on-line communication, "David" has learned to devise and deploy a much, much better slingshot.

Litigation Groups and Exchanges

In 1962, led by veteran litigator Paul D. Rheingold, attorneys involved in litigation against Richardson-Merrell formed the MER/29 group (Ranii 1984). MER/29, an early anti-cholesterol drug, caused numerous side effects, most notably the development of cataracts (*Toole v. Richardson-Merrell* 1967). The drug was approved by the FDA in 1960 on the basis of fraudulent information provided by Richardson-Merrell (*ibid.*, 696-97). The MER/29 litigation group, a confederation of thirty-three plaintiff lawyers, formed to coordinate discovery efforts. According to Howard Erichson (2000b, 393), "[t]he group provided its member lawyers with copies of key liability documents, trial transcripts, and other materials, submitted a standard set of interrogatories, and reached an agreement with the defendant that discovery could be carried out by the group's representatives on behalf of all the group's cases." The MER/29 group kept attorneys up to date with a newsletter and ran the "MER/29 school" to teach lawyers how to try the cases. The MER/29 litigation has been called "one of the great success stories of voluntary cooperation among litigants." The MER/29 group was significant because "it laid the groundwork for the growth of coordinated efforts by a cadre of elite lawyers in mass tort litigation. This corps of repeat players, many of whom handled MER/29 cases in the 1960s, then Dalkon Shield and asbestos cases, then breast implants, and most recently Fen-Phen and tobacco, succeeds by creating 'a high degree of informal coordination, continuity, and learning across different mass torts'" (*ibid.*).

Tobacco litigation has also spawned associations, foremost among them, the Castano Group. Founded in 1994 when New Orleans attorney Wendell

Gauthier convinced sixty law firms to contribute $100,000 each toward a coordinated assault on cigarette companies. The Castano Group more recently aimed its sights on gun makers (Segal 1999). Notably, Gauthier apparently views "the plaintiffs bar as a de facto fourth branch of government, one that achieved regulation through litigation where legislation failed" (Olson 1999, para. 12), much like the "private attorneys general" envisioned by Harry Kalven and Maurice Rosenfield (1941, 689).

Today, the organization of litigation groups is a primary focus of the AAJ, comprising more than a third of the association's annual convention activities (Association of Trial Lawyers of America 2004a). According to the AAJ, the nearly seventy groups now under its aegis "are voluntary networks of ATLA [now AAJ] members who share their accumulated information and experience regarding a specific type of case. Often, a litigation group will focus on a particular product, such as: breast implants, nail guns, cardiac devices, penile implants, or tobacco products. Other litigation groups are broader in scope, focusing on a category of claims, such as: construction site accidents, inadequate security, domestic violence, workplace injury, bad faith insurance, or nursing homes" (*ibid.*, para. 2). In short, litigation groups provide efficiencies for small practitioners who individually lack the resources of their corporate adversaries. Moreover, the AAJ hosts a fee-based legal research exchange, allowing members to "search thousands of depositions, pleadings, trial transcripts ... other court documents" as well as expert witness information, among other services (Association of Trial Lawyers of America 2004b).

Related to the advantages accrued by pooling resources, the relevant plaintiffs' bar has become more specialized over the past twenty years. Thus, John Heinz, Edward Laumann, Ethan Michelson, and Robert Nelson (1998, 760-62) report that from 1975 to 1995 the number of personal injury lawyers hired by plaintiffs who reported exclusive engagement in this field of law rose dramatically. While such numbers necessarily capture a population that is broader than the mass injury endeavours with which we are primarily concerned, it does suggest that this group of attorneys is increasingly recognizing the efficiencies of specialization that have long been enjoyed by the corporate bar (see, for example, Galanter 1974, 141ff). The cause-lawyering literature has observed a robust movement, which is now reaching global proportions, in which attorneys share information, resources, and strategies (for example, Sarat and Scheingold 2006; 2005; 2001; 1998).

Outreach and Advertising

Twenty-seven years ago, the Supreme Court of the United States put its imprimatur on attorney advertising (*Bates v. State Bar of Arizona* 1977). Since then, viewers of daytime and late night television have become accustomed to being told: "If you've got a phone, you've got a lawyer." Not surprisingly, however, the Internet has fostered much more sophisticated and potentially widespread outreach efforts. Take for example the law firm of Lieff, Cabraser, Heimann, and Bernstein, one of hundreds of personal injury law firms advertising on-line. Not only does the firm maintain a regular business website (http://www.lieffcabraser.com/), but it also supplies an impressive array of independent, subject-specific websites:

- AFjustice.com (Abercrombie and Fitch discrimination lawsuit)
- Carbon Monoxide Poisoning Lawsuits
- Discrimination Case against Johnson and Johnson
- Federal Express Race Discrimination
- Fen-Phen Legal Resources
- International Hemophilia Litigation
- Lieff Cabraser Securities (for Institutional Investors)
- Prescription Drugs Pricing Lawsuits
- Pap Smear Suit against Magee
- Popcorn Worker Butter Flavour Lung Injuries
- Pulmonary Hypertension and the Fen-Phen Connection
- Unnecessary Heart Surgery
- Vehicle Injuries and Suv Rollovers
- Welding Rod Injuries

Notably, a Google search of "Fen-Phen *and* legal" immediately yields the Lieff Cabraser site. So, too, does the search "popcorn workers *and* injuries," and so forth.

Other sites aggregate legal outreach. For instance, the website Big Class Action (http://www.bigclassaction.com/) offers potential plaintiffs a "free case evaluation" by a participating attorney. In addition, the site features so-called "hot issues," class categories, and the opportunity to sign up for a free e-newsletter that notifies recipients of "new class actions and class action settlements and verdicts." A similar service is provided by the website Class Action America (http://www.classactionamerica.com/), featuring the tagline: "Justice is now a click away" and the offer of a free desktop class action alert system. An Internet search will turn up a range of similar sites available to citizens in the United Kingdom, Canada, and Australia.

Forum Shopping
Among the oldest and most controversial plaintiff strategies is forum shopping – seeking the best venue in which to pursue litigation. This strategy may involve a horizontal move – picking from among courts within the same system – or it may occur vertically in attempts to move from state to federal court or federal to state (Algero 1999, 80). In any event, as the Supreme

Court of the United States has said, "[a]n opportunity for forum shopping exists whenever a party has a choice of forums that will apply different laws" (*Ferens v. John Deere Co.* 1990, 527). Indeed, for all of the negative onus surrounding the device, our federal system of independent, yet overlapping, jurisdiction encourages it. Of course, from the plaintiffs' perspective, the strategy is put in less loaded language – a smart litigant engages in "plaintiff's privilege" (Ryan 2000, 169) or in "forum choice" (Hensler et al. 2000, 24). And while this "choice" or "privilege" is important in all civil lawsuits, as Hensler et al. explain,

> class action attorneys often have greater latitude in their choice of forum or venue than their counterparts in traditional litigation. Under some circumstances, an attorney filing a statewide class action can file in any county of a state and an attorney filing a nationwide class action can file in virtually any state in the country, and perhaps any county in that state as well. In addition, class action attorneys often can file duplicative suits and pursue them simultaneously. These are powerful tools for shaping litigation, providing opportunities not only to seek out favorable law and positively disposed decisionmakers, but also to maintain (or wrest) control over high-stakes litigation from other class action lawyers. *(ibid.)*

A vivid illustration is provided by attorney Elisa Barnes, who represented both individual plaintiffs and the National Association for the Advancement of Colored People (NAACP) in lawsuits against the gun industry.[26] Ms. Barnes' original suit, brought in 1994 on behalf of the relatives of six people killed by handguns and one survivor, featured Beretta as the leading corporate defendant (*Hamilton v. Beretta* 2001b). Her subsequent suit for the NAACP was notable for the fact that Beretta, one of the largest gun makers, was absent from the list of defendants. Barnes was anxious for the suit to be heard by federal district judge Jack Weinstein under diversity jurisdiction.[27] Federal jurisdiction is disallowed, however, if any plaintiff shares common state residence with any defendant (*Strawbridge v. Curtiss* 1806). The NAACP and Beretta are both incorporated in Maryland – thus, the disappearance of Beretta.[28]

Defendants

Inasmuch as defendants in mass or class suits tend to be corporate or governmental entities, they have long had substantial advantages. This is precisely the argument that Marc Galanter (1974) makes in his classic treatise "Why the 'Haves' Come out Ahead."[29] While Galanter spells out in generalized terms the advantages of large institutional defendants, at least some of which would presumably be muted by mass and class plaintiff actions, he also identifies more specific strategies that can be employed by the big targets of litigation. Frequently, such strategies are aimed more at minimizing losses than at outright winning.

Secret Settlements

A time honoured, though potentially harmful and even ethically question-able, means of lessening litigation damage is the secret settlement. Infamously, in 1933 when workers brought compensation claims against Johns-Manville, the asbestos manufacturer, the company entered into a secret agreement, one aspect of which had the plaintiffs' attorney agreeing not to bring any more cases against the company (*Janssens v. Johns-Manville* 1984; *Fischer v. Johns-Manville* 1986). By the 1990s, "[t]he sealing of court records and the enforce-ment of covenants of silence ... [had become] increasingly common practices in the settlement of civil lawsuits" (Bechamps 1990, 117), and notorious examples included Dow Corning silicone gel implants and Bridgestone/Firestone tires on Ford Explorers (Smith 2004, 247). The benefits for corpor-ate defendants are substantial. Secret settlements often allow the defendant to steer clear of admitting legal liability, to get around divulging sensitive information, and, perhaps most important, to avoid adverse publicity. For their part, plaintiffs are frequently happy to enter into such agreements since they offer finality and, not infrequently, bigger pay-offs. Moreover, judges are not averse since any settlement reduces the docket. At the same time, such settlements have been the subject of increasing criticism and even some legislative and judicial limits,[30] particularly where, as in the early asbestos case, they conceal public health hazards.[31]

Bankruptcy

The asbestos tragedy is, among many other things, also an illustration of strategic bankruptcy on the part of defendant companies. From 1976 through 2003, seventy-one companies had gone into bankruptcy over asbestos claims (Asbestos Alliance 2004). And while the asbestos numbers are particularly dramatic, they are hardly unique. Thus, according to David Skeel (2001, 221; also see Delaney 1992), bankruptcy, today, is "the forum of choice for resolv-ing the modern dilemma of mass tort liability." Although bankruptcy sounds horrid to the layperson, signalling failure and insolvency, "the bankruptcy process can be used by firms that are not confronting financial failure. These firms ... employ bankruptcy to limit liability, even when they are not in danger of suffering financial or economic distress" (Cole 2002, 1248). This has certainly been the case in a great deal of mass tort litigation, including asbestos (see Delaney 1992). Such manoeuvring, according to Cole, "can be thought of as 'defensive bankruptcy filings' because they represent an at-tempt by mass tort defendants to reign in otherwise unmanageable litigation" (*ibid.*, 1270). According to Mark Plevin, Victor Schwartz, and Paul Kalish (2001, 68), "the Bankruptcy Code provides a palette of tools not available elsewhere," including an automatic stay of litigation; the centralization of all cases in one court; limitations and, in some cases, the elimination of punitive damages awards; the resolution of claims and issues more quickly and cheaply; and the provision of trusts to pay future claimants. Moreover, "if you are a company in financial trouble, it is much easier to get credit if you file for bankruptcy. This is called 'debtor in possession financing' and, as ordered by the Bankruptcy Court, money loaned on this basis is paid off ahead of all the other creditors" (Mesothelioma Legal Information Center 2004, para. 2).[32]

Defensive Legislation

As Galanter points out, large, well-resourced entities are in a good position to influence not only litigation but also legislation, some of which, in turn, is aimed at influencing litigation. The most ambitious and far-reaching attempts by the potential defendant bar fall under the general rubric of the "tort reform movement." Now, almost thirty years old, the movement is spearheaded nationally by the American Tort Reform Association (ATRA), a political advocacy group, which is heavily supported by industry, industry trade associations, insurance companies, and doctors' groups, as well as a variety of state groups at the local level, notably Citizens against Lawsuit Abuse.[33] In addition, tort reform is a major project of a number of conservative associations and think tanks, including the Federalist Society, the Heritage Foundation, the Cato Institute, the Washington Legal Foundation, the Manhattan Institute, and the American Legislative Exchange Council (see, for example, Haltom and McCann 2004a; Rustad and Koenig 2002; Johnson 2004; Landay 2000).

The tort reform movement has several aims, each pointed toward the overreaching goal of creating a more business-friendly legal environment. Obviously, in order to effectively pursue any reform agenda, a movement needs to influence opinion – both public and elite. Toward this end, the tort reform movement has been unremitting in highlighting so-called frivolous lawsuits,[34] painting trial attorneys as greedy ambulance chasers, and even sponsoring seminars for judges.[35] According to at least some accounts, it has been quite successful (see especially Haltom and McCann 2004a). Thus, a 2003 ATRA poll – the method and results of which have been heavily criticized by the AAJ – reported that "83 percent of those surveyed believe that there are too many lawsuits filed in America ... 76 percent believe that money spent to defend excessive lawsuits results in higher costs of goods and services for American consumers; [and] 67 percent agreed that excessive lawsuits are causing good companies to go bankrupt" (American Tort Reform Association 2003). In the same year, the Gallup poll found 72 percent of respondents favouring caps on non-economic damages (Albert 2003). And lawyering, always a profession about which Americans have been highly ambivalent,

Table 2.1

State tort reform limitations, 1986-2004

Type of limitation	Number of states adopting*
Punitive damages[1]	31
Non-economic damages[2]	18
Joint and several liability[3]	39
Prejudgment interest[4]	14
Collateral source rule[5]	23
Product liability[6]	15
Class action[7]	8
Attorney relation sunshine[8]	5
Appeal bond reform[9]	30
Jury service reform[10]	7

* Limitations found unconstitutional are not included.
1 Refers to caps, evidentiary rules, or other limits placed on the award of punitive damages.
2 Refers to caps or other limits placed on the award of damages for pain and suffering, emotional distress, loss of consortium, and so on.
3 The doctrine of joint and several liability makes multiple defendants liable at judgment. So, for example, if two defendants jointly share liability and the first becomes insolvent, her unpaid liabilities may be reallocated to the second solvent defendant. Limitations include banning or modifying the application of the rule in all or some types of cases.
4 Prejudgment interest refers to interest that accrues on a loss during a time prior to a court award of damages. Prejudgment interest limitations cap, set at current rates or otherwise, limit such interest.
5 A common law doctrine that there should be no reduction in damages should not be reduced simply because an injured person has received compensation from other sources such as insurance. Under application of the rule, evidence of collateral compensation may not be admitted at trial. Limitations on the rule include outright or partial abolishment.
6 Refers to a variety of limits on product liability claims.
7 Refers to changes making class certification more difficult.
8 Attorney "sunshine" legislation requires legislative approval of most large contingent fee contracts.
9 Refers to reductions on the amount of bond that must be posted to appeal a verdict.
10 On the theory that "unrepresentative" juries favour plaintiffs, jury service reforms make it more difficult for individuals to exempt themselves from service.
Source: Adapted from American Tort Reform Association (2004b), http://www.atra.org/files.cgi/7802_Record6-04.pdf.

by some estimates, is more unpopular today than ever (Cates and McIntosh 2001, 69-73; see, for example, Klein 1997).[36]

Regardless, or because, of the effect on public opinion, the tort reform movement has been quite successful in achieving both legislative and judicial limits on lawsuits. Thus, as Table 2.1 demonstrates, between 1986 and 2004 states enacted restrictions in a number of key areas, from placing caps on damages, to amending the rules on joint and several liability, to making it more difficult to certify classes. And while attempts to have Congress pass broad-based tort reforms have been somewhat less successful, the movement has many supporters among national lawmakers.[37]

In addition to more generalized limits on lawsuits, industry-specific shields have also been advocated and enacted. Most successful has been the National Rifle Association's (NRA) efforts to enact so-called "firearm industry relief acts," which are aimed at severely limiting the ability of local governments to bring lawsuits against gun manufacturers and dealers. As of 2003, the NRA had introduced such legislation in forty-six states, successfully passing acts in thirty-one states. In 2005, President Bush signed into law the *Protection of Lawful Commerce in Firearms Act,* asserting that "[a] qualified civil liability action that is pending on the date of enactment of this Act shall be immediately dismissed by the court in which the action was brought or is currently pending."[38] As of 2006, twenty-three states had enacted "obesity litigation reform acts," which are designed to shield manufacturers, distributors, and sellers of food and non-alcoholic drinks from health-based lawsuits (American Tort Reform Association 2004a). A typical example is Florida's legislation, which was signed into law by Governor Jeb Bush in May 2004:

> No manufacturer, distributor, or seller of foods or nonalcoholic beverages intended for human consumption shall be subject to civil liability for personal injury or wrongful death to the extent such liability is premised upon a person's weight gain or obesity, or a health condition related to weight gain or obesity, resulting from the person's long-term consumption of such foods or nonalcoholic beverages. For purposes of this section, the term "long-term" means the cumulative effect of multiple instances over a period of time and not the effect of a single or isolated instance. Such limitation on civil liability shall not bar a claim for damages if otherwise available under any other provision of law against a manufacturer, distributor, or seller of foods or nonalcoholic beverages if such manufacturer, distributor, or seller has failed to provide nutritional content information as required by any applicable state or federal statute or regulation, or has provided materially false or misleading information to the public.[39]

As part of his 2005 State of the Union message, President Bush announced that "[t]o make our economy stronger and more competitive, America must reward, not punish, the efforts and dreams of entrepreneurs. Small business is the path of advancement, especially for women and minorities, so we must free small businesses from needless regulation and protect honest job creators from junk lawsuits. Justice is distorted, and our economy is held back, by irresponsible class actions and frivolous asbestos claims and I urge Congress to pass legal reforms this year" (Bush 2005, para. 9). The embodiment of the president's call to action, the *Class Action Fairness Act,* which was passed in February 2005 due, in large part, to efforts by the US Chamber of Commerce, was estimated to have cost $40 million in lobbying for the bill (Birnbaum 2005). The act moves virtually all large-class actions out of state and into federal court, where judges traditionally have been less sympathetic to plaintiffs' claims (Harris 2005).[40]

Legal Precedent and Judicial Placement
Achieving favourable judicial rulings has also been a major goal of the tort reform movement, including efforts to limit forum shopping and prevent lawsuits by uninjured plaintiffs.[41] What is potentially the most far-reaching is what Michael Rustad and Thomas Koenig (2002, 54ff) term the "constitutionalization of punitive damages." Key among strategies to reverse plaintiff-friendly judicial rulings has been a three-decade effort by the US Chamber of Commerce to counter the influence of litigation groups. Jeffrey Rosen (2008, 2) explains:

> [By the late 1980s, t]he chamber started winning cases in part by refining its strategy. With [Robin] Conrad's[[42]] help, the chamber's Supreme Court litigation program began to offer practice moot-court arguments for lawyers scheduled to argue important cases. The chamber also began hiring the most-respected Democratic and Republican Supreme Court advocates to persuade the court to hear more business cases. Although many of the businesses that belong to the Chamber of Commerce have their own in-house lawyers, they would have the chamber file "friend of the court" briefs on their behalf. The chamber would decide which of the many cases brought to its attention were in the long-term strategic interest of American business and then hire the leading business lawyers to write supporting briefs or argue the case.
>
> Until the mid-'80s, there wasn't an organized group of law firms that specialized in arguing business cases before the Supreme Court. But in 1985, Rex Lee, the solicitor general under Reagan, left the government to start a Supreme Court appellate practice at the firm Sidley Austin. Lee's goal was to offer business clients the same level of expert representation before the Supreme Court that the solicitor general's office provides to federal agencies. Lee's success prompted other law firms to hire former Supreme Court clerks and former members of the solicitor general's office to start business practices. The Chamber of Commerce, for its part, began to coordinate the strategy of these lawyers in the most important business cases.

The strategy has paid off. The Supreme Court of the United States today is not only more likely to decide economic cases in favour of business but, generally, accepts more such cases for review than it did thirty years ago *(ibid.).* Punitive damages cases offer one such example. Traditionally grounded in common law and the strict purview of state courts, in recent years the Court has moved to attach due process rights to the awarding of punitive damages and thus "procedural and substantive limits on recovery" (*ibid.*, 60). Thus, for example, in *BMW of North America v. Gore* (1996, 517), the Court, for the first time, held a state jury award of punitive damages to be "grossly excessive and hence violative of due process." In so holding, the Court established "three guideposts" for determining excessiveness in jury awards: (1) the "degree of reprehensibility"; (2) the "ratio" between harm done and monetary award; and (3) legislative "sanctions for comparable misconduct" (*ibid.*, 575ff, 580ff, and 583ff).[43]

Again in 2003, the high court signalled its displeasure with large punitive damage awards in the case of *State Farm Mutual Automobile Insurance Company v. Campbell* (2003). In this case, reiterating *Gore,* the Court asserted that punitive damages of more than nine times the amount of compensatory damages will generally be considered an unconstitutional denial of property without due process of law. In 2007, the Court limited what juries may consider in assessing punitive damages. In *Philip Morris USA v. Williams* (2007a), a tobacco case, a jury used harm done to smokers not involved in the suit to calculate punitive damages, a calculation deemed to be in violation of the Fourteenth Amendment's due process clause. Finally, in 2008, nearly two decades after the tanker *Exxon Valdez* ran aground, spilling millions of gallons of crude oil into Prince William Sound in Alaska, the Court ruled that a $2.5 billion punitive damages award levied against Exxon was excessive as a matter of maritime common law and should be limited to an amount equal to compensatory damages (*Exxon Shipping Company v. Baker* 2008). Although the ruling is specific to maritime judgments, it is widely expected to have broader implications for punitive damage awards generally (see, for example, Yost 2008).[44]

One of the reasons that tort reform advocates have been keen to get class actions moved into federal courts is because of several Court rulings and subsequent changes in the *Federal Rules of Evidence,* which make it easier for defendants to successfully challenge expert witnesses in federal court. And while about half the states have followed suit, most of the largest – California, New York, Florida, and Illinois – have not. Recall the discussion in *Daubert v. Merrell Dow Pharmaceuticals, Inc.* (1993). This case both tightened rules for admissibility of expert testimony and gave district court judges a broad gatekeeping role in determining this admissibility. Four years later, the Court spoke again to the subject, mandating "abuse of discretion" as "the proper standard for an appellate court to apply in reviewing a Federal District Court's decision to admit or exclude expert scientific testimony at trial" (*General Electric v. Joiner* 1997, 136), thus, largely shielding trial court judgments from appellate review. This judgment was followed in 1999 with a decision to apply *Daubert* principles to "all expert testimony, not only scientific" (*Kumho Tire Company v. Carmichael* 1999, 137).[45]

Although the rules appear facially neutral, most observers believe they favour defendants. For example, Edward K. Cheng and Albert H. Yoon (2005, 473) note that

[t]he resulting effects of Daubert have been decidedly pro-defendant. In the civil context, Daubert has empowered defendants to exclude certain types of scientific evidence, substantially improving their chances of obtaining summary judgment and thereby avoiding what are perceived to be unpredictable and often plaintiff-friendly juries.

Tort reformers agree. Thus, David Bernstein (2002, para. 1), writing for the Washington Legal Foundation, asserts that "[t]he result [of *Daubert-Joiner-Kumho*] has been a crackdown on 'junk' expert testimony in federal courts." Notably, the *Daubert* hearings were instrumental in uncovering problems with silicosis claims.

Finally, the tort reform movement has been active in the judicial selection process. For example, the American Judicature Society (2004, para. 2) notes that in Alabama

[j]udicial races ... became increasingly politicized in the 1980s and 1990s, in large part because of the controversy over tort reform. The size of jury verdicts began to increase during this time, to the extent that Alabama was dubbed "Tort Hell" by Forbes magazine. The legislature passed a tort reform package in 1987, but many of its provisions were declared unconstitutional by the Alabama Supreme Court during the early 1990s. As judicial races took on heightened significance, campaign fundraising became more important. Between 1986 and 1996, expenditures by supreme court candidates grew by 776 percent. As campaigns became more expensive, they also became more contentious. The 1996 elections were dubbed "the year of the skunk" because of an ad run by an incumbent supreme court justice that alluded to his opponent and featured pictures of a skunk, accompanied by the caption "Some things you can smell a mile away."

For its part, the ATRA, not too subtly, has taken aim at what it refers to as six "judicial hellholes, cities, counties, or judicial districts that attract lawsuits from around the nation or the region because they are correctly perceived as very plaintiff-friendly jurisdictions" (American Tort Reform Association 2003, para. 1). Presumably, these "hellholes" could be transformed into more heavenly forums via pressure on, or replacement of, current judges – or via what the ATRA, in a more politick turn of phrase, advocates: "[T]he fair and full attention of the media and action by readers of this report" (*ibid.,* para. 8).

Just as important, the US Chamber of Commerce and other business entities have been highly successful in lobbying for the placement of business-sympathetic justices on the Supreme Court of the United States, including a formal endorsement process. Thus, the Chamber of Commerce endorsed both Ruth Bader Ginsburg (known for being "comfortable with the finer points of business litigation") and Stephen Breyer (praised for "truly underst[anding] business issues") during the Clinton administration (Rosen 2008, 3). During the George W. Bush administration, the Chamber of Commerce passed over Judge Michael Luttig, a conservative states' rights proponent, and instead backed John Roberts, "the go-to lawyer for the business community."[46] It also endorsed Samuel Alito, "whose 15-year record as an appellate judge showed a consistent skepticism of claims against large corporations" (*ibid.,* 4).

Population and Prestige

As suggested earlier, over the past thirty years or so, the plaintiff bar has found a number of means (for example, litigation groups, outreach) to strengthen its hand in battles with the defendant bar. Still, certain population and prestige advantages continue to accrue to corporate defendants. Indeed, in their study of Chicago lawyers, John Heinz et al. (1998, 767) report a rather dramatic leap in the percentage of time devoted to corporate clients as opposed to personal clients:

> In ... 1975 ... the estimate is that 53 percent of lawyers' time was allocated to corporate fields (including work for nonbusiness organizations such as unions and governmental entities), while 40 percent was devoted to the personal clients field and another 7 percent was not clearly assignable or was spread across a variety of small fields. By 1995, the disparity between the two sectors has increased considerably ... [T]he corporate sector consumed more than twice the amount of Chicago lawyers' time devoted to personal and small business client work in 1995 (64 percent vs. 29 percent). The "large corporate" cluster of fields increased most – from 18 percent of the total in 1975 to 32 percent in 1995 – while the "personal business" and "personal plight" [including personal injury] clusters both declined.

Many have noted the tendency of corporate lawyering to attract disproportionately graduates of elite, high-prestige law schools (see, for example, Heinz and Laumann 1994). This is clearly the case with the areas of litigation that we focus upon. Where 46 percent of our sample of defendant attorneys graduated from one of the top-twenty law schools, according to *US News and World Report,* only 17 percent of the plaintiff attorneys had.[47] While this statistic says nothing about the capabilities of the attorneys, as Galanter (1974, 116) says, attorneys who "make up 'lower echelons' of the legal profession ... [tend to] possess low prestige within the professions."

Conclusion

Politics may be many things, but, in the end, it all boils down to a struggle for power.[48] So, of course, does litigation – the quintessential fight well fought.[49] The two – politics and litigation – both involve competition, which is often over very high stakes. Indeed, in broad scale multi-party litigation, the stakes escalate significantly. And in both politics and litigation, there are bound to be winners and losers. Conversely, the two realms have traditionally operated very differently. Politics, generally, involves group struggle, where litigation, conventionally, is about the individual's day in court. Political struggle is normally resolved collectively by legislators or bureaucrats, where pre-appellate litigation is resolved by a single judge or by a jury, with the final call going to the judge. Politics is a collaborative, sometimes collusive, activity. Litigation is founded on an adversarial model. Politics strives for policy efficiencies; litigation strives for balanced justice.

As the foregoing suggests, and as subsequent chapters will demonstrate, the world of mass and class lawsuits much more closely resembles the traditional political model than it does the conventional litigation model. The group, and the larger policy questions, not the individual, are the focus of such litigation, causing some to worry about the loss of due process, which is the very centrepiece of the American legal motif. Moreover, mass and class litigation is frequently resolved in an almost legislative manner, with groups of attorneys hammering out compromises and settlements in the legal lingo. Indeed, not only does such litigation mimic the legislative process, as the tort reform movement and asbestos story demonstrate, but it also spills into the legislative agenda, departing from the contained nature of the traditional lawsuit. This, in short, is politics by another name. In this and the preceding chapter, we have tried to set the legal and strategic stages for our subsequent analysis. In the chapters that follow, we will take a more detailed look at several litigation scenarios. We begin with the tobacco wars of the past two decades. We move on in the following chapter to examine the efforts to hold gun manufacturers, distributors, and sellers liable for gun injuries. In Chapter 5, we assess food litigation. In Chapter 6, the growth of multi-party litigation in Canada, the United Kingdom, and Australia is explored.

Appendix 2.1

Asbestos timeline

1898	Lucy Deane, UK factory inspector, cites asbestos as damaging to bronchial tubes and lungs.
1906	Asbestos linked to the deaths of fifty French textile workers.
1935	Dr. A.J. Lanza conducts study of asbestos exposure, downplaying the deleterious affects. Results of the study are published by the United States Public Health Service. It is later learned that Vandiver Brown, Johns-Manville's vice-president, corporate secretary, and chief attorney, pressured Lanza to downplay the negative implications of asbestos exposure.
1930-60s	Johns-Manville maintains policy of not telling employees about the results of X-rays that showed they were suffering from asbestosis, so they "can live and work in peace and the company can benefit by [their] many years of experience" (*Johns-Manville Sales Corp. v. Janssens* 1984).
1965	Irving Selikoff, Jacob Churg, and E. Cuyler Hammond publish "The Occurrence of Asbestosis among Industrial Insulation Workers," finding that among examined insulation workers, evidence of pulmonary asbestosis was present in almost half the men examined.
1966	Claude Tomplait files suit against Johns-Manville, Fibreboard Paper Products Corporation, Owens Corning Fiberglas, and eight other manufacturers of asbestos-containing insulation products (*Tomplait v. Combustion Engineering, Inc.* 1968). Mr. Tomplait loses.
1969	Insulation worker Clarence Borel initiates a diversity action in the United States District Court for the Eastern District of Texas against a number of manufacturers including Fibreboard Paper Products Corporation, Johns-Manville Products Corporation, and Pittsburgh Corning Corporation. A jury awards Borel's widow about $80,000 in damages.
1972	Occupational Safety and Health Administration sets workplace asbestos exposure limits.
1973	On appeal, the Fifth Circuit Court upholds *Borel* decision, finding that "the danger to Borel and other insulation workers from inhaling asbestos dust was foreseeable to the defendants at the time the products causing Borel's injuries were sold" (*Borel v. Fibreboard Paper Products Corporation* 1973, 1093).
1982	The number of asbestos claimants reaches 20,000; defendant companies number 300.
1982	Johns-Manville goes into bankruptcy. Estimates put the number of asbestos-related bankruptcies at over seventy to date.
1983	Second wave of asbestos litigations begins.
1988	Manville Corporation (formerly Johns-Manville) emerges from Chapter 11.

1989	Environmental Protection Agency (EPA) bans most uses of asbestos and advises building owners and the industry on the handling of asbestos. The ban is overturned by the Fifth Circuit Court.

1989   Environmental Protection Agency (EPA) bans most uses of asbestos and advises building owners and the industry on the handling of asbestos. The ban is overturned by the Fifth Circuit Court.

1991   The EPA successfully bans all new uses of asbestos and promulgates regulations for inspecting and removing asbestos.

1991   Federal asbestos cases transferred to a single judge in a multi-district litigation procedure.

1991   Ad Hoc Committee on Asbestos Litigation, appointed by Chief Justice Rehnquist, issues report urging federal legislation, asserting that "[t]he most objectionable aspects of asbestos litigation can be briefly summarized: dockets in both federal and state courts continue to grow; long delays are routine; trials are too long; the same issues are litigated over and over; transaction costs exceed the victims' recovery by nearly two to one; exhaustion of assets threatens and distorts the process; and future claimants may lose altogether" (cited in *Amchem Products v. Windsor* 1997, 598).

1994   US District Court judge certifies an asbestos plaintiffs class for purposes of settlement (*Georgine v. Amchem Products, Inc.* 1994).

1996   Third Circuit Court vacates certification holding that it failed to meet the "typicality and adequacy of representation requirements" of *Rule 23* of the *Federal Rules of Civil Procedure* (*Georgine v. Amchem Products, Inc.* 1996).

1997   Supreme Court of the United States affirms Third Circuit Court decertification. Justice Ginsburg, writing for the six-to-two majority, urges Congress to step into the asbestos quagmire (*Amchem Products v. Windsor* 1997, 599).

1998   Despite *Amchem,* the Fifth Circuit Court upholds another class action settlement attempt *In re: Asbestos Litigation* 1998).

1999   Supreme Court of the United States again rejects class certification. In concurrence, Chief Justice Rehnquist echoes Justice Ginsburg's previous exhortation, noting that the asbestos litigation "cries out for a legislative solution" (*Ortiz v. Fibreboard Corporation* 1999, 865).

2001   W.R. Grace files for bankruptcy.

2002   Number of asbestos claimants has soared to at least 600,000, with defendant companies numbering about 6,000.

2003   Following several legislative failures, in December 2003, President George Bush chides congressional inaction saying: "It was a mistake not to ... get asbestos reform" (Press Conference of the President 2003, unpaginated webpage).

2006   Senator Arlen Specter introduces latest attempt at settlement, the *Fairness in Asbestos Injury Resolution Act of 2006* (109th, s. 3274). Opposed by labour unions, plaintiff attorneys, and many defendants, the effort stalls.

2008   W.R. Grace agrees to settle outstanding asbestos-related claims with payments to a victims' trust fund and ten million warrants, allowing claimants to buy company stock at a reduced price.

3
The Politics of Tobacco Litigation

In the previous two chapters, we explored generally the legal and strategic bases for multi-party litigation. Legally, much of the stage for the growth in multi-party lawsuits was set in the 1960s, with revisions to the *Federal Rules of Civil Procedure* and passage of the *Multi-District Litigation Act*.[1] Strategically, the groundwork was laid in a desire to even the litigation playing field through the coalescence of many small aggrieved parties hoping to make inroads against large institutional entities, whether African American families combining against southern school systems or injured individuals against big corporations. As we have seen, however, the development of law and strategy were hardly played out on a one-way street as evidenced by recent statutory enactments and judicial rulings limiting class actions and by the efforts of such organizations as the US Chamber of Commerce to match the coalitional politics of the plaintiffs' bar. With these generalities in mind, we now turn our attention to a series of specific legal battlefronts, beginning in this chapter with the politics of tobacco litigation.

If ever an industry knew how to play the game of politics old style, it is big tobacco. A textbook example of interest dominion under the regime of "iron triangles,"[2] the tobacco industry flourished throughout much of the twentieth century, the beneficiary of generous government subsidies and a scarcity of government regulations.[3] The political world, however, did not remain stagnant. New politics replaced the old and new winners were those that could adapt to new realities. The beneficiary of the old politics of iron triangles over the past three decades, the tobacco industry, has become the target of the new politics of litigation (see generally Derthick 2002). In this chapter, we explore the litigation explosion known as the tobacco wars. The chapter begins with a brief historical overview before assessing the contemporary landscape. Without cover of the iron triangle, one might have expected the cataclysmic collapse of the cigarette companies. Yet, as we shall see, while the old politics were vastly preferable from an industry perspective, tobacco has learned to play the new politics of litigation fairly well.

Although the tobacco litigation wars seem to be a wholly modern phenomenon, they actually are quite ancient. Indeed, the first tort action against a tobacco company was filed half a century ago in 1954, ten years before the first US Surgeon General's report causally relating smoking to lung cancer (United States, Department of Health and Human Services 1964). More notable, however, is the fact that of the 813 private claims filed against cigarette companies between 1954 and 1994, only twice did trial courts find for the plaintiffs, and, in both, the decisions were reversed on appeal (LaFrance 2000, 190-91) – quite a winning record for big tobacco!

In many ways, the most prominent of these early suits, *Cipollone v. Liggett Group, Inc.* (1988; 1992), is also a prime example of the ability of repeat players to trump "one shotters" (Galanter 1974). Rose Cipollone was fifty-eight years old in 1983 when she filed suit in federal court in New Jersey seeking compensation from the Liggett Group. At the time, Cipollone had been smoking for over forty years and had lost a lung to prove it. Indeed, she died during the course of the trial, leaving her husband, Antonio, to carry forth on behalf of the estate (*Cipollone v. Liggett Group, Inc.* 1988). In 1988, it appeared that the Cipollones were vindicated, when a jury awarded Antonio $400,000 in damages on grounds that the Liggett Group had failed to warn of the risks of their products prior to 1966, the year that labels began appearing on cigarette packages (see the *Federal Cigarette Labeling and Advertising Act of 1965*)[4] and that it had breached "an express warranty that the cigarettes were safe" (Jacobson 1989, 1023). Naturally, the tobacco company was not about to take the decision lying down – $400,000 was a pittance, however, the precedent was far from trivial. Thus, the Liggett Group argued that the Cipollones' claims, which were mostly based in state tort doctrines, were pre-empted by federal law. In what seemed like an early body blow to the industry, the Supreme Court of the United States ruled that much of the *Cipollone* case was *not* superceded (*Cipollone v. Liggett Group, Inc.* 1992, 524-31). The Court, however, remanded the case for a new trial, but this new trial never happened. Instead, after a bruising nine-year battle, the Cipollone family (now, the couple's son, since Antonio had also passed away) quietly settled the case when their law firm, citing losses of about $5 million, pulled the plug (Schroth 1992). Wall Street insiders also theorized that the firm's other clients – mostly major corporations – were tiring of its assault on one of their own (*ibid.*).

Whatever the reason, *Cipollone* is a clear illustration of the power of the wealthy established interest. The tobacco company was in the game for the long haul and far better able to withstand delays and appeals than the Cipollones, whose deaths during the process stood as a sad metaphor for the inability of the individual to play for "long-run interests." This ultimately placed the cigarette group in the driver's seat, steering the surviving son and his weary lawyers almost inevitably toward the outcome that was favoured by Liggett all along – a quiet settlement. Moreover, we must remember, that compared to the other 813 litigants, the Cipollones came out quite well – their estate at least got something. As a counsel to R.J. Reynolds put it, "[t]he aggressive posture we have taken regarding depositions and discovery in general continues to make these cases extremely burdensome and expensive for plaintiffs' lawyers, particularly sole practitioners. To paraphrase General Patton, the way we won these cases was not by spending all of [RJR]'s money, but by making that other son of a bitch spend all of his" (*Haines v. Liggett Group, Inc.* 1993, 421).

Individuals versus Tobacco: Contemporary Suits

While big tobacco traditionally fared well against small, individual claimants, it has had to face renewed battles with such smokers in recent years. Much of this new litigation has been spurred on by the discovery of internal documents revealing industry deception and misrepresentation. Where tobacco had prevailed for nearly four decades by blaming smokers for their ills, sufficient documentation of industry duplicity had been uncovered by the mid-1990s to embolden a new round of litigants (see, for example, Schwartz 1994). And on the face of things, these litigants have scored some big victories. Several major cases are generally cited as indications of tobacco's new vulnerability. In 1999, a San Francisco jury awarded a smoker $50 million in punitive damages (*Henley v. Philip Morris, Inc.* 1999)), while, in Oregon, a jury returned a judgment of $80 million (*Williams-Branch ex rel. Estate of Williams v. Philip Morris, Inc.* 1999). In 2000, another California jury found in favour of plaintiff Leslie Whiteley, awarding her $21.7 million (*Whiteley v. Raybestos-Manhattan Inc.* 2000). In 2002, a Los Angeles jury awarded a single plaintiff a record-breaking $28 billion in punitive damages (*Bullock v. Philip Morris* 2002). Despite these apparent anti-tobacco victories, however, the record of the cigarette giants remains quite impressive – even in the face of those damning internal documents. Big tobacco continues to win most of its cases at trial. Moreover, on appeal, its losses tend either to be greatly reduced or overturned outright.

On 6 July 2000, in a very closely watched case, a Brooklyn jury decided that thirty years worth of smoking was not related to the plaintiff's lung cancer (*Anderson v. Fortune Brands* 2000). Only two weeks later in Mississippi, home to crusading attorney general Mike Moore, a jury refused to hold cigarette companies responsible for the lung cancer death of a thirty-seven-year-old man, a smoker since childhood (*Nunnally v. R.J. Reynolds* 2000). Rather, the jury agreed with the industry that Joseph Nunnally had known the risks of smoking and willingly assumed those risks. Moreover, and significantly, the jury determined that the cigarettes were not defective (Tobacco.org 2000, para. 2). In 2003, a Philadelphia jury found Brown and Williamson not liable for the lung cancer death of a man who smoked

Carlton cigarettes, thinking that they were safer than other brands (*Eiser v. Brown and Williamson* 2003). Moreover, juries in Sacramento and Miami issued verdicts for Philip Morris and R.J. Reynolds, respectively (*Lucier v. Philip Morris* 2003; *Allen v. R.J. Reynolds Tobacco Company* 2003).

Equally important is the fact that, although the industry has clearly sustained some trial losses, these are all just *trial* losses. Not surprisingly, the tobacco companies have appealed them or are in the process of doing so. Thus, for example, in October 2003, the Supreme Court of the United States threw out an $80 million verdict against Philip Morris, ordering Oregon courts to review the award in light of *State Farm Insurance v. Preece* (2004; also see *Philip Morris USA Inc. v. Williams* 2004).[5] When the case appeared before the Court again in 2007, the high court overturned punitive damages against Philip Morris on grounds that jurors inappropriately calculated the figure to punish the cigarette manufacturer for the harm it caused to smokers, other than the deceased, for whom the suit was brought (*Philip Morris USA v. Williams* 2007b).

Although appeals are pending nationwide, it is crucial to note that as of 2007 tobacco has not lost a single appeal on final judgment. Moreover, those who watch the industry with particular interest – major Wall Street analysts – believe that tobacco will come out on top. Thus, for example, Martin Feldman of Salomon Smith Barney notes: "The industry is having to fight harder, but in the long run it will prevail. It's a mistake to believe that this industry won't come up with new effective defenses." Marc Cohen of Goldman Sachs agrees, pointing to the industry's "compelling batting average" (both quoted in Haddad 2000, para. 10). Moreover, even if tobacco has to settle up for really big bucks, "it is the smokers who will bear the cost of litigation" (quoted in *ibid.*, para. 12). Cohen thus estimates that even if the industry were to lose one hundred cases a year (and it would certainly settle if the legal tide appeared to be turning against it), "cigarette makers could – and would – recoup the cost of judgments through raising prices about 15 cents a pack" (paraphrased in *ibid.*). As the headline in *Business Week* put it in May 2003, "[t]he smoke around big tobacco clears" (Choe 2003).

Clearly, the repeat player – the "have" of the litigation world – would be most advantaged in squaring off against a one-shot litigant. And hundreds of individual litigants have filed tort actions against the cigarette companies in an attempt to have their own "day in court." Yet, just as clearly, the ravages of lung, mouth, and lip cancer, of emphysema, and of other tobacco-related health problems have ultimately reached proportions that far transcend the injuries to any single person. Thus, sometimes, Goliath is made to face Goliath in the judicial process. And, one might say that, at least generically and taken in toto, there is no greater Goliath (that is, repeat player) than the government. Government, after all, is party to hundreds upon hundreds of civil suits every year, and it prosecutes *all* criminal defendants.

Mass Tort Subrogation: Government versus Tobacco

Over the past decade, one of the hallmarks of the tobacco wars has been the active involvement of state and federal governments. A combination of increasing health care and productivity costs, the uncovering of those damning internal cigarette company documents, and growing public aversion to tobacco products has forced government – or at least a portion of government – into the fray against big tobacco.[6] The fray has been entered on multiple political fronts, including pre-emptive smoke-free indoor air laws promulgated by states and municipalities,[7] increased taxes on cigarettes,[8] and the implementation of smoking prevention and control programs (National Governors Association 2005). The most dramatic policy expressions, however, have come in the form of litigation. Legally promulgated under the theory of mass tort subrogation, government has been the winner on the face of it, but a closer look might well reveal otherwise.[9]

Food and Drug Administration (FDA) Case

Take, for example, one of the earliest government efforts, the FDA's attempt to regulate nicotine as a drug and cigarettes as drug delivery devices – an attempt upheld by a trial judge in North Carolina, the very cradle of American tobacco! No doubt, Judge Osteen's holding that the FDA *did* possess authority to regulate nicotine as a drug came as something of an unhappy surprise to the industry. After all, the cigarette companies' decision to file the complaint in North Carolina was hardly serendipitous – one might reasonably surmise that a tobacco country judge would be a bit more sympathetic to tobacco interests than, say, some northern urban or western jurist. Of course, trial decisions can be appealed, particularly by litigants with deep pockets, and the industry's appeal to the Fourth Circuit Court had a far more satisfactory outcome, with the appellate panel reversing the district court's ruling (*Brown and Williamson v. U.S. FDA* 1998). Even more satisfactory, however, when the FDA appealed the circuit court decision to the Supreme Court of the United States tobacco scored a huge victory. Thus, Justice O'Connor, writing for a narrow majority, concurred with the appeals court, ruling that "Congress has clearly precluded the FDA from asserting jurisdiction to regulate tobacco products" (*FDA v. Brown and Williamson* 2000). According to the Court, if the FDA wanted specific authority to regulate cigarettes as drugs, it must gain the power explicitly via the legislative process – traditionally, a process that has tended to favour tobacco.[10]

Master Settlement Agreement (MSA)

Still, one might argue that the FDA's loss was but a hollow victory for tobacco in light of other recent governmental developments – notably, the more than $240 billion and additional concessions extracted by the states in the *MSA* and the Department of Justice's litigation.[11] In the mid-1990s, tobacco interests were shaken when Mississippi attorney general Mike Moore filed suit against the cigarette industry (*Moore v. American Tobacco Company* 1994). Moore claimed that the industry had knowingly manufactured and marketed a harmful, addictive product causing major health damage to the citizens of the state. Indeed, Mississippi and several other deep south states, with very high rates of smoking,[12] suffered an incidence of lung and other tobacco-related cancers that was far beyond the national average (Division of Cancer Epidemiology and Genetics 2004).[13] Moore asked the court to assess economic damages sufficient to reimburse Mississippi for past and future expenses related to treating sick smokers[14] and for punitive damages "in such amount as will sufficiently punish the defendants for their conduct and as will serve as an example to prevent a repetition of such conduct in the future" (*ibid.*, paras. 83, 88, and 91). In addition, he asked the court to enjoin the industry from promoting or selling its product to minors (*ibid.*, para. 94). In what seemed to be a virtual steamroller bearing down on the beleaguered industry, nearly every other state attorney general had filed a similar suit by June 1997 (Kelder and Davidson 1999). Since large institutional entities generally prefer settlements to trials and because of the unwieldy nature of the multi-jurisdictional actions, the industry pushed for a general settlement proposal in order to conclude all state and class action claims against it. And because the proposed settlement would have to bind all fifty states, it had to be in the form of a congressional enactment. Thus, by mid-1997, the tobacco litigation wars had moved to Washington where a bipartisan settlement of $368.5 billion was initially proffered. By all accounts, the industry was agreeable to this amount.

Referred to the Senate Commerce Committee in 1998, however, the bill permuted into a different – and considerably larger – animal. Thus, the committee bill upped the ante by about $148 billion. Notably, the industry was not necessarily averse to the higher price tag. However, it was miffed by provisions that would raise federal cigarette taxes by $1.10 per pack, give the FDA regulatory authority, and drastically reduce cigarette marketing and advertising. Steven Goldstone, chairman of R.J.R. Nabisco, in rather imperious tones, informed Congress that "[t]he bill ... requires my signature and there is no chance in the world it's going to get my signature" (quoted in Rosenbaum 1998, 2). Thus, the congressional effort died in committee, sending the action back to the states. The ultimate result was the *MSA*, which was finalized on 23 November 1998, among industry participants and forty-six states. In what was hailed by the attorneys general as a major tobacco capitulation, the industry acceded to total payments to the states over a seventeen-year period of $206 billion; to fund a $1.5 billion anti-smoking campaign; to open previously secret industry documents; to curb significantly their advertising and marketing campaigns, including banning cartoon characters such as Joe Camel and paraphernalia aimed at youth; and to disband certain industry trade groups (National Association of Attorneys General 1998). The attorneys general, who were significant system repeat players themselves, had seemingly come out ahead.

Well, maybe – and maybe not. After all, the industry was powerful enough to tell Congress to "go take a hike" and, itself, to go hiking for a better deal. By most assessments, it got a better deal – in spades! Several facets of the agreement are particularly noteworthy. To begin, there is the problem of the schedule of payments. Naturally, the tobacco companies were loath to shell out a huge lump sum to the states. Thus, in order to seal the bargain, the attorneys general had to agree to a very long, drawn out system of compensation. The $206 billion is being paid out in instalments over a twenty-five-year period. Significantly, these payments are directly tied to the tobacco companies' continued fiscal well-being. The structure, then, sets up what amounts to a partnership between the states and the large cigarette manufacturers. State governments, salivating over millions of extra dollars flowing into their treasuries, actually have an enormous incentive to guarantee the financial health of their new partners. Take, for example, the relatively small case of Colorado, which is scheduled to receive about $2.9 billion over the time span. Flush with its tax-free windfall,[15] the state legislature was set in 2000 to fund a number of popular new programs including a third-grade reading program; children's health care plans; a tobacco and substance abuse research fund; and prescription drug subsidies for the elderly. Good stuff, but according to two members of that legislature, "Colorado's General Assembly now finds itself in a dilemma: By depending upon annual payments to fund new programs, the Legislature must expect – even hope that domestic tobacco sales remain relatively strong. If it chooses not to condone smoking and improve public health by promoting smoking cessation, the Legislature may watch the tobacco money disappear and find itself committed to new programs that it can no longer financially support" (Dean and Feeley 2000, B8).

Colorado is not alone. California, for example, "has sold $2.6 billion in bonds financed by payment from tobacco companies to fill past budget gaps" (Morain 2004, B1). Indeed, though not as dramatic, according to the National Conference of State Legislatures, closing budgetary gaps is the number one use of tobacco payment monies, far outstripping funding for health programs (National Conference of State Legislatures 2004). The states thus have a huge stake in the continued financial viability of tobacco. As one commentator put it, "[s]tate governments are now de facto shareholders in tobacco manufacturing companies, a relationship that necessarily conflicts with the traditional role of state governments in protecting the health and welfare of their constituencies. Every potential policy or program related to tobacco now carries a uniquely special price tag. In some states, even the protections afforded to an appellee in a lawsuit against a tobacco manufacturer may have changed, at least in part, to protect those states' property interests in the continued sale of cigarettes" (Harris 2001, 168).[16]

Just how huge this stake is was demonstrated in 2003 in the light cigarette case, *Price v. Philip Morris* (2003a; 2003b). In April of that year, an Illinois court awarded $10 billion in damages against Philip Morris for misleading consumers about the safety of light cigarettes. Pending appeal, the judge ordered the tobacco giant to post a $12 billion bond, an amount that Philip Morris said would force it into bankruptcy. True or not, the company's distress call was heard loud and clear by recession-wracked state governments. Should Philip Morris go under, one sure source of income for these states would go with it. Thus, in an *amicus* brief filed by the National Association of Attorneys General, Illinois circuit court judge Nicholas Byron was asked to set bond so as not to adversely affect state coffers. The judge did just that, slashing the bond in half (Luke 2003, 2). This decision was upheld by the Supreme Court of Illinois, which, in a further victory for Philip Morris, allowed the company to proceed on expedited appeal (Levin 2003, C-1). As an attorney who took part in the *MSA* negotiations noted, "[e]ach State now has an incentive to *increase* tobacco sales. This dampens any likelihood of a taxing or regulatory strategy to reduce the sales of tobacco and reverses the position that States should advance, putting them in partnership with the tobacco companies" (LaFrance 2000, 197-98). Moreover, if other provisions of the *MSA* are any indication, the states are *not* the senior partners!

Thus, for example, the *MSA* virtually guaranteed that there would be no federal tax increases on tobacco products for at least several years: "If within the next four years Congress increases the federal tax on cigarettes and shares the proceeds with the states, the companies will enjoy a dollar-for-dollar setoff against the payments to the states" (Galanter 1999, 55). In other words, if Congress did try to raise the federal cigarette tax, forty-six states would "lose a corresponding amount from their tobacco payments" (Nemitz 1998, 1B).[17]

Moreover, the *MSA* grants the large participating companies near oligopoly status in the market. In effect, under the terms of the *MSA*, the major cigarette manufacturers can raise prices in order to fund the settlement without losing market share to smaller discount companies that were not part of the agreement. Arguably, the big companies' preferred place in the market is guaranteed in two ways. First, the *MSA* strongly encourages the enactment of so-called "qualifying statutes," whereby states "effectively and fully neutralize ... the cost disadvantages that the Participating Manufacturers experience vis-à-vis Non-Participating Manufacturers within such Settling State as a result of the provisions of this Agreement."[18] Second, the *MSA* establishes a price cap on "subsequent participating manufacturers" (SPM) – legal terminology for all of the small companies who were not part of the original agreement. According to small wholesalers and retailers, this clause means that, "as a practical matter, if an SPM lowers its prices to expand its market share, its sales will quickly reach the market share cap and it will be forced to either pay a share of the *MSA* settlement payments or restrict its output. The actual penalty for any sales by an SPM in excess of its quota is about $.19 per pack of cigarettes ($1.90 per carton) or about one-third of the $5 whole-sale price of a carton of discount cigarettes" ("Tobacco Cases" 1999, 2).

Since implementation of the *MSA,* a number of small firms have launched antitrust actions against the large manufacturers. Thus far, they have either been unsuccessful (see *A.D. Bedell v. Philip Morris, Inc.* 2000) or quietly settled (*DeLoach v. Philip Morris* 2003). Hence, among other benefits, the *MSA* shields the tobacco industry from major litigation, for a time at least, from increased federal taxes, and from competition, and it draws forty-six state governments into a mutually beneficial alliance – all for the relatively cheap price of $206 billion, which is easily passed onto its addicted clientele (see, for example, Haddad 2000 and Galanter 1999).

The Federal Suit
As part of his 1999 State of the Union message, President Bill Clinton an-nounced the following:

> As everyone knows, our children are targets of a massive media campaign to hook them on cigarettes. Now, I ask this Congress to resist the tobacco lobby, to reaffirm the FDA's authority to protect our children from tobacco and to hold tobacco companies accountable, while protecting tobacco farm-ers. Smoking has cost taxpayers hundreds of billions of dollars under Medi-care and other programs. You know, the states have been right about this. Taxpayers shouldn't pay for the cost of lung cancer, emphysema, and other smoking-related illnesses, the tobacco companies should. So tonight I an-nounce that the Justice Department is preparing a litigation plan to take the tobacco companies to court and with the funds we recover to strengthen Medicare. (Clinton 1999a)

Nine months later, on 22 September 1999, the United States filed suit against six major cigarette manufacturers and two industry affiliates, the Council for Tobacco Research and the Tobacco Institute. The government's four-count case was based on three statutes, the *Medical Care Recovery Act (MCRA),* the *Medicare Secondary Payer Provisions (MSP),* and the *Racketeer Influenced and Corrupt Organizations Act,* better known by its acronym *RICO.*[19] The *MCRA,* the government claimed, gave it "a cause of action to recover certain speci-fied health care costs it pays to treat individuals injured by a third-party's tortuous conduct." The *MSP,* it said, provided cause "to recover Medicare expenditures when a third-party caused an injury requiring treatment and a 'primary payer' was obligated to pay for the treatment."[20] And, *RICO,* more commonly associated with mob-related activities, "provides parties with a cause of action to recover treble damages due to injuries they received from a defendant's unlawful racketeering activity, and to seek other equitable remedies to prevent future unlawful acts" (*United States v. Philip Morris* 2000, 2). For this, the United States was asking $280 billion in damages.[21]

The first round went to tobacco. On 28 September 2000, US district judge Gladys Kessler sided with the industry, ruling that much of the government's case was based on a misapplication of two laws, the *MCRA* and the *MSP*. The judge allowed the case to proceed on the racketeering counts, but the ruling seriously weakened the government's case (United States, Department of Justice 2004; Miller 2000). Nevertheless, the suit lumbered forward, beginning trial before Judge Kessler in September 2004 and lasting until August 2006. The government's case, then limited to *RICO*, was laid out in a whopping 2,500-plus page *Findings of Fact* (*United States v. Philip Morris* 2004a). In essence, the government accused defendants of having "engaged in and executed – and continu[ing] to engage in and execute – a massive 50-year scheme to defraud the public, including consumers of cigarettes, in violation of RICO." The government contended, moreover, that tobacco's "past and ongoing conduct indicates a reasonable likelihood of future violations" (*ibid.*, 33).[22]

For its part, tobacco assembled a "dream team" of attorneys, led by corporate "superlawyer" Dan Webb and including help from such Wall Street firms as Arnold and Porter, Hunton and Williams, and Paul, Weiss, Rifkind, Wharton, and Garrison. Webb, himself, deemed this case the "mother of all trials" (Beck 2004, 1). In any event, "[t]obacco companies were confident the defence [*sic*] honed in dozens of cases will prevail." According to William Ohlemeyer, vice president and associate general counsel of Altria Group, the parent company of Philip Morris, "[i]t is the exact same evidence that juries look at in other cases, and for the most part, they return defence [*sic*] verdicts" (Buckley 2004, 17).

In February 2005, most of the remaining legs were seemingly cut from under what was left of the government's case. Although the District of Columbia Circuit Court allowed the suit to proceed, the court barred the Department of Justice from seeking $280 billion in past profits as part of its fraud and racketeering case against the industry (*United States v. Philip Morris* 2005). In light of this development and the Bush administration's general lack of enthusiasm for the case, the Department of Justice in June 2005 reduced the amount of penalty sought to a relatively paltry $10 billion.[23] More than a year later, in August 2006, the case concluded with both a bang and a whimper. The bang came in Judge Kessler's scathing opinion (published in a massive 1,653 pages!),[24] finding that cigarette companies had conspired for decades to deceive the public, hiding or lying about the dangers of smoking. Kessler pulled no punches in asserting that over the course of more than 50 years, Defendants lied, misrepresented, and deceived the American public, including smokers and the young people they avidly sought as "replacement smokers," about the devastating health effects of smoking and environmental tobacco smoke, they suppressed research, they destroyed documents, they manipulated the use of nicotine so as to increase and perpetuate addiction, they distorted the truth about low tar and light cigarettes so as to discourage smokers from quitting, and they abused the legal system in order to achieve their goal – to make money with little, if any, regard for individual illness and suffering, soaring health costs, or the integrity of the legal system. (*United States v. Philip Morris* 2006a, 852)

Devastating words, indeed, but the bang was followed with a clear whimper when Kessler, claiming that her hands were tied by appellate rulings, issued a set of remedies so trifling that tobacco stocks rallied on news of the decision (Henderson 2006). Thus, she enjoined defendants from "participating in any way, directly or indirectly, in the management and/or control of any of the affairs of [the Center for Tobacco Research] CTR, [the Tobacco Institute] TI, or the Center for Indoor Air Research (CIAR), or any successor entities" (*United States v. Philip Morris* 2006b, 2). Defendants were also enjoined from making any misleading health claims about cigarettes, including labelling some products as "light," "low tar," "mild," "natural," or "any other words which reasonably could be expected to result in a consumer believing that smoking the cigarette brand using that descriptor may result in a lower risk of disease or be less hazardous to health than smoking other brands of cigarettes" (*ibid.*, 3-4). (Kessler later applied this portion of the ruling to overseas marketing as well as domestic sales ["US Judge Rules" 2007]). The companies were ordered to make public statements on cigarette packages, in major newspapers, on network television, and on their websites, correcting past misinformation (*United States v. Philip Morris* 2006b, 4-12). Moreover, Philip Morris, R.J. Reynolds, Lorillard, and Brown and Williamson were required to "maintain Internet Document Websites until September 1, 2016 at their expense" (*ibid.*, 12-18). The effects were summed up by David Adelman, an analyst with Morgan Stanley. "From a business perspective," Adelman asserted, "this is a complete win. [The tobacco companies are] not making any substantial payments. There's no threat of future substantial payments" (quoted in Henderson 2006, D1).[25] Even so, the industry is appealing.[26]

Classes versus Tobacco

Broin versus Philip Morris
On the (generally correct) assumption that juries will find individual smokers wholly or largely at fault for their own bad habits, the tobacco industry has

fought hard against class certifications. Indeed, a number of national polls taken during this era indicate that the general public overwhelmingly agreed (for example, Haltom and McCann 2004a, 254-55). And, using federal *Rule 23* and its state analogues to argue that smokers are too diverse to be adequately represented by a single settlement, the cigarette companies have been able to squash most class-making deals.[27] Moreover, the few class certifications that have been achieved have largely resulted in tobacco company wins, class legal limbo, or both.

Since juries have tended to fault individual smokers, it is perhaps not surprising that the first successful plaintiff class certification against cigarette manufacturers did not involve smokers but, rather, non-smokers. In 1991, with the counsel of Stanley and Susan Rosenblatt, well-known tobacco injury attorneys, 60,000 flight attendants sued nine tobacco companies for injuries resulting from second-hand cabin smoke.[28] The class was approved by the Florida Court of Appeal in 1994 (*Broin v. Philip Morris* 1994). The trial, which was scheduled to proceed in two phases, began and ended in 1997 with a settlement – both sides agreeing to major compromises.[29] For its part, the tobacco industry agreed, among other things, to a $300 million research effort on the effects of second-hand smoke, to pay class counsel $49 million in fees, to waive the statute of limitations, to allow class members to proceed with individual suits in their resident venues, and to "shift the burden of proof on generic causation as to lung cancer, chronic obstructive pulmonary disease, chronic bronchitis, chronic sinusitis and emphysema" from plaintiffs to defendants (*Philip Morris v. French* 2004). For their part, plaintiffs agreed to abandon any claims for punitive damages and to dismiss "fraud, misrepresentation and conspiracy claims" (*ibid.*, 6). Apparently, tobacco got the better end of the deal. Since 1997, 3,000 flight attendants have brought individual suits under the agreement. To date, only eight *Broin* cases have been tried, and, of those, only one plaintiff, Lynn French, has been successful against the cigarette companies.[30]

Castano Group Litigation

No doubt, the most ambitious of the tobacco litigations were those launched by the Castano Group. During the mid-1990s, New Orleans attorney Wendell Gauthier began soliciting fellow members of the plaintiffs' bar to engage in a large-scale assault against tobacco. Gauthier became interested in the fight in 1993, when his close friend, Peter Castano, died of lung cancer at the age of forty-seven (Woodyard 1997). Gauthier was further bolstered in his strategy when ABC News ran a documentary in 1994 suggesting the industry spiked cigarettes with nicotine to ensure an addicted clientele (Pringle 1999, 388). The result was one of the best-funded litigation coalitions in history, as Gauthier eventually persuaded sixty law firms to kick in $100,000 a year toward class action litigation. The group was impressive not only in numbers

but also in credentials, including Elizabeth Cabraser of class action special-
ists Lieff, Cabraser, and Heimann, mega-tort super-star Stanley Chesley,
Baltimore Orioles owner Peter Angelos, and Washington, DC's John Coale
(*ibid.*, 391).[31]

No shrinking violets, the group began its efforts on behalf of Castano's
widow, Dianne, and "[a]ll nicotine-dependent persons in the United States
... who have purchased and smoked cigarettes manufactured by the defendants; the estates, representatives, and administrators of these nicotine-
dependent cigarette smokers; and the spouses, children, relatives and
'significant others' of these nicotine-dependent cigarette smokers as their
heirs or survivors" (*Castano v. American Tobacco Company* 1996)! Estimates
of the size of the class ran to around 100 million, including forty million
current smokers and another sixty million who had quit or died since 1943
(Maclachlan 1995). Citing as causes of action, "fraud and deceit; negligent
misrepresentation; intentional infliction of emotional distress; negligence
and negligent infliction of emotional distress; violation of consumer protection statutes under state law; breach of express warranty; breach of implied
warranty; strict product liability," the suit sought compensatory and punitive damages, attorneys' fees, and equitable relief, as well as "a declaration
that defendants are financially responsible for notifying all class members
of nicotine's addictive nature, a declaration that the defendants manipulated
nicotine levels with the intent to sustain the addiction of plaintiffs and the
class members, an order that the defendants disgorge any profits made from
the sale of cigarettes, restitution for sums paid for cigarettes, and the establishment of a medical monitoring fund" (*Castano v. American Tobacco Company* 1996). According to the district court that granted certification, it was
"embark[ing] on a road certainly less traveled, if ever taken at all" (*Castano
v. American Tobacco Company* 1995). In the words of group member John
Coale, it was "the mother of all lawsuits" (quoted in Curriden 1995, A1).

Whatever it was, the strategy appeared to pay off in March 1996, when
the Liggett Group broke from industry ranks, agreeing to settle *Castano*
(Hansen 1996, 22).[32] The victory, however, may have been a pyrrhic one.
First, in exchange for settling, Liggett admitted no liability. Moreover, Liggett
agreed only "to help fund stop-smoking programs and to abide by proposed
federal regulations designed to keep minors from smoking" (*ibid.*, 22). While
the deal was applauded by many in the anti-tobacco community and be-
moaned by industry supporters, tobacco plaintiff attorney Stanley Rosenblatt
deemed it "a joke": "It's a great deal for Liggett, but it's a lousy deal for the
plaintiffs' ... Members of the class are being asked to give up their right to
sue ... in exchange for what amounts to a discount at a Smoke Enders program. 'It doesn't put 10 cents in the pocket of any afflicted individual' ...
'All it does is provide a tremendous amount of fodder for *The Wall Street*

Journal and others who view these class action cases as a vehicle to make lawyers rich'" (Rosenblatt quoted and paraphrased in Hansen 1996, 24).

Two months later, the Fifth Circuit Court joined the skirmish on interlocutory appeal, undoing the certification on grounds that "[t]he district court abused its discretion by ignoring variations in state law and how a trial on the alleged causes of action would be tried" (*Castano v. American Tobacco Company* 1996, 752). Undaunted, John Coale vowed to instigate suits on the state level: "We will start with Louisiana, and we will start filing in 10 states a week. With 60 law firms we cover most of the states" (quoted in Maclachlan and Blum 1996). Ultimately, the group filed twenty-five state class actions (*In re: Application of Brown and Williamson Tobacco Corporation v. Stanley M. Chesley* 2004). Only two of these cases proceeded to trial, one ending in a win for the plaintiffs (*Scott v. American Tobacco Company* 2004)[33] and the other a win for the defendants (*In re: Tobacco Litigation (Medical Monitoring Cases)* 2004).[34] The plaintiff victory is now pending appeal. Other group cases have largely been dismissed.[35] Nevertheless, the Castano Group has had a major impact in the tobacco litigation wars, primarily through their involvement with the public entity cases that led to the *MSA*. California's "Davis/Ellis" case is illustrative. Davis/Ellis was initially filed by the Castano Group during the summer of 1996 on behalf of the named plaintiff, James Ellis, an Orange County cancer patient. Several months later, the case was voluntarily dismissed and re-entered when then California attoneny general Gray Davis joined the case. Eventually, other such suits were consolidated with Davis/Ellis and became the basis for California's portion of the *MSA*.[36]

Engle versus Liggett Group

If the Castano filings were the most ambitious, the most dramatic class effort to date was offered by the case of Dr. Howard A. Engle. It may also be the most dramatic class win by tobacco. Represented by the Rosenblatts, Engle, a retired Miami pediatrician and emphysema sufferer originally filed suit in Florida in 1994 for himself, five other named plaintiffs, and a class of "[a]ll United States citizens and residents, and their survivors, who have suffered, presently suffer or have died from diseases and medical conditions caused by their addiction to cigarettes that contain nicotine" (*Liggett Group, Inc. v. Engle* 2003, 441). Two years later, the class was whittled down to Florida smokers only but was still an estimated 700,000 strong *(ibid.)*. The trial was to proceed in three phases, two of which actually occurred. In Phase 1, jurors were charged with determining whether defendants were grossly negligent. If so, Phase 2 was set to determine punitive damages due for the entire class. And, finally, Phase 3 would involve individual trials to assess compensatory damages for each class member (the judicial version of the cart leading the horse).

Needless to say, when the jury completed Phase 1 with a verdict finding for the class on all counts, the industry must have held its collective breath. However, if that were the case at the conclusion of Phase I, total loss of breath must have accompanied the jury's Phase II decision – a stunning $145 billion in punitive damages to be paid by the nation's five largest cigarette companies. It was, by far, the largest damage award ever handed down by *any* jury against *any* defendant. So huge was the award that, before the verdict came down and anticipating a *lesser* amount, a Philip Morris attorney warned that it would be a "'death warrant' for the industry" (Wilson 2000, para. 18). Of course, the defendants appealed. And staving off the death knell one more time, the state's Third District Court of Appeal not only tossed out the damages verdict but decertified the plaintiff class of smokers, thus, presumably ending the watershed event of anti-smoking litigation (*Liggett Group, Inc. v. Engle* 2003). The court found that the class ran afoul of Florida's *Rule 1.220* (the state's version of *Rule 23*) on several counts.[37] First and foremost among these, and echoing the concerns of the authors of *Rule 23*,[38] the Florida court asserted that "Rule 1.220 ... requires that class representation be superior to other available methods of fairly and efficiently adjudicating the claims presented ... If significant individual issues exist, little value is gained by proceeding as a class action. Not only would the lawsuit become unmanageable, it would further be unjust to bind absent class members to a negative decision where the class representative's claims present different individual issues than those of the absent members. Under these circumstances, class representation would not be 'superior' to individual suits for the fair and efficient adjudication of the controversy" (*ibid.*, 445). In July 2006, the Supreme Court of Florida upheld the ruling, holding that the issues in the case "are highly individualized and do not lend themselves to class action treatment" (*Engle v. Liggett Group* 2006, 1254).[39]

The Light Cigarette Cases
Also dead for plaintiffs is Illinois' light cigarette case – the one that brought the state attorneys general to the rescue of Philip Morris on an appeal bond amount. Brought under the state's *Consumer Fraud and Deceptive Business Practices Act,* the suit was filed on behalf of an estimated 1.14 million plaintiffs, who were former and current smokers of light cigarettes (*Price v. Philip Morris* 2003a; 2003b).[40] The question of class was first before Judge Nicholas Byron of the Illinois Circuit Court in Madison County.[41] As usual in such cases, the tobacco company argued that distinctions among the class members – current smokers versus those who had quit, those who smoked more cigarettes after switching to light versus those who smoked the same amount or fewer, and sick smokers versus well smokers – meant that each case should be tried separately. Plaintiffs, on the other hand, relying on scientific evidence and the tobacco company's own internal documents, argued that litigants

had enough in common to proceed as a class.[42] Judge Byron agreed with the latter.

While the class clash was familiar, the case differed from most tobacco suits, focusing on economic damages as opposed to health costs. According to the *Consumer Fraud and Deceptive Business Practices Act*, plaintiffs might recover under the so-called "benefit of the bargain rule ... the difference between the actual value of the property sold and the value the property would have had if [product] representations were actually true" (Vock 2004, 14). How this difference was to be calculated was, needless to say, a matter of dispute between the plaintiffs and the defendant. Thus, Philip Morris argued that the actual price of light cigarettes is what consumers pay now. The value they "would have had" is the price paid prior to the lawsuit. Since smokers paid as much, and more, for a pack in 2004 as they did in 2000, the cigarette company contended that they suffered no economic damages *(ibid.)*.

Plaintiffs offered a wholly different methodology. The actual value of light cigarettes, they argued, is how much smokers paid during the class period:

> Yet because they claim that no real-world cigarette exists that delivers lower tar and nicotine, the plaintiffs used a survey to determine how much more this "genuine" (but non-existent) light cigarette would be worth to smokers. They conducted a survey of 276 smokers nationwide that asked participants to compare the existing Marlboro Light cigarette to a hypothetical cigarette that tasted like a Marlboro Light but delivered less tar and nicotine. Respondents were asked how much of a discount they would need in order to buy existing Marlboro Light cigarettes over the imagined ones if they were told that the existing light cigarettes were "just as harmful" as regular Marlboros. The surveyors then asked them what discount would be needed to convince them to buy existing Marlboro Lights that "could be more harmful" than regular Marlboros. On average, the respondents said they would need a 78 percent price drop to buy the "just as harmful" Marlboro Lights instead of the imagined alternative. They wanted a deeper discount – 92 percent – to buy the "more harmful" Marlboro Lights. *(ibid.)*

Again, Judge Byron agreed with the plaintiffs, awarding compensatory damages of $7.1005 billion. Punitive damages in the amount of $3 billion were earmarked for the state treasury. In addition, Byron ruled that any unclaimed compensatory damages would be divided among "11 law schools, drug courts, domestic violence programs, legal-aid organizations and the Illinois Bar Foundation" (*ibid.*, 8). The Supreme Court of Illinois, however, was having none of it. Thus, in December 2005, the court ruled that under paragraph 10b(1) of the *Consumer Fraud and Deceptive Business Practices Act*, the Federal Trade Commission specifically allowed tobacco companies to use words such as "low," "reduced," and "light" if "the statement is accompanied by a clear and conspicuous disclosure of" tar and nicotine content (*Price v. Philip Morris* 2005, 196). As a result, it reversed the lower court judgment with instructions to dismiss.

Despite this ruling, and on the heels of Judge Kessler's findings in the federal case, on 25 September 2006, Judge Jack Weinstein of the US District Court in Brooklyn granted class action status to light cigarette smokers in a suit that might have potentially involved tens of millions of smokers seeking as much as $200 billion in damages (Hays 2006). In July 2007, however, a three-judge panel of the Second Circuit Court "gave a rough reception" during oral argument to the viability of the class and its potential for success against the tobacco companies. In April 2008, the class was decertified (*McLaughlin v. American Company* 2008, 215).

In re: Simon II Litigation

Indeed, Judge Weinstein's tobacco class certifications have been largely unsuccessful thus far. During the fall of 2002, Judge Weinstein certified a class action against eight defendant tobacco companies, two industry umbrella organizations, and the public relations firm that represented the tobacco industry from 1953 through 1968. Weinstein's decision was novel in at least two respects. First, it created the first nationwide smoking class consisting of "[a]ll persons residing in the United States, or who were residents of the United States at the time of their deaths, who smoke or smoked Defendants' cigarettes, and who have been diagnosed by a physician with one of a number of smoking related diseases" (*In re: Simon II Litigation* 2002a, 96).[43] Excluded from the class were persons who had already obtained judgments against, or settled with, the defendants; persons against whom the defendants have obtained judgments; the Florida *Engle* class; and persons whose diseases were diagnosed before they began using tobacco (*ibid.*, 96-97). This, then, created a non-opt-out class.

Second, the class was created for assessing and awarding *only* punitive damages, "a punishment on behalf of society generally," according to the judge. Responding to the Supreme Court of the United States' concerns about "grossly excessive" punitive damages (see *BMW of North America v. Gore* 1996), Weinstein reasoned that

> [a] national punitive damages verdict will ... tend to be (a) less than the sum of local jury verdicts, and (b) more readily controllable than geographically diverse local verdicts because of a greater universe of comparable decisions ... The class action now certified provides a reasonable and conservative solution consonant with legal and equitable tradition. Such a non-opt out punitive class provides an opportunity to effectively address problems of punitive damages in mass torts. The Tobacco litigation is a particularly useful

vehicle because it addresses a mature tort with many cases already tried, providing some benchmarks for both compensatory and punitive damages. An immature mass litigation, where an early punitive damage class is assembled without any testing of what juries will do, does not permit the mega-analysis appropriate in this mature dispute approaching its closing stages. (*In re: Simon II Litigation* 2002b, 18-19 [internal citations omitted])

The proceedings, according to Weinstein, would "perform the vital function of helping to close the book on a terrible chapter of American medical-legal-entrepreneurial failures in abuse of tobacco" (*ibid.,* 14).

Although the proposal was praised as a fair and innovative solution to the tobacco litigation problem, it faced some formidable hurdles. Thus, recall that the Supreme Court of the United States rejected a nationwide asbestos class in 1999 (see Chapter 2 in this text). And, while Weinstein was quick to distinguish the tobacco class action from the failed asbestos case, opponents were just as quick to point to similarities. Moreover, those opponents were composed of an impressive array of strange litigation bedfellows. Complaining that the plan was "an unfair limitation of victims' rights," the Association of Trial Lawyers of America and the American Cancer Society filed briefs backing the tobacco companies' position (Glaberson 2004, B1)!

Indeed, on 6 May 2005, the Second Circuit Court vacated the certification, remanding the case and holding that "there is no evidence by which the district court could ascertain the limits of either the fund or the aggregate value of punitive claims against it, such that the postulated fund could be deemed inadequate to pay all legitimate claims." In other words, plaintiffs failed to satisfy the *Ortiz v. Fibreboard Corp.* (1999) criteria, and, thus, the plaintiffs had failed to satisfy one of the presumptively necessary conditions for limited fund treatment under *Ortiz.* Moreover, the circuit court ruled that "the order fails to ensure that a potential punitive award in this action would bear a sufficient nexus, and be both reasonable and proportionate, to the harm or potential harm to the plaintiff class and to the general damages to be recovered, as required by *State Farm*" (*In re: Simon II Litigation* 2005, 127-28). The nail nearly in the coffin, several months later plaintiffs moved for dismissal of the action, a request granted by Judge Weinstein on 6 February 2006 (*In re: Simon II Litigation* 2006).

United Seniors Association, Inc. v. Philip Morris

On 4 August 2005, the United Seniors Association, a conservative alternative to the American Association of Retired Persons, filed suit against Philip Morris and other major manufacturers in federal court in Boston. Filing as a "private attorney general" acting under the authority of the *Medicare as Secondary Payer Act (MSP),* the group was seeking to recover $60 billion in Medicare payments for cigarette-related illnesses.[44] Not surprisingly, tobacco companies asked the court to dismiss the suit (Smyth 2006). The court complied, and, in August 2007, the First Circuit Court concurred, concluding "that United Seniors failed to establish Article III standing to bring an action under MSP" (*United Seniors Association v. Philip Morris* 2007).

Conclusion

In the tobacco wars, the line between litigation and politics has become increasingly blurred over the past two decades (Appendix 3.1 at the end of this chapter recaps the most significant events). Indeed, the struggle is a clear example of litigation *as* politics. By the last decade of the twentieth century, the classic litigant (for example, Rose Cipollone) had been dwarfed by the likes of 700,000 Floridians and most state attorneys general representing millions nationwide. Initial suits pitting individuals against the mighty tobacco industry were replaced by what presumably were more even matches – the Castano Group versus Big Tobacco, for example – on the theory that coalitional litigation was the only realistic response to the power of the tobacco industry. Deals mimicking the legislative process have been attempted in an effort at compromise, the very hallmark of advanced legislative politics. Moreover, tobacco litigation ultimately has spilled into the actual legislative process, departing from the contained nature of the traditional lawsuit.

And, not just any politics – modern tobacco litigation is based on a theory of *movement* politics, not unlike the civil rights lawsuits that spawned the modern class action. As former Mississippi attorney general Mike Moore (1998, para. 18) explains, tobacco litigation was

> the biggest challenge, the biggest legal challenge in history. If we could climb this mountain, so to speak, then there would never be one larger than this. No challenge greater. Nobody has ever beaten the tobacco industry before. We felt like we had a chance. We also knew if we won, we might just do more good than any lawyer had ever done in history. Might save more lives than most doctors have ever saved in history. So I mean, why not do that? Why not be a part of that? And as the movement grew through the years I became more and more convinced we were going to be successful.

Litigation as Regulation

The question remains whether tobacco litigation has been an effective means of regulation. The answer is hardly straightforward. Legislation may have a variety of regulatory goals, and so it was with tobacco litigators, whose ends broadly could be seen as fiscal, health, and morality based. For the largest litigation groups, notably the state attorneys general and the US Department of Justice, fiscal regulation was a primary goal. In short, they sought reimbursement for Medicaid, Medicare, and other smoking-related costs borne by the government. The *MSA* settlement of $206 billion, the largest settlement that most states had ever received, was hardly chump change and could certainly be viewed as a regulatory victory, particularly given the expectations for industry actions that accompanied it. On the other hand, numerous commentators have demurred. Some, for example, point to the fact that state settlement revenues have been fungible to say the least – used to shore up budgets that have little or nothing to do with smoking prevention or smoking-related medical costs. On this count, the Campaign for Tobacco Free Kids gives thirty-seven states and the District of Columbia a failing grade, noting that in the fiscal year of 2005, for the third year in a row, "states have cut funding for tobacco prevention programs" (Campaign for Tobacco-Free Kids 2005, para. 3).

Indeed, none other than Mississippi's Mike Moore, progenitor of the states' suit and resulting *MSA*, has testified that "[s]ince the Tobacco Settlements I have been in 44 states giving a speech called 'spend the money on what the fight was about.' I have discovered that some governors and state legislators must believe that the tobacco settlement dollars fell out of heaven ... that the dollars have no connection to the public health lawsuit that we brought. The money is being spent on one-time budget deficits, college scholarships, tobacco warehouses, roads, anything but prevention, cessation, and improving public health of this country" (Moore 2003).[45] Others insist that whether or not states use the settlement money for health-related purposes is beside the point. Smokers, according to Kip Viscusi (2002, 9), are actually doing government a fiscal favour: "[I]n considering economic cost externalities arising from cigarettes, there is no net cost imposed on the states or on the federal government, even if one excludes excise taxes. Proper recognition of the full health consequences of smoking indicates that smokers will live shorter lives than nonsmokers and consequently will generate fewer nursing home expenses and lower pension and social security costs than nonsmokers. Indeed, smokers are self-financing for every state and for the federal government, even excluding the role of excise taxes already in place."

Similarly, the impact of the litigation on health is not altogether clear. Presumably, health could be affected in a number of direct and indirect ways. Most evidently, the increased costs of cigarettes anticipated from the tobacco industry's big pay-out was expected to suppress smoking.[46] Whether this has been the case, however, is difficult to gauge. The percentage of smokers in the population has been on a fairly steady decline for several decades (Saad 2008, 1). Regulation may also be morality-based – aimed at exposing and punishing wrongdoers. Here, the case for litigation as an effective regulatory device may be somewhat clearer. Litigation, after all, exposed the fact that the cigarette companies spiked nicotine levels, an allegation that was long denied by the industry. It also brought to light the enormity of tobacco company advertising, especially that aimed at the young, such as the Joe Camel campaign. Moreover, it is hard to deny that the combined effects of the *MSA* and the many defences waged by the industry have been demanding.

Of course, whether for treasury, public well-being, or ethical concerns, regulation is supposed to change the behaviour of the regulated entity. So, the question remains, has coalitional litigation managed to substantially alter cigarette companies' activities? Certainly, superficially, industry participants look to have become better corporate citizens. The enticing Joe Camel is a thing of the past. A click onto the Philip Morris USA homepage reveals a site that, on the face, looks as if it were sponsored by an anti-tobacco organization, featuring warnings about the dire consequences of smoking, a how-to-quit guide, and tips for parents seeking to discourage their children from smoking. Similarly, linked to its website, R.J. Reynolds features a smoking and health guide. And, in 2006, breaking for the first time with industry allies, Philip Morris announced that it now backs the FDA regulation of cigarettes (Szymanczyk 2007).

On the other hand (and a large other hand it is), the industry would appear to have changed very little. Thus, for example, as late as 2007, before entering the R.J. Reynolds website, the visitor was greeted with a full-page popup, alerting her to the fact that "a 156 percent tax cut!" is being considered by "some politicians in Washington, D.C." and informing smokers that "[b]etween federal, state, and local taxes, and tobacco settlement payments, government entities raked in more than $33 *billion* from smokers in 2006" (quoted in Kasperowicz 2007, para. 1). More telling, the Harvard School of Public Health found in 2005 "that cigarette makers [were] targeting young smokers with candy and liqueur-flavored new brands that mask the harsh and toxic properties found in tobacco smoke, and in one case, embedding a hidden flavor pellet within the filter" (Harvard School of Health 2005, para. 1). Although R.J. Reynolds agreed to stop the sale of its candy-flavoured cigarettes a year later, it has continued to pursue marketing strategies clearly contrary to the aims of would-be tobacco regulators. For example, in 2007, the company introduced "Camel No. 9," a name meant to evoke "fragrances like Chanel No. 19, as well as a song about romance, 'Love Potion No. 9'" (Elliott 2007, para. 2). The cigarettes come packaged in shiny black with hot pink fuchsia foil and the slogan "light and luscious." Obviously designed to appeal to women, both the Harvard School of Public Health and the Campaign for Tobacco-Free Kids, among others, contend that the targeted consumers are not women but, rather, girls: "While RJR claims that it is marketing only to women, its advertising and promotions tell a different story. Slick ads for Camel No. 9 have run in magazines popular with girls, including Vogue, Glamour, Cosmopolitan, Marie Claire and InStyle. Promotional giveaways include berry lip balm, cell phone jewelry, cute little purses and wristbands, all in hot pink. As the Oregonian newspaper put it, the company that once marketed to kids with the Joe Camel cartoon character is doing it again with 'Barbie Camel'" (Campaign for Tobacco-Free Kids 2007a, para. 3).

In addition, the major cigarette companies are actively growing the smoke-less segment of the industry, repacking and remarketing snuff in moist, "spitless" form. The strategy appears to be meeting with considerable suc-cess. Sales of the new snuff more than doubled from 1986 to 2005, and in-dustry promotional spending on the products has risen more than five-fold. According to Bill Phelps, spokesman for Philip Morris USA, "this is a growth strategy for us" (Koch 2007, para. 18).

Winners and Losers

All of this discussion finally begs the question, has tobacco litigation pro-duced winners and losers? Clearly, litigation (brought by an individual or by a class) and politics share in common the tendency to produce winners and losers. What has distinguished the two traditionally was litigation's much clearer outcomes as opposed to the often ambiguous verdicts of pol-itics. Here, too, the modern tobacco wars look more like politics than any kind of traditional litigation, marked by coalition building, strategic decision making, public posturing, and complex negotiation. At the same time, al-though there have always been winners and losers, the real winners and losers in tobacco litigations were not always apparent. On the one hand, the litigation has cost the industry much – in defences, settlements, and appeals. On the other hand, tobacco has thus far won many more cases than it has lost. What accounts for tobacco's continued ability to come out ahead – or at least to hold the line? Where we would have expected the early vic-tories against sporadic individual plaintiffs, certainly less expected has been the cigarette companies' ability to hold the line in the wake of the virtual onslaught of individual and class claims over the past two decades – claims that have been well armed with all kinds of compelling evidence. Even more surprising, perhaps, is the fact that the industry has come out of litigation and negotiations with the government, an even larger entity than the ciga-rette industry, smelling more like a rose than like stale tobacco. We are thus reminded of Marc Galanter's words in the introduction to this book. Indeed, addressing the tobacco wars of the 1990s, Galanter notes that the course of tobacco litigation only serves as a reminder of the great disparity between an industry worth billions of dollars and replete with in-house and out-of-house talent devoted to nothing but its survival and a plaintiffs' bar that, even when coalesced, has fewer resources and more diffuse interests. True, by the 1990s, plaintiffs had been strengthened "by formidable players like state attorneys general and lawyers made wealthy by asbestos cases. But public lawyers are under-financed and anxious about political risks: with a single exception, none of the state AG offices was prepared to handle this litigation in house and turned to the plaintiffs bar to do the job. A few plaintiffs firms can finance such major litigation, but the more of their assets they have riding on it, the greater the pressure to be risk averse" (Galanter 1999, 56).

Unquestionably, without grand coalitions, the odds of success against tobacco companies have been stacked exceptionally high against the individual claimant. However, even when amassed with others, the individual smoking plaintiff has not fared well. Recall, that the largest classes have been decertified on appeal. In the few cases where settlements have been achieved, little to nothing has redounded to any individual. The flight attendant suit resulted in a settlement of $349 million, most of which went into research on second-hand smoke, with the remainder reimbursing attorneys. Nor did individuals get anything out of the Castano Group litigation, the main result of which was the Liggett Group's concession to fund anti-smoking programs. And, of course, the government suits were never designed to recompense individuals. Thus, while victory and defeat accrued to many over the course of the tobacco litigation saga (to the industry, to governments, and to attorneys), one clear set of losers emerged from the battles – the individual smokers for whom the war was presumably begun in the first place. In the next chapter, we turn our attention to the politics of gun litigation, a politics born of, and very much formed by, the politics of tobacco litigation.

Appendix 3.1

Tobacco litigation timeline

1954   Ira C. Lowe, a factory worker, files suit against R.J. Reynolds Tobacco Company, charging that Camel cigarettes caused his lung cancer (*Lowe v. R.J. Reynolds Tobacco Company* 1954). Thought to be the first product liability action against a tobacco company, the suit was dismissed before trial.

1960   In the first tobacco product liability case to go to trial, the widow of Edwin Green sues the American Tobacco Company for causing her husband's lung cancer. Although the jury finds that the smoking of Lucky Strikes was the proximate cause of Mr. Green's disease, it determines that the tobacco company could not have known that users of Lucky Strike cigarettes would be in danger of contracting lung cancer. The Greens are subsequently assessed $1,969.74 for costs incurred by the American Tobacco Company (*Green v. American Tobacco Company* 1962).

1964   US Surgeon General concludes that smoking is tied to lung cancer and other illnesses.

1965   Congress enacts the *Federal Cigarette Labeling and Advertising Act of 1965*, 15 U.S.C.S. 1331-40.

1983   Rose Cipollone files suit against the Liggett Group in federal court in New Jersey seeking compensation for smoking-related illness.

1988   A jury awards Cipollone's heir $400,000 in damages on grounds that the Liggett Group had failed to warn of the risks of their products prior to 1966.

1991   Flight attendants gain class certification in suit for injuries resulting from second-hand cabin smoke.

1992   Against the Liggett Group's appeal in the Cipollone matter, the Supreme Court of the United States rules that federally mandated warnings do not bar smokers from suing manufacturers under state personal injury laws. Individuals may press claims alleging that the tobacco companies made fraudulent or inaccurate statements in their advertising or that the companies conspired to mislead people about the health hazards of smoking (*Cipollone v. Liggett Group* 1992).

The Cipollone family settles.

1994   Internal documents from Brown and Williamson Tobacco Company leaked to Congress and the press indicate that senior executives had knowledge of nicotine's addictive nature for over thirty years. Documents indicate that corporate officials hid research that might have saved lives because the evidence could damage them in the courts.

Mississippi Attorney General Mike Moore files suit against the cigarette industry (*Moore v. American Tobacco Company* 1994), claiming that the industry had knowingly manufactured and marketed a harmful, addictive product causing major health damage to the citizens of the state.

Wendell Gauthier begins forming the Castano Group to sue the tobacco industry. Subsequently, Dianne A. Castano, representing her deceased husband and all nicotine-dependent persons in the United States, their estates, and relatives since 1943 files suit against tobacco companies. The claimants contend that defendants fraudulently failed to inform consumers that nicotine is addictive and manipulated the level of nicotine in cigarettes to sustain their addictive nature.

Dr. Howard A. Engle, a retired Miami pediatrician and emphysema sufferer, files suit in Florida in 1994 for himself, five other named plaintiffs and a class of "[a]ll United States citizens and residents, and their survivors, who have suffered, presently suffer or have died from diseases and medical conditions caused by their addiction to cigarettes that contain nicotine" (*Engle v. R.J. Reynolds Tobacco Co.* 1996, 39).

1996   Breaking with other industry participants, Liggett agrees to settle the Castano lawsuit.

The Fifth Circuit Court decertifies the Castano class (*Castano v. American Tobacco Company* 1996). In response, the group files twenty-five state class actions. Only two proceed to trial, one a win for the plaintiffs, the other a win for the defendants. The plaintiff victory is now pending appeal. Other group cases have largely been dismissed.

Food and Drug Administration (FDA) asserts jurisdiction to regulate tobacco products.

Engle class action reduced to Florida smokers.

1997   Tobacco companies file suit against the FDA in federal court, claiming the regulations exceeded the agency's authority.

Nearly every state attorney general has now filed suit against the tobacco companies.

Flight attendants and tobacco companies settle.

1998   Effort to reach a congressionally directed settlement between the states and cigarette companies dies in committee.

Forty-six states and tobacco industry participants reach a *Master Settlement Agreement*. The industry accedes to total payments to the states, over a seventeen-year period, of $206 billion; to fund a $1.5 billion anti-smoking campaign; to open previously secret industry documents; to curb significantly their advertising and marketing campaigns, including banning cartoon characters such as Joe Camel and paraphernalia aimed at youth; and to disband certain industry trade groups.

1999   The United States files suit against six major cigarette manufacturers and two industry affiliates, the Council for Tobacco Research and the Tobacco Institute. The government seeks $280 billion in damages.

San Francisco jury awards smoker and lung cancer patient Patricia Henley $1.5 million in compensatory and $50 million in punitive damages on claims against Philip Morris of product liability, failure to warn, negligence, breach of express warranty, intentional and negligent misrepresentation, fraudulent concealment, and fraudulent promise (*Henley v. Philip Morris, Inc.* 1999).

An Oregon jury awards the widow of Jesse Williams $79.5 million in punitive damages for Philip Morris' history of systemic fraud affecting not only Williams but also smokers generally (*Williams-Branch ex rel. Estate of Williams v. Philip Morris, Inc.* 1999).

2000   Judge Gladys Kessler rules that two of three government counts against tobacco companies were misapplied.

Supreme Court of the United States sides with tobacco companies in the FDA suit, ruling that "Congress has not given the FDA the authority to regulate tobacco products as customarily marketed" (*FDA v. Brown and Williamson* 2000,120).

A Florida jury finds in favour of the *Engle* plaintiffs, awarding $145 billion in punitive damages to be paid by the nation's five largest cigarette companies. It is the largest damage award ever handed down by *any* jury against *any* defendant.

California jury awards Leslie Whiteley $21.7 million (*Whiteley v. Raybestos-Manhattan Inc.* 2000).

Brooklyn jury finds in favour of Fortune Brands, deciding that Danny Anderson's smoking is unrelated to his lung cancer (*Anderson v. Fortune Brands, Inc.* 2000).

Mississippi jury refuses to hold cigarette companies responsible for the lung cancer death of a thirty-seven-year-old man, a smoker since childhood (*Nunnally v. R.J. Reynolds* 2000).

2002   Judge Jack Weinstein of the US District Court in Brooklyn certifies a class consisting of "[a]ll persons residing in the United States, or who were residents of the United States at the time of their deaths, who smoke or smoked Defendants' cigarettes, and who have been diagnosed by a physician with one of a number of smoking related diseases" (*In re: Simon II Litigation* 2002a, 96).

Los Angeles jury awards a single plaintiff, Betty Bullock, a record breaking $28 billion in punitive damages (*Bullock v. Philip Morris* 2002).

2003   A Florida Court of Appeals decertifies the *Engle* class, a holding upheld by the Supreme Court of Florida. The case is ended (*Engle v. Liggett Group* 2006).

An Illinois court awards $10 billion in damages against Philip Morris for misleading consumers about the safety of light cigarettes (*Price v. Philip Morris* 2003).

Philadelphia jury finds Brown and Williamson not liable for the lung cancer death of a man who smoked Carlton cigarettes thinking that they were safer than other brands (*Eiser v. Brown and Williamson* 2003).

Sacramento jury returns verdict in favour of Philip Morris, against cancer victim claiming negligence, strict liability, false representation, deceit, fraudulent concealment, breach of express warranty, and loss of consortium (*Lucier v. Philip Morris* 2003).

Miami jury returns verdict in favour of R.J. Reynolds, against death of smoker claiming strict liability, failure to warn, negligence, and conspiracy (*Allen v. R.J. Reynolds Tobacco Company* 2003).

2005   Supreme Court of Illinois dismisses light cigarette case (*Price v. Philip Morris* 2005).

Second Circuit Court vacates *In re: Simon II* class, remanding the case.

In light of adverse rulings and a lack of Bush administration support, the Department of Justice lowers the government's requested damages from $280 billion to $10 billion.

United Seniors Association files suit against Philip Morris and other major manufacturers in federal court in Boston.

After several judicial reductions in punitive damages, Philip Morris pays Patricia Henley a total of $16.7 million, down about $35 million from the original jury's judgment.

2006   *In re: Simon II* plaintiffs move for dismissal of their action, a request granted by Judge Weinstein.

Judge Kessler issues scathing opinion in government's tobacco case, asserting that "over the course of more than 50 years, Defendants lied, misrepresented, and deceived the American public, including smokers and the young people they avidly sought as 'replacement smokers,' about the devastating health effects of smoking and environmental tobacco smoke" (*United States v. Philip Morris* 2006a, 105-6). Nonetheless, penalties are so paltry that an industry analyst deems the suit "a complete win" for tobacco.

A federal court in Brooklyn certifies a class of potentially tens of millions of light cigarette smokers seeking as much as $200 billion in damages (*Schwab v. Philip Morris USA, Inc.* 2006).

2007   Court of Appeals rules against United Seniors Association, asserting the group failed to establish Article III standing (*United Seniors Association v. Philip Morris* 2007).

In the case of Jesse Williams, the Supreme Court of the United States finds that jury consideration of non-parties in assessing punitive damages against Philip Morris amounts to a taking of property from the manufacturer without due process. The Court vacates the punitive damages and remands for reconsideration (*Philip Morris USA v. Williams* 2007a).

2008   Second Circuit Court of Appeals decertifies *Schwab* light cigarette class (*McLaughlin v. American Company* 2008).

Following a retrial, punitive damages in the 2000 *Whiteley* case are reduced to $250,000. Enforcement stayed until 6 June 2008.

California Court of Appeals (Second Appellate District, Division Three) reverses $28 million punitive damages award in *Bullock*, remanding the case for a new trial.

In its annual tobacco settlement report, the Campaign for Tobacco-Free Kids finds that "most states still fail to fund tobacco prevention programs at minimum levels recommended by the U.S. Centers for Disease Control and Prevention (CDC), and altogether, the states are providing less than half what the CDC has recommended" (Campaign for Tobacco Free Kids (2007, i).

4
The Politics of Gun Litigation

[S]omething clicked in my mind. If there was some substantial
basis for the state lawsuits against the tobacco industry, perhaps
there was a basis for a city suing gun manufacturers. I started to
look into it ... I found that the best theories were the most
traditional torts. No law reform was required. Public nuisance and
negligence. Those are the theories that would be developed in this
litigation.
> – David Kairys, James E. Beasley Professor of Law,
> Beasley School of Law, Temple University, 1998

[G]uns have become the next tobacco.
> – Brian J. Siebel, Legal Action Project,
> Center to Prevent Handgun Violence, 1999

If tobacco litigation was born as a series of small traditional torts, morphing,
only after decades, into a major political fight, gun litigation was virtually
conceived as grand political strategy. True, some precedent was provided by
individual suits, but, as the foregoing quotes suggest, the idea of mass action
based on the tobacco model bloomed very quickly and full-blown.[1] In this
chapter, we explore litigation against the gun industry, focusing primarily
on suits brought by cities and states and the aggressive and ultimately successful gun lobby counterattack.

Individuals versus the Gun Industry: Contemporary Suits
The gun market, like the tobacco industry, began facing serious challenges
during the mid-to-late 1990s when several sets of individuals filed suit.[2] The
seminal case, *Hamilton v. Accu-tek* (1999) (later, *Hamilton v. Beretta* [2001a])
was launched in 1994, when relatives of six people killed by handguns and
one survivor of gun violence filed suit against twenty-five handgun makers,

claiming they were collectively liable for "negligent marketing." Following a four-week trial in 1999, a jury found fifteen of the defendants negligent: "[N]ine were found to have proximately caused injury to one ... plaintiff." The jury subsequently awarded damages of $520,000 to the injured plaintiff, holding three manufacturers to have been "thirteen percent responsible" for the injuries of the plaintiff, based on the market share liability doctrine – a loss for the gun industry but, certainly, not a big one (*ibid.*, 808).[3] One attorney representing the gun manufacturers stated: "I just walked out of [Judge] Jack Weinstein's courtroom, and a Brooklyn jury had cut my people loose out of six wrongful-death cases. And I said, 'That's great'" (quoted in Van Voris 1999, 1). Needless to say, however, the whole bunch walked straight to the court of appeals. The resulting disposition was not kind to the plaintiffs.

Thus, the Second Circuit Court, after certifying and accepting questions of state law to the Court of Appeals of New York, determined unequivocally "that defendants' relationships with their dealers and distributors did not 'place the defendants in the best position to protect against the risk of harm,' given the 'very large' pool of potential plaintiffs and the 'remote' connection between defendants, the criminal wrongdoers, and plaintiffs" (*Hamilton v. Beretta* 2001a, 28, citing *Hamilton v. Beretta* 2001b). In other words, plaintiffs failed to show that gun manufacturers owed a *specific* duty to them, as opposed to a more general duty to society from which tort liability does not arise.

Other litigation followed. In the same year that the *Hamilton* suit was initiated, relatives of a number of people killed in a San Francisco office building by a deranged individual toting military assault pistols sued the weapons' manufacturer (*Merrill v. Navegar, Inc. (In re: 101 California Street Litigation)* 1999). A year later, the parents of Kenzo Dix sued Beretta after Kenzo was unintentionally killed by a fourteen-year-old friend playing with his parents' semi-automatic handgun (*Dix v. Beretta U.S.A. Corp.* 1997). Similarly, in Massachusetts, the parents of twelve-year-old Ross Mathieu sued Beretta after his best friend fatally wounded him with a 950BS pistol (*Mathieu v. Fabrica D'Armi Pietro Beretta SPA and Beretta U.S.A.* 2000). In 1997, in New Mexico, another unintentional shooting prompted parents to sue manufacturers of "Saturday Night Specials" (*Smith v. Bryco Arms* 2001). In 2000, families of the victims of white supremacist Benjamin Nathaniel Smith's three-day 1999 shooting rampage began litigation against manufacturer Bryco Arms (*Anderson v. Bryco Arms Corp.* 2000). Also in 2000, track star Bryant Lawson and other victims of high profile shootings in Washington, DC, filed suit in District of Columbia Superior Court (*Lawson v. Beretta* 2004).[4] In 2001, three victims and relatives of a deceased fourth victim of a racially motivated shooting in California lodged a complaint against several companies involved in the manufacture, marketing, and distribution of various firearms found in the shooter's possession (*Ileto v. Glock* 2003). And in 2003, victims, and the families of the victims of the DC area snipers, filed suit against the gun shop Bull's Eye Shooter Supply and rifle manufacturer Bushmaster Firearms (*Conrad Johnson et al. v. Bull's Eye Shooter Supply* 2003). The family of another sniper victim filed a separate wrongful death suit (*Estate of Pascal Charlot v. Bushmaster Firearms, Inc.* 2003).

As the sniper litigation suggests, litigation has not been confined solely to the makers of guns. Distributors and dealers too have been under fire. A dealer in Michigan was sued for selling a pistol to an individual despite being warned by the purchaser's sister that he was mentally ill. The man later shot several people in his psychologist's office (*Rissman v. Target Sports, Inc.* 2000). In Texas, the family of Alek Ambrosio sued a Houston dealer over Ambrosio's murder by a gun stolen from the store (*Ambrosio v. Carter's Country* 2000). In Kentucky, Jennifer Hicks sued TandM Jewelry for knowingly selling a gun to an under-aged individual who later shot her in the face (*Hicks v. TandM Jewelry, Inc.* 1999). In 1997, Deborah Kitchen brought a negligence suit against K-Mart for selling a gun to her clearly intoxicated ex-boyfriend, which was later used to severely injure her (*Kitchen v. K-Mart Corp.* 1997). In 1998, the parents of the late Sherry Lee White sued Wal-Mart for selling a shotgun to her estranged husband, then under a domestic violence restraining order (*Hopper v. Wal-Mart Stores, Inc.* 1999). In 2001, Pam Grunow, the widow of a Florida middle-school teacher shot by one of his students, sued Valor Corporation, a gun distributor, for negligence (*Grunow v. Valor Corp. of Florida* 2000). And in 2002, two New Jersey police officers, seriously wounded on duty, filed a complaint against Will Jewelry and Loan for selling the guns that shot them in an obvious straw purchase (*Lemongello and McGuire v. Will Jewelry and Loan et al.* 2003).[5]

It all sounds pretty bad for the industry. Yet the outcomes to date have tended heavily to favour the defendants, particularly the manufacturers and wholesale distributors. The scattershot litigation of individual plaintiffs has generally missed the mark. Indeed, manufacturers and distributors have fared *quite* well to date. In *Merrill v. Navegar, Inc. (In re: 101 California Street Litigation)* (1999), the Supreme Court of California upheld the trial court's grant of summary judgment to the defendant gun maker. In the police shooting case, a judge ruled gun maker Sturm Ruger not liable for the officers' injuries. And the lawsuit brought by families of the victims of Benjamin Nathaniel Smith was effectively abrogated by a ruling of the Supreme Court of Illinois against the city of Chicago (see discussion later in this chapter). The case of Kenzo Dix was ultimately decided by a jury in favour of Beretta. Conversely, a Florida jury awarded Pam Grunow millions in damages against distributor Valor Corporation, only to have the judge throw out the verdict. Valor is now suing Grunow for its legal fees! And the most promising of the suits, *Ileto v. Glock* (2006), was dismissed in 2006, the victim of federal legislation. The remaining cases are in various stages of discovery, motions, or settlement.

104 Multi-Party Litigation

Individuals have been more successful in aiming at gun sellers whose role is much less attenuated than that of manufacturers and wholesale distributors. The tendency here has been toward settlement. Thus, New Jersey police officers Lemongello and McGuire, while losing their case against Sturm Rugers, were able to extract a $1 million settlement from the seller Will Jewelry and Loan. Similarly, the high profile District of Columbia sniper case yielded the victims' families $2.5 million in settlement from Bull's Eye Shooter Supply. Target Sports of Michigan entered into a confidential settlement with the victims of a psychologist's office shooting. And Wal-Mart agreed to pay $16 million to the children of Sherry White, after selling to her estranged husband the gun that killed her.

The biggest loss to hit gun dealers came in the 1997 K-Mart case. A Florida jury awarded Deborah Kitchen a $12.5 million verdict against K-Mart after her ex-boyfriend left her a quadriplegic. The case was particularly egregious – prior to purchasing the gun, the boyfriend consumed a fifth of a bottle of whiskey and a case of beer. Indeed, Kitchen's assailant was so drunk that a clerk had to fill out the required federal firearms form for him (*Kitchen v. K-Mart Corp.* 1997)! The company appealed, but, in 1997, the Supreme Court of Florida ruled that a retail gun dealer has a legal duty to refrain from selling a firearm to an intoxicated buyer. Unfortunately for Kitchen, the case was remanded for further proceedings – proceedings indefinitely interrupted by K-Mart's recent bankruptcy, reorganization, and merger with Sears.

Mass Tort Subrogration: Government versus Guns

The Department of Housing and Urban Development (HUD) Threat

However successful the gun industry, and particularly its manufacturing side, has been to date in its dealings with individual litigants, these battles have not been the only legal troubles facing it. In December 1999, the HUD, with explicit White House backing, threatened to file suit against the gun industry on behalf of over 3,000 public housing authorities with a history of gun violence. The HUD estimated that it spent over $1 billion annually providing security to housing projects. The Clinton administration was attempting to pressure the industry into changing its "irresponsible marketing practices" and into adding safety features to its products (Clinton 1999b para. 16) – in other words, to hold the industry accountable for the consequences of its actions.

The threat, which was aimed specifically at forcing settlement, had some impact (Stout 1999). Notably, Smith and Wesson, the nation's largest gun manufacturer, agreed in March 2000 to a number of government requests. Hoping to insulate itself against the onslaught of litigation, Smith and Wesson acceded to demands to place hidden, difficult-to-remove serial numbers and trigger locks on all of its weapons. The company also agreed to implement so-called "smart gun" technology, permitting the operation of guns only by authorized users, within the next three years (United States, Department of Treasury 2000). The agreement settled disputes between Smith and Wesson, fifteen cities, and the states of New York and Connecticut. One might assume tough times for a beleaguered Smith and Wesson, that is until reading the company's "clarification" of the agreement. A few major examples suffice to make the point. Smith and Wesson agreed to add hidden serial numbers to its weapons, something it "is already doing ... on many of its firearms" (see Violence Policy Center 2000). The company also agreed to manufacture guns with external locking devices. Notably, it "has been including trigger locks in all of its handguns for several years" (*ibid.,* para. IA1b). Additionally, Smith and Wesson consented to installing internal locking devices, several types of which were already available to the company and which could be easily "incorporated in ... designs over the next 24 months" (*ibid.,* para. IA1c). Moreover, the company currently meets standards "acceded to" in much ballyhooed portions of the agreement such as child safety mechanisms, minimum barrel lengths, performance and drop testing. In other words, Smith and Wesson has shielded itself from major litigation pretty much by agreeing to do what it was already doing. And, putting icing on the cake, the Bush administration downgraded the agreement in 2001 to a "memorandum of understanding" and even then decided not to do anything to pursue it (Page 2001).[6]

State and Local Suits

There was still what would seem to be the biggest problem for big guns – remaining large institutional suits aimed at manufacturers, distributors, and dealers. By 2003, twenty-three local governments, the state of New York, and the National Association for the Advancement of Colored People (NAACP) and the National Spinal Cord Injury Association had launched litigation accusing major industry participants of, among other things, public nuisance, negligence, deceptive advertising, and defective design. The idea had two notable forebears. As early as 1996, David Kairys (1998, 4) a Temple University law professor, had begun looking to tobacco-death litigation as an analogue to the urban gun-death problem. Indeed, Kairys was convinced that gun manufacturers and dealers would make *better* legal targets than the cigarette makers:

> In tobacco, you can substantially undercut the causation and duty problems when the government brings the lawsuit. That's what I started looking at in the gun industry situation. Whatever the particulars of a case – who shot whom, whether or not there was a crime – the manufacturers are causing

direct harm to the cities and are quite aware of it. Without knowing who is going to shoot whom, or exactly when or where it is going to happen, the city of Philadelphia is going to incur costs connected with the product, starting with a 911 call, cleaning up blood off the streets, medical costs, which in some cities are borne by the city, all the way to the support of a child who might be orphaned as a result of gun violence.

Beginning in Philadelphia, Kairys would go on to serve on the legal teams in most of the municipal lawsuits.[7]

In addition to Kairys, the notion of a broad-based litigation assault on guns was proffered and acted on by the Castano Group. Founded by Louisiana attorney Wendell Gauthier,[8] the group originally formed to coordinate lawsuits against tobacco, reforming in the late 1990s as the Castano Safe Gun Litigation Group (Erichson 2005, 130). In 1998, it represented the city of New Orleans in the first municipal suit against gun makers (*Morial v. Smith and Wesson Corp.* 1998). Just as it made sense as a policy matter for Mississippi to be in the forefront of tobacco litigation, it made sense for large municipalities to take the lead in gun litigation. Between 1972 and 2002, 57.3 percent of homicides nationwide occurred in big cities and nearly 60 percent of gun-related homicides were urban events (Bureau of Justice Statistics 2004). In one year, in a single city (Chicago), 8,866 robberies, 4,390 aggravated batteries, and 3,963 aggravated assaults involved gun use (*Chicago v. Beretta* 1998).

The economic costs of gun violence are considerable and borne largely by government. Thus, more than half of the costs of medically treating gun injury victims fall to government (Cook and Ludwig 2000, 65). Moreover, government assumes all of the costs of prevention, investigation, judicial processing, and incarceration of those found guilty of firearms violations.[9] Thus, while individuals who filed suit suffered significant personal injuries as a result of the misuse of firearms, the pervasiveness of guns, especially in heavily populated urban areas, multiplies those incidents of individual tragedy and trauma. Indeed, viewed in the aggregate, the consequences of widespread, easy access to personal weapons have broader public policy implications.

Yet, while similarities between guns and tobacco may have seemed obvious, there are important differences between the two. For example, the gun industry does not have "deep pockets" in the same way that the tobacco industry does. Thus, where Smith and Wesson, the largest US producer of firearms, reported an estimated gross profit of $31.8 million in fiscal year 2004 (Smith and Wesson 2005), the Altria Group, owner of Philip Morris USA (the largest American cigarette company) and Philip Morris International reported 2004 earnings of $9.4 billion (Altria Group 2005a). In addition, while both industries sport powerful lobbies, the tobacco industry's has mostly been on the defensive in recent years, while the gun industry's has mostly stayed on the offensive. No one (not even Philip Morris)[10] suggests that cigarettes are safe, healthful products. On the other hand, gun manufacturers and distributors, along with their interest group allies, not only tout the complete safety of their products in the right hands but claim a constitutional right to ownership. Indeed, the industry has been positively blessed by its connection with, and backing by, one of the nation's most effective independent lobbying organizations, the National Rifle Association (NRA) (Wilcox 1998, 99) as well as several other well-funded sports-oriented groups. The NRA alone boasts an annual budget of about $200 million and an impressive voluntary membership of nearly four million politically active gun owners, aided often by "another 14 million Americans [who] think they are NRA members, and an additional 28 million [who] think they are affiliated in some way with the NRA because of their membership in one or more of the 35,000 shooting and hunting clubs" (Edsall and Grimaldi 2004, A1; see also Will 2004; Powell 2000).

Perhaps most important, though, is the perceived difference between the two in their relation to tort law. A credible – if not necessarily winning – case can be made that cigarettes generally are harmful, "defective products." After all, Philip Morris itself says that "[t]here is no safe cigarette" (Philip Morris USA 2008). Thus, individual suits, as well as the multi-state effort, could be premised on product liability law. Guns are a different matter altogether. According to Kairys (1998, 5), "product liability law doesn't help you in this case. If a product doesn't have a defect, you don't get anywhere under product liability law. Of course, the problem of handguns is that they work too well. Some are defective, and you can go after the manufacturer in those cases under product liability law. But in most cases, the handguns work too well, they are too cheap, they are too accessible." In fact, however, the first city to file suit, New Orleans, *did* premise its complaint on product liability, arguing that firearms are "unreasonably dangerous under Louisiana law" (*Morial v. Smith and Wesson Corp.* 1998). The pitfalls of the approach became apparent when, during the following year, the Louisiana legislature "preempted and precluded" the "governing authority of any political subdivision or local or other governmental authority of the state ... from bringing suit to recover against any firearms or ammunition manufacturer, trade association, or dealer for damages for injury, death, or loss or to seek other injunctive relief resulting from or relating to the lawful design, manufacture, marketing, or sale of firearms or ammunition."[11] Moreover, adding to the difficulties of pressing product liability claims on gun manufacturers, the *Restatement (Third) of Torts: Products Liability* has "taken the paradoxical position that inherently dangerous products do not fall within the definition of 'abnormally dangerous'" (Eggen and Culhane 2002, 119).[12]

However, if not product liability, then what? Two legal notions – nuisance abatement and negligence – have become the lynchpins. Of the two, negligence is perhaps the more conventional. Thus, a number of recent suits have been aimed at firearms distributors for negligence in sales – that is, knowingly selling guns to criminals, drunks, the mentally unstable, and the like (see, for example, *Hicks v. TandM Jewelry, Inc.* 1999). A more attenuated claim of negligence or negligent marketing might be, and has been, made against gun manufacturers themselves. So, for example, Chicago, in its suit against the industry, complained that manufacturers "owe a duty of care to the City of Chicago and its residents and the County of Cook and its residents living within Chicago to exercise reasonable care to prevent their firearms from ending up in the hands of persons who use and possess them illegally" (*Chicago v. Beretta U.S.A.* 2004, 362). A more novel approach rests on the theory of nuisance abatement. So, for example, Chicago additionally based its suit on the allegation that guns create a nuisance, the costly abatement of which fell to the city ($433 million between 1994 and 1998) *(ibid.)*. The approach is particularly tricky because, as one treatise on torts puts it, "[t]here is perhaps no more impenetrable jungle in the entire law than that which surrounds the word "nuisance." It has meant all things to all people, and has been applied indiscriminately to everything from an alarming advertisement to a cockroach baked in a pie. There is general agreement that it is incapable of any exact or comprehensive definition" (Keeton and Prosser 1984, 616, para. 86, cited in *ibid.*, 16).

However promising or pliable the legal theories, the plaintiff record in such suits has been dismal. The Chicago case is illustrative of one set of problems. The city and Cook County launched litigation in 1998 against eighteen manufacturers, four distributors, and eleven dealers, seeking injunctive relief and compensatory and punitive damages[13] on grounds that the defendants "knowingly and deliberately, and for their own financial benefit, created a public *nuisance* ... [and] *negligently* supplied firearms to Chicago residents who they know or have reason to know will illegally use, possess, transfer, or resell the firearms in Chicago" (*Chicago v. Beretta* 1998). The city based its case entirely on national and local statistics relating guns to death, injury, and criminal activity. The first blow to the city came in February 2000, when Judge Stephen A. Schiller dismissed its negligence claim. Seven months later, Judge Schiller dealt the second blow, rejecting the city's nuisance claim and thus dismissing the case in toto, citing Chicago's heavy use of statistics, "which a court, given Illinois's aversion to statistical bases for cause of actions ... can[not] use as essentially almost the sole basis for deciding whether individual parties are responsible for a public nuisance" (*Chicago v. Beretta* 2000, 5).

Two years later, the city appeared vindicated in a ruling by the appellate court. Relying largely on definitions of nuisance in the *Restatement (Second) of Torts*,[14] the court found a public nuisance to be "an unreasonable interference with a right common to the general public": "A sufficient pleading for a public nuisance cause of action consists of facts alleging a right common to the general public, a transgression of those rights by the defendant and resulting damages ... Rights of the general public entitled to protection include the right to 'the public health, the public safety, the public peace, the public comfort or the public convenience'" (*Chicago v. Beretta* 2002, 25). Moreover, the court rejected the defendants' contention that because the manufacture, distribution, and sale of firearms are legal, their actions could not constitute a public nuisance. According to the court, "common law public nuisance is 'not limited to those activities the legislature has declared [to be] public nuisances.' [C]ompliance with the law is not dispositive of whether a public nuisance exists, but merely serves as a 'guideline' in determining whether an unreasonable interference has occurred ... [L]iability for either public or private nuisance arises because one person's acts set in motion a force or chain of events resulting in the invasion or interference" (*ibid.*, 13 and citing the *Restatement (Second) of Torts*). As such, in what appeared to be a rather sweeping victory, the court held that "with regard to all three classes, manufacturers, distributors, and dealers ... the [city's] ... complaint states a cause of action for public nuisance under Illinois law (*ibid.*, 18).

The city's good ride, however, ended in 2004 with a ruling by the Supreme Court of Illinois. The court ruled against the city and county for several reasons. For one, the court determined that the defendants did not have any specific duty to the public. Moreover, the justices held that gun crime results from any number of acts by third parties that are not under the control of gun manufacturers, distributors, or dealers – the connection, in other words, is simply too remote. In general, the court worried about the applicability of the city's theory to future law. "If there is a public right to be free from the threat that others may use a lawful product to break the law," asserted Justice Garman, "that right would include the right to drive upon the highways, free from the risk of injury posed by drunk drivers":

This public right to safe passage on the highways would provide the basis for public nuisance claims against brewers and distillers, distributing companies, and proprietors of bars, taverns, liquor stores, and restaurants with liquor licenses, all of whom could be said to contribute to an interference with the public right. Similarly, cell phones, DVD players, and other lawful products may be misused by drivers, creating a risk of harm to others. In an increasing number of jurisdictions, state legislatures have acted to ban the use of these otherwise legal products while driving. A public right to be free from the threat that other drivers may defy these laws would permit nuisance liability to be imposed on an endless list of manufacturers, distributors, and retailers of manufactured products that are intended to be, or are likely to be, used by drivers, distracting them and causing injury to others. (*Chicago v. Beretta U.S.A.* 2004, 375)

Adding to the city's loss was the fact that its theory of damages was rejected and barred, according to the court "by the municipal cost recovery rule ... under which public expenditures made in the performance of governmental functions are not recoverable in tort" (*ibid.,* 118).

A similar fate was suffered by Philadelphia, though in federal, not state, court. In 2000, the city, along with five civic associations, sued fourteen gun manufacturers, claiming that the "industry's methods for distributing guns are negligent and a public nuisance" (*Philadelphia v. Beretta* 2000, 886).[15] US district judge Berle Schiller ruled the city's suit was barred by state law, specifically the Pennsylvania *Uniform Firearms Act.*[16] Philadelphia, according to Schiller, was preempted in several respects. First, the Supreme Court of Pennsylvania had previously found that the *Uniform Firearms Act* superceded municipal regulatory schemes. According to Schiller, the city's lawsuit was simply a backdoor form of regulation and thus could not stand under state law (*ibid.,* 889-90). Moreover, a 1999 amendment to the *Uniform Firearms Act* "specifically bars a variety of municipal suits against gun manufacturers" (*ibid.,* 890).

Having so found, Schiller nonetheless went on to address the substance of the city's claim.[17] First, the court addressed the negligence allegation, focusing on whether the gun industry owed a duty of care to Philadelphia. It did not, according to the court, because its relation to the city is tenuous, most of its vendees operate lawfully and its connection to harm done is tangential and unforeseeable (*ibid.,* 899-902). Moreover, the court found the city's related claim of negligent entrustment wanting for lack of proximate cause (*ibid.,* 903-5).[18] Similarly, the court rejected the city's nuisance complaint, finding that "defendants' actions do not constitute a nuisance under any recognized theory in Pennsylvania" and adding further that the plaintiffs' claim "is nothing more than a clever, but transparent attempt at an end run around the legislature's statutory prerogatives" (*ibid.,* 911).[19] The following year, the Third Circuit Court agreed, putting an end to the city's venture (*Philadelphia v. Beretta* 2002). Other governmental suits that have fully and finally adjudicated to the advantage of the gun industry include those brought in Atlanta, Bridgeport, Camden City, Camden County, Cincinnati, Detroit, Jersey City, Los Angeles and San Francisco, Miami-Dade County, Newark, New York State, St. Louis, and Wilmington.[20]

Indeed, as late as 2005, only four suits by public entities survived. New York City's case, begun by former mayor Rudy Giuliani in 2000, "requests an injunction enjoining the public nuisance by requiring defendants to adopt a variety of prudent marketing practices including the monitoring and supervision of distributors and retailers with whom defendants do business" (*New York City v. Beretta* 2004, 263). Delayed by the events of 11 September 2001, the case came before federal district judge Jack Weinstein in 2004 on the defendants' motion to dismiss.[21] The judge denied the motion, and a trial date of 4 April 2005 was scheduled. Similarly, the city of Cleveland awaited trial in federal court, having sued under state product liability law as well as under city and common law nuisance and negligence theories (*White v. Smith and Wesson* 2000). After being dismissed by a trial court, the Washington, DC, case was reinstated, although in much truncated form (*District of Columbia v. Beretta* 2004). And Gary, Indiana, having had its case reinstated by the state supreme court, was crawling toward a trial date set for June 2009 (*Gary v. Smith and Wesson* 1999; Browing 2004)! Even these frail hangers-on would be largely eviscerated by the events that were to take place in Washington, DC, the following year.

NAACP

In 1999, the NAACP filed suit against most of the main manufacturers, importers, and distributors of handguns in the United States. Although the case was ultimately dismissed because the organization "failed to demonstrate ... that it has suffered harm different in kind from that suffered by the public at large" (*NAACP v. A.A. Arms* 2003, 435), it is interesting in several respects and offered a rare ray of hope to gun opponents. First, the case was an interesting example of forum shopping. Brought by Elisa Barnes, the attorney who had earlier represented Hamilton et al. against the gun makers (*Hamilton v. Beretta* 2001a), the NAACP suit was notable for the fact that Beretta, one of the largest of those makers and a lead defendant in *Hamilton,* was absent from the list. Barnes was anxious for the suit to be heard by US district judge Jack Weinstein under diversity jurisdiction. Federal jurisdiction is disallowed, however, if any plaintiff shares common state residence with any defendant. The NAACP and Beretta are both incorporated in Maryland and, thus, the disappearance of Beretta.

Second, the case was significant because it marked the first, and one of the last (see discussion later in this chapter), cases accorded access to tracing data collected by the Bureau of Alcohol, Tobacco, and Firearms (ATF).[22] Major portions of the databases were made available during discovery, becoming the basis for statistical analyses by the parties. Previously, the ATF had demurred at providing the information to litigants.

Third, although he dismissed the case on standing grounds, Judge Weinstein wrote an exhaustive opinion on the merits. And this opinion was generally favourable to the would-be plaintiffs, going so far as to say that "[t]he evidence presented at trial demonstrated that defendants are responsible for the creation of a public nuisance and could – voluntarily and through easily implemented changes in marketing and more discriminating control of the sales practices of those to whom they sell their guns – substantially reduce the harm occasioned by the diversion of guns to the illegal market and by the criminal possession and use of those guns" (*NAACP v. A.A. Arms* 2003, 446). Absent blanket immunity, Judge Weinstein's ruling may have had some impact on other pending litigation, particularly the New York City case. Although he stopped short of applying the NAACP nuisance finding to the city's suit as a matter of collateral estoppel, the ATF data may have proven useful to New York – that is, if the city had been able to use it ("Top Cases" 2004).

Legislative Challenges
Indeed, whether New York or other jurisdictions would have been able to utilize ATF information under any circumstances has been cast into considerable doubt. The gun industry and its allied lobbies have been able to attain favourable protective acts from the nation's legislatures for far longer than the tobacco industry has. Access to ATF data is one small, but significant, example. As part of the *Consolidated Appropriations Act of 2005,* Congress sent a clear signal to courts that trace data are not appropriate evidentiary material.[23] Going even further, Congress held that, as part of the 2006 appropriations,

[n]o funds appropriated under this or any other Act with respect to any fiscal year may be used to disclose part or all of the contents of the Firearms Trace System database maintained by the National Trace Center of the Bureau of Alcohol, Tobacco, Firearms and Explosives or any information required to be kept by licensees pursuant to section 923(g) of title 18, United States Code, or required to be reported pursuant to paragraphs (3) and (7) of such section 923(g), to anyone other than a Federal, State, or local law enforcement agency or a prosecutor solely in connection with and for use in a bona fide criminal investigation or prosecution and then only such information as pertains to the geographic jurisdiction of the law enforcement agency requesting the disclosure and not for use in any civil action or proceeding other than an action or proceeding commenced by the Bureau of Alcohol, Tobacco, Firearms and Explosives, or a review of such an action or proceeding, to enforce the provisions of chapter 44 of such title, and all such data shall be immune from legal process and shall not be subject to subpoena or other discovery, shall be inadmissible in evidence, and shall not be used, relied on, or disclosed in any manner, nor shall testimony or other evidence be permitted based upon such data, in any civil action pending on or filed after the effective date of this Act in any State (including the District of Columbia) or Federal court or in any administrative proceeding other than a proceeding commenced by the Bureau of Alcohol, Tobacco,

Firearms and Explosives to enforce the provisions of that chapter, or a review
of such an action or proceeding; except that this proviso shall not be construed to prevent the disclosure of statistical information concerning total
production, importation, and exportation by each licensed importer (as
defined in section 921(a)(9) of such title) and licensed manufacturer (as defined in section 921(a)(10) of such title).

More impressive, as the New Orleans and Philadelphia suits demonstrated,
the gun lobby has been very successful in getting state legislatures to shield
the industry from liability through the passage of so-called "firearm industry
relief acts," which have been aimed at severely limiting the ability of local
governments to bring lawsuits. Claiming that "[f]irearms manufacturers
have already spent more than $200 million in legal fees," as of 2005, the
NRA had ensured such legislation was introduced in forty-six states, with
successful enactments in thirty-three (National Rifle Association 2005b, para.
8). Such laws, while varying in their restrictiveness, generally prevent local-
ities from suing gun companies without the express permission of the state's
attorney general and limit grounds to matters such as manufacturing defects,
breach of contract, or breach of warranty.[24]

In addition, the NRA and the National Shooting Sports Foundation, a
trade association for the manufacturers and sellers of firearms, were behind
efforts to pass federal legislation in this area, a prize they achieved late in
2005. Thus, in 2003, the House of Representatives easily passed (285 to 140)
the *Protection of Lawful Commerce in Arms Act (PLCAA)*, which was designed
"[t]o prohibit civil liability actions from being brought or continued against
manufacturers, distributors, dealers, or importers of firearms or ammunition
for damages resulting from the misuse of their products by others."[25] In the
Senate, too, the bill had broad bi-partisan support, boasting fifty-five co-
sponsors including then Democratic minority leader, Tom Daschle (South
Dakota) (Eilperin 2003, A21). The measure would have passed easily but for
an amendment offered by Senator Diane Feinstein (Democrat, Califonia) in
2004, renewing a soon-to-lapse ban on assault weapons. When the amendment passed, members, at the strong urging of the NRA, which had long
fought against the assault ban,[26] killed the entire bill in an impressive ninety-
to-eight vote (Epstein 2004).

The bill was reintroduced in the 109th Congress, featuring 111 House and
thirty-one Senate sponsors. Strongly backed by President George Bush because "[j]unk and frivolous lawsuits like [those against the gun industry] are
an abuse of the legal system" (Bush 2004, para. 14), the Senate passed the
bill in July, followed by passage in the House of Representatives and presidential signature in October 2005.[27] And it became immediately effective,
asserting that "[a] qualified civil liability action that is pending on the date

of enactment of this Act shall be immediately dismissed by the court in which the action was brought or is currently pending."[28] The legislation has mostly met its intended effect, taking the wind out of the sails of the few remaining litigations. Thus, for example, in May 2006, District of Columbia superior court judge Brook Hedge, dismissing Washington, DC's suit, ruled that Congress had "trumped local law by passing legislation to protect the profits of [gun] manufacturers" (Cauvin 2006, B4).

At least one judge, however, was not quite so willing to throw in the towel. Roughly a month after the *PLCAA* was signed into law, Judge Weinstein ruled that the New York City suit could proceed, holding that the city's litigation may fall under the so-called "predicate exception," presumably allowing suits where the sale of marketing of guns is done in "knowing violation" of the law.[29] The *New York Penal Law* provides that "[a] person is guilty of criminal nuisance in the second degree when: By conduct either unlawful in itself or unreasonable under all the circumstances, he knowingly or recklessly creates or maintains a condition which endangers the safety or health of a considerable number of persons."[30] According to Weinstein, though "there is a substantial ground for disagreement" on the issue, "[b]y its plain meaning, [the New York law] satisfies the language of the predicate exception" (*New York City v. Beretta* 2005, 262 and 298). As a result of the grounds for disagreement, Weinstein granted a stay of all proceedings, allowing defendants to proceed with an interlocutory appeal to the federal Second Circuit Court.[31]

Not brought up by either plaintiffs or defendants, and thus unknown to Judge Weinstein, was the *Appropriations Act* ban on the use of trace data as evidentiary material.[32] Thus, in a series of rulings in 2006, he was forced to consider defendants' contention that even if the predicate exception to the *PLCAA* was sufficient to keep the New York suit alive, the barring of trace data left the city with no case. Weinstein again disagreed, holding "that the rider does not prevent the City's action from proceeding [because] the restrictions in the 2006 rider cannot be read to encompass the trace data already in the City's possession and sought to be admitted in this pending case" (*New York City v. Beretta* 2006, 519). Nevertheless, the city's suit was finally brought to an end in April 2008 when the Second Circuit Court ordered Weinstein to dismiss the case as barred by the *PLCAA* (*New York City v. Beretta USA* 2008). The dismissal leaves Gary, Indiana, as the only municipality with a surviving case.[33]

Living up to New Yorkers' reputation for moxie, Mayor Michael Bloomberg launched yet another lawsuit in federal district court in May 2006, accusing twenty-seven out-of-state gun dealers of allowing "straw purchases." The suit is based on sting operations conducted by city officers, private investigators employed by New York, and gun control advocates in Georgia, Ohio,

Pennsylvania, South Carolina, and Virginia. Guns sold to the twenty-seven dealers have been linked to hundreds of crimes committed in New York from 1994 to 2001. The city called for "the appointment of a special master to monitor [the dealers'] sales closely" (Cardwell 2006, B5).

Not without considerable controversy (in April 2007, Virginia's attorney general threatened legal action against New York City [Craig 2007]), Bloomberg's efforts have resulted in settlements with a number of out-of-state dealers who have agreed to enhanced employee training and monitoring by a court-appointed special master. Several others have gone out of business on the heels of the investigation (Bloomberg 2007). Moreover, in August 2007, Judge Weinstein ruled against out-of-state sellers' claims that they could not be sued in a New York court, holding that "the city had demonstrated 'with a high degree of probability' that the shops' behavior had been 'responsible for the funneling into New York of large quantities of handguns used by local criminals' ... and [t]hat 'knowing' conduct brought the out-of-state dealers under New York jurisdiction" (Lee 2007, B6). Trial was set for 21 July 2008 (*New York City v. Bob Moates' Sport Shop, Inc.* 2008).

The Constitutional Wrinkle

In 1999, the gun lobby won a stunning legal decision when US district judge Sam R. Cummings declared unconstitutional a federal law banning individuals under court restraining orders from possessing firearms.[34] Cummings based the decision on his determination that the Second Amendment guarantees an *individual's* right to own a gun, marking the first ever such finding by a federal judge (*United States v. Emerson* 1999). Judge Cummings' decision was reversed by the Fifth Circuit Court in 2001 (*United States v. Emerson* 2001). However, the New Orleans-based appeals court did assert that "[i]t appears clear that 'the people,' as used in the Constitution, including the Second Amendment, refers to *individual* Americans" (*ibid.*, 230), placing it at variance with every other circuit court. Interestingly, in 2003, in briefs asking it not to review *Emerson* or a companion case (*Haney v. United States* 2002)), US solicitor general Ted Olson signalled to the Supreme Court of the United States the view of the Bush administration that the Second Amendment was an individual, not a militia, right (Mauro 2003, para. 25).

To clarify the administration's position further, the Department of Justice published in 2004 a *Memorandum Opinion for the Attorney General,* concluding that "the Second Amendment secures an individual right to keep and to bear arms" (United States, Department of Justice 2004, 1). Later that year, the president himself was unequivocal in his support for this position: "[The Attorney General's view] was a clear reversal [of the Clinton Administration's position]. It was a position that needed to be reversed – the prior Administration had taken the position that the Second Amendment only applies to state militias and doesn't protect an individual right to bear arms ... The Constitution gives people a personal right to bear arms. So we did reverse the Clinton Administration's position, and I think that was the right thing to do" (Bush 2004, para. 4). Notably, too, the liability shield law recently passed by Congress finds that "[t]he Second Amendment to the United States Constitution protects the rights of individuals, including those who are not members of a militia or engaged in military service or training, to keep and bear arms."[35]

The same year that the Department of Justice and President Bush asserted a personal right to bear arms, several residents of the District of Columbia challenged the city's restrictions on gun ownership, claiming an individual right to keep "functional firearms."[36] The district court dismissed the plaintiffs' suit on grounds that the Second Amendment does not protect "an individual right to bear arms separate and apart from Militia use" (*Parker v. District of Columbia* 2004, 108). The Court of Appeals of the District of Columbia disagreed, becoming the second federal appeals court to challenge the reading of the Second Amendment as a collective right and concluding that

> the Second Amendment protects an individual right to keep and bear arms. That right existed prior to the formation of the new government under the Constitution and was premised on the private use of arms for activities such as hunting and self-defense, the latter being understood as resistance to either private lawlessness or the depredations of a tyrannical government (or a threat from abroad). In addition, the right to keep and bear arms had the important and salutary civic purpose of helping to preserve the citizen militia. The civic purpose was also a political expedient for the Federalists in the First Congress as it served, in part, to placate their Antifederalist opponents. The individual right facilitated militia service by ensuring that citizens would not be barred from keeping the arms they would need when called forth for militia duty. Despite the importance of the Second Amendment's civic purpose, however, the activities it protects are not limited to militia service, nor is an individual's enjoyment of the right contingent upon his or her continued or intermittent enrollment in the militia. (*Parker v. District of Columbia* 2007, 395)

In one of the most anticipated decisions of the 2007-08 term, the Supreme Court of the United States affirmed. Writing for the five-person majority, Justice Scalia asserted "that the Second Amendment right is exercised individually and belongs to all Americans" (*District of Columbia v. Heller* 2008, 16). Though Scalia allowed that "[l]ike most rights, the right secured by the Second Amendment is not unlimited" (*ibid.*, 94), the Court's decision is likely to have widespread reverberations, particularly for other large cities with relatively strict gun control laws. Indeed, the day following the Court's decision in *Heller,* the NRA filed suit against Chicago, San Francisco, and several suburban jurisdictions challenging gun bans (Ahmed 2008).

Conclusion

Almost from the start, the gun litigation strategy was more than a search for courtroom justice – it was politics – politics as a struggle for power; politics as the means to policy. As one commentator described John Coale, the Gauthier Group attorney quoted at the beginning of the chapter, he intended "to set the agenda, to create a bandwagon that [would] sweep political and journalistic rivals down his chosen path ("John Coale's Next Case" 1999, 32). We summarize the major points in the history of litigation against the gun industry in Appendix 4.1 at the end of this chapter.

For gun litigation advocates, the 1990s, as a political moment, must have seemed very propitious indeed. Firearm-related crimes had reached a peak in the mid-1990s. This peak was followed in the latter part of the decade by a string of school shootings that shocked the country. After the Columbine High School massacre, in particular, support for gun control soared in public opinion polls (Butterfield 2000). On Mother's Day in 2000, hundreds of thousands gathered on the Mall in Washington in support of stricter gun regulations (Toner 2000). Shortly after, Michael Moore's film on American gun violence, *Bowling for Columbine* (2002), won the Academy Award for best documentary feature. During the late 1980s and 1990s, the gun control lobby emerged as a seemingly formidable opponent to the gun ownership lobby, winning, over the strong objections of the NRA, several major legislative victories.[37] Indeed, the richest and most prominent of the gun control groups, the Brady Center to Prevent Gun Violence, supported, and continues to support, a number of the gun litigations. As promising as the times seemed to be, however, the gun litigation effort may, in the end, be regarded as one of the great strategic political failures of the turn of the century. Indeed, not only did the gun lobby (most notably, the NRA) wage a winning defensive strategy, it delivered several ultimately fatal offensive blows, crafting broad legislative immunities from most lawsuits and scoring a victory in the Supreme Court of the United States against the most restrictive of municipal gun regulations.

Litigation as Regulation

Just as the political atmosphere seemed promising to the plaintiffs, the litigation also made sense from a regulatory policy perspective. Municipalities, counties, and states expend considerable resources in response, treatment, prosecution, defence, and incarceration related to gun violence. Big city mayors and county executives, in particular, were keen to recoup some of their losses and were far less beholden politically to the gun lobby than state or federal officials. Like state attorneys general, these entities coalesced in what should have been a powerful force for regulatory change.

As we have noted, those who organized litigation efforts against the gun industry did so explicitly to utilize the legal process as a regulatory mechanism in order to hold the industry accountable for the consequences of pervasive access to firearms, especially in big urban areas. According to Wendell Gauthier, the gun litigation "fit the Castano philosophy of the plaintiffs' bar as a de facto fourth branch of government, achieving by litigation what had failed legislatively" (cited in Erichson 2005, 136). In dismissing cases, a number·of judges viewed the litigation in precisely these terms and were quite prepared to defer to legislatures.

Winners and Losers

In many ways, gun litigation politics mimicked (quite purposively) tobacco litigation politics. However, as noted earlier, there were profound differences. And, in the end, those differences have produced far clearer results – results that manifestly have favoured the defendants. Big tobacco, a much larger corporate presence than the gun industry, had nothing as powerful as the NRA and its affiliates fighting on its behalf. Using superior organization and the ability to turn out votes, the NRA remains, after more than seven decades, one of the nation's most effective lobbying groups – one that politicians oppose at considerable career risk.[38] As President Clinton said of the 1994 mid-term elections: "The NRA had a great night. They beat both Speaker Tom Foley and Jack Brooks ... who had warned me this would happen. Foley was the first Speaker to be defeated in more than a century. [But t]he NRA was an unforgiving master: one strike and you're out. The gun lobby claimed to have defeated nineteen of the twenty-four members on its hit list. They did at least that much damage and could rightly claim to have made [Newt] Gingrich the House Speaker" (Clinton 2004, 629-30).

But for the most zealous libertarian, few would frame tobacco usage in terms of an unexpurgated individual right. Yet, the NRA and other gun rights groups have increasingly cast gun ownership in such terms. And they have both the will and the skill to exact political punishment – in the end, making it highly unlikely, legislation or no, that litigation against manufacturers and distributors can stand. In the following chapter, we look to one of the newest fronts in the history of coalitional litigation, that seeking healthier foods. In part modeled on tobacco and guns, the food litigators appear to have learned some valuable lessons from their predecessors – lessons that arguably have brought greater, if relatively more modest, success.

Appendix 4.1

Gun litigation timeline

1994   Relatives of six people killed by handguns and one survivor of gun vio-
        lence file suit against twenty-five handgun makers, claiming they were
        collectively liable for "negligent marketing" (*Hamilton v. Accu-tek*
        1999).

1995   The parents of Kenzo Dix sue Beretta after their son is unintentionally
        killed by a fourteen-year-old friend playing with his parents' semi-
        automatic handgun (*Dix v. Beretta U.S.A. Corp.* 1998).

1997   The parents of twelve-year-old Ross Mathieu sue Beretta after his best
        friend fatally wounds him with a 950BS pistol (*Mathieu v. Fabrica D'Armi
        Pietro Beretta SPA and Beretta U.S.A.* 2000).

        In New Mexico, the parents of Sean Smith file suit against Bryco Arms
        when their son is accidentally shot in the face with a J-22 handgun. The
        judge enters summary judgment in favour of defendant Bryco Arms (*Smith
        v. Bryco Arms* 2001).

1998   California jury rules in favour of defendant Beretta in *Kenzo Dix* case.
        Subsequent retrials also favour the gun manufacturer.

        New Orleans, represented by the Castano Group, becomes the first pub-
        lic jurisdiction to file suit against the gun industry, arguing that firearms
        are "unreasonably dangerous under Louisiana law" (*Morial v. Smith &
        Wesson Corp.* 1998).

        Chicago and Cook County file a $433 million negligence and nuisance
        suit against gun manufacturers, distributors, and dealers (*Chicago v. Beretta*
        1998).

1999   Brooklyn jury finds fifteen *Accu-tek* defendants negligent, awarding
        $520,000 to injured plaintiff (*Hamilton v. Accu-tek* 1999).

        Court of Appeals in California rules that victims of a deranged mass
        shooter armed with TEC-9/DC9 assault weapons have a cause of action
        against gun manufacturer Navegar for negligent distribution (*Merrill v.
        Navegar, Inc. (In Re 101 California Street Litigation* 1999).

        Louisiana Legislature ends New Orleans' gun suit by preempting and
        precluding the "governing authority of any political subdivision or local
        or other governmental authority of the state ... from bringing suit to
        recover against any firearms or ammunition manufacturer, trade asso-
        ciation, or dealer for damages for injury, death, or loss or to seek other
        injunctive relief resulting from or relating to the lawful design, manu-
        facture, marketing, or sale of firearms or ammunition" (*Preemption of State
        Law; Liability of Manufacturer, Trade Association, or Dealer of Firearms and
        Ammunition*, La. R.S. 40:1799 (2004)).

        Clinton Department of Housing and Urban Development (HUD) threat-
        ens to file suit against gun industry on behalf of over 3,000 public hous-
        ing authorities with a history of gun violence.

        Atlanta files suit against fourteen gun manufacturers alleging they manu-
        factured, distributed, marketed, promoted, and sold firearms that were

defective, unreasonably dangerous, and negligently designed (*City of Atlanta v. Smith and Wesson Corp.* 2002).

Bridgeport, CT, sues Smith and Wesson, among others, for costs incurred as a result of the design, production, marketing, and distribution of handguns without safety devices (*Ganim v. Smith and Wesson* 1999).

The city of Camden, NJ, sues Beretta and others to obtain relief from "the defendants' willful, deliberate, reckless, and/or negligent marketing and distribution of guns, which injure Camden and its citizens" (*Camden v. Beretta* 1999).

Cincinnati sues firearms manufacturers, a distributor, and three trade associations for costs incurred in providing police, emergency, court, prison, and other related services in connection with shootings (*Cincinnati v. Beretta* 1999).

Boston launches legal action against gun manufacturers, distributors, and trade groups seeking damages for the municipal costs of gun violence (*Boston v. Smith and Wesson Corp.* 1999).

Gary, IN, sues Smith and Wesson among others (*Gary v. Smith and Wesson* 2003; Browning 2004).

The National Association for the Advancement of Colored People (NAACP) files suit against most of the main manufacturers, importers, and distributors of handguns in the United States (*NAACP v. A.A. Arms* 2003).

2000   Beretta settles *Mathieu* case by announcing it will no longer sell pistols without either a magazine disconnect safety or a warning label.

Smith and Wesson breaks with other gun manufacturers agreeing to a number of HUD requests. The resulting "Clarification" agreement does little more than implement existing gun safety mechanisms.

Philadelphia sues fourteen gun manufacturers, claiming that the "industry's methods for distributing guns are negligent and a public nuisance" (*Philadelphia v. Beretta* 2000, 886).

Mayor Giuliani sues handgun manufacturers in federal court, seeking damages to compensate New York City for injuries and other damage from illegal gun use (*New York City v. Beretta* 2004).

New York State sues (the first state to do so), charging that handgun manufacturers' and wholesalers' sales and distribution practices violate New York State laws (*New York v. Sturm, Ruger and Co., Inc.* 2001).

Washington, DC, files suit against Beretta and others (*District of Columbia v. Beretta* 2004).

US District Court of New Jersey dismisses Camden's claims against firearms manufacturers (*Camden County Board of Chosen Freeholders v. Beretta U. S.A. Corp.* 2000).

2001   Three victims and relatives of a deceased fourth victim of a racially motivated shooting in California lodge a complaint against several companies involved in the manufacture, marketing, and distribution of various firearms found in the shooter's possession (*Ileto v. Glock* 2002).

Court of Appeals in New Mexico reverses trial court in *Smith v. Bryco,* ruling that juries may determine if gun makers can be held liable for failing to include feasible safety devices (*Smith v. Bryco Arms* 2001).

Second Circuit Court of Appeals overturns *Accu-tek* verdict, asserting that plaintiffs failed to show that gun manufacturers owed a *specific* duty to them, as opposed to a more general duty to society from which tort liability does not arise (*Hamilton v. Beretta* 2001a).

Supreme Court of California overturns *Navegar* decision on grounds that California law bars lawsuits against gun companies for their alleged negligent marketing and distribution of firearms (*Merrill v. Navegar, Inc.* 2001).

Supreme Court of Connecticut dismisses *Bridgeport* suit against gun makers (*Ganin v. Smith and Wesson* 2001) of *Camden* gun suit.

Ohio legislature passes gun litigation shield law in effect ending Cincinnati law suit.

Bush administration downgrades Smith and Wesson agreement to a "memorandum of understanding" and determines to pursue no further action.

2002   District court judge dismisses claims against gun manufacturers in *Ileto v. Glock* (2002).

Philadelphia gun suit ends when Third Circuit Court upholds lower court decisions ruling "that the absence of proximate cause barred plaintiffs' claims in negligence and that the gun manufacturers were under no legal duty to protect citizens from the deliberate and unlawful use of their products" (*Philadelphia v. Beretta* 2002, para. 18).

Court of Appeals in Georgia dismisses all Atlanta claims against gun industry (*Sturm, Ruger and Company, Inc. v. Atlanta* 2002).

Citing financial concerns, Boston becomes first city to voluntarily drop a gun industry suit.

2003   Supreme Court of New York State, Appellate Division, dismisses New York State's lawsuit against gun makers, saying that it was "legally inappropriate, impractical and unrealistic to mandate that defendants undertake, and the courts enforce, unspecified measures urged by plaintiff in order to abate the conceded availability and criminal use of illegal handguns" (*New York v. Sturm, Ruger and Company, Inc.* 2003).

Federal judge dismisses *NAACP* lawsuit against gun industry on standing grounds (*NAACP v. A.A. Arms* 2003).

Ninth Circuit Court reinstates Ileto's claims against three manufacturers (*Ileto v. Glock* 2003).

2004   Supreme Court of Illinois dismisses Chicago/Cook County law suit, rejecting all of the city's claims (*Chicago v. Beretta U.S.A.* 2004).

2005   Thirty-three states have passed legislation barring or limiting the ability of local governments to bring lawsuits against the gun industry.

President George Bush signs into law the *Protection of Lawful Commerce in Arms Act* (Public Law no. 109-092, 2005). The law prohibits "causes of action against manufacturers, distributors, dealers, and importers of firearms or ammunition products, and their trade associations, for the harm solely caused by the criminal or unlawful misuse of firearm products or ammunition products by others when the product functioned as designed and intended." The law effectively ends almost all remaining individual, municipal, county, and state suits against gun industry.

2006   Congress bans the use of trace data as evidence.

New York Mayor Michael Bloomberg launches series of lawsuits in federal district court accusing out-of-state gun dealers of allowing "straw purchases" (see, for example, *New York City v. A-1 Jewelry & Pawn, Inc.* 2007).

2007   Contrary to other courts, the Indiana Court of Appeals allows Gary's suit to proceed in spite of *Protection of Lawful Commerce in Arms Act* (*Smith and Wesson v. Gary* 2007).

2008   Second Circuit Court ends New York City's 2000 gun suit (*City of New York v. Beretta USA* 2008).

Denying defendants' motions to dismiss, Federal District Court in Brooklyn sets trial date of 21 July 2008 for New York City lawsuit against out-of-state dealers (*New York City v. Bob Moates' Sport Shop, Inc.* 2008).

In a five-to-four decision, the Supreme Court of the United States rules that the "Second Amendment *protects an individual right to possess a firearm* unconnected with service in a militia" (*District of Columbia v. Heller* 2008).

5
The Politics of Food Litigation

In the previous chapter, we examined the largely failed attempt to regulate the gun industry through a regime of litigation. In this chapter, we turn our attention to food. We begin with a brief overview of the long history of litigation over tainted food products. We then look at contemporary litigation with a much more overtly regulatory aim, starting with concerns over genetically modified crops and then moving on to efforts to make fast food and junk food more healthy.

Food Litigation: Traditional Claims

Historically, food has been a much-regulated commodity. After all, it is both essential to life and highly susceptible to adulteration. Thus, even in antiquity, governments acted to insure the integrity of food and drink (Burditt 1995; Wilson 2002).[1] More than a decade before signing the Magna Carta, King John decreed the *Assize of Bread,* prohibiting the "adulteration of bread with such ingredients as ground peas or beans" and ushering in a long English tradition of food regulation (Food and Drug Administration 1999, para. 1). This concern for at least minimal food safety and purity was adopted in the colonies and, later, by the individual states, which quickly "began to regulate food and drugs ... primarily to address basic consumer protection and trade concerns" (Mueller 2001, 4). Throughout the nineteenth century, federal regulation of food was spotty and weak, in keeping with the general premise that health and welfare were primarily state concerns. Then in 1906, Upton Sinclair published *The Jungle,* his graphic exposé of the Chicago stockyards. Widely read, including by President Theodore Roosevelt, the book prompted an outcry for immediate federal intervention. And this intervention was indeed immediate – during the same year, Congress passed the *Food and Drugs Act,* prohibiting "interstate commerce in misbranded and adulterated foods, drinks and drugs" (Food and Drug Administration 1999, para. 11) and the *Meat Inspection Act,* "providing for the inspection of all meat products sold in interstate commerce" (United States, Department of

Agriculture, Food Safety and Inspection Service 2006, para. 2).[2] Thereafter, throughout the twentieth century, Congress passed dozens of major food regulatory acts,[3] inspiring thousands of rules by agencies charged with implementation.[4]

Litigation, too, has a long relationship with food. As early as 1606, an English court wrote that "[i]f a man sells victuals which is corrupt without warranty an action lies, because it is against the commonwealth" (*Roswell v. Vaughn* 1606, cited in *Friend v. Childs Dining Hall Co.* 1918). Indeed, according to Jeffery Lyons (1998, 742), the whole "concept of product liability 'originated in English common law, in which the brewer, butcher, cook, or other person was held responsible for tainted or adulterated drink or food.'" Needless to say, legal actions over food made the jump across "the pond" rather effortlessly and have remained a mainstay of civil litigation, often contributing to legal theory more generally. For example, in 1939, a New York woman brought suit against a delicatessen after biting into a Danish pastry, the yummy inside of which contained not only cream cheese but also a tack. The deli, for its part, interpleaded the bakery from which it had purchased the Danish. In its defence, the bakery noted that it included a statement on the back of all of its invoices expressly stating that it gave no guarantee "as to quality, description, merchantability or fitness for purpose intended and will in no way be responsible for damages or allowances." In ruling for both the woman and the delicatessen, however, the municipal court called such a disclaimer "contrary to natural justice and good morals and against public policy" (*Linn v. Radio Center Delicatessen, Inc.* 1939, 880).

A food (specifically, a beverage) problem is generally cited as the impetus for the theory of strict liability. Thus, when a waitress was injured by an exploding bottle of Coca Cola, the Supreme Court of California sided with her against the company. Justice Traynor, however, in concurrence, went further:

> [I]t should now be recognized that a manufacturer incurs an absolute liability when an article that he has placed on the market, knowing that it is to be used without inspection, proves to have a defect that causes injury to human beings ... Even if there is no negligence ... public policy demands that responsibility be fixed wherever it will most effectively reduce the hazards to life and health inherent in defective products that reach the market. It is evident that the manufacturer can anticipate some hazards and guard against the recurrence of others, as the public cannot. Those who suffer injury from defective products are unprepared to meet its consequences. The cost of an injury and the loss of time or health may be an overwhelming misfortune to the person injured, and a needless one, for the risk of injury can be insured by the manufacturer and distributed among the public as a cost of doing business. It is to the public interest to discourage the marketing of products

having defects that are a menace to the public. If such products nevertheless find their way into the market it is to the public interest to place the responsibility for whatever injury they may cause upon the manufacturer, who, even if he is not negligent in the manufacture of the product, is responsible for its reaching the market. However intermittently such injuries may occur and however haphazardly they may strike, the risk of their occurrence is a constant risk and a general one. Against such a risk there should be general and constant protection and the manufacturer is best situated to afford such protection. (*Escola v. Coca Cola Bottling Company* 1944, 462 [Traynor, J., concurring])

Of course, the consequences of a sandwich containing some foreign object or of the occasional exploding soft drink are clearly undesirable, but they are isolated. Observers of the process generally agree that food substances intended for public consumption have, by and large, become fairly reliable and safe as a result of legislative regulations and product liability litigation. However, there is a world of difference between the isolated occurrences of certain bad episodes and a wide-scale adulteration that affects thousands – even millions – of consumers. And the possibility of such widespread defilement are increasing constantly as the distribution of food, like other commodities, becomes more and more globalized, and regulators are unable to inspect more than a fraction of the imports (MSN Broadcast Company 2007).[5]

Thus, today, food litigation, particularly that inspired by food-borne illnesses, continues to be filed in US courts, which is not surprising, given that food pathogens are both pervasive and frequently the result of human mishandling (Buzby, Frenzen, and Rasco 2001).[6] According to the Centers for Disease Control and Prevention (CDC), "[a]n estimated 76 million cases of foodborne disease occur each year in the United States." And while "[t]he great majority of these cases are mild and cause symptoms for only a day or two, [some] cases are more serious ... CDC estimates that there are 325,000 hospitalizations and 5,000 deaths related to foodborne diseases each year" (Centers for Disease Control and Prevention 2005c, para. 20). Indeed, the Consumer Product Safety Commission reports that "contaminated food products cause more deaths each year than the combined totals of all 15,000 products" it regulates (Buzby, Frenzen, and Rasco 2001, 5).

Of course, when food producers, distributors, restaurants, and institutional facilities such as schools, hospitals, and prisons are responsible for adulterating food, we would expect multiple people (and, potentially, multiple litigants) to be affected. And this is not an uncommon occurrence. According to the CDC, in 2004 alone, 1,319 known food-borne disease outbreaks occurred, affecting more than 28,000 individuals (Centers for Disease Control and Prevention 2005d).[7] Moreover, in an era of mass marketing and globalized food distribution, we would anticipate further occurrences. Thus, for example, numerous law firms are recruiting clients for lawsuits over the spinach E. coli outbreak of 2006, which resulted in 205 confirmed illnesses and three deaths (Food and Drug Administration 2007).[8] In August 2007, San Francisco attorney William Audet launched the first, of what will no doubt be many, lawsuit against a Chinese company that had provided contaminated pet food ingredients to American and Canadian producers, resulting in the deaths of hundreds of dogs and cats and a massive product recall. Dozens of pet food lawsuits have been instituted against manufacturers in the United States and Canada (Bailey 2007). And it took no time at all for tomatosalmonellalawyer.com, among other websites, to appear online following the FDA's announcement in June 2008 that tomatoes may have sickened people in forty states (Food and Drug Administration 2008).

Relatively speaking, product liability claims involving food have traditionally been straightforward and, in a very general sense, uncontroversial. Victims of tainted food, after all, tend to become manifestly sick within hours or days of ingestion. The typical case of E. coli or salmonella poisoning is not, shall we say, subtle. As the cases noted earlier suggest, food lawsuits have tended to be of the more customary reactive sort, brought by a fairly easily identifiable group of plaintiffs, and susceptible of contained and finite settlements or judgments.[9] However, in recent years, food litigation has begun to assume a more overtly regulatory tone. This has been notably true in two areas: genetically modified foods and foods produced for mass markets and their association with obesity and related health issues.

Genetically Modified (GM) or Genetically Engineered (GE) Foods

Under US law, GE refers to "[t]he genetic modification of organisms by recombinant DNA techniques."[10] This may include the production of transgenic plants resulting "from the insertion of genetic material from another organism so that the plant will exhibit a desired trait" (Europa 2008, para. 25). Similarly, transgenic animals are produced by introducing new genes. Although the FDA (Center for Veterinary Medicine) has thus far not approved any transgenic animals for use as human food,[11] in a relatively short period of time, GM plant crops have become more and more pervasive: "In 2006, 252 million acres of transgenic crops were planted in 22 countries by 10.3 million farmers ... [C]ountries that grew 97% of the global transgenic crops were the United States (53%), Argentina (17%), Brazil (11%), Canada (6%), India (4%), China (3%), Paraguay (2%) and South Africa (1%). Although growth is expected to plateau in industrialized nations, it is increasing in developing countries. The next decade will see exponential progress in GM product development as researchers gain increasing and unprecedented access to genomic resources that are applicable to organisms beyond the scope of individual projects" (Human Genome Project 2008, paras. 4 and 6).[12]

Major producers of GM crops herald their seed technology as both environmentally beneficial and crucial to the alleviation of world hunger. Thus, for example, Monsanto, the largest GM seed producer, claims that its products "increase productivity or reduce cost by increasing yield, improving protection from insects and disease, or increasing their crops' tolerance to heat, drought, and other environmental stress. For many farmers, especially small-scale growers, our products help improve their lives by helping them produce more while conserving more time and inputs" (Monsanto 2008, para. 2). Some individuals, particularly environmentalists, have dismissed such assertions. Friends of the Earth International, for instance, maintains that "[c]ontrary to the promises made by the biotech industry, the reality of the last ten years shows that the safety of GM crops cannot be ensured and that these crops are neither cheaper nor better quality. Biotech crops are not a solution to solve hunger in Africa or elsewhere ... The biotech industry continues to misleadingly claim that GM crops play a role in solving world hunger, and the world's largest producer of GM seeds, Monsanto Company ... keeps an objectionable influence over agriculture and food policies in many countries and international bodies" (Friends of the Earth International 2006, cited in Ecomall 2008, para. 3).

Among consumers, genetic engineering has been most widely resisted in Europe. Especially since the movement toward unification has fostered the freer flow of goods across national borders, concern over GM and other food-related issues has prompted considerable administrative scrutiny. And this reticence has been reflected in governmental policy. Hence, following the limited approval of some GM foodstuffs beginning in the 1990s, the European Union in 1998 placed a *de facto* moratorium on further authorizations (European Commission 2003). The freeze lasted until May 2004 when the commission approved the sale of a GM sweet corn (Sparshott 2004). Even so, opposition to GM products remains relatively high in Europe.[13] Hostility toward GM crops has been far less widespread and far more muted in the United States. This relative complacency, however, has not kept the issue out of court.[14] Of particular note are the Alliance for Bio-Integrity lawsuit and the StarLink saga.

Alliance for Bio-Integrity v. Shalala (2000)

In September 2000, Judge Colleen Kollar-Kotelly of the US District Court for the District of Columbia considered a complaint brought by a coalition of scientists and religious leaders under the umbrella of the Alliance for Bio-Integrity.[15] The group, seeking tighter restrictions on GM foods, sued the secretary of health and human services over alleged FDA improprieties on a number of counts. In general, the alliance was concerned with an FDA statement of policy dated 29 May 1992 in which the agency announced that it would "presume that foods produced through the rDNA process [genetically-modified foods] were 'generally recognized as safe' (GRAS) under the *Federal Food, Drug and Cosmetic Act* ("FDCA"), 21 U.S.C. § 321(s), and therefore not subject to regulation [or labeling] as food additives" (*Alliance for Bio-Integrity v. Shalala* 2000, 170). Specifically, the group alleged that the FDA's statement was not properly subjected to notice-and-comment procedures; that the FDA did not comply with the *National Environmental Protection Act* by compiling an environmental assessment or environmental impact statement; that the FDA's presumption that rDNA-developed foods are GRAS and therefore do not require food additive petitions was arbitrary and capricious; that the agency's decision not to require labelling for rDNA-developed foods was arbitrary and capricious; that its decision not to regulate or require labelling for rDNA-developed foods violated the Free Exercise Clause; and that the decision not to regulate or require labelling for rDNA-developed foods violated the *Religious Freedom Restoration Act* (*ibid.*, 170).[16] The judge disagreed on every count, finding that the FDA had acted in accordance with statutory requirements. The alliance did not appeal.

The StarLink Crisis

In the same month that Judge Kollar-Kotelly handed down her decision, an event occurred that garnered far more attention and had a more far-reaching impact than the Bio-Integrity case. During this month, the public first became aware of something called StarLink. StarLink, a type of corn patented by Aventis Crop Science,[17] was genetically modified to contain an insecticidal protein, Cry9C. The downside of the development was that Cry9C "shared several molecular properties with proteins that are known food allergens" (Centers for Disease Control and Prevention 2005e, para. 1). In 1998, the product was licensed by the US Environmental Protection Agency (EPA) for limited use in animal feed, industrial non-food uses, and seed increase. Notably, because of the allergen issue, StarLink was not licensed for human consumption (*ibid.*). It was also placed under a number of special regulations designed to keep it strictly segregated from other corn. Two years later, however, in September 2000, a coalition of biotech critics convened a press conference to announce their discovery that the corn had been detected in Taco Bell taco shells for sale in grocery stores (Kaufman 2001). Ultimately, hundreds of corn products were discovered to be adulterated, prompting a massive nationwide recall (Food and Drug Administration 2000).

In order to avert lawsuits with farmers directly affected by StarLink – StarLink growers and buffer growers[18] – Aventis took a number of early actions. First, the company, upon the urging of the EPA, withdrew StarLink from the market. Second, in September, the US Department of Agriculture agreed to purchase StarLink corn from farmers at a 25-cents-per-bushel premium above the posted county price to ensure that StarLink corn was fed to the farmers' own animals, sold to feed outlets, or sold to the Commodity Credit

Corporation. Aventis reimbursed the Department of Agriculture for the costs of the program, which were estimated at about $100 million (Segarra and Rawson 2001). Finally, in January 2001, Aventis entered into an agreement with the attorneys general of seventeen states to pay 25 cents per bushel to growers and buffer growers to control corn grown from StarLink hybrids and corn grown within 660 feet of corn grown with StarLink hybrids.[19] Growers and elevators were also eligible for reimbursement of StarLink costs or losses. Program estimates ran as high as billions of dollars (Laidlaw 2001).

By November, several dozen people had lodged complaints with the FDA claiming allergic reactions, including anaphylactic shock ("44 Claim Illness" 2000), and traces of the product were found in snack foods as far away as Japan. The US corn market suffered, as many American and foreign producers shied away from US domestic corn because of the possibility that it might be polluted. Litigation was not far behind as a complex and sometimes cross-cutting amalgam of consumers, farmers who used or discovered Star-Link in their crops, corn growers not directly affected but claiming to have suffered from changes in the US corn market, and some franchisees and corn product manufacturers filed suit against Aventis, Garst Seed (the licensee who produced and distributed StarLink seeds), taco shell suppliers, and corn product manufacturers.

Consumers
The most easily and cheaply concluded of the suits was that brought by consumers. As noted earlier, a number of individuals reported allergic reactions to StarLink-adulterated products. Several of those people brought suit on behalf of themselves and others similarly situated against not only Aventis but also the major food product manufacturers, including Kraft, Kellogg, Mission Foods, and Aztec Foods (*In re: Starlink Corn Products Liability Litigation* 2002). In fact, consumers were not in a great position to delve into the corporate pockets too deeply. In June 2001, the CDC published a report that cast considerable doubt on the proposition that anyone had experienced an allergic reaction to the StarLink infected products (Centers for Disease Control and Prevention 2001).[20] Nevertheless, in 2002, district court judge James Moran approved a $9 million settlement, directing $6 million into customer coupons to be placed on taco shell, taco chip, and other product packages and $3 million into administrative costs and attorneys fees (Carroll 2002).

Taco Bell
Despite the fact that restaurant tacos were ultimately found not to be contaminated, the connection between StarLink and the Taco Bell name adversely affected business at a number of fast food franchises. As a result, a group of franchisees sued Aventis, Garst, and taco shell suppliers. Like the consumer suit, the Taco Bell action was fairly quickly concluded when

suppliers agreed to a $60 million settlement for lost business ("U.S. Taco Bell Franchisees" 2001).

Non-StarLink Farmers

If the consumer suit was relatively easy, cheaply concluded, and legally inconsequential, the class action brought by so-called non-StarLink farmers was its opposite in every respect. Brought by a class of about 400,000 corn farmers nationwide, the "non-StarLink farmer suit" against Aventis and Garst Seed claimed broad economic harm to the plaintiffs based on a number of legal theories. While dismissing some portions of the suit, Judge James Moran of the District Court for the Northern District Court of Illinois allowed the complaint to proceed on a number of grounds, including a far-reaching theory of nuisance not unknown to other recent class actions and presenting clear regulatory potential. Thus, the farmers claimed harm under a common law theory of public nuisance.[21] A public nuisance is "'an unreasonable interference with a right common to the general public' ... including 'the public health, the public safety, the public peace, the public comfort or the public convenience'" (*In re: Starlink Corn Products Liability Litigation* 2002, 848). Judge Moran concluded that the widespread StarLink contamination satisfied the criteria of public nuisance. More difficult, however, was the farmers' *private* public nuisance claim, for to sustain such allegations plaintiffs must demonstrate that "they have been harmed differently than the general public" both in terms of severity and in terms of their share of the overall burden (*ibid.*, 847). Siding with the farmers, Moran concluded that "[w]hile the general public has a right to safe food, plaintiffs depend on the integrity of the corn supply for their livelihood" (*ibid.*, 848). Judge Moran's expansive reading of nuisance led fairly quickly to settlement, culminating in early 2003 with Aventis and Garst Seed agreeing to a payout of roughly $112 million (*In re: Starlink Corn Products Liability Litigation* 2003).

The McLawsuits

> As a last resort, and only if – as with the problem of smoking – the government does little to reduce the problem, law suits could be brought, especially against companies which misrepresent their foods.
> — John F. Banzhaf III, Professor, George Washington
> University Law School, 2002

> McDonald's double cheeseburgers [are] a weapon of mass destruction.
> — Ralph Nader, 2002

[F]rivolous lawsuits ... only enrich the trial bar at the expense of
the restaurant operators and their employees, who are the hardest
working Americans.
>   – Steven C. Anderson, President and CEO,
>   National Restaurant Association, 2003

What we think is counterproductive is finger-pointing, reckless
accusations, and lawsuits that won't make anyone any thinner.
>   – Spokesperson for the Grocery Manufacturers of
>   America, 2003

A man in New York is suing four fast food restaurants, and he's
claiming they made him obese. Reportedly, the man is suing for
$1 million, but said he'd settle for six large burritos.
>   – Conan O'Brien, Late Night with Conan O'Brien

We hear it over and over: America is fat and getting fatter. According to the
CDC, "[i]n 2007, only one state (Colorado) had a prevalence of obesity less
than 20%. Thirty states had a prevalence equal to or greater than 25%; three
of these states (Alabama, Mississippi and Tennessee) had a prevalence of
obesity equal to or greater than 30%" (Centers for Disease Control and Prevention 2008, para. 2). And, statistics released in 2007 showed us getting
even larger (Centers for Disease Control and Prevention 2007)! Nor is this
simply an American phenomenon. The International Obesity Task Force
(2008) estimates that worldwide 300 million people are obese. In nearly
every developed country, the term "epidemic" is used to describe our increasing poundage. Thus, calling it an epidemic, a paper prepared for the Canadian
Parliamentary Information and Research Service estimated that "6.8 million
Canadian adults ages 20 to 64 were overweight, and an additional 4.5 million were obese" (Starky 2005, para. 1). The Health Survey for England found
that 38 percent of English adults were overweight and another 24 percent
were classified as obese. In addition, almost 30 percent of English children
were deemed overweight or obese (United Kingdom, Department of Health
2008). Nearly 33 percent of Australian adults are overweight, with obesity
affecting about 16 percent of adults, 25 percent of Australian boys and 23.3
percent of Australian girls are either overweight or obese (Biggs 2006).

Of course, this is more than just a problem of aesthetics. The US Surgeon
General reports that

- 300,000 deaths each year in the United States are associated with
  obesity

- overweight and obesity are associated with heart disease, certain types of cancer, type 2 diabetes, stroke, arthritis, breathing problems, and psychological disorders, such as depression
- the economic cost of obesity in the United States was about $117 billion in 2000 (United States, Department of Health and Human Services 2006).

Indeed, according to Rand researchers, obesity is a more serious health problem than smoking, heavy drinking, or living in poverty (Sturm et al. 2004). The causes of the epidemic are, at once, fairly straightforward ("an imbalance involving excessive calorie consumption and/or inadequate physical activity") and very complex ("for each individual, body weight is the result of a combination of genetic, metabolic, behavioral, environmental, cultural, and socioeconomic influences") (United States, Department of Health and Human Services 2006, para. 3).[22] Whatever the combination of factors, however, much of the blame has been placed on fast food, packaged snacks, and sugary drinks.[23]

The "McDonald's" Suits
Numerous medical studies have demonstrated a link between fast food consumption and obesity. For example, Britain's Medical Research Council found that fast foods that tend to be "energy dense ... fool people into consuming more calories than the body needs" (British Broadcasting Corporation 2003, para. 2). Research out of Boston's Children's Hospital found, among other things, that people who eat fast food more than twice a week "have a 50 percent greater risk of obesity than do those who eat this way once or less [and that t]heir risk of abnormal glucose control, an inability to break down sugar efficiently that often foreshadows diabetes, is double" (Cable News Network 2003, para. 8). Moreover, "a single meal from [a fast food] restaurant often contains enough calories to satisfy a person's caloric requirement for an entire day" (National Institute of Health 2004, para. 5).[24] Although McDonald's is hardly the only purveyor of fast food, as the largest such entity in the world its name is synonymous with the genre, and it could expect to find itself the first named defendant on any lawsuit targeting fast food. The restaurant colossus operates and franchises more than 30,000 facilities in 118 countries, serving roughly fifty million customers a day. In 2007, the company reported revenues in excess of $23 billion (McDonald's Corporation 2007). Other industry giants, though operating in the shadow of McDonald's, report very healthy business as well.[25]

Not surprisingly, the notion that fast food purveyors might be targeted by litigation came from some of the individuals who had been in the front lines of the tobacco wars. Notable in this regard were two law professors, John Banzhaf, III, of George Washington University and Richard Daynard of

Northwestern University. Banzhaf, who founded Action on Smoking and Health over thirty-six years ago and remains an anti-tobacco activist, first took on the fast food industry in the early 1990s over the issue of second-hand smoke.[26] By early in this decade, Banzhaf had begun making the connection between legal action against cigarette companies and a possible litigation strategy aimed at fast food. Hence, in January 2002, he fired an opening salvo, asserting that "as we're getting more and more figures saying just how dangerous obesity is, people are wondering if tactics used against the tobacco industry very successfully and other problems such as guns less successfully could be used against the problem of obesity" (Park 2002, para. 4). His plan of attack was fourfold, starting "with the relatively easy stuff":

> The first line of attack is to go after food companies that misrepresent their products by understating the fat content or omitting to mention ingredients ... The second, slightly harder, line of attack is to accuse companies of making misleading health claims for their products – proclaiming pork to be "the other white meat," for example, when its fat and cholesterol content are in fact closer to beef than to chicken. The third approach would be to pick up on a failure to warn consumers of certain health risks ... And finally, the real zinger, if it can be made to work: an onslaught on the fast-food industry as a whole, in which it would be made to pay its share of responsibility for type-two diabetes, sclerotic arteries, heart attacks and strokes. (Gumbel 2002, 16)

Daynard, too, has been a long-time anti-tobacco activist, having founded the Tobacco Products Liability Project in 1984 "to establish the legal responsibility of the tobacco industry for tobacco-induced disease, death and disability" (American Bar Association 2008, para. 25). Like Banzhaf, Daynard sees a link between the litigation aimed at cigarette manufacturers and fast food lawsuits. According to his Public Health Advocacy Institute (2006),

> [t]obacco litigation focused on the tobacco industry's behaviors that interfered with the consumer's ability to make a free and informed choice. As in tobacco, there is a similar concern with the food industry. Heavy marketing of high calorie-dense foods to children is dismaying. Additionally, it is unclear if some foods with added sugars and fat are addictive. If the food industry believes this to be true, there is an obligation to inform their customers. Finally, the industry often markets particular foods as health-enhancing. Often this marketing approach is simply misleading. What is clear is that the food industry is in the best position to understand the health effects of their products.

The Hindu French Fry Suit

McDonald's own claim to be serving healthier food kicked off the first of the contemporary wave of suits. On 23 July 1990, Ed Rensi, the president of McDonald's USA, released a press statement, proclaiming that "the best french fries in the world have just gotten better ... Now our customers can enjoy the same great taste they've known and loved for 35 years, but without any cholesterol and with 45 percent less saturated fat per serving ... Our customers want to be comfortable that they're getting not only great-tasting food but good nutrition, too. At McDonald's, they get both!" (quoted in *Pelman v. McDonald's* 2003c, C(1)). The fries had gotten better, McDonald's claimed, because they would no longer be cooked in animal fat. Instead, the restaurant would begin using "100 percent vegetable oil." The assertion was reiterated numerous times.

What McDonald's did not tell its customers, however, was that the "natural flavor" that made its popular product "the best french fries in the world," was beef tallow, a fact that once revealed did not sit well with vegetarians or observant Hindus. In India, the news caused riots, with "restaurant windows ... smashed and statues of Ronald McDonald smeared with cow dung" (Goodstein 2001, para. 6). In the United States, of course, it caused a lawsuit. Thus, on 6 June 2001, a proposed class action lawsuit was commenced against McDonald's Corporation asserting claims for violations of the consumer fraud laws and common law principles of all fifty states and alleging that the restaurant chain provided false and misleading nutritional information to consumers. The class included American vegetarians and Hindus who had consumed McDonald's french fries or hash browns since 23 July 1990 and who had dietary, ethical, moral, religious, philosophical, or health-related concerns about the consumption of beef or meat (*Block v. McDonald's* 2002). Eager to avoid a fight of international proportions, McDonald's quickly agreed to a settlement that included the company's denial of all allegations and liability in exchange for $10 million in charitable donations to vegetarian, Hindu, child nutrition, and Jewish educational organizations, a corporate apology to Hindus and vegetarians,[27] and the establishment of "an advisory board to make reports and recommendations to McDonald's about dietary restrictions that apply to various types of vegetarians, as well as guidelines for companies who market to vegetarians" (*ibid.*, para. 4).

The Obesity Suits

On 23 July 2002, Caesar Barber distinguished himself by becoming the first obese American to file suit against the fast food industry, including McDonald's, Burger King, KFC, and Wendy's.[28] Weighing in at over 270 pounds and having barely survived two heart attacks, Barber attributed his ill health to having eaten fast food four to five times per week for twenty years (Sixty Minutes, Australia 2002). His complaint, lodged for himself and all other persons similarly situated, was filed in New York State court by Samuel Hirsch, an attorney with no previous class action experience (Parloff 2003). Ultimately, the lawsuit, alleging negligent and deceptive marketing of unsafe products and failure to warn of product risk (*Barber v. McDonald's* 2002), generated a great deal more media attention than legal action, as varying combinations of "Team Barber, Hirsch, and Banzhaf" made the rounds of talk and interview programs[29] and as Barber suffered the indignity of becoming the summer's national joke.[30] Indeed, within weeks, Barber had become such "Leno-fodder" that Banzhaf convinced Hirsch to withdraw the suit, acknowledging that "Barber was an adult, and people could say, 'Well, he should be held responsible for the consequences of his own actions'" (Ferguson 2002, para. 3). Rather, Banzhaf set his sights on a more vulnerable, sympathetic, and, presumably, more winning demographic.

At nineteen years of age, Jazlyn Bradley weighed in at 270 pounds and Ashley Pelman, just fourteen years old and only four feet, ten inches tall, tipped the scales at 170. Both girls had already "developed diabetes, coronary heart disease, high blood pressure, and elevated cholesterol intake," among other indicators of ill health (*Pelman v. McDonald's* 2003b, 519). In federal district court,[31] Pelman and Bradley, representing the class of minors in New York State who purchased and consumed McDonald's products, claimed (1) that the fast food giant marketed its product as nutritious while failing to disclose deleterious health effects in violation of New York law; and (2) that its promotional techniques, including the ubiquitous "Happy Meal," particularly aimed to induce children to ingest its product, also in contravention of state statute. Additionally, at common law, plaintiffs alleged (3) that McDonald's acted "negligently in selling food products that are high in cholesterol, fat, salt and sugar when studies show that such foods cause obesity and detrimental health effects"; (4) that it failed to warn consumers that its ingredients could lead to obesity and associated health problems; and (5) that it "acted negligently in marketing food products that were physically and psychologically addictive" (*ibid.*, 520).

As initially presented, the arguments were hardly convincing, and Judge Robert Sweet dismissed the complaint in its entirety for lack of specificity on every count. The judge, however, decided to allow plaintiffs to submit an amended complaint addressing deficiencies in the original. Indeed, Sweet was quite generous in offering suggestions to plaintiffs. For example, as to the state statutory claims, Sweet pointed the litigants in the direction of earlier evidence of McDonald's advertising practices gathered by a former attorney general, suggesting this data as a starting point, but warning that it might be legally stale (*ibid.*, 530). Similarly, he made very specific suggestions with regard to each of the common law complaints (see *ibid.*, 536-43).

Unfortunately for the plaintiffs, their amended complaint, now limited only to state statutory claims, faired no better with Judge Sweet who exhibited some irritation at the litigants' failure to substantially improve on the first effort (*Pelman v. McDonald's* 2003c). Thus, while *Pelman III* made some effort to present data on misleading advertising practices, it failed to heed Sweet's "warning" about statutes of limitation (*ibid.,* 13).[32] Sweet also admonished plaintiffs for failing to pinpoint, with particularity, any deceptive act that caused injury (*ibid.,* 22ff). The plaintiffs failed to show plainly that they relied upon, or were aware of, specific health misrepresentations when purchasing McDonald's products (*ibid.,* 20). And the court rebuked plaintiffs for failing to "address the role that 'a number of other factors other than diet may come to play in obesity and the health problems of which the plaintiffs complain'" and thus falling short on establishing causation (*ibid.,* 31-33). In again dismissing the claims, a clearly exasperated Sweet noted:

> The plaintiffs have not only been given a chance to amend their complaint in order to state a claim, but this Court laid out in some detail the elements that a properly pleaded complaint would need to contain. Despite this guidance, plaintiffs have failed to allege a cause of action for violations of New York's consumer protection laws with respect to McDonald's advertisements and other publicity. The plaintiffs have made no explicit allegations that they witnessed any particular deceptive advertisement, and they have not provided McDonald's with enough information to determine whether its products are the cause of the alleged injuries. Finally, the one advertisement which plaintiffs implicitly allege to have caused their injuries is objectively non-deceptive. (*ibid.,* 40-41)

Notwithstanding such arguments, early in 2005 the Second Circuit Court considered Pelman's appeal, holding that the overweight minors could proceed with their suit. Sweet had erred, the Court of Appeals held, because New York's deceptive practices law "does not require proof of actual reliance" on the plaintiffs' part in order to launch a suit (*Pelman v. McDonald's* 2005a, 508). At the same time, the court acknowledged that the plaintiffs' allegations were fuzzy and strongly suggested that "the cure for such deficiencies, in a claim not required to be plead with particularity, is a motion for a more definite statement under Rule 12(e)" (*ibid.,* 514).[33] Remanded for further proceedings, not surprisingly, McDonald's moved for the more definitive statement – a motion granted by Judge Sweet (*Pelman v. McDonald's* 2005b). The case remains in discovery.

Corporate and political reaction to *Pelman* and other attacks on the fast food industry such as Morgan Spurlock's (2004) award-winning documentary, *Super Size Me,* and Eric Schlosser's (2001) book, *Fast Food Nation,* has been swift and broad-based. On the one hand, McDonald's and other fast food giants have moved to include, and aggressively advertise, healthier – or at least healthier looking – items on the menu. For example, one of McDonald's newest ubiquitous billboard campaigns promotes an "Asian Salad," featuring "a harmonious blend of crisp greens, warm orange-glazed chicken (grilled or crispy), snow peas, edamame, mandarin oranges, and toasted almonds." And if that were not enough to demonstrate the company's bona fides as a health food vendor and good corporate citizen, the salad is served with one of Paul Newman's dressings.[34] Moreover, in 2004, the chain announced plans to eliminate "supersizing" from its menu choices (Fauber and Johnson 2004),[35] and, recently, it began allowing consumers to "mix and match" Happy Meal items, substituting juice for soda and apples for French fries.[36]

Additionally, McDonald's announced in October 2005 that it would begin putting nutritional labels on most of its packaged foods, promising implementation in "20,000 of its 30,000 restaurants worldwide by the end of 2006," which specifically aims at averting the *Pelman*-type "failure to warn" claims (Warner 2005a, C1). Moreover, the company website features a nutrition page with information on most of its products, tips from a nutritionist and a "personal trainer," and a virtual "Bag a Meal," allowing consumers to view the food value of an entire preferred McDonald's meal.[37] Public relations aside, the restaurant industry has waged an aggressive legislative strategy. Thus, taking a page from the playbook of the other NRA, the National Restaurant Association has promoted so-called "commonsense consumption laws," which would limit the liability of food companies for obesity and obesity-related illnesses (Warner 2005b). As of 2007, in various forms, the legislation had passed in twenty-three states, had been defeated in eight states, and was pending in eight others (National Restaurant Association 2008).

Federal legislation is being pursued as well, although it has yet to emerge from committees in final form. In October 2005, the House of Representatives passed the *Personal Responsibility in Food Consumption Act* on a vote of 306 to 120.[38] The bill would have prohibited "civil liability actions brought or continued against food manufacturers, marketers, distributors, advertisers, sellers, and trade associations for claims of injury relating to a person's weight gain, obesity, or any health condition associated with weight gain or obesity."[39] A similar bill, the *Commonsense Consumption Act* was referred to the Senate Judiciary Committee where it stalled. In 2007, the bill re-emerged as the *Commonsense Consumption Act of 2005*.[40] The Senate bill was referred to the Judiciary Committee in May; the House of Representatives bill to the Subcommittee on Commercial and Administrative Law (Judiciary) in June. As of 2008, additional action is pending.[41]

"Attractive Nuisances": Soda and Saturday Morning Cartoons

Of course, Big Macs are hardly the only potential temptation for America's rapidly expanding youth. Sugary soft drinks, pre-packaged sweets, and that perennial source of slothfulness, television, along with its newer partner, video games, have all been deemed culprits in the obesity epidemic. And all have been the recent targets of litigation or of litigation threats.

The Coke and Pepsi Suit

By mid-decade, numerous studies had begun to sound alarms about soft drink consumption among children and adolescents in the United States. Surveys indicated not only that young people had "excessively high" intake of discretionary sugar (see, for example, Muñoz et al. 1997; Subar et al. 1998; Cavadini, Siega-Riz, and Popkin 2000; Borrud, Enns, and Mickle 1996; Mickle, Nowverl, and Tippett 1998; Lytle et al. 2000) but also that the major source of this bad sugar was soft drinks (Guthrie and Morton 2000). Moreover, serving sizes had increased dramatically over a fifty-year period (Gleason and Suitor 2001). Indeed, between 1977 and 2001, calories obtained from sweetened beverages had risen a whopping 135 percent (Columbia Broadcasting System News 2006)![42] This escalation was linked to obesity and its associated diseases (Ludwig, Peterson, and Gortmaker 2001), dental problems (Heller, Burt, and Eklund 2001), and a decrease in milk consumption and thus calcium intake (Cavadini, Siega-Riz, and Popkin 2000). At the same time, and also contributing to the problem, soda machines were becoming ubiquitous in the nation's schools, as cash-strapped educators increasingly entered into exclusive contracts with Coke or Pepsi as a means of enhancing revenues (see, for example, Kaufman 1999).

Responding to these indicators, late in 2005, attorneys at the Center for Science in the Public Interest (CSPI), along with Stephen Sheller, a Philadelphia lawyer and yet another long-time tobacco warrior, and Northwestern University's Daynard announced plans to file a lawsuit in Massachusetts against Coke and Pepsi (Mayer 2005).[43] The attorneys planned to sue under the doctrine of "attractive nuisance" a tort traditionally used against property owners whose holdings contain some potentially unsafe object that may attract children, for example, an unguarded swimming pool or a discarded refrigerator. According to Daynard, "[y]ou want to keep kids away from dangerous objects, and a soda machine is demonstrated to be a dangerous object for kids" (*ibid.*, D2).

The response of the American Beverage Association (ABA) was swift. First, it released its own study reporting "a 24 percent drop in purchases of full-calorie carbonated soft drinks at schools from 2002 to 2004" (*ibid.*). More promising, however, from the perspective of the potential litigants, was the ABA's announcement in May 2006 that it had developed school guidelines in conjunction with the Alliance for a Healthier Generation, a joint initiative of the American Heart Association and the William Jefferson Clinton Foundation.[44] At the same time, the soft drink companies agreed to pull their high-calorie drinks from schools. As a result, the CSPI dropped the planned litigation (Center for Science in the Public Interest 2006a).[45]

SpongeBob: If Only He Were Hawking Pineapples [46]

In January 2006, the CSPI, the Campaign for a Commercial-Free Childhood, and two Massachusetts parents announced plans to sue Viacom, the parent company of Nickelodeon Television, and Kellogg's, the maker of such kid-directed delectables as SpongeBob SquarePants Wild Bubble-Berry Pop-Tarts and frequent Nickelodeon sponsor. The aim was a class action representing all Massachusetts [47] parents and guardians with children less than eight years of age "who have (1) seen an advertisement for a nutritionally poor food on Nickelodeon or in another Viacom medium, (2) seen an advertisement for a nutritionally poor Kellogg product during children's programming in any other media, or (3) seen or purchased a nutritionally poor Kellogg or other product emblazoned with a Nickelodeon character" (Center for Science in the Public Interest 2006b, para. 2).[48] According to the CSPI, "100 percent (21/21) of Kellogg's websites for children feature foods of poor nutritional value. One study found that 98 percent of Kellogg's commercials on Saturday morning television were for foods of poor nutritional content. In 28 hours of Nickelodeon, of 168 food commercials – 148 (88 percent) were for foods of low nutritional value. Nickelodeon has partnered with both McDonald's and Burger King and its characters can be found on many packages of food of low nutritional value. Junk food is advertised extensively on Nick.com, and Nickjr.com which are among the most popular websites for kids" (Campaign for a Commercial-Free Childhood 2006, para. 3).

The plaintiffs alleged that Viacom and Kellogg's market "nutritionally poor" food to children who are unable to recognize such promotions as advertising, particularly when they "feature fun and adventure, are often colorful and musical ... include well-loved 'spokes-characters' ... and are incorporated 'into the theme or plot of stories, books, movies, Internet sites, or video games'" (Center for Science in the Public Interest 2006b, 4). They planned to "ask a Massachusetts court to enjoin the companies from marketing junk foods to audiences where 15 percent or more of the audience is under age eight, and to cease marketing junk foods through web sites, toy giveaways, contests, and other techniques aimed at that age group" (*ibid.*, 9). The statute under which the suit would be brought "provides for damages of $25 per violation of unfair or deceptive advertising."[49] In other words, it would apply "each time that a Massachusetts child sees an ad for a junk food on Nickelodeon, sees a Kellogg junk-food ad on that or another network, or sees Kellogg junk-food packaging that bears SpongeBob SquarePants, Dora the Explorer, or other cartoon characters" (Center for Science in the Public Interest 2006c). This could have amounted to billions of dollars, although the plaintiffs said they "would settle for a commitment from the companies to change their marketing practices" (Center for Science in the Public Interest 2006b, para. 15). The industry response, if not a total capitulation, was nonetheless pretty astounding.

Hence, following extensive negotiations with the CSPI, the Kellogg Company announced in June 2007 that it would phase out advertising worldwide of products to children under the age of twelve unless foods met nutritional guidelines for caloric, fat, sugar, and sodium content. Affected foods include such long-time childhood favourites as Pop-Tarts and Froot Loops cereal (Martin 2007). As a result, the CSPI dropped its suit against the food giant (Center for Science in the Public Interest 2007b). The Kellogg move, moreover, had something of a steamroller affect throughout the summer of 2007. First, Massachusetts congressman Ed Markey (Democrat), chairman of the House Subcommittee on Telecommunications and the Internet, added to the ominous threat of still pending litigation against such entities as Nickelodeon, praising Kellogg's "important first step" and warning that "[i]f the rest of the industry does not act quickly, the Congress or the Federal Communications Commission might have to take steps to safeguard kids from junk food ads during children's television programming" ("Chairman Markey Responds" 2007, para. 4). Roughly a month later, eleven large food and drink manufacturers, including General Mills, McDonald's, Campbell Soups, PepsiCola, Coca-Cola, and the Hershey Company agreed to limit their advertising to children (Tong 2007).

This move was followed after another month by the Discovery Channel's announcement that it would "license its name and characters for use only in connection with healthy food and beverage products" (Discovery Communications 2007, para. 1). Several days later, Nickelodeon promised to quit licensing its characters (including SpongeBob, Dora, and the Rugrats) for use on junk food products "except on special occasions such as Halloween" (United Press International 2007, para. 1). The Cartoon Network got on board shortly thereafter.

Trans Fats

Obesity aside, certain food products have been known for some time to pose long-term health risks. High on the list of such products is trans fat, "made when manufacturers add hydrogen to vegetable oil – a process called hydrogenation." In turn, hydrogenation "increases the shelf life and flavor stability of foods containing [the] fats" (Food and Drug Administration 2004, para. 4). Trans fats are known to increase low-density lipoprotein cholesterol levels (the so-called dangerous cholesterol) and thus are linked to coronary heart disease. Trans fats are typically found in shortening and packaged snacks.

Oreos, America's self-proclaimed "favorite cookie," was long an orgy of hydrogenation, with both the chocolate wafer and the creamy centre containing trans fats. As a result, in May 2003, San Francisco attorney Stephen Joseph, a crusader against trans fats, announced plans to sue Kraft Foods, maker of Oreos, in California.[50] At the time, trans fats were not listed on food labels and Kraft actively promoted the cookies to children, including in-school marketing. California law shields manufacturers and vendors from liability for "inherently unsafe ... product[s] ... known to be unsafe by the ordinary consumer who consumes the product with the ordinary knowledge common to the community."[51] Obviously aimed at shielding tobacco companies, the law presumably would shield other unsafe products as well – for example, liquor and fireworks. Joseph, however, pointed to the fact that there was no common knowledge about trans fats. The suit sought no damages but, instead, asked for an injunction ordering Kraft "after the expiration of a reasonable grace period to cease and desist from marketing and selling Oreo Cookies to children in the State of California, until such cookies contain no partially hydrogenated oil or other *trans* fat" (Ban Trans Fats 2006, para. 4).

In remarkably short order (fourteen days, to be exact), Joseph dropped the suit, claiming a major victory, both in concessions from Kraft and in media coverage. "The incredible national and international publicity that the lawsuit received," according to Joseph, had sufficiently alerted the public to the dangers of trans fats. "[W]e could no longer honestly tell a judge that *trans* fats were not known to be unsafe by the ordinary consumer. The lawsuit was a victim of its own success" (*ibid.*, para. 8). Moreover, according to Joseph, "[j]ust one day after the media coverage about the lawsuit began, Kraft announced that it would reduce or eliminate the *trans* fat in the Oreo" (*ibid.*, para. 6). While the timing of Kraft's decision was not quite as clear cut as Joseph would have it, the giant food maker did announce plans to undertake "a sweeping, global overhaul of the way it creates, packages, and promotes its foods[,]" including "eliminate[ing] – or greatly reduce[ing] – *trans* fats in all of its cookies and crackers" (Horovitz 2003, 1A).[52]

Given the ubiquity of trans fats in processed foods, McDonald's was destined to find itself in the crosshairs of this litigation front as well. And, so, in the summer of 2004, Joseph trained his sights on the giant fast food vendor. Filed in California court on behalf of Katherine Fettke and a potentially enormous class of McDonald's customers, *Fettke v. McDonald's Corp.* (2004) charged "false advertising" and "fraud" (O'Leary 2004). Two years earlier, following the Hindu french fry suit, McDonald's had pledged, among other things and to great fanfare, that it would significantly reduce trans fatty acids in its fried products with the introduction of improved cooking oil – a major step toward the company's avowed goal of completely eliminating trans fats (PR Newswire 2002). According to *Fettke,* the fact that McDonald's had failed to keep its promise, "caused the individual plaintiff and other consumers to unwittingly eat foods loaded with *trans* fats." The "chain's announcement [that] it would change to healthier cooking oil," the suit alleged, "was so widely disseminated that it became common knowledge among the consuming public" (O'Leary 2004, 66). Within six months, McDonald's had settled, agreeing to donate $7 million to the American Heart Association and to spend $1.5 million notifying the public as to the status of its progress in reducing trans fats. The company also agreed to pay $7,500 to Ban Trans Fat and $7,500 to Ms. Fettke as well as to pay for the plaintiffs' legal fees (Garofoli 2005). Moreover, the fast food giant later agreed to eliminate trans fats from its menu items by 2008. In 2007, it settled on a canola oil blend, containing 0 grams of trans fat. All fried menu items are now trans fat-free, and the restaurant chain promises that all baked goods will be similarly "reformulated by the end of 2008" (McDonald's Corporation 2008a, para. 2).

In one of the latest battles over trans fats, a Washington, DC, physician, with backing from the CSPI, filed suit in June 2006) in the Superior Court of the District of Columbia against Yum! Brands, the parent of KFC, for himself and all Washington consumers of the popular chicken franchise (*Hoyte v. Yum! Brands. d/b/a KFC* 2006). Initially, the corporation had little to say other than that the suit was "frivolous" (Hirsch 2006). However, in April 2007, it announced that both KFC and Taco Bell had ceased using trans fats. US district judge James Robertson dismissed the lawsuit several days later. Meanwhile, the CSPI has launched a suit against Burger King that, while complying with no trans fats ordinances in New York and Philadelphia, continues to use partially hydrogenated oils elsewhere (*CSPI v. Burger King Corp.* 2008; Center for Science in the Public Interest 2007a).[53]

I Just Ate How Much??? Putting Calories on Menus
In order to maintain a healthy weight, the government recommends that a moderately active adult woman consume no more than about 2,000 calories a day; a moderately active adult man, roughly 2,500 (United States, Department of Health and Human Services and Department of Agriculture 2005, 23). A single McDonald's meal of a double quarter-pounder with cheese, large fries with ketchup, a large classic Coke, and a McFlurry with M and M's provides 2,180 calories (McDonald's Corporation 2008b). Although many fast food chains post nutritional information on their websites, including caloric and fat data,[54] and some provide such information on in-store wallboards,[55] restaurants have been resistant to the idea of posting such figures directly on in-store menus or on over-the-counter menu displays (National Restaurant Association 2008).

Believing that such readily available statistics are important to stemming the obesity epidemic, a number of jurisdictions have moved to require (or are considering moving toward requiring) that eating establishments (particularly fast food chains) provide nutritional facts on menus and menu boards. The industry has decided to fight back. Thus, for example, in December 2006, the New York City Board of Health passed an ordinance (Regulation 81.50) that would have required many of the city's fast food chains to list calories on menus (Severson 2006). The rule was quickly challenged by the New York State Restaurant Association on grounds that it was "expressly preempted by the Nutrition Labeling and Education Act of 1990 ... (21 U.S.C. §§ 301, 343, 343-1 (2006)," as well as on the basis that the regulation violated "its members' First Amendment rights" (*New York State Restaurant Association v. New York City Board of Health* 2007a, 352). Declining to reach the First Amendment claim, the court did acknowledge the city's authority to "mandate nutritional labeling by restaurants" but found the manner in which it had done so preempted by federal law (*ibid.*, 353). In January 2008, the city tried again, requiring large national chains to provide "point of purchase" nutritional information (New York City Law Department 2008). The move was immediately challenged by the New York State Restaurant Association, once more claiming federal preemption and First Amendment violation. This time, however, the court sided with the city (*New York State Restaurant Association v. New York City Board of Health* 2007b). The restaurant association has appealed.

Meanwhile, in March 2008, the San Francisco Board of Supervisors passed an ordinance requiring food chains with at least twenty restaurants state wide to display nutritional information. The California Restaurant Association is suing on grounds similar to those posed by its New York counterpart (Tucker 2008). According to the CSPI, more than twenty states, cities, and counties are currently considering legislation similar to that enacted in New York City and San Francisco (Center for Science in the Public Interest 2008).

Conclusion

Winners and Losers

For all the late night gag lines, and despite the lack of many actual cases, of the three US litigation fronts examined herein, plaintiffs in the food movement have been the most successful (for a summary of these cases, see Appendix 5.1 at the end of this chapter). Indeed, one could say that modern food litigation has mostly produced winners. From the perspective of plaintiff groups, wins can be counted in terms of such things as the ever-decreasing amount of trans fats in food products and the disappearance of high calorie sodas from school vending machines. Defendant industries also can probably count themselves winners. With only gentle nudging and at relatively little cost, they can now at least claim, as McDonald's does, "to fit every active lifestyle" and to provide "a range of quality foods" that fit nicely "into a balanced diet."[56] In fact, if there are losers, in this scenario, they are neither the plaintiff coalitions nor the defendant industries but, rather, the individuals such as Mr. Barber, who gained little beyond national ridicule (see, for example, Haltom and McCann 2004b).

The success of coalition plaintiffs in food litigation is admittedly clouded by a number of contributing factors – for example, the success of films such as Spurlock's *Super Size Me* and books such as Schlosser's *Fast Food Nation,* considerable news media attention to obesity and its attendant problems, a growing public consciousness about health, and, until recently, sluggish-to-flagging fast food sales.[57]

Litigation as Regulation

Nevertheless, undoubtedly, the threat of litigation has had a major role in recent agreements by food companies to modify their unhealthy ways. It also has presaged legislative regulations such as the New York and San Francisco menu mandates and, more recently, California's ban on cooking with trans fats (McGreevy 2008). Certainly, the industry has reacted in some predictable ways. Like tobacco (after all, until 2007 Altria owned Kraft as well as Philip Morris), fast food companies and junk food manufacturers have repeatedly invoked the "personal responsibility" mantra, and, like its fellow NRA though not quite as successfully, the restaurant association has pushed *for* liability shield laws and *against* menu nutritional information. At the same time, however, fast- and snack-food purveyors have been far more likely than their counterparts to concede fairly quickly to the demands of would-be litigators. Moreover, the food litigators, with very explicit regulatory intent, have cleverly avoided accusations that they are merely money-grubbing lawyers – for the most part, shunning direct payment. They have also avoided the spotlight that accompanies jury trials ending with massive awards and especially punitive damages. Indeed, industry defendants have opted for relatively quick settlement.

The reasons are several fold. First, everybody eats. Despite pretty obvious marketing to teenagers, tobacco is largely considered the problem of a weak-willed 25 percent of the adult population – a group that, despite the fact that it generally began using the highly addictive product as children, is supposed to know better by this point in history. As litigants, smokers tend to be fairly unsympathetic. And in spite of the pervasiveness of gun violence, most people are never faced down by a firearm – gun violence is usually "somebody else's problem." On the other hand, the threat of gun regulation *is* somebody else's problem, and those somebodies are highly interested and easily mobilized. Second, food litigators have tended to focus on children. These, after all, are the true innocents. And while the tactic has yet to yield fruit in *Pelman,* it has been quite successful in the soda and advertising arenas. Third, no doubt, one of the reasons that *Pelman* lagged was in mimicking so closely the tobacco litigations. Of particular importance, Bradley and Pelman requested of the court unspecified monetary damages. As Bryce Jensen (2001, 1379) notes, "[a] primary goal of litigation is to compensate an aggrieved party for past wrongs, and [that] can cause a plaintiff's focus to shift from public policy objectives to monetary damages." Moreover, children or no, litigants and attorneys seeking large money awards from institutional giants (especially such culturally embedded icons as McDonald's) can be rather easily portrayed as gold diggers – witness the "McDonald's coffee lady." On the other hand, as observed earlier in this chapter, the food litigators, having learned from the mistakes of their cigarette and gun brethren, largely eschewed monetary recompense, preferring actual public policy change.

Finally, the changes asked of the food industry have frankly been relatively easy to do. Philip Morris did not have a safe cigarette waiting in the wings. And one must recall that one of the few gun successes, the Smith and Wesson agreement, included promises by the gun maker to do what it was already planning on doing. On the other hand, the modifications requested of big food have either cost little and/or redounded to the goodwill of the industry. For example, for all of the initial hue and cry about the difficulty of eliminating trans fats, it has been fairly painless in the end. According to the New York City Department of Health and Mental Hygiene (2007, para. 10), "[t]he cost of healthier replacement products should not affect the price of menu items. Widely available, traditional vegetable oils, such as corn and soy, are already used extensively by New York City restaurants. Newly marketed *trans* fat-free oils with longer fry lives may cost more per gallon, but may also last longer, potentially making them cost-neutral." Moreover, while PepsiCola may have had to remove Pepsi from school vending machines, the drink was easily replaced by Gatorade, Tropicana Pure Premium, and Aquafina water, just to name a few permitted and Pepsi-owned alternatives.

The differences and similarities among the three litigation fronts we have examined suggest interesting conclusions about the possibilities for successful litigation strategies (see Table 5.1). First, it helps if plaintiffs or potential plaintiffs are perceived as being universal or, frankly, likable and acting in good faith. If the general public is unable to empathize or sympathize with the litigators, the well-resourced opposing side can easily mobilize public

Table 5.1

Comparison of multi-party litigation characteristics in tobacco, gun, and food cases

Litigation issue	Tobacco	Guns	Fast food
Potential plaintiffs perceived universal or sympathetic	no	no	yes
Large plaintiff attorney payoffs	yes	no	no
Public-private litigation partnership	yes	yes	no
Aggressive defendant legal strategy	yes	yes	yes
Aggressive defendant legislative strategy	yes	yes	yes
International implications	yes	no	yes

relations strategies that demonize their foes (for example, Haltom and McCann 2004a). This is particularly true in the context of American politics where "personal responsibility," if not always practised, is nonetheless thoroughly rooted in the national psyche.

Moreover, consenting adults, who presumably understand the consequences of their actions, face a rather straightforward and extremely aggressive product liability defence to their injury claims. Nonetheless, claims by unsuspecting consumers are harder to defend (also clearly the case with pharmaceuticals). Here, child victims are the most sympathetic. Their inclusion among plaintiffs elevates the political stakes and makes a case more difficult to defend. Indeed, among the most combustible elements in the issues we have assessed have been tobacco advertising directed to young people (for example, Joe Camel). The immediate result was that industry participants in the *Master Settlement Agreement* agreed to change their policy and come to terms in relatively short order.[58] With regard to junk food, where children and adolescents represent a vast proportion of the market, focus on their consumption habits and health consequences were certainly an effective part of the political strategy of those who sought industry changes.

Similarly rooted is the long-standing love-hate relationship that Americans have with the legal profession, the hate portion of which tends to emerge most forcefully when trial lawyers actually make money. Large attorney pay-offs, particularly such as those garnered in the *Master Settlement Agreement* can be easily exploited by defendant allies in the media (see, for example, Contrubis 1997; O'Beirne 2001). They have also fuelled efforts to enact legislative limitations on potential claims (shield laws, caps on punitive damages, and the like), and they have been used as effective examples of excess in the American system by those charged with developing "access to justice" reforms elsewhere. In all politics, might frequently makes right. But, might comes in many guises. Logically, it would seem that pairing the might of the plaintiffs bar with that of big city mayors or entire state governments would overwhelm the resources and political acumen of even the wealthiest and savviest of defendants. This, however, was only partially the case with tobacco and most decidedly not so with guns. Ironically, perhaps, the most successful of our plaintiffs, the CSPI, accepts no corporate or government grants.

Of course, the strategic moves of defendants are just as important as those of plaintiffs. As Marc Galanter (1974) suggests, the most powerful parties are those that can successfully exploit and shape the rules in multiple venues. Thus, we would expect, and the case studies demonstrate, that defendants in the position to act aggressively on more than one front will certainly do so. Finally, with the exception of guns, which are heavily regulated outside the United States in the systems we assess, the actions in American courts have implications that extend beyond national borders. In part, this is an obvious result of the reach of economic markets. Tobacco and food corporations (especially the fast food industry) are trans-national, extending as far and wide as profits will take them. This is equally true of a growing list of commodities, whose production and distributional networks are truly expansive. The consequences of product use that is observable in one location can be directly extrapolated to others. Whether legal liability traverses a corresponding itinerary depends upon local law regimes and institutional rules governing the accessibility of courts. Since the last quarter of the twentieth century, constitutional changes have occurred across a range of countries. Courts have achieved greater independence and are engaging politically significant issues that were traditionally addressed through the legislative and regulatory processes. This has helped to stimulate continued growth in trans-national networks of legal advocates and has encouraged judges to view themselves as members of an expanding community. Indeed, as early as 1994, Anne-Marie Slaughter (1994, 99) recognized that "[c]ourts are talking to one another all over the world" as they find themselves addressing similar issues.

Up until this point, we have been primarily concerned with the politics and policy aims of litigation in America, which has the most extensively developed multi-party litigation system in the world. As we have seen in the three preceding case studies, the results have been mixed on all counts – on political efficacy, regulatory effectiveness, and litigant success. However, what of the other advanced industrial nations, particularly those that share a common law tradition? In the following chapter, we turn our attention north to Canada, east to the United Kingdom, and west to Australia.

Appendix 5.1

Food litigation timeline

1998   StarLink genetically modified corn licensed by the US Environmental Protection Agency for limited use in animal feed, industrial non-food uses, and seed increase.

2000   Alliance for Bio-Integrity sues Food and Drug Administration (FDA) for, among other things, failure to subject safety statement on genetically modified foods (GM) to proper notice-and-comment procedures. Judge finds that the FDA had acted in accordance with statutory requirements (*Alliance for Bio-Integrity v. Shalala* 2000, 170).

StarLink discovered in Taco Bell taco shells for sale in grocery stores. StarLink-adulterated corn products subject to massive recall.

2001   Aventis, maker of StarLink, enters into agreement with the attorneys general of seventeen states to pay 25 cents per bushel to growers and buffer growers to control corn grown from StarLink hybrids and corn grown within 660 feet of corn grown with StarLink hybrids.

Aventis settles with Taco Bell franchisees agreeing to a $60 million payment for lost business.

A class, including American vegetarians and Hindus, sues McDonald's Corporation over French fries, asserting claims for violations of the consumer fraud laws and common law principles of all fifty states and alleging that the restaurant chain provided false and misleading nutritional information to consumers (*Block v. McDonald's* 2002).

2002   StarLink consumer lawsuit settled for $9 million, mostly consisting of customer coupons (*In re: Starlink Corn Products Liability Litigation* 2002).

In large class action, non-StarLink farmers, claiming broad economic harm, sue Aventis and Garst Seed. Farmers base suit on theories of public nuisance and private public nuisance (*In re: Starlink Corn Products Liability Litigation* 2002).

McDonald's settles Hindu French fries suit with denial of all allegations and liability in exchange for $10 million in charitable donations to vegetarian, Hindu, child nutrition, and Jewish educational organizations, a corporate apology to Hindus and vegetarians, and the establishment of "an advisory board to make reports and recommendations to McDonald's about dietary restrictions that apply to various types of vegetarians, as well as guidelines for companies who market to vegetarians" (*Block v. McDonald's* 2002, 2).

Caesar Barber sues fast food industry participants for himself and other similarly situated individuals, claiming that consumption of their products are responsible for his obesity-related health problems (*Barber v. McDonald's* 2002).

Barber drops fast food suit.

2003   Aventis and Garst agree to settle with farmer class for about $112 million (*In re: Starlink Corn Products Liability Litigation* 2003).

Obese teenagers, Jazlyn Bradley and Ashley Pelman, sue McDonald's claiming that the fast food giant marketed its product as nutritious while failing to disclose deleterious health effects in violation of New York law; that its promotional techniques, including the ubiquitous "Happy Meal," particularly aimed to induce children to ingest its product, also in contravention of state statute; that it acted "negligently in selling food products that are high in cholesterol, fat, salt and sugar when studies show that such foods cause obesity and detrimental health effects"; that it failed to warn consumers that its ingredients could lead to obesity and associated health problems; and that it "acted negligently in marketing food products that were physically and psychologically addictive" (*Pelman v. McDonald's* 2003b).

District court judge rejects *Pelman* claims.

San Francisco attorney Stephen Joseph announces plans to sue Kraft Foods for the use of trans fats in Oreos.

Kraft announces plans to undertake "a sweeping, global overhaul of the way it creates, packages, and promotes its foods," including "eliminate[ing] – or greatly reduce[ing] – *trans* fats in all of its cookies and crackers" (Horovitz 2003, 1).

Joseph drops plans to sue Kraft.

2004   McDonald's announces phase-out of super-sized menu items.

Representing a potentially large class, Katherine Fettke files suit against McDonald's for failure to keep promise of reducing use of trans fats (*Fettke v. McDonald's Corp.* 2004).

2005   Second Circuit Court reinstates *Pelman* and remands for further proceedings (*Pelman v. McDonald's* 2005a).

Center for Science in the Public Interest (CSPI) announces plans to sue Pepsi and Coke in Massachusetts court for selling soda in schools.

McDonald's settles *Fettke* case, agreeing to donate $7 million to the American Heart Association and to spend $1.5 million notifying the public as to the status of its progress in reducing trans fats. The company also agrees to pay $7,500 to BanTransFat.com and $7,500 to Ms. Fettke as well as to pay the plaintiffs' legal fees.

2006   District Court allows *Pelman* to proceed. Case remains in discovery phase.

American Beverage Association announces plans to develop school guidelines for soft drink sales.

Soft drink companies agree to pull high-calorie drinks from schools.

The CPSI drops Massachusetts soda litigation.

The CPSI issues letter of intent to pursue a class action suit against Viacom and Kellogg's for marketing unhealthy food to children.

The CPSI backs trans fat suit brought by Washington, DC, physician and all District of Columbia consumers of Yum! Brand products, including KFC and Taco Bell (*Hoyte v. Yum! Brands d/b/a KFC* 2006).

New York City Board of Health passes ordinance forcing fast food chains to post nutritional facts on menus and menu boards.

2007   Kellogg's announces worldwide phase-out of advertising to children under the age of twelve unless foods met nutrition guidelines for caloric, fat, sugar, and sodium content. Affected foods include such long-time childhood favourites as Pop-Tarts and Froot Loops cereal.

The CSPI drops suit against Kellogg's.

Additional food companies, including General Mills, and television stations, including Viacom-owned Nickelodeon, agree to limit advertising and licensing of children's characters on junk food.

Yum! Brands announces that both KFC and Taco Bell have ceased using trans fats. *Hoyte v. Yum! Brands* dismissed.

"Commonsense consumption laws," which limit "the civil liability of any manufacturer, distributor, seller, or retailer of food or nonalcoholic beverages in cases in which liability is based on an individual's weight gain, obesity, or obesity-related health condition that results from that individual's long-term consumption of a food or beverage," passed in twenty-three states and are pending in eight others.

US District Court rules New York City menu law preempted by federal statute.

2008   The CSPI launches trans fat suit against Burger King over continued use of partially hydrogenated oils (*CSPI v. Burger King Corp.* 2008).

New York City announces new menu ordinance.

New York City menu ordinance upheld by district court. Case is currently on appeal.

San Francisco Board of Supervisors passes ordinance requiring food chains with at least twenty restaurants statewide to display nutritional information. California State Restaurant Association sues.

6
International Developments in the Politics of Litigation

Thus far, the focus of our analysis has been on group-based litigation in the United States. We have seen an ongoing struggle to reconcile the tension between dealing with large-scale conflict and the broader social and economic problems such episodes entail and addressing the individual issues that can be dwarfed or minimized when consolidated with many others. We have also seen the nakedly political nature of such litigation. As we noted earlier, although the typical lawsuit is best represented as a dyadic conflict, with one plaintiff and one defendant, the need has arisen historically to accommodate other scenarios, particularly those in which multiple plaintiffs who have similar complaints against a common defendant are consolidated into a single action. Indeed, such cases pepper the agenda of nineteenth-century American courts, and those that have been charged with dealing with the problem have referred to earlier conflicts etched into British legal history for guidance. Although the two systems can point to a common historical legacy, by the early twentieth century it was clear that they would take divergent paths.

As we discussed in Chapter 1, the general trend in the United States until recently has been to further accommodate mass litigation, leading some observers to project that a collective format could serve an important regulatory function by providing a means of accessing the courts to individuals whose claims were too small to pursue individually (for example, Kalven and Rosenfield 1941). In this way, a mechanism was created to exert pressure on a relatively powerful entity (usually a large corporation or industry group or a government department), whose activities cut a wide swath through the community, in order to change its course (or, at the very least, to reflect upon its impact). Meanwhile, the British high bench delivered a severely restrictive interpretation of key language in its *Civil Procedure Rules* that required "same interest in a claim" among "more than one person" in order to proceed with a representative action. Indeed, in *Markt and Co. v. Knight Steamship Co.* (1910), the Court interpreted the "same interest" clause quite literally. Thus, by mid-century, the class action form was embraced in the United States, while representative actions languished under the weight of nearly impenetrable threshold criteria in the United Kingdom and, by extension, in the commonwealth jurisdictions where judges looked to legal precedent emanating from London for guidance. At the turn of the twenty-first century, the US system of class actions and consolidated mass litigation was by far the most developed in the world, but political and economic conditions had changed and demand for structural legal reforms stretched across the globe. For a somewhat broader perspective on the issues, we first consider the various activities that were taking place, most of which have occurred since the 1990s, in a range of systems beyond the United States and then explore the British situation a bit more closely. Finally, we consider parallel developments in Canada and Australia, whose systems, like that in the United States, were heavily influenced by the British legacy.

Taking a Wider View

A number of scholars have argued that the processes of globalization, which include the cross-border transportation of goods and capital, the international movement of people, the development of new information technologies, and a heightened interest in issues such as intellectual property and human rights, have corroded traditional notions of sovereignty and are fashioning a new global legal order (Shapiro 1993; Tate and Vallinder 1995; Teubner 1997; Buxbaum 2004). At the least, these issues have piqued scholarly interest in international law and tribunals (for example, Unah 1998; Schulte 2004; Kennedy 2004). At the same time, international and domestic courts have been empowered with more significant and independent decisional authority, as constitutional reform movements swept the globe in the late twentieth and early twenty-first centuries (for example, Hirschl 2004; Dickson 2007; Russell and O'Brien 2001; Stone Sweet 2000). These dynamics have a number of important implications in national and international politics, as courts become higher-level players in governance and policy-making. Indeed, as new justices have assumed positions on their nation's high courts under conditions of enhanced institutional independence, some have led their colleagues in more assertive directions, entertaining a wider array of legal challenges, especially to actions and products of relatively powerful entities, and thus drawing fire from critics for engaging in judicial activism (for example, Dickson 2007; Russell and O'Brien 2001).

Moreover, Anne-Marie Slaughter (2003; 2004) has observed that judges, particularly those who sit on their nations' highest tribunals, are drawn to view themselves as holding membership in a shared community. As early as 1994, she observed that "[c]ourts are talking to one another all over the world" in a process of cross-fertilization that has continued apace (Slaughter

1994, 99; compare with Goldsworthy 2006; Opeskin 2001; Manfredi 1990). Several current justices of the Supreme Court of the United States, where the·issues of independence and authority were resolved long ago, openly admit that the jurisprudential experience of the courts of other nations, while not determinative, can be relevant to their own deliberations regarding strictly domestic issues (at least on their face) (for example, Justice Kennedy's majority opinion in *Lawrence v. Texas* (2003) (sodomy); Justice Ginsberg's dissent in *Gratz v. Bollinger* (2003) (affirmative action); and Justice Kennedy's majority opinion in *Roper v. Simmons* (2005)· (juvenile capital punishment).[1] Moreover, in his remarks to a 2003 meeting of the American Society of International Law, Justice Breyer had this to say:

> [W]e find an increasing number of issues, including constitutional issues, where the decisions of foreign courts help by offering points of comparison. This change reflects the "globalization" of human rights, a phrase that refers to the ever-stronger consensus (now nearly worldwide) as to the importance of protecting basic human rights, the embodiment of that consensus in legal documents, such as national constitutions and international treaties, and the related decision to enlist judges – i.e., independent judiciaries – as instruments to help make that protection effective in practice. Judges in different countries increasingly apply somewhat similar legal phrases to somewhat similar circumstances, for example in respect to multi-racial populations, growing immigration, economic demands, environmental concerns, modern technologies, and instantaneous media communication. Thus, it is not surprising to find that the European Court of Human Rights has issued decisions involving, for example, campaign finance laws and free expression or that the Supreme Court of India has written extensively about "affirmative action." (Breyer 2003; also see Badinter and Breyer 2004)

As we have noted, the search for universality, or at least a wider perspective, is not confined to the Supreme Court of the United States (see, for example, Galanter 1966). Jurists, lawyers, and lawmakers in other systems are also engaged in a similar quest as they address issues in the making (Slaughter 2003; 2004). Indeed, some courts have a long-established tradition of drawing upon the experience and jurisprudence of sister tribunals.[2] Robert Kagan (1996, 7) has observed that, although a range of forces push toward international convergence of law and legal solutions, national identities and cultures have produced idiosyncratic "legal styles and institutions [that] stubbornly resist homogenization." In comparison to others, the US system assumes, even encourages, a high degree of contentiousness. It is a system of "adversarial legalism" (see especially Kagan 2001). "American judges are more diverse, more political, more autonomous than" their counterparts in other countries, "and their decisions are less uniform. Law in the United States is more malleable, open to novel legal and policy arguments put forth by parties and their lawyers" (Kagan 1996, 9).[3]

Although hierarchically structured, legal institutions are far from being politically unified, encouraging innovative advocacy by parties at each stage. The American political culture and federal structure chafes at centralized decision-making power and holds out the expectation that the decision-making process is not beyond an individual's reach and that she can have her "day in court." Other cultures place more trust and responsibility in concentrated government authority, and so their law tends to derive from a more centralized process that is not subject to ongoing challenge and interpretation. This means that adjudication – and thus, litigants, lawyers, and judges – are not as prominent in the law-making process as they are in the United States. It also means that litigation has been de-emphasized as a problem-solving strategy. However, those traditional markers seem to be fading (for example, Heaps and Jackson 2007), and symptoms hint that the malleability and openness virus may be infecting court systems in other developed states, leading some observers to ask: "Are we becoming more American?" (Betts 2006, unpaginated webpage). Courts, whose members do not reflexively back away from legal challenges to legislative actions or from engaging controversies spun off from hotly contested political issues generate expectations and signal the legal community that it may be worthwhile to pursue cases at law that otherwise would be directed to other institutions.

With regard to collective litigation, the US system clearly has a wealth of experience, thus providing a point of reference, if often a negative one, that can be useful. As Kagan (2001, 120) astutely notes, "[t]he class action is a distinctively American legal invention, generally eschewed by other political systems but quite congruent with American political propensities" (also see Sherman 2002). A few jurisdictions adopted procedures to address such issues in the late 1970s to early 1980s, openly acknowledging the American model in doing so.[4] There was a flurry of activity, however, in the late 1990s, as judges and lawmakers, particularly across the developed world, finally recognized that some adjustment to accommodate group litigation was essential. For the most part, architects of reform acknowledged the US experience while explicitly stating their intention to avoid what were by then widely understood to be gross excesses embedded in the American model. Writing in 1996, as the European Union (EU) was considering the adoption of procedural law changes to recognize representative litigation as a cause of action, a leading Swedish scholar observed: "In modern society, which is directed towards mass production, mass distribution, mass information, and mass consumption of goods and services, it is much more common than before for large numbers of people to be injured by a defective product or otherwise negatively affected by incidents or measures taken. In such situations, claims or disputes arise that are similar for large numbers of people. The existing European litigation procedures, the principles of which were laid down more than half a century ago in most countries, are not structured to accommodate these kinds of disputes" (Lindblom 1996, 10). Per Henrik Lindblom (*ibid.*, 14) goes on to note that, although the "class action was certainly born in mediaeval England," the rules became so severe that it was nearly non-existent in that country for some time and that the civil law countries of Europe have only recently begun to consider it. In addition, he confirms that the American system has attracted many critics, with the "most discussed abuse of the class action [being] the risk that the lawyers for the plaintiffs (the group members) will accept a bad settlement in order to avoid the trial and earn fast money for themselves" (Lindblom 1997, 823).

As the twentieth century drew to a close, an increasing number of decision makers around the globe had begun to take the reform process seriously and to consider the options for allowing easier entrée to representative litigation. Lindblom's observations regarding the underlying social and economic realities were shared by many. The processes of mass production, distribution, and consumption, as well as a general swell in the number of mass accidents and product injuries, which were occurring in a legal context of increasingly independent and invigorated judicial institutions, had created conditions leading to waves of litigation and growing demand to accommodate multi-party actions in a wide array of systems.[5] To do so would enhance access to a broader range of individuals who had experienced harm, particularly those without the financial means to pursue a grievance alone and/or whose claims were sufficiently small that they simply would not justify the effort to file as individual actions. In addition, it had become clear that consolidation of similar claims made good sense for pragmatic reasons. From the courts' perspective, trying a single bundle of claims together is far less time consuming and costly than trying them each individually. Moreover, addressing a series of similar cases holds the undesirable potential for producing different outcomes and likely extends the life of a broad-based and repeating conflict indefinitely. Whereas, consolidation can yield a single result, which, even if appealed, has a manageable life cycle. Thus, encouraging consolidation of multi-party litigation has considerable appeal for reasons of economy, consistency, efficiency, and access to justice. In addition, some of those charged with developing a model for reform also noted that allowing individual plaintiffs to pool their claims and resources would give them greater leverage to negotiate, thus effecting a general deterrent influence against wrongdoing by powerful parties (usually large corporations) that were faced with enhanced potential risk – a regulatory influence not unlike that envisioned by Harry Kalven and Maurice Rosenfield (1941) for the American class action.

On the other hand, the US approach is often viewed with a degree of skepticism at home as well as abroad.[6] Individualized justice may not be realized. Indeed, claimants whose cases are consolidated with many others may well find their particular grievance and story of hardship entirely lost in the interest of achieving a global resolution. This consequence of aggregating claims has due process implications and has produced ongoing debates regarding the relative merits of notification procedures and "opt in" and "opt out" regimes. Courts in most countries require that potential class members be notified of the pending action and affirmatively opt in, agreeing to be represented and to be bound by the outcome, as opposed to being provided the opportunity to opt out under the US model. Moreover, if multiple parties' access to the courts to consolidate claims is too liberal, undue pressure can be brought to bear on defendant corporations, raising the stakes so much that it forces them to settle or risk bankruptcy (see, for example, Schuck 1995, 958). Some view this action as little more than legal hostage taking or "judicial blackmail" by plaintiff attorneys (Friendly 1973, 120). This refrain has, on occasion, been sounded in the United States and echoed by those considering reform in other systems.[7]

For example, in overturning certification of a truly massive class, consisting of all nicotine-dependent people in the United States, and the estates and family members of those who had died after years of tobacco use, a Fifth Circuit Court panel stated bluntly: "[C]lass certification creates insurmountable pressure on defendants to settle, whereas individual trials would not. The risk of facing an all-or-nothing verdict presents too high a risk, even when the probability of an adverse judgment is low. These settlements have been referred to as judicial blackmail" (*Castano v. American Tobacco Company* 1996, 746; also see, for example, Sobol 1991). In addition, in another often-cited opinion, Judge Richard Posner, writing for a Seventh Circuit Court panel to reverse a district court's class certification of haemophiliacs who had contracted HIV aids from a contaminated blood supply, stated: "One jury, consisting of six persons (the standard federal civil jury nowadays consists of six regular jurors and two alternates), will hold the fate of an industry in the palm of its hand ... With the aggregate stakes in the tens or hundreds of millions of dollars, or even in the billions, it is not a waste of judicial resources to conduct more than one trial, before more than six jurors, to determine whether a major segment of the international pharmaceutical industry is to follow the asbestos manufacturers into Chapter 11" (*In re: Rhone-Poulenc Rorer, Inc.* 1995, 1300). Indeed, in its 2003 report, recommending reforms to ease restrictions on multi-party litigation, the Law Reform Commission of Ireland (2003, 36) used Posner's "fate of an industry" quote in noting serious criticisms of the American system. Law reformers generally have stood firmly against the notion of introducing juries to their systems, particularly in complex, multi-party actions, where they would hold considerable power. Juries are perceived to be far too receptive to claims against deep-pocketed defendant corporations in such cases. Moreover, British Lord Denning, in an often quoted comment on the attractiveness of the US contingency fee system to plaintiffs, stated in a 1983 opinion: "As a moth is drawn to the light, so is a litigant drawn to the United States. If he can only get his case into their courts, he stands to win a fortune" (*Smith Kline and French Lab. Ltd. v. Bloch* 1983, 74).

In addition, most economically advanced countries outside the United States have long-standing and well-developed medical and social welfare programs, providing administrative remedies for harms and grievances that are generally addressed by litigation in the United States (part of Kagan's [2001] notion of "adversarial legalism"). Indeed, nations across the EU have set up extensive public insurance systems to compensate individuals for occupation-related injuries and disabilities.[8] Often, litigation is also allowed, and, in many cases, it is supported by labour unions and other organizations, but compensation is generally limited to lost wages and medical expenses associated with the disability.[9] Most systems are also quite flexible, allowing new and unanticipated issues to arise. This was the case with the asbestos problem, where symptoms were occuring decades after exposure, and the number of related claims has escalated considerably since the 1990s, as it has in the United States. A few large awards have resulted, but such cases tend to be filed exclusively by individuals presenting unusual and extenuating circumstances (see, for example, *Ward v. Newalls Insulation Co and Cape Contracts Ltd* [1998], in which £700,000 was awarded).[10]

Nonetheless, the regulation and enforcement regime has been far from flawless. As we shall discuss in this chapter, the British system fell grimly short in heading off litigation, and Cristina Poncibò (2005) reports that a series of regulatory failures since the 1990s have highlighted imperfections in the European system and shaken confidence among the population that they will be protected from unforeseeable harm, thus leading some to call for reforms to allow wider access to the courts. Among the more serious incidents were those involving food safety and health regulations. The British bout with mad cow disease, unclear messages from officials regarding its transmissibility to humans, and, finally, a delayed ban on all beef imports from the United Kingdom with wide-scale eradication of suspect animals in farms across several EU countries, has constituted an unwelcome drama that has done little to reassure the public (*ibid.*, 13; see, for example, Ratzan 1997). Other recent incidents involving foot and mouth disease, E. coli, and avian flu, among others, have given the appearance of a system lurching from one emergency to another and have shaken confidence among some quarters in the EU regulatory regime (MacMaoláin 2007). Indeed, mass production and distribution of food products, as well as controversies regarding genetic modification and broad-scale use of pesticides, not only exacerbate this type of problem but also challenge the ability of regulation and enforcement to keep pace (Holland and Pope 2003; Alemanno 2007). Although obesity represents a mounting health problem in the United Kingdom, the trans fat issue has thus far not translated into litigation. Despite the fact that two of its European neighbours have initiated nation-wide bans (Denmark in 2003 and Switzerland in 2008) and several countries have enacted strict labelling laws, the British approach has thus far relied upon voluntary change within the food industry, and evidence suggests that some degree of movement is occurring, likely an effort to avoid government regulation and legal liability (for example, Blake 2007; Food Standards Agency 2007).

For those situations that end in litigation, many governments have provided public legal aid to enhance the accessibility of the system.[11] In early 2003, the European Commission issued a directive on legal aid to improve "access to justice" by establishing "minimum standard rules for the availability of legal aid for litigants in cross-border civil and commercial lawsuits ... to assure that all persons can assert their rights in the courts even if their personal financial situation makes it impossible for them to bear the costs of the proceedings. Legal aid would cover all court costs from pre-litigation advice to appeal costs to costs directly connected with the cross-border dimension of the dispute."[12] However, in the United Kingdom, given the growing financial burden associated with such programs, recent years have seen declines in their overall coverage and benefits. For example, Christopher Hodges (2001, 308) reports that "[l]egal aid began as a post-war welfare benefit covering 80 percent of the population ... Its scope expanded to the mid-1980s but then reached a crisis up to the mid-1990s, by which time eligibility had fallen to 48 percent of households." Coupled with the "loser pays" rule and restrictions in most jurisdictions against American-style contingency fee agreements, the system, while ostensibly providing "access to justice" to a large portion of the population, actually served as a deterrent to all but the claims most likely to be successful. By the early 1990s, a few systems had allowed some form of contingency fees (for example, Ontario and Australia), and, with its 1998 reform legislation directed at accommodating a form of multi-party action, the British House of Commons also enacted provisions to allow conditional fee agreements in most civil litigation circumstances. In addition, the 2003 EC directive also allowed contingency fees in order to promote access to justice.[13]

In an attempt to address the rapidly changing realities of life, the European Parliament and Council issued a directive to member states in 1998 for enactment of a policy to allow some form of collective litigation by the end of 2000.[14] EC Directive 98/27 on Injunctions for the Protection of Consumers'

Interests suggests that "qualified entities" – either organizations (for example, consumer associations) or independent public trustees (for example, administrative agencies) – should be assigned rights of action, allowing them to file "group litigation" on behalf of a collection of consumers harmed in some way by a defendant's conduct, such as by unfair sales and contract practices (Sherman 2002, 418; Koch 2001). This prompted reform across Europe to allow for injunctive relief, as suggested by the directive, with most countries taking care to avoid creating incentives for entrepreneurial lawyering and legal blackmail, limiting the options for seeking damages. As Harald Koch (2001, 357-58) describes the primary thrust,

> group representation in Europe differ[s] from American and Canadian class actions in two important ways. First, there is no method of self-appointment of an individual champion (plaintiff) and no concept of an individual private Attorney General, whose initiative is fostered by fee incentives or by an alluring contingency fee arrangement. To be sure, this may be well-deserved because of the risk assumed and the attorney's hard work; however, in the European tradition – although this may be slightly over-simplified – we entrust the public interest to public institutions rather than to private law enforcers ... There is a second crucial difference between the class action and the European style collective actions, and that is the latter's emphasis on injunctive relief rather than on damages (although in some countries, damages, especially symbolic and non-material, can also be sought by an association).

Thus, representative litigation, under this scheme, is overtly regulatory (for example, see Garth, Nagel, and Plager 1988). The primary thrust is to provide a mechanism for seeking injunctive relief that is in the "public interest." Damage awards are generally connected to individual actions, with judgments tailored to specific circumstances. A few jurisdictions (for example, France, Greece, Norway, and Sweden) allow group damage claims, but awards tend to be small (symbolic), and punitive damages can be awarded with the provision that lump sums be donated for charitable purposes rather than distributed among the claimants (*ibid.,* 359-60). The initial approach taken in several other countries (for example, Germany and Italy) is to address the problem of unfair, even illegal, terms often written into consumer contracts, a situation that is unlikely to produce individual litigation and thus is best addressed on a mass scale, with clear regulatory implications (see, for example, Taruffo 2001, 411-12; Poncibò 2005). As the member states experiment with varying forms, the likelihood is that the European Commission will find it necessary to harmonize in order to help simplify what can be quite complex legal issues. In addition, the EU will likely face the same problem that has arisen in the United States, of similar cases flowing through courts in different jurisdictions that carry the potential for conflicting outcomes, giving rise to multi-district consolidation procedures.

Despite considerable differences in tradition, history, and social and political cultures as well as variations in legal forms and structures, the worldwide trend seems to be in the direction of accommodating, even if in small ways, group litigation. Indeed, with the exception of litigation against the gun industry (among those issues we have considered in this text) and others that might be highly context-driven, the core issue of group claims is clearly transnational – for example, the effects of substances or products on human life and economic well-being. This is probably a reflection of the growth of global markets and the reach of international corporations, the transnational flow of capital, goods, and people, the relative ease of transactions of all types (facilitated by the development of the Internet and other communication technologies), and related activities. The importance of the judiciary to the process of addressing such controversies also reflects constitutional reform and an enhanced centrality of courts in the governing system. The British provided early guidance, as we have seen, but then moved to minimize group procedures at the turn of the twentieth century. Recent reforms, however, have produced a new shift toward a more accommodating format.

United Kingdom

The United Kingdom has a long-recorded history of group-based legal actions, dating to the time of feudal lords and tenants, whereby the landlords provided protection and access to manorial lands in exchange for a tithe – a portion of whatever was produced from the use of the land, labour on behalf of the manor, or other like payment. By banding together, tenants not only enhanced their bargaining power but also gradually accrued sets of basic privileges under the law that could be invoked against unfair actions by landlords. Two types of courts operated in medieval England. The common law courts generally held to the standard dyadic form, with one plaintiff and a single defendant, unless there were parties in joint ownership or otherwise identically situated. The chancery courts of equity utilized a more flexible approach to avoid a multiplicity of proceedings where there were many with a similar claim or interest in a dispute (see, for example, Kazanjian 1973, 411).[15] As Lord Cottenham stated in *Wallworth v. Holt* (1841, 244), "I think it is the duty of this Court to adapt its practice and course of proceeding to the existing state of society, and not by too strict an adherence to forms and rules, established under different circumstances, to decline to administer justice, and to enforce rights for which there is no other remedy."[16] In 1873, the chancery and common law courts were consolidated under a single set of rules.[17] Although early decisions continued to apply a liberal principle in representative actions,[18] the House of Lords eventually imposed a more restrictive approach. At the turn of the twenty-first century, their now long-departed legal engagements, understood as a precursor to today's group litigation scenario, are part of the documented history and are occasionally referenced by judges trying to address often difficult and complex questions.

Judges at the turn of the last century were considerably less distant from those precedential etchings, and some left opinion brush strokes indicating the early skirmishes as useful points of reference.[19] One particularly good example is found in a House of Lords decision in 1901, *Bedford v. Ellis* (1901, 1). The case was brought by a group of farmers against the Duke of Bedford under provisions of an 1828 act of Parliament, establishing access to the public Covent Garden Market for purposes of selling produce. For his part, the duke was recognized as the owner and manager of the market. As Lord Macnaghten noted in his opinion, the act distinguished between "those who sell their own produce and those who are ordinary dealers in the market or middlemen," allowing the latter to be taxed by the duke but protecting the former from any such toll. However, despite this legislation, the farmers were being taxed. Arguing that their statutory rights had been infringed, "Ellis and five other persons, on behalf of themselves and all others, the growers of fruit, flowers, vegetables, roots or herbs ... brought an action against ... the Duke of Bedford." The duke contended that the growers held no proprietary rights and that he should determine who should pay a toll for a market slot (he was the duke, after all). Moreover, the petitioners were in varying positions (for example, some held permanent stalls, some seasonal; some sold directly to the public, and others both to the public and to the middlemen who resold to the public), and their claims should have been separated for individual consideration. Lord Macnaghten rejected both arguments. On the second question, he cited several nineteenth-century precedents, noting:

> I doubt whether it is accurate to say that in the case of representative suits we have advanced a long way since the days of Lord Eldon [1751-1838]. It is, of course, not necessary nowadays to go to a Court of Law in order to establish legal rights. But in all other respects I think the rule as to representative suits remains very much as it was a hundred years ago. From the time it was first established it has been recognised as a simple rule resting merely upon convenience. It is impossible, I think, to read such judgments as those delivered by Lord Eldon in *Adair v. New River Co.*, in 1805, and in *Cockburn v. Thompson,* in 1809, without seeing that Lord Eldon took as broad and liberal a view on this subject as anybody could desire. "The strict rule," he said, "was that all persons materially interested in the subject of the suit, however numerous, ought to be parties ... but that being a general rule established for the convenient administration of justice must not be adhered

to in cases to which consistently with practical convenience it is incapable of application." "It was better," he added, "to go as far as possible towards justice than to deny it altogether." He laid out of consideration the case of persons suing on behalf of themselves and all others, "for in a sense," he said, "they are before the Court." (*ibid.*, 2)

Thus, as of 1901, the propriety of representative action was considered settled law. However, it was also under challenge, and Macnaghten did not write for a unanimous panel. Indeed, a short ten years later, the British high bench issued a much less "broad and liberal view."

The *Markt* Principle

In *Markt* (1910), in which the owners of cargo on a sunken ship attempted to sue on behalf of forty-four others, Lord Justice Moulton, for the majority in the English Court of Appeals, stated that the requirement for a "common interest" meant that there must be issues common to all group members and the relief sought must be the same. This definition meant that representative or class actions would be virtually impossible except in those rare instances when the class members' claims were identical. Moreover, because Lord Moulton asserted that "damages are personal," each claim must be addressed individually in order to make the correct assessment (*ibid.*, 1041). The defendants were the owners of the steamship *Knight Commander*, which set off from New York in 1904 laden with cargo destined for delivery in Japan. The plaintiffs were merchants doing business in the United States and Japan, each of which had contracted individually with the defendant. Unfortunately, the *Knight Commander*'s trip took place during the Russo-Japanese war, and it was stopped and sunk by a Russian cruiser on the ground that the ship's papers were not satisfactory and that it was carrying contraband of war. Two merchants filed suit on behalf of all of the others for damages resulting from breach of contract and for secreting contraband items among the legal cargo, thus jeopardizing the entire shipment, relying upon *Duke of Bedford* (1901) as the controlling precedent. However, Lord Moulton read the prior case law differently:

> The essential condition of a representative action is that the persons who are to be represented have the same interests as the plaintiff in one and the same cause or matter. There must therefore be a common interest alike in the sense that its subject and its relation to that subject must be the same. As I have already stated, Lord Macnaghten phrases it thus: "Given a common interest and a common grievance, a representative suit is in order if the relief sought is in its nature beneficial to all whom the plaintiff proposes to represent."

Whether we start from the language of the rule or from this authoritative interpretation of it, the present actions ... fail in every particular to answer the necessary condition of a representative action. The counsel for the plaintiffs suggests that the people in the list are in similar circumstances, because they shipped goods under similar bills of lading in the same ship. Assuming, for the sake of argument, that this is so ... each of these parties made a separate contract of shipment in respect of different goods entitling him to its performance by the defendants and to damages in case of non-performance. It may be that the claims are alike in nature, and that the litigation in respect of them will have much in common. But they are in no way connected; there is no common interest. Defences may exist against some of the shippers which do not exist against the others ... so that no representative action can settle the rights of the individual members of the class ... The proper domain of a representative action is where there are like rights against a common fund, or where a class of people have a community of interest in some subject-matter. Here there is nothing of the kind. The defendants have made separate contracts which may or may not be identical in form with different persons. And that is all. (*ibid.*, 1040-41)

Thus, according to the Court in *Markt,* representative actions can go forward if the individual claimants have essentially identical cases against a common defendant. Lord Vaughan Williams, in the lead opinion, was also skeptical that one litigant could adequately represent the interests of others, especially without their informed consent. To have similar claims does not create a "community of interest." The 1910 precedent has proven to be a serious deterrent to representative litigation in the United Kingdom, particularly when combined with the "loser pays" fee scheme. And although *Markt* was not considered binding precedent across the British Commonwealth, it was considered authoritative and dampened group actions in a number of countries for the better part of the twentieth century.

Finally, in 1981, a full seventy years later, some changes began to take shape (Andrews 2001, 253-55). One small, but important, change arose from a public company shareholder case in the Chancery Division of the High Court (*Prudential Assurance v. Newman Industries* 1981, 255). A group of plaintiffs filed a representative action on behalf of all of the other shareholders, charging the corporate board with misrepresentation. Judge Vinelott, rejecting the *Markt* "identical interest" rule, found that if there is a "common ingredient in the cause of action of each" plaintiff the case could go forward on the question of fraud. Since damages must be calculated precisely for each party, class members could follow after the first stage of the case was completed with individual negligence claims, establishing an entitlement to damages.

Another 1981 decision (*E.M.I. Records v. Riley* 1981) reinforced this change in direction. This case involved wide-scale pirating of recorded music. A few artists filed a representative action on behalf of all of the members of the British Phonographic Industry (BPI) for copyright violations and to recover losses attributable to improper sales. The court awarded damages, with the money placed into an account controlled by BPI, whose members made and distributed most recorded music in the United Kingdom and who had agreed that damages from the litigation be pooled to support any related legal actions on their behalf.[20] Moreover, in a pivotal defendant representative action, *Irish Shipping Ltd. v. Commercial Union Assurance Co (The Irish Rowan)* (1991), the Court of Appeals distinguished *Markt* and allowed the case to proceed because it would be exceedingly inconvenient to do otherwise. The *Irish Rowan* involved a group of plaintiff ship owners and seventy-seven defendant insurance companies, each with separate contracts and no overlapping coverage. The court found that, because of a common provision (an underwriter clause) in each insurance contract, members of the defendant class had the same interest. Indeed, the clause stated that any settlement of a claim by one insurer would be considered binding upon all of the others. Given this fact, the court held that a representative action was the proper form, and the logic of the *Irish Rowan* decision has been extended ever since (see, for example, *Bank of America National Trust and Savings Association v. Taylor* 1992; *National Bank of Greece SA v. RM Outhwaite* 2001).

Contemporary Issues
Asbestos has produced some difficult legal issues in the United Kingdom, as it has around the globe, and, not unlike the stories elsewhere, the British record is something less than stellar. Asbestos consumption, and thus exposure, was higher in the United Kingdom and Europe than it was in the United States from the initial periods of use in the early twentieth century, and it declined more slowly (for example, White 2004, 189-90). Although a workers compensation system was instituted early on, paid benefits were small and hard to get (Castleman 1996; Tweedale 2000). As an indication of loss of faith in the regulatory system to provide adequate and timely remedies, and a sign that courts had become more significant players in the governing process, claimants (individually and in combination) began to focus more attention on the judicial process. In the early 2000s, asbestos litigation was the impetus for a rather dramatic shift in British liability law, when two surviving spouses and a current sufferer of mesothelioma brought suit against several employers. Given the long gestation period of asbestos-caused cancer, it was impossible to identify with any precision the employer who had exposed the men to the disease. Under existing tort principles, if a duty to protect an employee "was broken by two tortfeasors and not only

one ... [the employee was] held to be entitled to recover against neither, because of his inability to prove what is scientifically unprovable" (*Fairchild v. Glenhaven Funeral Services Ltd.* 2002b, para. 9 [Lord Bingham of Cornhill]). However, in 2002, the House of Lords Judicial Committee determined that "[i]f the mechanical application of generally accepted rules leads to such a result, there must be room to question the appropriateness of such an approach in such a case" (*ibid.*, para. 9). According to Lord Cornhill,

> [i]t can properly be said to be unjust to impose liability on a party who has not been shown, even on a balance of probabilities, to have caused the damage complained of. On the other hand, there is a strong policy argument in favour of compensating those who have suffered grave harm, at the expense of their employers who owed them a duty to protect them against that very harm and failed to do so, when the harm can only have been caused by breach of that duty and when science does not permit the victim accurately to attribute, as between several employers, the precise responsibility for the harm he has suffered. I am of the opinion that such injustice as may be involved in imposing liability on a duty-breaking employer in these circumstances is heavily outweighed by the injustice of denying redress to a victim. Were the law otherwise, an employer exposing his employee to asbestos dust could obtain complete immunity against mesothelioma (but not asbestosis) claims by employing only those who had previously been exposed to excessive quantities of asbestos dust. Such a result would reflect no credit on the law. (*ibid.*, para. 33)

In 2006, the Law Lords considered the limits of the *Fairchild* (2002a; 2002b) exception. Specifically, should each employer be responsible in full for a litigant's damages? The answer, much to the chagrin of asbestos disease sufferers, was "no." Instead, in a four-to-one ruling, the Court ruled that liability should be apportioned according to the relative degree to which any given company contributed to an employee's exposure to asbestos. According to Lord Hoffman, "fairness suggests that if more than one person may have been responsible, liability should be divided according to the probability that one or other caused the harm" (*Barker v. Corus* 2006, para. 43). He noted, approvingly, moreover, the American courts' doctrine of several liability, citing in particular, the diethylstilbestrol (DES), a birth defect-causing drug, cases (*ibid.*, 44-46). For its part, however, the House of Commons moved swiftly to overturn the decision, passing legislation that allowed patients with asbestos-related illnesses to claim full compensation (Hall and Peel 2006; McHugh 2006).

The global implications of corporate misconduct and the global complexities of assigning corporate liability were manifest in the case of *Lubbe v.*

Cape PLC (2000a). British-based Cape PLC was founded in 1893 as a producer of asbestos-based insulation products. Key to its success were its South African mining operations, employing local workers as extremely cheap labour to dig and process blue asbestos, including children. Though the dangers of asbestos were well known for decades, Cape PLC continued to keep its increasingly sick African employees in the dark about it well into the 1960s, suppressing reports of its deadliness and exposing people to exorbitant amounts of the substance (Steele 2001). Although Cape PLC sold its South African mining operations in 1979 (Cape PLC 2008), it continued to hold an interest in several South African companies until 1989 (*Lubbe v. Cape, Plc.* 2000b, para. 4 [Lord Bingham of Cornhill]). Indeed, the purchasing company's shares were held by another South African asbestos mining corporation, whose shares were, in turn, held by Cape PLC.

Meanwhile, under a similarly structured corporate veil, Cape Industries also created a US subsidiary, North American Asbestos Corporation (NAAC), for marketing purposes in the United States. In 1974, a class action was commenced against Cape PLC and the NAAC in US District Court (in Tyler, Texas). Cape PLC presented a jurisdiction argument but ultimately settled in 1978. A second class action was filed in 1979, led by petitioner Jimmy Wayne Adams. Cape PLC again challenged jurisdiction, refused to settle, but this time sold its US holdings. A default judgment was entered against Cape PLC in 1983. However, with no remaining assets there, the company evaded distribution of any payments. Adams subsequently sought enforcement in the British courts. After a thirty-five-day trial, the case was dismissed (*Adams v. Cape Industries PLC* 1990, ch. 433). Justice Scott issued a lengthy opinion, found the issues to be very complex, some of the defense presented by Cape to be quite disingenuous, but also entirely within the parameters of English law. Case dismissed. Venturing further, Adams appealed, but the Court of Appeals upheld Scott's decision and dismissed the appeal (*Adams and Others v. Cape Industries PLC and Anor* 1991).

To return to a discussion of *Lubbe*, in 1997 thousands of South Africans sought to hold Cape PLC legally accountable for their illnesses or the deaths of family members. The path to trial or settlement was a long one, however – the major sticking point being in which country to hold the proceedings. Claiming that they could not receive adequate legal assistance in South African courts and citing the lack of established procedures in South Africa for dealing with group actions, the plaintiffs wished to proceed in English courts. For its part, Cape PLC, citing the long-established principle of *forum non-conveniens*, insisted that South Africa was the only appropriate venue, a position upheld in the lower courts. In 2000, however, the House of Lords disagreed, allowing the plaintiffs to proceed before the British judiciary. Citing, among other factors, Article 6 of the *European Convention on Human Rights*, Lord Bingham of Cornhill determined that the plaintiffs, most of whom were "black and of modest means" would probably "have no means of obtaining the professional representation and the expert evidence [in South Africa] which would be essential if these claims were to be justly decided" (*Lubbe v. Cape PLC*. 2000b, paras. 2 and 28i).[21] In 2003, Cape settled, agreeing to pay the claimants £7.5 million (Tait 2003).

A number of multi-party cases were litigated in the 1980s and 1990s, involving significant large-scale issues, including pharmaceutical product liability,[22] workplace safety,[23] and tobacco[24] – not unlike litigation during the same era in the United States. Indeed, the first major case against big British tobacco was brought after the Supreme Court of the United States found in *Cipollone v. Liggett* (1992) that product warning labels were insufficient to insulate the manufacturers from liability in light of evidence of public deception (*Hodgson v. Imperial Tobacco Ltd*. 1998).[25] Without clear guidance, judges were left with wide latitude to address complicated multi-party litigation as they could – to improvise procedures and solutions. Lord Steyn, writing in 1993, stated it in this way: "Subject to the duty to act fairly, the judge may and often must improvise: sometimes that will involve the adoption of entirely new procedures. The judge's procedural powers in group actions are untrammeled by the distinctive features of the adversarial system. The judge's powers are as wide as may be necessary to control the litigation fairly and efficiently" (*AB v. John Wyeth and Brothers Ltd*. 1993, 6).

After considerable study and prodded by EC Directive 98/27 on Injunctions for the Protection of Consumers' Interests (see Woolf 1996), a new version of the *Civil Procedure Rules* went into effect in 2000, largely retaining the old form for representative actions, allowing litigation to proceed only "where more than one person has the same interest in a claim."[26] Although this language, as we have discussed, has discouraged group litigation in the United Kingdom, another section of the law is much more flexible. Under Part 19.11 of the amended rules, the courts can issue a group litigation order (GLO), which bears considerable similarity to the multi-district litigation format in the United States, providing for "the case management of claims which give rise to related issues of fact or law" (*ibid.*). The new procedures enable the court to issue a GLO, including the establishment of a group register to manage the process and specifying the claims to be administered as a group in the case. An application for a GLO, submitted by a solicitor acting for one of the parties to a proposed group claim, is considered by a judge and requires approval from the lord chief justice (if the case arises in the Chancery Division) or from the vice-chancellor (if the case arises in a county court).[27] Once the GLO is issued, parties with similar and/or related claims must opt in to become part of the cluster, in direct contrast to the US model. Moreover, a managing judge is assigned with the responsibility for orchestrating the process and hearing the issues. Among the objectives of the system is to allow judges freedom to manage their dockets and equip them with flexible tools to do so. As Lord Woolf (1996, ch. 17, para. 32) noted in his report, "the need for imagination and creativity in dealing with [multi-party litigation] is attested to by every judge who has tried such a case." Thus, the managing judge can weed out meritless cases, assign variable liability as warranted by differing facts in multiple claims, distribute fees and awards equally or differentially among successful claimants, and, in general, craft outcomes that, in the judge's view, further the cause of justice.

As we have noted, contingency fee arrangements were historically banned in the United Kingdom, where there was a long-standing system of public legal aid. In addition, there was widespread belief that American-style contingency fees encourage entrepreneurial lawyers to launch frivolous litigation, leverage the process to exact huge settlements from deep-pocketed defendants (blackmail), and encourage premature settlements that deny clients fair compensation for their injuries. By the mid-1980s, however, the legal aid system was in financial trouble, and parliamentary reforms restricted availability except among the poor, thus leaving the large middle class to pay their own way (Epp 1998, ch. 7). Given the unavoidable access-to-justice implications, decision makers began to reconsider the system's fee structure. In 1987, the Law Society of England and Wales changed its rules to allow contingency fees for solicitors representing clients in a foreign jurisdiction where this type of arrangement was permitted (Hodges 2001, 140). In 1990, justified as a way to extend legal services to both the poor and middle classes, the *Courts and Legal Services Act* (section 58) was passed, allowing a conditional fee arrangement (CFA) in several areas of practice.[28] The law went into effect in 1995 and was extended in 1998.[29]

The first multi-party action to arise under the CFA provisions was *Hodgson v. Imperial Tobacco Ltd.* (1998), the case against the tobacco industry that we noted earlier. *Hodgson and Ors v. Imperial Tobacco Ltd. and Gallaher Group PLC* (1999a) was dismissed in 1999. After six years of preparation, the court at pretrial, relying on the statute of limitations, dismissed a majority of the claimants' cases, stating that they were prevented from suit because they were diagnosed with lung cancer more than three years prior to filing the suit.[30] Moreover, a number of representative group members had already abandoned the suit because it had been held hostage to such lengthy procedural manoeuvrings, with only six remaining plaintiffs, and the lawyers (Leigh, Day and Company), who had filed the action on a "no-win, no-fee" basis and were already facing more than £750,000 out-of-pocket expenses, decided that it was simply too risky to continue. Indeed, while British governments have not followed the American model of partnering with law firms to engage the tobacco industry, litigation initiated by smokers, individually and collectively, has fared no better than parallel efforts in the United States.[31]

The *Markt* reasoning has had a long-lasting effect, rendering the representative action largely useless as a group litigation mechanism in England

and Wales. As a consequence, and in light of the clear need for some way to deal with the inevitable, British lawmakers developed the GLO procedure, with the express intention of providing a set of mechanisms and tools that are flexible and give judges the ability to address multi-party actions effectively and fairly. This format has proven to be versatile, and it has allowed a number of substantial cases to be filed and consolidated. The fourth such action aggregated thousands of claims by South African asbestos miners in the *Lubbe* case that we discussed earlier. In the first seven years, some sixty-five GLOs were authorized, representing a range of issues, including *Royal Liverpool Children's Litigation* (2000), dealing with organ and body tissue harvesting of stillborn and deceased children unbeknownst to parents and relatives; *Persona Group Litigation* (2001), dealing with a defective contraceptive device; *McDonalds Hot Drinks* (2001), concerning excessively hot drinks and defective containers that led to scalding and significant burns; *Deep Vein Thrombosis and Air Travel Group Litigation* (2002), dealing with blood clots developed by international flight passengers due to overcrowded and cramped conditions, known as "economy class syndrome," resulting in at least one death; *Coal Mining Contractors Contribution Group Litigation* (2002), concerning the respiratory illnesses of coal miners; *Trilucent Breast Implant Litigation* (2003), dealing with problems with peanut oil and soya oil breast implants; and *DePuy Hylamer Group Litigation* (2005), dealing with faulty hip replacements.[32] While these cases represent a significant movement toward acceptance of the group litigation format, there has clearly been no explosion of activity as opponents had warned.

However, recent changes may signal a more energetic and involved judiciary. The *Constitutional Reform Act 2005* goes into effect in 2009, when the Supreme Court of the United Kingdom will take to the bench for the first time and begin deciding cases.[33] Moreover, Brice Dickson (2007, 363ff) finds recent decisions by the Law Lords to indicate a new-found inclination toward assertiveness, highlighted by *Jackson v. Attorney General* (2005), in which the Court upheld an act of Parliament. Although guns, strictly regulated in the United Kingdom, have not been a focus of litigation, this case was initiated by a group of fox hunters who questioned the constitutional validity of the *Hunting Act 2004*, which effectively makes their sport illegal.[34] Jackson and his co-plaintiffs[35] directly challenged the procedures by which the act had become law.[36] The Law Lords unanimously upheld the constitutionality of the act and, in the process, noted that parliamentary supremacy, long sacrosanct in British jurisprudence, was a principle of common law *created by judges* and, as such, could be revisited. Indeed, as Lord Steyn noted in his opinion, under the principle of judicial review, any act of Parliament must be "consistent with the rule of law" and subject to assessment by the Court to ensure there has been "no breach of constitutional propriety" (*ibid.*, para. 27) [emphasis added].[37]

Canada

Courts in Canada and Australia have historically referred to British legal precedent for guidance, and, although both countries achieved political independence much earlier, they did not fully cut their constitutional ties until the 1980s.[38] Nonetheless, by the 1970s, recognizing the necessity for change, lawmakers in both countries began to reassess their court rules, generally based on the inherited language of the *Supreme Court of Judicature Act* from the Victorian era.[39] Moreover, understood in light of the restrictive *Markt* precedent, the group litigation form was generally not a viable option. Looking to the US example where *Rule 23* had gone into effect in the previous decade, Québec adopted legislation in 1979, allowing class actions to proceed in the provincial courts.[40] However, lacking experience of their own, the courts struggled with the issues in the early going.[41] After expressing its initial reticence, the Court of Appeal for Québec issued a landmark decision in 1990, taking an expansive view that allowed a class action to proceed against the manufacturer of the Dalkon Shield birth control device (*Tremaine v. A.H. Robins Canada Inc.* 1990, 570). Indeed, the court stated that, although "the evidence may well vary from one member to the next ... the legislator of 1978 did not want to limit the class action to stereotypical cases."[42]

Meanwhile, an important case was brewing in Ontario, where, like all of the other provinces except Québec, representative actions were governed by a briefly worded provision based largely on the old 1873 English *Rule 10* and burdened by *Markt*.[43] The plaintiff sought approval to proceed on behalf of nearly 5,000 Oldsmobile Firenza purchasers upon the allegation that General Motors had breached its warranty and engaged in false advertisements, promoting the vehicle as "durable" and "reliable." Plaintiffs argued that the relatively small amount of each claim made it impossible to file separate actions. The Court of Appeal for Ontario ruled that a group action could go forward if confined to purchasers who had seen a written warranty in advertisements and, on that basis, had bought the automobile, thus placing them in a very similar relation to General Motors (*Naken v. General Motors of Canada Ltd.* 1979). The Supreme Court of Canada, however, determined the current rules regarding class actions to be "totally inadequate" and that the responsibility for changing them were "more fittingly the subject of scrutiny in the legislative rather than the judicial chamber" (*Naken v. General Motors of Canada Ltd.* 1983, 408). Justice Estey, for the Court, found that

> it is not enough that the group share a "similar interest" in the sense that they have varying contractual arrangements with the appellant which give rise to different but similar claims in contract relating to the same model of automobile ... [S]ome members of the class may have seen some but not all of the appellant's advertisements. Some may have made inquiries of the

appellant or its representatives. Others may have seen all the public releases in question and made no inquiries of anyone ...

It is my conclusion that the rule, consisting as it does of one sentence of some thirty words, is totally inadequate for employment as the base from which to launch an action of the complexity and uncertainty of this one. For these reasons, therefore, I would conclude that the action may not be framed as a class action under Rule 75. (*ibid.*, 408-10)

The attorney general had asked the Ontario Law Reform Commission (OLRC) to study the class action issue in 1976, and a very extensive, three-volume report, detailing the restrictive history of the current rules, assessing the need for reform, and proposing draft legislation that borrowed liberally from American *Rule 23,* was published in 1982 (Ontario Law Reform Commission 1982). Nonetheless, the legislature failed to act – a fact not lost on the *Naken* Court, whose opinion not only drew attention to the problem but also put real faces on it.[44] Ultimately, legislation was adopted in 1992 after further study from the OLRC, with rules largely based on the earlier report,[45] and the law quickly became a model for other provinces.

The Canadian provisions bear some similarities to those in the United States. For example, class members must opt out, and attorneys are compensated through court-awarded contingency fees, but fees vary considerably across the provinces. In an Ontario class action brought by a large number of plaintiffs who had contracted Hepatitis C through the national blood bank system, the attorneys' fees amounted to only about 4 percent (*Parsons v. Canadian Red Cross Society* 1999). In British Columbia and Québec, however, attorneys can generally expect to recover upwards of 25 percent, which is closer to the US norm. In addition, Canada utilizes a modified "loser pays" rule, in which liability for a defendant's attorney fees and costs extend only to the representative plaintiff. Moreover, Canadian courts rarely award punitive damages, and most civil trials are conducted by a judge without a jury. Factored together, these provisions mean that fees and awards in Canada are generally lower than in the United States.[46] As few as two parties can proceed as a class, as long as the claims raise common issues and the representative plaintiff is truly representative and presents a feasible course of action. Moreover, *Naken* had been decided only months after the *Canadian Charter of Rights and Freedoms* went into effect and by an essentially pre-*Charter* court.[47] By century's end, the political-legal context had changed dramatically, finding a more powerful and assertive judiciary, many of whom were willing to address issues of significance without the traditional reticence of their predecessors to take bold action.

In 2001, the Supreme Court of Canada unanimously decided three significant cases, with Chief Justice Beverley McLachlin writing the opinion in each: *Western Canadian Shopping Centres Inc. v. Dutton* (2001); *Hollick v. Toronto (City)* (2001); and *Rumley v. British Columbia* (2001). All three are important cases and, taken together, have created a noteworthy trilogy, but *Dutton* is particularly significant. The case arose in Alberta, which had not updated its class action rules and was still governed under the old *Naken* (1983) era provisions – indeed, the defendant argued that *Naken* precluded a class procedure. The court, however, felt otherwise, taking a very different approach than it had done in 1983: "Absent comprehensive legislation, the courts must fill the void under their inherent power to settle the rules of practice and procedure as to disputes brought before them" (*Western Canadian Shopping Centres Inc. v. Dutton* 2001, para. 34).[48] Justice McLachlin presents an extensive review of the "history and functions of class actions" dating back to seventeenth-century England (*ibid.*, para. 19-29). She also notes the critical importance of class actions in a world dominated by large corporations that affect vast numbers of individuals at once:

> The class action plays an important role in today's world. The rise of mass production, the diversification of corporate ownership, the advent of the mega-corporation, and the recognition of environmental wrongs have all contributed to its growth. A faulty product may be sold to numerous consumers. Corporate mismanagement may bring loss to a large number of shareholders. Discriminatory policies may affect entire categories of employees. Environmental pollution may have consequences for citizens all over the country. Conflicts like these pit a large group of complainants against the alleged wrongdoer. Sometimes, the complainants are identically situated vis-à-vis the defendants. In other cases, an important aspect of their claim is common to all complainants. (*ibid.*, para. 26)

In light of these conditions, the aggregation of claims is useful to judges and represents a practical and economical method of addressing far-reaching problems. It also provides access to the courts in cases involving many individual small claims, and it represents a potent mechanism for holding powerful "mega-corporations" accountable for their actions and misdeeds, serving as a way of ensuring that they "do not ignore their obligations to the public. Without class actions, those who cause widespread but individually minimal harm might not take into account the full costs of their conduct, because for any one plaintiff the expense of bringing suit would far exceed the likely recovery" (*ibid.*, para. 27-29).

Hollick and *Rumley* also took an expansive view of class action proceedings. *Rumley* represented a collective claim against British Columbia regarding the operation of a public school for the deaf that was alleged to have engaged in sexual, emotional, and physical abuse of students and staff over a forty-two-year period. The facts were not in dispute, but the trial judge denied class certification on the theory that, because of the wide time frame, claims would necessarily vary widely. The Supreme Court of Canada disagreed, finding commonality criteria to have been satisfied and that the class action form was preferable from the courts' perspective rather than face the prospect of trying hundreds of cases individually. *Hollick* was a nuisance and negligence action filed against the city of Toronto on behalf of 30,000 residents who lived near a landfill. The trial court certified the class but was overturned on appeal. The Supreme Court of Canada determined that the class format was not preferable in this case, as viewed "through the lens of the three principal advantages of class actions – judicial economy, access to justice, and behaviour modification" (*Hollick v. Toronto (City)* 2001, para. 27). Toronto had set up a special small claims trust fund to pay individual claims up to $5,000. However, no complaints had been filed. The Court reasoned from this that either there were no small claims or the claims were individually large enough to warrant separate review. Thus, access to justice was not an issue.[49]

As we noted earlier, Newfoundland and Labrador, Saskatchewan, Manitoba, and Alberta all passed comprehensive class action legislation very soon after *Dutton* and its companion decisions.[50] Acceptance of the form has created a much more friendly atmosphere for class actions, and the ensuing years have seen the number of cases increase substantially on issues mirroring those brought in the United States (for example, Watson 2001, 278-79). Indeed, the influx of litigation has produced a need for coordination across the court system, as courts in different provinces face similar cases. For example, a 2005 report by the Uniform Law Conference of Canada (2005, 5) notes that "in early 2004 ... courts in six provinces struggled to manage the litigation surrounding Baycol, an allegedly defective anti-cholesterol drug."[51] Similarly, the *Canadian Medical Association Journal* reported in November 2004 that within days of pharmaceutical giant Merck's decision to withdraw its Vioxx anti-arthritis drug from the market at least ten class actions were filed in four provinces and in federal court (with more likely to come in) against the company's Canadian subsidiary (Kondro 2004, 1335). Indeed, the growing number of such parallel actions makes reaching decisions more complicated and has led to proposals for the creation of a national class mechanism by which multi-district litigation can be consolidated and addressed more efficiently and fairly – all of the same reasons that this model was put into play in the United States (Uniform Law Conference of Canada 2005; Saumier 2005).[52]

Although gun ownership is common in Canada, it is not considered an inviolable right (handguns are not so commonplace), so firearms are heavily regulated. At one time, the Canadian government apparently considered litigation against the US gun industry because of a significant flow of illegal weapons across the border, but it is simply not an issue that the courts have faced (Delacourt and Whittington 2005, A1). In addition, although asbestos has taken a toll on Canadian workers as it has elsewhere, the government early on initiated a no-fault workers' compensation program to address it, thus rendering litigation unnecessary (Watson 2001, 271). Other issues, however, have gravitated to the courts, invigorated in the post-*Charter* era and encouraged by a high court willing to assume a serious role in the governing process.

The first Canadian tobacco class action, *Caputo v. Imperial Tobacco Ltd.* (1997) was filed in 1995 on behalf of all nicotine dependent smokers and their families in Ontario, approximately 2.4 million people. After nine years of legal manoeuvring by the three defendant multi-national tobacco corporations, Justice Warren Winkler of the Superior Court of Ontario finally decided that the proposed class actually combined several potential classes, lacked sufficient commonality, and could not be rendered "manageable, efficient and fair," as required under Canadian law. The court thus dismissed the plaintiff's application for class certification. As it has in the US courts, big tobacco has generally used the litigation process quite effectively. Nonetheless, several class actions have since been pursued before the Canadian judiciary,[53] with two large classes certified in Québec in 2005, after enduring six years of preliminary motions (*Blais v. Imperial Tobacco* 2005; *Létourneau v. Imperial Tobacco* 2005). The two cases, claiming millions of dollars in damages as a result of addiction and smoking-related illnesses, were filed against JTI MacDonald, Imperial Tobacco, and Rothmans, Benson and Hedges. Despite the shared complexities with the case that was ultimately dismissed in Ontario, the Québec court decided that the cases should move forward, but the process will likely be a protracted one.

Canadian lawyers and lawmakers obviously watch developments in the United States closely. This was certainly the case as the consolidated actions by the states to recover costs associated with tobacco use moved toward a global settlement in 1997. Indeed, the provincial government of British Columbia very quickly enacted legislation creating a cause of action by the government against the industry.[54] The attorney general immediately moved to court, but the Supreme Court of British Columbia found the act to be unconstitutional because it created extra-provincial civil rights (*JTI-Macdonald Corp. v. British Columbia* 2000). The legislature responded with a new statute – the *Tobacco Damages and Health Care Costs Recovery Act* – clearly specifying liability within the province.[55] The government then sued the largest Canadian tobacco companies, but the new legislation met the same fate as the earlier version (*British Columbia v. Imperial Tobacco* 2003). The Court of Appeals for British Columbia reversed, however, and the Supreme Court of Canada upheld the constitutionality of the act in 2005 (*British Columbia v. Imperial Tobacco Canada Ltd.* 2005).[56]

Ontario took a different approach. Assuming the US courts to be more receptive, the provincial government filed an ill-fated claim under the *Racketeer Influenced and Corrupt Organizations Act* in the US District Court in 2000, alleging that the tobacco industry had "participated in an international conspiracy to ensure a market for their hazardous products" and that they had hidden information about the addictive qualities of nicotine, calculating damages at $40 billion (*Ontario, The Minister of Health and Long Term Care v. Imperial Tobacco* 2000, 1). The Ontario government retained the services of a South Carolina law firm that had represented twenty-five states in US tobacco litigation, but the claim suffered the same fate as an earlier case consolidating claims by the governments of Guatemala, Panama, Brazil, Bolivia, and Colombia, testing the ability of foreign governments to sue American tobacco companies before American courts. The cases were dismissed by the district court, which found that the proper jurisdiction lay in the respective national court systems.[57]

On the food front, the Canadian courts have hosted litigation that parallel cases in the United States. For example, in 2004, a group of organic farmers in Saskatchewan, claiming negligence, strict liability, nuisance, trespass, and violations of the *Environmental Assessment Act* and the *Environmental Management and Protection Act,* sought class status in a suit against Monsanto and Bayer.[58] The two agricultural products giants had developed and released, with government approval, genetically modified (GM) canola plants. The farmers maintained that contamination from the GM crop made it impossible for them to market certified organic canola. The claims have been roundly rejected by Canadian courts. Thus, in the first round, Justice Smith of the Court of Queen's Bench of Saskatchewan considered the farmers' claims against each of the criteria for certification of a class action:

(a) the pleadings disclose a cause of action; (b) there is an identifiable class; (c) the claims of the class members raise common issues, whether or not the common issues predominate over other issues affecting individual members; (d) a class action would be the preferable procedure for the resolution of the common issues; and (e) there is a person willing to be appointed as a representative plaintiff who (i) would fairly and adequately represent the interests of the class; (ii) has produced a plan for the class action that sets out a workable method of advancing the action on behalf of the class and of notifying class members of the action; and (iii) does not have, on the common issues, an interest that is in conflict with the interests of other class members. (*Hoffman v. Monsanto* 2005, para. 25)

Justice Smith began with the question of whether the plaintiffs had causes of action on any of the common law or statutory claims. On the issue of negligence, she determined that the farmers "failed to establish a prima facie duty of care" and that, in any event, "compelling policy reasons" excluded a duty of care on the parts of defendants (*ibid.*, para. 70 and 81).[59] Indeed, Justice Smith ruled against the plaintiffs on each of the common law claims, finding, in turn, "no liability under the strict liability rule ... no reasonable claim in nuisance" and no evidence that Monsanto's or Bayer's actions constituted a trespass (*ibid.*). And while Smith did allow that the two statutory claims might reveal a reasonable cause of action, she subsequently found that the plaintiffs "failed to provide a factual basis upon which [to assert] an identifiable class in relation to the claims asserted" (*ibid.*, 246). That being the case, "no issue can be common across a class" not properly identified, which, in turn, obviates a class action as the preferable procedure (*ibid.*, 310 and 328). In 2006, the Court of Appeals for Saskatchewan upheld Justice Smith's denial of the class (*Hoffman v. Monsanto* 2006), as did the Supreme Court of Canada in 2007 (*Hoffman v. Monsanto* 2007).

The trans fat story in Canada is similar to that of its neighbour to the south. A combination of voluntary changes within the industry and proactive regulatory measures has minimized the likelihood of litigation. The Trans Fat Task Force (2006) began work in early 2005 and issued its final report to the minister of health in June 2006, calling for extensive labelling and the elimination of the additive from the nation's processed food supply.[60] According to a Canadian Broadcasting Corporation (2008) news report, a strict labelling law had gone into effect by July 2008, federal health minister Tony Clement had given restaurants and food processors until 2009 to eliminate trans fats voluntarily or face legislative mandates, and surveys had suggested quick compliance within the restaurant industry. Calgary health officials were not impressed, however, and initiated stringent regulations (maximum 2 percent content, effectively constituting a ban), which applied to all restaurants across the region by December 2007 (Canadian Broadcasting Corporation 2007).

Perhaps in part because of the close proximity and the high degree of economic and cultural exchange between the two countries, the Canadian approach to class actions shows considerable similarity to that in the United States.[61] True, the Canadian courts do not use juries, legal fees are often capped at a relatively low rate, and punitive damage awards are not routine. However, the scheme that has been developed across the provinces and embraced by the courts explicitly adopts the notion that small wrongs, when aggregated, quickly become major ones on a wide scale and that litigation is an important mechanism by which to hold mega-corporations accountable.

Australia

Like Canada, Australia inherited considerable legal tradition from the English common law system, but, in the last two decades, rules governing representative litigation have been heavily influenced by the US class action model. Australia has a federal structure, including six states and two self-governing territories, with corresponding federal, state, and territorial hierarchically arrayed courts. A number of structural alterations in the last quarter of the twentieth century, in addition to changes in membership on the nation's High Court, have set the stage for a more independent and active judiciary. In 1977, legislative reform established the Federal Court of Australia, thereby relieving the High Court of Australia from having to hear a range of issues under its original jurisdiction requirement, and a 1984 reform provided the justices with further control over their appellate docket. Most importantly, constitutional change enacted in 1986 gave the High Court of Australia independence from review by the Privy Council of the British House of Lords. Anthony Mason was appointed chief justice in 1987, and, under his leadership over the next seven years, the Court exerted its independence, moving boldly to distance itself from earlier more conservative and restrained predecessors (see, for example, Wheeler and Williams 2007; Pierce 2006; Oliver 2005). Arguably its most important decision came in 1992 in *Mabo v. Queensland (No. 2)* (1992), where the Court acknowledged Aboriginal land rights after more than a century of denial (see Russell 2005). The case did not provoke rejoicing in all political and legal circles, however, and, as we shall see, in the post-reform era the Court has played a significant role in developing class action jurisprudence, transgressing boundaries created by its own historical passivity and leading to charges of excessive "activism" by critics.

Australian judges often look beyond their borders for guidance. British precedent is considered persuasive but not binding, and Canadian and US case law has been noted with some degree of regularity in recent years, particularly in federal representative and class actions.[62] The *Federal Court of Australia Act of 1976* defines a class as seven or more persons who have a claim against the same party arising from substantially the same or related circumstances and involving common or similar factual or legal issues.[63] Moreover, Australian federal procedures do not require that a judge certify the class, and like the US and Canadian models, Australia applies the opt-out rule to govern the exclusion of class members.[64] Together, these provisions suggest a litigation-friendly system, but the Australian federal regime incorporates the loser-pay rule for attorneys' fees, which is a clear countervailing disincentive to would-be plaintiffs and, unlike in the US system, juries are not empanelled. In addition, the courts were not initially receptive to the expansion of collective litigation procedures, despite the enactment of legislative reforms.

The precedent of the British *Markt* case (1910) and the governing rules of court procedure requiring "identical" claims in representative litigation, although not strictly binding, have long been followed in Australian jurisdictions.[65] An indication of the restrictive judicial view is found as recently as

1981, where the High Court of Australia held in *Payne v. Young* (1981) that claims filed by a number of slaughterhouse owners challenging fees imposed upon them by the Western Australian government could not be joined as a combined claim, because the fee structure created separate contracts rather than a "series of transactions."[66] In response, the Labour government in Victoria enacted a statutory revision *(Supreme Court Act),*[67] but the Supreme Court of Victoria negated the legislature, relying heavily upon the High Court's decision in *Payne* to find that separate debt contracts, even involving the same financial institution, simply could not be construed as a transaction series for the purposes of group proceedings (*Marino v. Esanda LTD* 1986).

Thus, despite the 1976 legislation,[68] which was modeled loosely on the US system, the courts continued to take a restrictive view, prompting the Australian Law Reform Commission (ALRC) to issue a report in 1979 indicating procedural changes that would be essential to enhance access to the courts. Indeed the commission aptly titled its report *Access to the Courts – II* (Class Actions) (Australian Law Reform Commission 1979). Although there was some parliamentary movement, the courts were clearly reluctant to embrace a new, more flexible, regime. In 1988, the ALRC issued another report, once again calling for extensive reforms, this time explicitly rejecting the American model.[69] Finally, new rules were adopted as Part IVA of the *Federal Court of Australia Amendment Act 1991,* which went into effect in March 1992.[70]

At about the same time, a case that would prove to be pivotal to Australian group action law development was working its way through the courts. In 1986, Ainsley and Diane Carnie entered into a loan contract with Esanda Finance Corporation to purchase harvesting equipment for their wheat farm. Unable to meet the first annual instalment, they signed a variation agreement to extend payments and avoid default. They discovered too late that under the terms of the extension agreement, their original principal and unpaid interest were bundled, with new interest added to the calculation. They filed a claim in New South Wales on behalf of all others who had entered into similar variation agreements with Esanda, charging the financial institution with violating provisions of the *Credit Act 1984.*[71] Esanda moved to quash the litigation, noting that there were no class action rules in place in New South Wales and that prevailing precedent prevented consolidation of the alleged claims unless they were identical *(Markt)* or parts of a single transaction series *(Payne)*. After following a "tortuous course," prompted by multiple procedural manoeuvres by Esanda, a divided Court of Appeals for New South Wales subsequently rejected the notion of allowing a consolidated claim (*Esanda Finance Corporation Ltd v. Carnie* 1992).[72]

Chief Justice Gleeson, for the majority, borrowing directly from the Supreme Court of Canada's *Naken* (1983) opinion, found the current rules to be entirely inadequate but that to allow a group action to proceed would implicate the court in policy-making, an activity more appropriately within the legislative domain:

> What the respondents seek to achieve in the present case is a good example of what is ordinarily termed a class action. Each of the persons whom the respondents claim to represent had a separate contract with the appellant. The respondents do not know who such persons are, or how many of them there might be. Most of them, for their part, know nothing of, and have to date shown no interest in the current proceedings. What they have in common with the respondents is that the appellant has, on some past occasion, made with them the same kind of contract as it made with the respondents ... If class actions of the kind now available in the Federal Court are to be permitted in New South Wales (and there are large policy issues involved in that decision), then this should only be done with the backing of appropriate legislation or rules of court, adequate to the complexity of the problem, and appropriate to the requirements of justice. (*ibid.*, 388-90)

In dissent, Justice Kirby argued that changed social and economic conditions had significantly dimmed the relevance of the central premise of *Markt* and that the courts do have the authority to adjust procedures in a case such as this, particularly when it presents clear issues of justice. Indeed, he directly challenged the current relevance of the *Markt* precedent: "The decision coincided almost exactly with the advent of mass production of goods, such as cars. The mass provision of services (such as banking, finance, insurance, and government services) was to follow during the course of this century ... the *Markt* decision narrowed the availability of the representative action in a way congenial to common law procedures but frustrating the rule of court and of the procedures of Chancery from which that rule had been derived. *Markt* was followed throughout the British Empire ... Gradually over a period of more than 80 years, the judges of common law countries have been struggling to recover from the set-back of *Markt*" (*ibid.*, 395 [Kirby, J., dissenting]; cited in Mulheron 2004, 79). Moreover, Justice Kirby also contended that, although there was no existing rule in New South Wales to accommodate a "class action" and notwithstanding the relatively recent *Payne* precedent, it was clear that numerous parties had a common interest in the proceedings initiated by the Carnies and that a "representative action" should be allowed (*ibid.*, 394).

Upon appeal, the High Court of Australia unanimously agreed with Justice Kirby (*Carnie v. Esanda* 1995), finding that the Court of Appeals for New South Wales should properly consider the claim to be a representative action. In so doing, the Court presented a sweeping review of group litigation, dating back to early British history, through *Bedford v. Ellis* (1901) and *Markt* (1910), and more recent attempts by courts (since the 1970s) to deal with group litigation issues in the United Kingdom, Canada, New Zealand, and Malaysia, with the discernable trend across jurisdictions being to provide greater latitude to multiple party suits against a common defendant.[73] Notably, although the Court gave considerable attention to these external decisional activities, no US courts were cited and *Rule 23* was given only passing reference. The Court also addressed the concerns voiced by Chief Justice Gleeson in the earlier proceeding, asserting that questions of how to manage notice to potentially interested parties, whether consent is required of group members, whether they should be allowed to opt out, and the like, while complex, are within judicial competency to sort through and should not prevent the litigation from proceeding.

The matter then was sent back to the Court of Appeals, which, in turn, referred it to Justice Young for further consideration. Justice Young focused on the procedural questions noted earlier, deciding that the other now identified eighty-eight debtors should be notified of the litigation and given the option of whether they should be represented by the Carnies (and thus be bound by the result), go it alone, or drop out altogether, and that the plaintiffs should pay for the legal notice (*Carnie v. Esanda* 1996).[74] The Carnies, already in considerable debt, informed the court that they could not afford to do so, and Justice Young entered an order nullifying their claim to represent anyone other than themselves. In the end, a consent decree was filed under which the Carnies agreed to pay not only their debt (with compounded interest) but also Esanda's court costs.

The High Court of Australia's position notwithstanding, the ultimate outcome in *Carnie* served as a clear warning to would-be representative litigation plaintiffs. However, by 2000, reform came to Victoria in recognition of the growing need for something like a class action procedure. The Supreme Court of Victoria adjusted its rules, and the Victorian *Supreme Court Act 1986* was amended to replicate the recently updated federal *Rule IVA,* allowing explicitly for group proceedings when at least seven parties have a similar or related claim against a single defendant under a common set of legal or factual issues.[75] Moreover, among the changes was a switch from requiring all members of the represented group to opt in to allowing them to opt out. Both legislative acts met with legal challenge and both were upheld in the courts (*Femcare Ltd. v. Bright* 2000 [upholding federal *Rule IVA*]; *Mobil Oil Australia Pty. Ltd. v. Victoria* 2002 [upholding *Supreme Court Act 1986,* pt. 4A]). The High Court of Australia also made it clear that the reform was intended to liberalize the procedure for class actions rather than make it more onerous. In *Wong v. Silkfield Pty. Ltd.* (1999), the Court was asked to construe the meaning of "substantial interest" to determine whether James Wong could represent others who had also signed contracts to purchase units in a Queensland high-rise residential building, which he now alleged were based on false representations. The lower court had ruled against Wong because all of the individual contracts had been negotiated separately and contained different provisions. The High Court of Australia, however, found differently: "Clearly, the purpose of the enactment of Part IVA was not to narrow access to the new form of representative proceedings beyond that which applied under [earlier] regimes. This suggests that, when used to identify the threshold requirements of section 33C(1), 'substantial' does not indicate that which is 'large' or 'of special significance' or would 'have a major impact on the ... litigation' but, rather, is directed to issues which are 'real or of substance'" (*ibid.*, 267).

Thus, the legal reforms have survived court challenge, but we see in these cases the hallmarks of a very effective litigation strategy by well-heeled respondent corporations – if the plaintiff is forced to sustain sufficiently high procedural costs and attorney fees up front, they may be able to avoid addressing the central legal issues. It is part of the now familiar "haves come out ahead" scenario. This is precisely what happened, as we have seen, in the Carnies' hapless effort against Esanda. Effective use of the rules to wage an aggressive and costly procedural defence is not unusual in the United States, and it is apparently prominent in Australia as well. As Justice Finkelstein of the Federal Court of Australia recently observed in a class action brought against the manufacturer of the Filshie clip contraceptive device, on behalf of sixty-one women,

> [t]here is a disturbing trend that is emerging in representative proceedings which is best brought to an end. I refer to the numerous interlocutory applications, including interlocutory appeals that occur in such proceedings. This case is a particularly good example. The respondents have not yet delivered their defences yet there have been approximately seven or eight interlocutory hearings before a single judge, one application to a Full Court and one appeal to the High Court ... This is an intolerable situation, and one which the court is under a duty to prevent, if at all possible ... What I say should not be taken as a particular criticism of the present respondents. But it is not unknown for respondents in class actions to do whatever is necessary to avoid a trial, usually by causing the applicants to incur prohibitive legal costs. (*Bright v. Femcare, Ltd.* 2002, 607-8)

The Australian system has also seen other issues and manoeuvres that are now quite familiar to observers in the United States. Asbestos mining and use in building materials has led to serious health issues around the world, including Australia. Mining operations were carried out principally at Wittenoom (Western Australia) and Baryulgil (New South Wales) in the early to mid-twentieth century.[76] The health issues first came to light in 1974, and a range of legislative remedies were passed in individual states and territories over the next five years. The first successful negligence claim in relation to an asbestos disease was heard in 1985, and damages of AUS $222,500 were awarded.[77] Finally, most uses (and importation) of asbestos were banned by the Australian Parliament in 2003, and, the following year, a compensation fund was created to address the injuries of the individuals.[78] One commentator has noted that Australian corporations watched the legal developments in the United States and the United Kingdom very closely and quickly took steps to minimize their own liability, such as under-capitalizing subsidiaries involved with asbestos, thus raising the spectre of bankruptcy and promoting the general compensation fund idea – in addition to utilizing a process-based strategy (filing motions, delay, and so on) to drive up costs to plaintiffs (Spender 2003; Gibson 2000).

Similarly, tobacco litigation has a substantial history in Australia. In 1991, Justice Morling of the Federal Court of Australia found that a series of 1986 Tobacco Institute of Australia advertisements, denying adverse health effects of tobacco smoke, were misleading and deceptive and granted an injunction against further ads (*Australian Federation of Consumer Organizations Inc. v. Tobacco Institute of Australia Ltd* 1991).[79] The story of Rolah Ann McCabe also has a familiar ring to it. A long-time smoker, she developed cancer and filed suit against British American Tobacco Australia (BAT). Unfortunately, McCabe died before the litigation ran its full course. After a series of procedural motions by defendants, the trial judge finally entered a $700,000 judgment in her favour in 2002, with a strong reprimand of the company's legal tactics and other activities related to the litigation, including the destruction of thousands of internal documents dating to 1986. BAT appealed, and the Supreme Court of Victoria overturned the lower court's judgment because it was not absolutely clear that the document destruction was related to this particular case (*McCabe v. British American Tobacco Australia Services Ltd.* 2002).[80]

In 1999, the first class action against the major Australian tobacco companies was initiated in federal court, alleging negligence and misleading and deceptive marketing conduct, on behalf of all persons (some 60,000 people) suffering from a lengthy list of smoking-related diseases. As usual, the tobacco industry filed motions to dismiss the claims, but the court ruled in favour of allowing the proceeding to move forward (*Nixon v. Philip Morris (Australia) Ltd.* 1999). On appeal, however, the defendants prevailed. Indeed, the full Federal Court of Australia found the complaints to be defective, as it was doubtful that each plaintiff had suffered as a result of the actions by all of the defendants (*Philip Morris (Australia) v. Nixon* 2000).[81]

On a broader front, the class action (or representative litigation) form seems to have taken firm root in Australia. One commentator, a practitioner in a leading law firm, notes that US class action developments are closely watched by Australian lawyers, judges, and lawmakers and that "class action litigation ... in one sense is creating a new atmosphere of 'regulation' through private litigation ... Class action litigation is emerging globally as a de facto tool of industry regulation that is frequently supported by governments across a variety of jurisdictions in which traditional legislative regulation is perceived to be ineffective" (Betts 2006, unpaginated webpage). Indeed, litigation involving such issues as asbestos, tobacco, pharmaceuticals, insurance, corporate governance, health care, and medical devices is becoming increasingly prominent, and it seems that a number of distinguished Australian class action lawyers have significant ties to the United States.[82]

The constitutional changes of the 1980s, which enhanced the courts' power and their independence, in addition to "access to justice" reforms of the early 1990s, which facilitated the aggregation of claims, created opportunities for an increasing number of Australian lawyers and law firms to develop class action and representative litigation expertise. Although the range and volume of collective litigation has not approximated the proportions seen in the United States, Australian courts did witness a rise in activities, most notably in product liability and shareholder claims. Indeed, the immediate post-reform decade produced a range of important multi-party cases (with plaintiff class members often numbering in the tens of thousands) against major corporate interests, including cases involving tobacco (*Nixon v. Philip Morris (Australia) Ltd.* 1999), heart pacemakers (*Courtney v. Medtel* 2003; *Darcy v. Medtel* 2001), Filshie applicator and clip contraceptive device (*Bright v. Femcare* 1999) as well as salmonella poisoning from peanut butter (*Butler v. Kraft Foods Ltd.*, settled in 1997), fruit juice (*Dowdell v. Knispel Fruit Juices Pty Ltd.* 2003), and oysters contaminated with the Hepatitis A virus (*Graham Barclay Oysters v. Ryan* 2000).

Gun ownership is tightly regulated, and the gun industry has not faced litigation efforts like those occurring in the United States. However, the changing nature of food markets is reflected in the case law in Australia, as it is elsewhere. For example, in 1995, New South Wales ranchers, Brian and Leone McMullin, filed a representative suit in federal court against chemical manufacturer ICI Australia (now Orica Limited) and other respondents.[83] The McMullins cited losses suffered "as a result of the accumulation of chlorfluazuron in the tissues of cattle ... [which they said] occurred when the cattle were fed cotton waste that had been sprayed with an insecticide marketed under the name 'Helix'" (*McMullin v. ICI Australia Operations Pty Ltd.* 1996, 1511). Despite vigorous opposition, Justice Wilcox found in favour of the class, efficiently steering the case toward settlement:

> [T]he parties selected a few cases that raised major points of principle. These were heard over a few days and rulings made. The parties then entered into negotiations in relation to individual cases, exchanging information in accordance with directions made by the Court and with mediation of many cases by a Court officer. Two or three cases were not resolved by agreement.

The damages in those cases had to be determined by a judge. All the rest were agreed. Towards the end of the process of negotiating settlements, the Court ordered publication of advertisements in newspapers circulating amongst graziers notifying group members that they must submit outstanding claims by a particular date, or be excluded from the benefit of the judgment. By the time that date arrived, 499 claims had been received. After the last of them was resolved, the total payout reached some $100 million. Total court time for the whole operation was only about 30 days. (cited in Morabito 2007, 52 [Wilcox J.])

In another class action, filed in 1997, 2,500 Australians joined suit against Kraft, claiming injuries from eating contaminated peanut butter. Justice Raymond Northrop of the Federal Court of Australia oversaw an opt-in/opt-out settlement in which Kraft agreed to pay claimants between AUS $500 and AUS $50,000 depending on the seriousness of their illness (*Butler v. Kraft Foods Ltd.*, settled in 1997). Two years after the *Butler* suit was filed, consumers of Nippy's orange juice launched a class action seeking medical costs, economic damages, and pain and injury compensation for salmonella poisoning after they became sick from drinking the defendant's beverage (*Dowdell v. Knispel Fruit Juices Pty Ltd.* 2003). The parent company, Knispel Fruit Juices, initially denied liability. By 2000, it admitted "strict liability," though without negligence, again clearing the way for settlements averaging between AUS $2,000 and $4,000 per injured party ("Trial Likely in Class Action" 1999; Kibble 2000; Uren 2001).[84]

The Australian state governments have been divided on the issue of allowing genetically modified (GM) agricultural crops to be imported or grown domestically. As they are introduced, it would seem a matter of time before we see the issue taken to court. Ongoing drought conditions and increased worldwide demand for grains have led to some proposals to introduce GM wheat that might produce higher yields despite low-rainfall conditions, but thus far those proposals have been rejected.

As with other issues, the obesity litigation against the fast food industry in the United States has been closely monitored in Australia. Mirko Bagaric and Sharon Erbacher (2005) suggest that, although obesity is a rising problem across the country, the Australian approach is more likely to place responsibility for regulation upon the legislature rather than upon the courts (also see Erbacher and Bagaric 2006). In response to extensive pressure from health and consumer organizations, state and federal parliaments have considered a number of regulatory measures, including restrictions on advertising to children. In November 2002, amid rising calls for government action, the Australian Health Ministers Conference created the National Obesity Task Force to assess the effectiveness of current food standards (with particular attention to advertising and fast food) and to recommend new ones if warranted. In 2006, the University of Sydney's Faculty of Law hosted an academic conference that drew further attention to the issues, particularly among the law communities in Australia and New Zealand.[85] More generally, the food industry has engaged in an aggressive campaign to self-regulate (for example, limiting advertising, changing menus, more extensive labelling, and reducing trans fat content) in order to pre-empt potential litigation (see, for example, Ashton, Morton, and Mithen 2003; Carter 2006).

Although the nation's courts had hosted a number of significant cases since the class action form became available in 1992, Bernard Murphy (2005, 7; also see Sherman 2002, 426), writing in December 2005, notes that the litigation represented "more of a trickle than a flood." To present the case in more concrete terms, he goes on to offer the following estimates: "Between 1992 and 1997 there were approximately 30 class actions commenced. [According to a 2000 ALRC report (at 7.91)] there were 20 class actions [currently] before the Federal Court. In 2002 an experienced class action litigator [Peter Cashman] estimated that there had been only approximately 75 class actions commenced by that time. Even if the estimate was wrong by 33 percent it would still mean that there had not been more than 100 class actions in a ten year period" (Murphy 2005, 7; Australian Law Reform Commission 2000). Nonetheless, an indication of effectiveness is probably found in the fact that reportage has been laced with the same kind of elevated hyperbole and intense lobbying to which American lawmakers have grown accustomed.[86] Just as their counterparts in the United States have responded by passing tort and class action reforms, the Australian Parliament and every Australian state and territory has also enacted tort system changes in 2003-04, significantly raising damage thresholds and thus diminishing the ability to launch mass tort claims (for example, *ibid.*, 3).

Conclusions

In this chapter, we have explored the challenge of group litigation in a comparative transnational context, with special focus on developments in the United Kingdom, Canada, and Australia. To be sure, all three systems share historical roots that are not entirely foreign to the United States. Indeed, American judges, particularly in the nineteenth century, took lessons from their British predecessors to develop principles for dealing with multiple parties presenting closely related legal claims. By the early twentieth century, it was clear that the United States would follow its own path toward accommodating the multi-party format, fostering the expectation that the rules (even if somewhat confusing) could effectively enhance access to the law in situations involving a large number of parties who had incurred a relatively small injury as a consequence of a similar transaction or set of events and that the process could have a regulatory impact. Institutional structures and rules systems create opportunities for those with the ability and resources to develop strategies to exploit them. A significant policy role was assumed by US courts early on, and, in its formative years, the Supreme Court of the United States was staffed by a number of jurists willing to develop judicial power and assert institutional independence. Aggregating similar claims had clear administrative benefits and often worked to the advantage of the entity whose dealings had produced a multitude of legal adversaries – as long as the multitude were disorganized. So far, so good, however, the collective format also represents a potentially exploitable opportunity for similarly situated weaker parties to gain leverage over a stronger opponent, if they can successfully pool their resources. This situation sets the stage for meeting strategy with counter-strategy, which has played out in the American system as it developed, especially through the twentieth century. The British courts operated within a markedly different structural system, in which lawmaking was unambiguously parliamentary centred.

The British courts gave their rules a different spin (in the 1910 *Markt* decision), requiring that all claims must be identical in order to be combined, essentially shutting off collective litigation as a possibility until reform came in the final decade of the century. Indeed, the owners of the *Knight Commander* steamship represented significant shipping interests with considerable political capital. It is not surprising that the court was receptive to their defence, but it probably had not counted on creating such a long-lasting legal precedent. By the mid-1990s, contingency fee restrictions were eased, and, in 2000, the GLO format went into effect, allowing similar claims against a common defendant to be bundled for consideration under the jurisdiction of a single court. This was a considerable step toward the acceptance of something like the class action. However, the British system requires litigants to opt *in* if they wish to be included in the GLO process. Lawmakers were keen to avoid what they perceived to be excesses in the American model, and the GLO formula has not released a flood of activity but, rather, a steady issuance of about ten orders per year. The British courts may be poised to enter a new era of independence and serious engagement with controversial issues, which would likely encourage litigants to seek redress in cases that historically have been routed through the legislative-regulatory system. *Jackson v. Attorney General* (2005) suggests that parliamentary supremacy was a common law principle, constructed by judges and thus subject to court review, setting an intriguing stage for the newly created Supreme Court of the United Kingdom, which will hear its first cases in 2009.[87]

Both Canadian and Australian judges followed the *Markt* doctrine until it became clear that it neither promoted justice nor enhanced procedural efficiency, as situations prompting large numbers of similar cases surfaced to highlight weaknesses in a system that essentially required individuals to seek their own individual redress, even if their claims were against a common defendant. Indeed, as we have found in the US experience, problems can quickly rise to a policy level warranting regional or national attention when considered in the aggregate, even though they are rather insignificant in isolation. Legislation allowing group claims went into effect in Québec in 1979, but the courts struggled with the issue, as judges were reticent to move too quickly, finally adopting a more liberal approach in 1990 (similar to the US regime). The Ontario provincial government, after a series of stops and starts, enacted reforms in the early 1990s, but other jurisdictions lagged behind. The Supreme Court of Canada ultimately forced the issue with a trilogy of decisions in 2001, finding that with or without the benefit of legislation group litigation must be an active option in all provinces for three inter-related reasons: to enhance access to justice, to avoid redundant costs that diminish court efficiencies, and to provide a means by which large corporations could be held accountable – a regulatory function. Note that all of the most significant jurisprudential changes have occurred in the post-*Charter* period and after newly appointed jurists replaced predecessors who were more securely tethered to old regime politics and formulas. Indeed, a range of scholars has observed the Court to have embarked upon a course of unprecedented "activism" in this era (see, for example, Hirschl 2004; Manfredi 2001; Martin 2005; Songer 2009).

Australian judges were at least as cautious as their Canadian counterparts. Despite legislative reforms enacted by the national legislature in 1976 and the Victoria parliament in 1984, the High Court of Australia continued to issue restrictive decisions based largely on the British *Markt* precedent, setting off further calls for real reform. In response, the federal Parliament adopted new rules in 1991 (the Victorian government did so in 2000), and the High Court finally took a strong position in 1995.[88] Again, the most significant changes in judicial direction have come under conditions of enhanced institutional independence (see, for example, Pierce 2006; Williams 2001; Wheeler and Williams 2007).

Thus, all three systems we have observed moved, if rather haltingly, toward acceptance of a group litigation model. Although the initial signals in Canada and Australia (in the mid-1970s) were positive, and US *Rule 23* seemed to have been a useful guide to legislators, the courts, led by holdover pre-reform era jurists, held to more restrictive parameters found in aging, and increasingly outdated, judicial precedent. By the 1990s, lawmakers in both countries openly expressed their desire to avoid the perceived abuses and extremes associated with American-style class action and voiced concern for opening the litigation floodgates. The British never warmed to the notion of allowing class actions, but, in the face of an EU mandate and realities of a global economy, reforms were finally put into place at the turn of the century.

Perhaps due to the geographic proximity, close economic connections between the two countries, and the likely overlap in consumer class memberships, the Canadians embraced the class action more completely and earlier than either the British or Australians, although they did not accept the full package. There are serious restrictions, particularly in the area of legal fee structures and damage awards, but, since the Supreme Court of Canada assumed a more activist posture in the late 1990s, the number and range of collective litigation activities have increased significantly. The Canadian model places a high premium on access to courts, and the opt-out formula assumes class membership among all similarly situated litigants and allows those with special circumstances warranting special consideration to pursue their own individual claim. Moreover, judicial efficiency is another important consideration, and the Canadian courts have recently taken measures to allow consolidation of similar class actions filed in different provinces to avoid duplicative effort and minimize the likelihood of conflicting outcomes.

The Australian system has also adopted the opt-out model but has remained more true to the loser-pays fee structure and retains limits on awards. The threshold for class formation is relatively low and the rules are flexible. There have been a number of significant cases, especially since 2001, but no sign of a litigation explosion. Both the British and Australian approaches show a longer-lasting preference for a legislative-based regulatory regime to address market-related consumer economic, health, and social problems that frequently represent core class action issues in the United States and increasingly so in Canada. The structure in each of the three systems reflects a political culture that has historically held greater faith (compared to the United States) in relatively centralized parliamentary and regulatory (especially Australia) and judicial (British) decision makers to sort through complex and competing sets of claims and analyze event chains to make appropriate assessments (for example, Flemming 1994). In the face of a series of significant regulatory failures, however, this faith seems to be weakening. Moreover, the Supreme Court of Canada has explicitly assigned regulatory value to the process itself. All three systems place a high premium on individual justice (due process), very likely enhanced by constitutional reforms that elevate the judicial role and by general recognition and the growing force of the *Universal Declaration of Human Rights,* although they address it in different ways.[89] For example, the British GLO formula requires litigants to make a conscious and deliberate choice to opt in, rather than simply find themselves bound by the outcome in a legal action, with which they were entirely unengaged and about which, perhaps, they were largely oblivious. The Canadians and Australians have adopted an opt-out model (more like that in the United States) that makes it easier to construct a class for action but that has greater restrictions on fee structures to discourage aggressive and entrepreneurial manoeuvring among the plaintiff bar. None have embraced the American-style punitive damage system, but this has been undergoing serious legislative revision across the United States in recent years, suggesting that all systems are converging toward a similar legal model.

To the extent that policies developed in all three systems were devised in response to the spectre of a legal mobilization onslaught, they appear to have largely succeeded. However, aggressive manoeuvring on the defence side was not part of the decision equation that produced the reforms, and judges in each system have voiced their frustration, finding defence tactics in some instances effectively yield unjust results. This is not to suggest that plaintiffs must always prevail. However, despite a first-glance plaintiff-friendly appearance, the "haves" have often found ways to render the schemes defender-friendly – to come out ahead, regardless of structural edifice.

7
Conclusions

We have addressed a complex tangle of issues related to multi-party litigation across several dimensions. The conventional format for court proceedings has always been based upon a triadic formula in which two adversaries present their competing claims for resolution (Shapiro 1981).[1] Many variations on this central theme, of course, do occur, as there can be more than one plaintiff and more than one defendant. However, the core notion is that a qualifying claim is one that arose from a single event or a tightly entwined series of actions. When this condition is not met, the court faces difficulty in assigning rights and responsibilities and determining an appropriate outcome for each party. Moreover, if a conflict is allowed to collect a large number of participants, fanning across a wide range of the community, the menu of possible solutions will, by definition, reach beyond parochial interests of individuals and take on characteristics of generalized policy. Indeed, we have seen courts in all contexts grapple with these issues and reach different conclusions.

Early evidence from England indicates some judges were prepared to acknowledge that, on occasion, conflict can involve multiple parties and were receptive to adapting court procedures in order to achieve a "global" outcome – a far more efficient approach than trying to separate out each claim for individual consideration. Case records involving such situations date to well before the first colonial ships ventured into the Atlantic. Thus, the underlying conditions that give rise to, and propel, multi-party conflict are clearly not a new phenomenon. However, the spate of reform activities to accommodate group litigation virtually everywhere in the late twentieth and early twenty-first centuries suggest that the distribution and consumption patterns inherent in the structure of a global economy considerably enhance these conditions.

In all of the courts we studied, and in all historical periods, a foremost issue that has accompanied the presentation of group-based litigation is how to reconcile and balance individual rights against larger demands – that is, system efficiency and major player (governments and corporations) account-ability. Indeed, resolving this dilemma has plagued judges and law reformers repeatedly. In the United States, principles of due process suggest that each party should be provided an opportunity to construct a claim or defence appropriate to that party's interests. This process has produced ongoing complaints about the group litigation model and an unending stream of questions. For example, is it fair to bind class members to outcomes, even when they are unaware that their interests are represented by someone else or they do not have the opportunity to tell their own story? The US model calls for notice to all potential class members and allows individual litigants to opt out in order to pursue their own claim separately.

In the other systems we have studied, similar issues also figure promin-ently in devising procedures to deal with multi-party legal conflicts. Indeed, the British high bench took these issues to an extreme position in 1910 (*Markt and Co. v. Knight Steamship Co.* 1910), requiring that, in order to be consolidated as a group action, all claims must be identical. On the one hand, this requirement acknowledges the idiosyncratic qualities of individual cases and rests upon the assumption that each party is best situated to pres-ent and protect her own parochial interests and should control her own fate in the process. However, it also denies the larger public policy reality associ-ated with a scenario in which the actions of one (or a few) major entity af-fects many relational partners.[2] Indeed, this feature of collective (class or representative) litigation expands the scope of the outcome landscape and, in the process, highlights the political dimension of the conflict. Even among the earliest of cases, such as the one brought by Father Martin against his parishioners in twelfth-century England, we see this dynamic,[3] and it has not been lost on scholars and other observers who have assessed class action and representative litigation in a wide variety of venues. Moreover, this aspect of group-based action was noted directly by Harry Kalven and Maurice Rosenfield (1941) in their reflection on the first twentieth-century revisions to the procedure in the United States, in which they envisioned a role for private attorneys general who might work on behalf of consumers and shareholders to hold large corporations accountable.

Rosenberg's (1991) thesis suggests that such hope for influence through litigation is "hollow." On this score, we find mixed results. With regard to tobacco and gun litigation campaigns, the limitations for lasting change are rather clear. What appeared to be a big victory against the US tobacco in-dustry seems to have been just that – an appearance of victory – and litigation in Australia, Canada, and the United Kingdom follows a very similar track. Anti-gun forces have been utterly outflanked through the legislative process. Even in a historically strong-court system, legislative lawmaking can be marshalled to trump the judicial process. The courts are too scattered and decentralized to develop systematic policy change. The trans fat story has played out somewhat differently. Indeed, the food industry has changed its course in all of the jusrisdictions we reviewed, as litigation forces gathered in preparation for major actions. The industry, of course, argues that it is simply doing the right thing in light of medical scientific evidence. And it makes good marketing sense. However, the move took place after some initial legal actions and has pre-empted a larger, more concerted, and expensive campaign in the courts.

Political and social expectations that judicial institutions will act as independent agents of policy have historically been relatively weak in the commonwealth jurisdictions, especially compared to the United States. Mounting pressures for constitutional change and more extensive recognition of individual rights in the late twentieth century have given courts more authority and independence. Coincidental to these developments, procedural changes were enacted, largely through the legislative system, in Australia and the United Kingdom, and the courts have hosted a rising (although not huge) number of aggregated claims against politically and economically potent defendants. The Supreme Court of Canada, by contrast and on its own initiative, mandated shifts to facilitate access to the courts, enhance greater efficiency, and, in so doing, expressed hope that litigation might serve an effective regulatory function against increasingly powerful corporate giants. Such rule changes have encouraged consumer organizations and the plaintiff bar to gear up for collective actions, and the signals of political mobilization efforts are clearly evident in all three countries. However, procedural changes do not necessarily translate into substantive changes. Despite the fact that class action-type litigation has occurred with some regularity in the United Kingdom and Australia, and has multiplied quickly in Canada, we have detected few signs of lasting significant policy influence. Courts in each system have recently exerted greater independence and willingness to engage major, politically charged issues. No doubt, Rosenberg's model of institutional weakness applies well to systems in which the courts have a tradition of weakness.

Although we have not systematically surveyed all multi-party litigation, we have noted and summarized many of the more important ones, both historical and recent, across several jurisdictions. A common feature that appears repeatedly, throughout our observations and, in some cases, those of presiding jurists, is that the more powerful parties find ways to make the legal process work in their favour – that is, the "haves" seem consistently to come out ahead. This is certainly not a startling conclusion, as it follows expectations of the process articulated by Marc Galanter (1974) and others who have applied his model to study US litigation, but the scenarios in these terms look strikingly similar in each of the systems we assessed. In the pages that remain, we summarize our chief observations and present a number of issues that follow from our research and that deserve further investigation.

Summary of Observations

Throughout this book, we have assumed that litigation is a form of politics. Thus, we would expect certain resource and structural advantages to accrue to larger, wealthier, more experienced entities with influence in other political arenas. Unquestionably, in each of our American case studies, major plaintiffs' attorneys, and, in many cases, the plaintiffs themselves, viewed the litigation effort as a political exercise – a means of fighting an enemy partisan on judicial, rather than legislative, turf. Thus, frustration over a perceived lack of regulation fuelled Wendell Gauthier's coalition against tobacco, big city mayors' fight with guns, and John F. Banzhaf's battle with fast food.

Winners and Losers

Clearly, the defendants saw the struggles as more than just courtroom drama, in each case wide-ranging counter-attacks were waged not only in court but also in the legislative and public relations arenas. And, here, of course, is the rub. In each case, the politically and legally more experienced and re-sourced party, if not always a clear winner, was always at least able to cut its losses to the disadvantage of the would-be regulators. In some instances, the sheer mismatch in experience and resources was overwhelming. When Samuel Hirsch put poor Cesar Barber on display in the first fast-food obesity case, his client became the object of ridicule almost overnight, setting an inauspicious precedent for future efforts. In other cases, the disparities were perhaps less blatant but, nevertheless, accrued to the enormous advantage of the defendants. Take for example, the gun litigation. Big city mayors, the likes of Rudy Giuliani and Mike Bloomberg in New York and Richard Daley in Chicago, are hardly political neophytes. Yet, the gun industry, abetted significantly by the National Rifle Association (NRA), has out-manoeuvred them at nearly every step, even to the point of achieving broad legislative bans on legal regulatory efforts.

Even what might from a certain perspective be deemed a plaintiff political success story – the tobacco litigation – has hardly been a slam dunk. Un-questionably, the cigarette companies have suffered some legal losses, but these setbacks have hardly crippled them. Indeed, after Judge Kessler's final ruling in the government's case against tobacco, chastising the industry but assessing virtually nothing in damages, Wall Street saw tobacco stocks stage a significant rally. As a Morgan Stanley analyst put it, "[f]rom a business perspective, this is a complete win. [The tobacco companies] not making any substantial payments. There's no threat of future substantial payments" (Henderson 2006, D1). Clearly, this is not to say that defendants have gone unscathed. The food industry, for example, faced with threats of litigation, has spent a considerable amount in removing or reducing trans fats and has no doubt lost revenues in removing sugary soft drinks from school vending machines. On the other hand, the industry was not merely responding to legal threats. Almost non-stop media reporting of the so-called "obesity crisis" certainly has played a role, as have the public demands for more "natural," nutritious food and drink. In the end, the industry response was simply good marketing. And because the issues and the markets span the globe, particularly in economically developed areas, similar actions have occurred nearly simultaneously in all of the jurisdictions we considered.

Of all of the defendant businesses, cigarettes undoubtedly took the biggest hit. The *Master Settlement Agreement (MSA)*, after all, was no small potatoes even for an industry as wealthy as tobacco.[4] On the other hand, the cigarette companies had put aside in escrow an amount in excess of the final *MSA* total, and, notwithstanding substantial legal fees, have not had to make another big payout since. Moreover, tobacco revenues have been increasing. For example, domestically, the Altria Group, parent company of Philip Morris USA, continues to see healthy annual revenue increases (Altria Group 2007). And Philip Morris International reported an earnings rise of 23 percent during the second quarter of 2008 (Wardell 2008).[5]

More broadly, the United States is becoming a less friendly environment for large-scale litigation. This, of course, has not been a serendipitous development. As Jeffrey Rosen (2008) reports, business-friendly and conservative groups (for example, the Chamber of Commerce, the America Tort Reform Association, and the Federalist Society) have waged a concerted campaign over the past several decades to influence both legislatures and courts. Until recently, consistent Republican rule at the national level and in many state houses (abetted in part by the electoral strategies of such groups) has made the campaign considerably easier and quite successful. Specific and general tort reform measures have been widely passed over the course of the decade, and the Supreme Court of the United States has clearly signalled its displeasure with punitive damages. The result is that "[c]ompanies involved in many of the largest and most controversial legal clashes of recent decades are seeing a sharp decline in the number of lawsuits against them" (Davies 2006, A1).

Litigation Coalitions

As in any political venue, success in the judicial arena depends on strength. In one form or another, strength is measured in numbers. For the defendants, the numbers come in many varieties. There are, of course, numbers in the form of financial resources. As we suggest in this chapter, big tobacco has big bucks – bucks that can be deployed toward top-drawer counsel, information gathering, and lobbying. The food industry enjoys similar financial reserve. Then there are constituent numbers, an advantage especially enjoyed by the gun industry. And these numbers are particularly muscular. When the NRA speaks, policy-makers listen – gun owners vote and vote with passion. Not surprisingly, then, the firearms industry has been most successful at garnering legislative assistance in thwarting the threat of litigation. Of course, the fact that it also got the US Constitution interpreted to its satisfaction furthers the cause as well. Then there are the numbers in the form of "friends," the stuff of powerful alliances. When Philip Morris went to battle over punitive damages in *Williams-Branch ex rel. Estate of Williams v. Philip Morris, Inc.* (1999), it did not go it alone. On the contrary, it enlisted powerful *amici* including the US Chamber of Commerce, the Business Roundtable, the National Association of Manufacturers, the Pharmaceutical Research and Manufacturers of America, the American Chemistry Council, the American Tort Reform Association, the Washington Legal Foundation, and the Cato Institute. As we have seen, plaintiffs have been at a considerable disadvantage on most counts. Yet, they have come increasingly to coalesce in order, at least somewhat, to balance the numbers scale. During the 1990s, there were, of course, the tobacco coalitions, notably the Castano Group. Food reformers also, and with greater success, learned the value of alliances following the disasters of *Barber v. McDonald's* (2002) and *Pelman v. McDonald's* (2005b). The gun wars have been led by coalitions of mayors and governors. And allied state attorneys general, together with private tobacco coalition attorneys, launched what arguably was one of the few plaintiff successes in the fight against cigarettes.

Litigation as Regulation

The question remains, however, can litigation produce an effective form of regulation? Defendants, of course, have always found the legislative regulatory environment to be the most promising – certainly, the most friendly and least onerous. Spending habits bear witness. Between 1998 and 2005, Philip Morris alone spent over $75 million lobbying Congress and federal agencies. During the same time frame, the tobacco industry as a whole flooded Washington with almost $224 million to advance its interests. And while cigarette company spending dwarfs that of the food industry and gun rights lobby, the others have spent healthy sums as well.[6] Moreover, in all three cases, congressional and agency spending was at its highest at precisely the times that the litigation threat loomed largest. Thus, tobacco companies peaked in the money devoted to national lobbying efforts in 1998 (roughly $64 million), the year that the *MSA* moved to Congress. The food, beverage, and restaurant industries, always fairly big spenders, began increasing their lobbying efforts between 2002 and 2003 when litigation started to get serious. Moreover, the gun rights lobby, led by the NRA, substantially augmented spending in 2000, the very time a critical mass of state and local suits had accumulated.[7] All of this money is just from lobbying and does not include substantial legislative campaign contributions!

The picture is different on the plaintiff side. Self-styled consumer rights, health advocacy groups, and the like have frequently felt stymied in the legislative and executive arenas. Moreover, they tend to get hugely outspent by their adversaries. For example, in 2005, gun control advocacy groups spent $180,000 lobbying Washington entities; gun rights organizations spent more than sixteen times that amount. In the same year, the Center for Science in the Public Interest funded lobbying efforts to the tune of about $212,000. Coke and Pepsi weighed in at over $2 million. Compared to K Street-style efforts, launching and funding litigation is a really cheap means to a regulatory end.

Cheap, however, does not always get you what you want. Obviously, in a case like that of the gun industry, litigation as regulation has been a complete bust. If would-be plaintiff-regulators are unable to score any victories, regulatory designs never get on the table. However, nor does lavish spending always result in desirable outcomes, particularly if a group cannot get the desired officeholders elected. The trial lawyers' association (the American Association for Justice [AAJ]), for example, has made campaign contributions of almost $30 million over the past ten electoral cycles primarily aimed at staving off tort reform – an obviously unsuccessful effort in the area of guns and even larger-scale develoments such as the *Class Action Fairness Act* (OpenSecrets. com 2008b).[8] Tobacco, on the hand, would seem to suggest something different. After all, the *MSA* exacted a huge, if clearly manageable, cost on the industry, as well as extracting agreements on the use of child-friendly advertising and posting smoking cessation information on cigarette company websites. For its part, the federal lawsuit, though failing to obtain any meaningful financial penalties from tobacco companies, may require them to stop marketing some cigarettes as "low tar," "light," "natural," or any other moniker suggesting good health.

On the other hand, the lion's share of state *MSA* monies has not gone into the kinds of anti-smoking and health-related programs that reformers had hoped they would. Indeed, the money has put states in a kind of perverse partnership with the tobacco industry – giving them an actual stake in the continued well-being of the cigarette business. Moreover, during the same time period that the tobacco companies have supposedly faced the greatest litigation-regulatory threat – 1998 to the present – the industry has actually been increasing the amount of nicotine in cigarettes – an average of 10 percent overall, with some brands packing a spike of up to 30 percent over the nine years (Brown 2006)! This is hardly the sort of activity that might be expected under a truly effective regulatory regime.

Attempts to control the practices of the food and drink industry through litigation present yet another murkier picture. In some ways, the threat of litigation on this front has resulted in very favourable outcomes. Notwithstanding the liability shield laws that the restaurant association have pursued, the industry overall has tried assiduously to stay out of court by capitulating to the demands of its opponents. Kraft has been far more compliant in removing the most unhealthy elements of its products than its Altria partner

Philip Morris has been in its. So, too, the soft drink industry has moved fairly swiftly to remove sugar-laden sodas from schools.

In part, as we have noted, this positive, compliant behaviour is probably due to other factors – lagging sales and obesity-related publicity (the litigators were particularly aggressive in promoting adverse publicity about the health effects of trans fats), especially among children and adolescents, to name two. Moreover, a number of governments have instituted labelling requirements (a few have banned trans fats from fast food menus), but most actions have come from voluntary changes from within the food industry. At the same time, and notwithstanding the botched *Barber* and *Pelman* fat suits, potential litigator-regulators appear to have learned valuable lessons from tobacco and guns. Most, after all, were veterans of the cigarette and firearms battles. Thus, they have been ready to enter into compromise agreements and, by eschewing payment, have been able to deflect the usual "greedy lawyer" accusations. In the end, however, how successful the food litigation efforts will have been in actually regulating industry remains to be seen.

Future Research
As economic globalization continues and expands, we are likely to see more consumer-related issues affecting larger populations of consumers and increasingly crossing jurisdictional boundaries. Lawrence Friedman (1973) observed that, as the US economic development began to reach across state boundaries, especially in the post-Civil War period, demand for unification and standardization of law was generated. Indeed, the business community wanted standardized and legally enforceable contracts to enhance the security of transactions with an increasing array of new trading partners. One of the first priorities of the American Bar Foundation, when it organized in 1878, was to promote the uniformity of law across the states. Similar trends have occurred in other nations with a federal structure in order to standardize law across states and territories, such as Australia, Canada, and Germany in the mid-twentieth century (for example, Leach 1963; Cranston 1997).

More recently, a major component of European Union unification has been harmonization of law across member states (for example, Falkner et al. 2005; Dingel 1999). There has been considerable movement in this direction with regard to such issues as intellectual property rights (for example, Keeling 2004; Vaver and Bently 2004). Assuming that the internationalization of commerce continues apace, corporations will seek out lower cost labour, develop distribution networks for both production and marketing purposes, and identify more consumer markets, wherever they can do so – all accompanied by an increased likelihood of group-based claims. As Supreme Court of Canada Justice McLachlin wrote in 2001: "The rise of mass production, the diversification of corporate ownership, the advent of the mega-corporation, and the recognition of environmental wrongs have all contributed to its [the class action's] growth. A faulty product may be sold to numerous consumers. Corporate mismanagement may bring loss to a large number of shareholders. Discriminatory policies may affect entire categories of employees ... Conflicts like these pit a large group of complainants against the alleged wrongdoer" (*Western Canadian Shopping Centres Inc. v. Dutton* 2001, para. 26).

Thus, the conditions that are conducive to group litigation seem destined to become increasingly pervasive. A case in point occurred in mid-September 2006 when news broke regarding E. coli-tainted spinach, originating from California. The California spinach was very quickly linked to the death of three people and illness of at least 166 others across a number of states (for example, Waters 2006; MSN Broadcasting Company 2006). The initial federal investigation pointed to a product distributed by Natural Selection Foods, with a distribution network that stretched across the United States, Canada, and Mexico as a probable source. Nearly as quickly, news surfaced that a Chicago restaurant had filed a class action claim against Natural Selection to recover the cost of the discarded spinach, with more cases likely to come (for example, Herman 2006). In addition, as we observed earlier in the introduction, Vioxx litigation forces mobilized in the United States, United Kingdom, Canada, and Australia within days of Merck's decision to withdraw the drug from the market.

At the same time, as we noted earlier, labour production and consumption matrices are growing in complexity, evolving with little regard for legal and political boundaries. Indeed, as national and regional laws are harmonized to accommodate business and commercial development, transnational activity and exchange is encouraged and proliferates, thus setting the stage for the types of litigation to which Justice McLachlin refers. Such activity means that we should expect multi-party actions to appear in greater numbers in all jurisdictions. As we observed in Chapter 6, there was considerable reform activity directed toward creating devices to allow for aggregated litigation models in the 1990s and early 2000s. The widespread reticence to emulate the US system notwithstanding, this trend should continue, and litigation activity is likely to grow more robust. The clear historical preference across European jurisdictions, including the United Kingdom and Australia, has been to address broad issues of industry-related liability (for example, asbestos-associated illness), stockholder complaints, and product-specific consumer claims through the legislative and administrative processes. However, creating mechanisms to facilitate the bundling of large numbers of individual complaints for consideration by courts has implications for the future that warrant further assessment. Although a menu of brakes (award caps, contingency fee restrictions, and the like) is the general rule, we have already seen some of them be relaxed in the interest of enhancing "access to justice."

In both the United Kingdom and Australia, as well as across the European Union, group litigation is underway – not a flood but at least a trickle. The Canadian courts have seen more activity, although not yet approaching the US volume. In part, this direction may represent deterioration in traditional and historical barriers to "adversarial legalism," which as Robert Kagan (2001) has noted, is quintessentially American and an early signal of convergence toward an invigorated court model. Kagan argues that the forces of tradition and local cultures are sufficiently strong to resist incursions of foreign influence (also see Kagan 1996; Kagan and Axelrad 2000; Legrand 1996), but others find evidence of movement (see, for example, Galanter 1992; Keleman 2006; Keleman and Sibbitt 2004; Shapiro 1993). Moreover, there are many indications of an enhanced judicial role in the public policy process in established democracies, especially since the post-Second World War era (for example, Dickson 2007; Pierce 2006; Hirschl 2004; Howe and Russell 2001; Russell and O'Brien 2001; Morton and Knopff 2000; Stone Sweet 2000; Tate and Vallinder 1995).

All of the systems from which we drew observations have a common law tradition, which places high value on principles articulated in previously decided cases and in which judges generally follow the doctrine of *stare decisis*. In the United States, this foundation, of course, does not etch precedent into stone, but it does provide a semblance of stability and predictability in the law. Indeed, Justice Story in 1820 reasoned that "where the parties are very numerous, and the court perceives, that it will be almost impossible to bring them all before the court; or where the question is of general interest, and a few may sue for the benefit of the whole; or where the parties form a part of a voluntary association for public or private purposes, and may be fairly supposed to represent the rights and interests of the whole; in these and analogous cases, if the bill purports to be not merely in behalf of the plaintiffs, but of all others interested ... the court will proceed to a decree" (*West v. Randall* 1820, 722). Although the number of parties has grown exponentially and case contours have become exceedingly complex, Story's core reasoning continues to resonate with American judges.[9] Moreover, the notion that both litigants should bear their own costs was noted to be the "general practice in the United States" by the Supreme Court of the United States in 1796 in *Arcambel v. Wiseman* (1796), and, although fee structures have also become more complicated and intricate, particularly in multi-party cases, it remains the general rule.

With regard to both issues – whether a group model of litigation can proceed, and who will pay the freight – a multitude of questions have arisen to produce a myriad of variations of the central themes. Indeed, the US legal tradition seems to encourage ongoing challenge and reinterpretation of rules (see, for example, Kagan 1996). By contrast, the rules governing procedures in the Australian, British, and Canadian systems have tended to be more fixed, with judges less receptive to the notion of revisiting them. This was certainly the case with regard to collective litigation and the influence of the 1910 *Markt* precedent. Although the question did arise from time to time in all three countries, the courts generally held to the *Markt* rule that claims should not be joined unless they presented identical issues until late in the century.[10]

The Supreme Court of Canada's decision in *Naken v. General Motors of Canada Ltd.* (1983) is a clear and prominent example. The justices found existing rules to be outdated and stifling, but they were not prepared to engage in the type of policy-making that would be necessary to change them. This set of legal actions also has additional features that are not uncommon among cases of its genre. First, it had moved with glacier-like speed for about a decade, resulting in a knot of episodically published opinions on procedural questions in varying courts along the way. Ultimately, the corporation prevailed over a band of consumers (the "haves" came out ahead).[11] Note also that the defendant was a Canadian branch of a US concern, and a big one at that. Given the defendant's status and the clear connections and proximity to the United States, one would expect there to have been significant sharing of strategic and information resources, particularly on the defence side.[12] Moreover, although the opinions of the Ontario courts, as well as the Supreme Court of Canada, cite the centrality of *Markt* and its British and Canadian progeny, they also pay considerable attention to recent experience in the United States (at both the federal and state levels) as useful points of reference. This scenario signals a process of cross-fertilization of ideas and experience, which is noticeable among the judicial opinions of Canada and Australia but far less so in those we reviewed from the British and US courts (except among the early cases). Whether the interest expressed in decisions in non-domestic jurisdictions is a product of the judges' own research or the presentations by attorneys is an interesting question, but it will require more extensive and systematic assessment of advocacy briefs and opinions.

We observed extensive indications of coordination of effort and pooling of resources among the legal community (among both the plaintiff and defence bar) as well as cross-venue references in opinions among the US cases we reviewed.[13] Indeed, the practice of information sharing and coordination of effort by otherwise unconnected advocates dates at least to the early 1960s in the United States, facilitated by the American Trial Lawyers' Association (ATLA). Among the progenitors was attorney Paul Rheingold, who, in 1962, created a clearinghouse operation to coordinate discovery proceedings in the myriad of cases that had been filed following disclosure of health dangers associated with the use of MER/29, a popular anti-cholesterol drug (see, for example, Rheingold 1968; Ranii 1984). In addition to the ATLA (now the AAJ), a number of umbrella organizations and clearinghouse groups have organized as ongoing concerns, holding regular workshops and providing staging areas for the exchange of ideas and strategic information. When specific issues arise, such entities serve as network hubs, points of reference for the coordination of activities and the sharing of expertise and technical information regarding the most current and pending trial and appellate actions, whatever the venue. This was precisely the function of the Rheingold MER/29 group, and we observed lawyers and organizations playing a similar role (sometimes an escalated one) in the tobacco, firearm, and food-related litigation upon which we focused.

Given the nature of the underlying causes, the probability of multi-venue litigation of similar issues is growing, with or without coordination. Indeed, the phenomenon took on such proportions in the United States that a special procedure was developed in 1968 in order to address it, thus allowing the courts to minimize duplicated effort and pre-empt the confusion that would follow from conflicting outcomes (Chapter 1). In more recent years, collateral litigation across Canada has produced calls for an official means to consolidate under a special judicial procedure, and the British general litigation order system is designed, in part, with a managerial purpose, so that similar claims that would otherwise be filed in different jurisdictions can be bundled (Chapter 6). Thus, even if there was no initial synchronization, multi-district consolidation demands it.

Moreover, because issues affecting large numbers of people are likely to occur simultaneously across jurisdictions, organizations at the international level assume a parallel posture, such as those with an interest in human rights (for example, Human Rights Watch, Amnesty International), environmental protection (for example, Greenpeace, Friends of the Earth), and a range of others whose agendas include combating tobacco consumption and other health-related problems, thus providing easily recognizable and accessible mechanisms for coordination and dialogue regarding legal challenges around the globe.[14] It is not surprising, then, that we notice a number of advocates whose connections extend beyond their own national borders, often linking to related actions in the United States. With the continued globalization of markets and law, these networks are only going to grow more extensive and active, and, as they do so, we are likely to see greater harmonization of litigation across jurisdictions – better coordination of effort and perhaps simultaneity in addressing the courts. A case in point (and there are likely others) occurred in the United States and Canada, and nearly as quickly in Australia and the United Kingdom, during the days following the publication of Merck's decision to withdraw its Vioxx anti-arthritis drug from the market because of negative side effects (see the introduction in this text).

Simply the occurrence of collateral litigation does not necessarily imply coordination, however, and such activities warrant further assessment. Simultaneous filings might be strategically useful with regard to product liability involving multi-national corporations, where the larger objective is to achieve global policy change. This is similar to the approach taken at the national level that we have observed, especially in the United States. However, serial litigation is also a strategic option. Since judges, especially those who preside over their respective system's highest court, as well as members of the legal community who have an active group litigation port-folio, represent an attentive audience, we may well observe a form of inter-national forum shopping. Indeed, plaintiff attorneys may wish to initialize their assault in a system where they believe they have a good chance of success, thus creating leverage elsewhere. This seems to have been among the strategies deployed by the Ontario government against the tobacco in-dustry in the late 1990s (see Chapter 6), and Carol Harlow and Richard Rawlings (1992, 131) report a similar early move by the British Opren litiga-tion team in the 1980s. Both cases resulted in negative outcomes in US Dis-trict Court, but their approach is suggestive and is, we hypothesize, not isolated.

Similar claims in multiple locations also produce incentives for the defence to coordinate the sharing of technical and legal expertise across jurisdictions – very likely, internationally. Indeed, the defence bar has organized in much the same way as plaintiff attorneys, forming such groups as Lawyers for Civil Justice (national, United States), the Defense Research Institute (mostly centred in the United States, but with an international component), the International Association of Defense Counsel (international), Association of Defense Trial Attorneys (international), the Federation of Defense and Corporate Counsel (international), all of which hold regular conferences and workshops, offer litigation coordination, research, and preparation as-sistance, build issue-related coalitions for better defence co-operation, and the like. In addition, major law firms generally have affiliates in a range of other strategically located countries. Again, this facilitates transnational coordination of effort across national venues.

We have noted the processes of globalization on a number of occasions, particularly as a confluence of activities that enhance conditions likely to stimulate multi-party litigation. An additional and oft-cited concomitant is easier travel and faster communications. To the extent that judges across systems wish to compare experiences and share visions, particularly in the developed parts of the world, they are able to do so quite extensively. Indeed, according to Anne-Marie Slaughter (2004, 69), several developments in recent decades – the proliferation of "constitutional cross-fertilization," the con-struction of a global community of human rights law, deepened relations between national courts and the international tribunals, the rise of private transnational litigation, and the emergence of face-to-face meetings among judges around the world – are constitutive of "the beginnings of a global legal system" in which "courts interact quasi-autonomously with other courts – national and international" (also see Alston 1997; Raustiala 2002; Harlow 2005; Saunders 2006).

This is probably an optimistic view of an expansive meeting of the judicial mind and the convergence of legal principles. Indeed, it is emphatically not shared by some members of the Supreme Court of the United States.[15] Nonetheless, judges do acknowledge the experiences and decisions of courts from external jurisdictions with some degree of frequency, even if they are of questionable precedential value. This has been the case across venues in the United States for some time, a practice that has no doubt been facilitated by judicial conferences and electronic legal databases (for example, Caldeira 1985; Landes, Lessig, and Solimine 1998). The degree to which judges cite sources beyond their own national system is a question that has received scant scholarly attention (but see, La Forest 1988; Opeskin 2001; Zaring 2006). In any event, because many systems have revised their procedural rules in recent years (in most cases since the late 1990s), providing a mechanism for collective litigation, judges are presented issues with which they have relatively little experience. Generally speaking, the revisions have been implemented to foster greater access to justice and to enhance efficiency. However, opening access to justice also has the effect of encouraging the legal community to mobilize for action in the courts as problems arise (see, for example, Epp 1998), perhaps inviting entrepreneurial lawyering and certainly presenting due process issues. Given the nature of multi-party litigation (class, representative, multi-district, and so on) and the breadth of the problems they signal across the community (increasingly, across communities), the controversies are fully laden with public policy implications, and they are inherently complex. As transnational advocacy networks continue to develop and to sponsor litigation, we should expect them to draw upon case law experience friendly to their respective position, thus furthering the notion of a "global legal system."

Notes

Introduction

1   There are many examples of holding individual plaintiffs aloft to public ridicule. The American Tort Reform Association maintains as part of its website a section entitled Loony Lawsuits, http://atra.org/display/13. Of course, no plaintiff has been more maligned by politicians, talk show hosts, and late night comics than Stella Liebeck, the "McDonald's coffee lady." However, she is not alone in being the target of ridicule and distortion. William Haltom and Michael McCann (2004a) present an excellent analysis of the Liebeck case and a range of others that are part of a very successful media campaign to portray (distort) the American tort system as a feeding frenzy by insatiably greedy people who clog the courts with questionable, often ludicrous, claims.

2   *Canadian Charter of Rights and Freedoms*, Part 1 of the *Constitution Act 1982*, being Schedule B to the *Canada Act, 1982* (U.K.), 1982, c. 11.

3   The *Constitutional Reform Act 2005*, c. 4, among other changes, creates a new high court that will assume most of the important judicial functions historically performed by the Privy Council Law Lords of the upper parliamentary chamber. It is available online at http://www.opsi.gov.uk/acts/acts2005/ukpga_20050004_en_1.

4   Determination of multi-district litigations is governed by the Judicial Panel on Multidistrict Litigation, a group created by Congress in 1968 (*Multidistrict Litigation*, 28 U.S.C. §1407) and comprised of seven sitting federal judges, who are appointed to serve on the panel by the chief justice of the United States. See generally, http://www.jpml.uscourts.gov/.

5   *Rule 23* of the *US Federal Rules of Civil Procedure*, http://www.law.cornell.edu/rules/frcp/, contemplates defendant classes as well, but modern attempts at such classes have been few and unsuccessful (see, for example, *Tilley v. TJX Companies* 2003a).

6   See chapters 1 and 2 in this text for further general discussions of large-scale litigation.

7   See, for example, *White et al. v. Mattel Inc.* (2007); *Mayhew v. Mattel, Inc.* (2007); *Monroe ex. rel. Monroe* (2007); *Sarjent v. Fisher-Price, Inc.* (2007); *Shoukry v. Fisher-Price, Inc.* (2007).

8   In the first major case to go to trial, a Texas jury awarded the widow of a Vioxx user $253 million. This award was later reversed on appeal (*Merck v. Ernst* 2008).

9   For example, in 2005, a New Jersey judge ruled that health plans that covered members' Vioxx prescriptions could sue Merck as a class ("New Jersey Judge Rules" 2005).

10 For current developments, see http://vioxx.laed.uscourts.gov/.

11 One such class, certified recently in the Superior Court of Justice in Ontario is being appealed by Merck Frosst Canada Limited (Merck Frosst 2008).

12 *Consumer Protection Act*, 1987, c. 43.

13 A group of UK citizens took their case to court in New Jersey, hoping to take advantage of the state's plaintiff-friendly rules. New Jersey courts, however, barred the plaintiffs' action under the doctrine of *forum non conveniens* (Gottlieb 2007).

14 *Canadian Bill of Rights*, S.C. 1960, c. 44.

15 *Due Process of Law Act 1368* (U.K.), 42 Edw. 3, c. 3.

16 On the notion of access to justice, see, for example, EC Directive 2003/8 to Improve Access to Justice in Cross-Border Disputes by Establishing Minimum Common Rules Relating to Legal Aid for Such Disputes, O.J. L26/41, 31 January 2003, http://eur-lex.europa.eu/LexUriServ/LexUriServ.do?uri=CELEX:32003L0008:EN:HTML.

17 See, for example, Justice Souter's discussion in *Ortiz v. Fibreboard Corporation* (1999).

18 The Center for Public Integrity found that nearly $13 billion was spent by organizations lobbying the US federal government in a five-and-a-half-year period from 1998 to mid-2004. Center for Public Integrity, http://www.publicintegrity.org/lobby/.

19 Indeed, Justice Brennan observed that the world had changed dramatically:

> Whatever the justification advanced in earlier days for refusing to recognize the rights and interests in land of the indigenous inhabitants of settled colonies, an unjust and discriminatory doctrine of that kind can no longer be accepted ... The common law does not necessarily conform with international law, but international law is a legitimate and important influence on the development of the common law, especially when international law declares the existence of universal human rights. A common law doctrine founded on unjust discrimination in the enjoyment of civil and political rights demands reconsideration. It is contrary both to international standards and to the fundamental values of our common law to entrench a discriminatory rule which, because of the supposed position on the scale of social organization of the indigenous inhabitants of a settled colony, denies them a right to occupy their traditional lands. (*Mabo v. Queensland (No. 2)* 1992, 42)

In May 2006, the Canadian government agreed to a resolution that became the largest class action settlement in the nation's history, thus ending lengthy litigation regarding the treatment of Indian residents at government-sponsored schools, which operated into the 1970s and are now acknowledged to constitute human rights violations. On 11 June 2008, Prime Minister Stephen Harper apologized "to former students of Indian Residential Schools and sought forgiveness for the students' suffering and for the damaging impact the schools had on Aboriginal culture, heritage and language" (Harper 2008). Full discussion of the *Indian Residential Schools Settlement Agreement* is available on the Indian and Northern Affairs Canada website, http://www.ainc-inac.gc.ca/rqpi/index-eng.asp.

20 In fact, the real story of Stella Liebeck, also known as the "McDonald's coffee lady," is quite different than the popular mythology would have it. In fact, Liebeck was very seriously burned and had tried to settle modestly with McDonald's before taking them to court, and McDonald's had received many previous complaints about the temperature of their coffee before Liebeck's mishap. Moreover, the multimillion dollars awarded to Liebeck by the jury was reduced to a few hundred thousand by the judge (*Liebeck v. McDonald's Restaurants* 1994; see also Haltom and McCann 2004a, especially Chapter 6).

The British courts also hosted litigation against McDonald's in a product liability multiparty action, alleging that their coffee was excessively hot and the drink containers faulty. The case has been noted on websites that belittle plaintiffs, but it has failed to get a lot of traction as most of the thirty-six claimants were children who suffered severe burns, with some requiring skin grafts. It was among the first cluster of claims consolidated for consideration under the UK's Group Litigation Order system in 2001. After a four-day hearing, the trial judge found for the defendant on each of the plaintiffs' charges (*Bogle v. McDonalds Restaurants Limited* 2002).

21 See Department of Justice Canada, http://laws.justice.gc.ca.

Chapter 1: Theoretical, Historical, and Legal Underpinnings

1 Stephen Yeazell (1987, 17) refers to conferring temporary corporate status to unincorporated groups for purposes of litigation as a sanction of "underground incorporation." Moreover, although the overwhelming majority of cases today involve plaintiff classes, defendant classes were not at all uncommon in earlier eras.

2 Writing for the Court in *Ortiz v. Fibreboard Corporation* (1999, 846), Justice Souter observes that "mandatory class actions aggregating damage claims implicate the due process 'principle of general application in Anglo-American jurisprudence that one is not bound by a

judgment *in personam* in a litigation in which he is not designated as a party or to which he has not been made a party by service or process,' it being our 'deep-rooted historic tradition that everyone should have his own day in court'" [citations and references deleted]. Dissenting in the same case, Justice Breyer offers the following counter-argument: "[T]he alternative to class-action settlement is not a fair opportunity for each potential plaintiff to have his or her own day in court. Unusually high litigation costs, unusually long delays, and limitations upon the total amount of resources available for payment, together mean that most potential plaintiffs may not have a realistic alternative" (*ibid.*, 867-68).

3 See, for example, *Galpin v. Page* (1873) (citing both US and British precedent from much earlier). In addition, see *Phillips Petroleum Co. v. Shutts* (1985, 812) for a much more recent case where the issue of proper notice was a central issue. Indeed, Justice Rehnquist, for the Court elaborated thusly: "The plaintiff must receive notice plus an opportunity to be heard and participate in the litigation, whether in person or through counsel. The notice must be the best practicable, 'reasonably calculated, under all the circumstances, to apprise interested parties of the pendency of the action and afford them an opportunity to present their objections.' The notice should describe the action and the plaintiffs' rights in it. Additionally, we hold that due process requires at a minimum that an absent plaintiff be provided with an opportunity to remove himself from the class by executing and returning an 'opt out' or 'request for exclusion' form to the court. Finally, the Due Process Clause of course requires that the named plaintiff at all times adequately represent the interests of the absent class members" [references deleted].

4 The "takings clause" – "nor shall private property be taken for public use, without just compensation" – is generally understood to mean that, while government can seize privately owned land for the betterment of the whole, the owner must be properly paid for the loss.

5 *Federal Rules of Civil Procedure* (1938), http://www.law.cornell.edu/rules/frcp/.

6 *Universal Declaration of Human Rights,* UN Resolution 217 A (III), 10 December 1948.

7 Haltom and McCann (2004a, 86-87) refer to class actions and mass torts as the "third world of torts" because of the high stakes and far-reaching implications.

8 The US Constitution and the various state constitutions formally grant rights to individual citizens and restrict the power of the state. By the same token, people are held individually responsible under criminal statutes, and they are expected to abide by their individually agreed-upon contractual obligations.

9 Marriage also falls into this category, but it has become quite contentious of late, due to the controversy surrounding the issue of gay rights.

10 US Constitution, Article 4, section 1, includes the "full faith and credit" clause, indicating that each state is obliged to recognize "the public Acts, Records, and judicial Proceedings of every other State." Moreover, section 2 guarantees that citizenship is transferable from one state to the next. In general, this has meant that rights conferred by one state are acknowledged in another, but it has become an issue of some debate recently regarding the question of gay marriage. The *Defense of Marriage Act,* 110 Stat. 2419 (1996), was intended to limit the reach of the "full faith and credit" clause.

11 Indeed, the Utah trial of uber-polygamist Warren Jeffs is not overtly about multiple marriages but, rather, about coercing young girls into relationships (Dobner 2007).

12 Apparently, Martin's congregants were not bringing their dead to his cemetery, where he would perform a service and collect a death tax, and he was suing to enforce his tax on them. See also *Martin, Rector of Barkway v. Parishioners of Nuthamstead* (1199).

13 Not surprisingly, the King's Council found in favour of Sir Otes.

14 The necessary party rule was deemed flexible, however, when the reality of a situation made it impossible to comply – for example, where the identity of one or more defendants was not known or one defendant was outside the jurisdiction, a case could proceed against those who could be identified or who were within jurisdictional reach.

15 The earliest recorded case on this issue is apparently *Brown v. Vermuden* (1676). The vicar of Worselworth had successfully sued his parishioners as a class for non-payment of tithes. Vermuden objected, arguing that he was not named in the original case and should not therefore be bound by the outcome. The court ruled against him, finding that to allow him

to prevail would open the courts to an unlimited flood of litigation (see, for example, Marcin 1974; Yeazell 1987, 134-35).

16 There were, of course, exceptions, particularly in the context of shareholders attempting to hold business officers accountable for their actions. The exceptions ultimately overwhelmed the rule. See, for example, *Chancey v. May* (1722); *Hitchens v. Congreve* (1828).

17 Yeazell (1987, 216-17) contends that although Justice Story "had read widely in preparation for writing his two equity treatises ... in this instance learning did not bring understanding." Hazard, Gedid, and Sowle (1998, 1878) explain the situation in this way: "His thoughts about representative suits were incompletely formed, tentative, and ambivalent. Nevertheless, he devised a classification of class suits that has descended into modern times."

18 Indeed, the court was clearly appalled by the cemetery intrusions: "This is not the case of a mere private trespass; but a public nuisance, going to the irreparable injury of the Georgetown congregation of Lutherans. The property consecrated to their use by a perpetual servitude or easement, is to be taken from them; the sepulchres of the dead are to be violated; the feelings of religion, and the sentiment of natural affection of the kindred and friends of the deceased are to be wounded; and the memorials erected by piety or love, to the memory of the good, are to be removed so as to leave no trace of the last home of their ancestry to those who may visit the spot in future generations" (*Beatty v. Kurtz* 1829, 584).

19 As of 17 October 2007, the number of subsequent cases citing *Beatty v. Kurtz* (1829) stood at 185, according to *Westlaw*.

20 *Federal Equity Rule 48*, 42 U.S. xlvi 1842 (repealed 1912).

21 Ibid., xlii, xlvi.

22 The case was, thus, remanded for trial. For a good discussion of this interesting and important case, see Hazard, Gedid, and Sowle (1998, 1897-1901); Yeazell (1987, 221-22).

23 *Swormstedt* lived a much longer life, however, because, according to our search of the *Lexis* database, it was cited in eighty-one additional federal court opinions between 1913 and 2003. *Rule 48* was revised in 1912.

24 See Chapter 6 for a discussion of *Markt and Co. v. Knight Steamship Co.* (1910) and its long-term impacts.

25 Diversity cases generally were filed in federal courts. However, there was no shortage of group-based conflicts within those categories where diversity was not an issue.

26 *Federal Equity Rule 38*, 226 U.S. 659 (1912).

27 *Supreme Council of the Royal Arcanum v. Green* (1915); *Hartford Life Ins. Co. v. Ibs* (1915); *Supreme Tribe of Ben-Hur v. Cauble* (1921) all involved the reorganization and distribution of member benefits of fraternal orders. The *Green, Ibs, Ben-Hur,* and *United Mine Workers v. Coronado Coal* (1922) opinions all referred positively to the *Swormstedt* logic, and the latter two noted the provisions of recently revised *Rule 38*. Moreover, all four were unanimous.

28 He also references the following previously decided state cases as authority: *Pickett v. Walsh* (1906); *Karges Furniture Co. v. Amalgamated Woodworkers Local Union* (1905); *Baskins v. United Mine Workers* (1921).

29 In fact, Taft quoted directly from Justice Farwell's opinion in *Taff Vale Co. v. Amalgamated Society of Railway Servants* (1901, 390), where the rationale was quite similar to, and supported, his own: "If the contention of the defendant society were well founded, the Legislature has authorized the creation of numerous bodies of men capable of owning great wealth and of action by agents with absolutely no responsibility for the wrongs that they may do to other persons by the use of that wealth and the employment of those agents."

30 In fact, the Court has consistently followed this logic. See, for example, *Harrison v. Perea* (1897); *United States v. Equitable Trust Co.* (1931); *Sprague v. Ticonic National Bank* (1939); *Mills v. Electric Auto-Lite Co.* (1970); and *Hall v. Cole* (1973).

31 In light of growing differences among the states and the practice by federal judges of deferring to state rules, Congress passed "far-reaching" legislation in an attempt to standardize the federal system (*Act of February 26, 1853,* 10 Stat. 161). The Court was reluctant to entertain questions of fee shifting, finding that such issues have been considered primarily legislative terrain and should remain so. Also see Chief Justice Warren's opinion for the Court in *Fleischmann Distilling Corp. v. Maier Brewing Co.* (1967), the first reference to the

practice as the "American rule," thereby distinguishing it from the "English rule." In discussing some of the historical development, Justice Warren also notes that "[i]n support of the American rule, it has been argued that since litigation is at best uncertain one should not be penalized for merely defending or prosecuting a lawsuit, and that the poor might be unjustly discouraged from instituting actions to vindicate their rights if the penalty for losing included the fees of their opponents' counsel" (*ibid.*, 717).

32 Apparently the "loser pays" rationale dates back to fifth-century Roman law and is now the prevailing practice across Europe, Canada, and a number of other countries around the globe (see, for example, Pfennigstorf 1984).

33 *Rule 23* of the *Federal Rules of Civil Procedure, supra* note 5.

34 Such analytical distinctions were first created by Thomas Atkins Street (1909) in his *Federal Equity Practice,* a treatise published in 1909. Street considered "true" cases to be based on property issues, noting *Swormstedt* as a good example of this type, and "spurious" class litigation, according to his scheme, was based on personal liability, with *American Steel and Wire Co. v. Wire Drawers' and Die Makers' Unions* (1898) being an example of this category.

35 Indeed, Levi and Moore (1937) published a law review article in 1937 that differentiated class litigation with the scheme that was employed in *Rule 23.*

36 Curiously, although the court agreed that the *Burke v. Kleiman* (1934) stipulation was untrue, it disagreed with the trial court's conclusion that it was fraudulent and collusive.

37 Moreover, racially restrictive housing covenants were found to violate the US Constitution in *Shelley v. Kraemer* (1948), in a case that was argued by Thurgood Marshall.

38 "Administrative law," they observe, "removes the obstacles of insufficient funds and insufficient knowledge by shifting the responsibility for protecting the interests of the individuals comprising the group to a public body which has ample funds and adequate powers of investigation" (Kalven and Rosenfield 1941, 686).

39 As Yeazell (1987, 237) observes, there was an occasional exception, but "such adventurousness was rare ... The original version of Rule 23, bolstered by the now constitutionalized individualism of *Hansberry,* froze the class action in place for thirty years."

40 There are many other examples of such expressions. For instance, in 1990, Justice Howerton, writing for an unanimous panel of the Illinois Court of Appeals (5th District), stated: "No matter how refined, how revised, or how evolved this flashy import becomes, the goal of the class action remains the same – justice for the lowly, the tenants, the parishioners, the multitudes" (*Wood River Area Dev. Corp. v. Germania Fed. Sav. and Loan Ass'n* 1990). Chief Justice McLachlin, writing for an unanimous Supreme Court of Canada in 2001, stated: "The class action plays an important role in today's world. The rise of mass production, the diversification of corporate ownership, the advent of the mega-corporation, and the recognition of environmental wrongs have all contributed to its growth. A faulty product may be sold to numerous consumers. Corporate mismanagement may bring loss to a large number of shareholders. Discriminatory policies may affect entire categories of employees. Environmental pollution may have consequences for citizens all over the country" (*Western Canadian Shopping Centres Inc. v. Dutton* 2001, para. 26).

41 See, for example, *Smith v. Allwright* (1944) (successfully challenging Texas Democratic Party rules restricting membership to whites only); *Missouri ex. rel. Gaines v. Canada* (1938) (striking down the University of Missouri law school admission policy that barred African-American students); *Shelley v. Kraemer* (1948) (striking down restrictive racial covenants in housing); *Sweatt v. Painter* (1950) (finding that separate Texas law schools, hastily created to avoid desegregation at the University of Texas, was clearly unequal); and *Brown v. Board of Education* (1954) (finding racially segregated elementary schools inherently unequal).

42 Historically, courts at all levels have hosted litigation initiated – and defended – by corporations, whose legal personhood was authenticated by the Supreme Court of the United States in 1886 (*Santa Clara County v. Southern Pacific Railroad Company* 1886). Indeed, large and small entities from the business community have long engaged the legal system. In keeping with litigation trends that have been unearthed by a variety of social scientists working in a range of judicial venues, a number of the more prominent Supreme Court of the United States cases in our earliest era involved parties that today would be recognized as business enterprises.

Corporations, for their part, have a long history of using the American courts to their advantage. While market firms have been active in the court system, they clearly are not the only collectivized parties to engage the process. Indeed, the press, political parties, state and local governments, labour unions, religious organizations, among many others, have been frequent litigants.

43 Of course, we could trace the Court's recognition of the importance of associational groupings to the famous footnote 4 in Justice Stone's opinion for the Court in *United States v. Carolene Products* (1938), where he stated in part: "Nor need we enquire whether similar considerations enter into the review of statutes directed at particular religious, or national, or racial minorities, whether prejudice against discrete and insular minorities may be a special condition, which tends seriously to curtail the operation of those political processes ordinarily to be relied upon to protect minorities, and which may call for a correspondingly more searching judicial inquiry."

44 The Supreme Court of the United States invalidated Alabama's statute that demanded the membership roles of the National Association for the Advancement of Colored People and recognized, for the first time, a constitutionally protected right of association under the First Amendment.

45 Four cases challenging state laws were decided collectively by the Supreme Court of the United States under the one case title *Brown v. Board of Education* (1954): *Belton v. Gebhart* (Delaware), *Briggs v. Elliot* (South Carolina), *Davis v. County School Board of Prince Edward County* (Virginia), and *Brown v. Board of Education* (Kansas). In addition, *Bolling v. Sharpe* (1954), challenging federal law in the nation's capitol, was argued with the others but was decided with a separate opinion. All were class actions.

46 We should note that success in this case only means that the litigation produced favourable judicial outcomes. Implementation of these decisions was another matter entirely (for example, Kluger 1976; Klarman 2004). Despite the foot dragging on this front, civil rights remained one of the most significant political and legal issues of the 1960s. Congress passed several major pieces of legislation, the first since the Civil War, beginning with the *Civil Rights Act of 1964*, PL 88-352.

47 The case before the Supreme Court of the United States centred on the size of the class, proper notice requirements, and the distribution of costs related to notice. A majority voted to dismiss the action without prejudice, thus allowing the plaintiffs to redefine the class.

48 Indeed, Public Citizen, the consumer organization founded by Nader, maintains an active litigation group, http://www.citizen.org/litigation/.

49 *National Environmental Policy Act*, 42 U.S.C. 4321-47 (1970). We have seen a wide range of interest groups engage the political process through the courts, and litigation has become an integral component of interest group politics. This process has also been extensively investigated, with research addressing litigation campaigns, and various strategic manoeuvres by organized groups, ranging from bringing test cases, providing mutual support, participating as *amici curiae* at various court levels and at various stages of agenda setting and decisional processes at the Supreme Court of the United States. The early civil rights litigation model was developed as a way to approximate (or at least offer some counter-weight to the organizational power of the forces aligned on the other side. Indeed, government is a formidable political-legal opponent and so too are the members of the corporate sector. Although they are relative latecomers to the arena, interest groups have become very frequent participants in litigation – especially before the Supreme Court of the United States.

50 Section (b) specifies four situations where litigation may proceed as a class action. An action may be maintained as a class action if the prerequisites of subdivision (a) are satisfied, and in addition: (1) the prosecution of separate actions by or against individual members of the class would create a risk of (a) inconsistent or varying adjudications with respect to individual members of the class which would establish incompatible standards of conduct for the party opposing the class, or (b) adjudications with respect to individual members of the class which would as a practical matter be dispositive of the interests of the other members not parties to the adjudications or substantially impair or impede their ability to protect their interests; or (2) the party opposing the class has acted or refused to act on

grounds generally applicable to the class, thereby making appropriate final injunctive relief or corresponding declaratory relief with respect to the class as a whole; or (3) the court finds that the questions of law or fact common to the members of the class predominate over any questions affecting only individual members, and that a class action is superior to other available methods for the fair and efficient adjudication of the controversy. The matters pertinent to the findings include: (a) the interest of members of the class in individually controlling the prosecution or defence of separate actions; (b) the extent and nature of any litigation concerning the controversy already commenced by or against members of the class; (c) the desirability or undesirability of concentrating the litigation of the claims in the particular forum; (d) the difficulties likely to be encountered in the management of a class action. *Federal Rules of Civil Procedure, supra* note 5, *Rule 23.*

51 If the litigation does not involve a bankruptcy, a trust or estate administered by the court, or a limited fund, the prevailing understanding is that all unnamed and absent members of the class must be notified and given an opportunity to opt out.

52 *Advisory Committee's Note to Proposed Rule of Civil Procedure 23,* 39 F.R.D. 69, 103 (1966).

53 For a summary of current procedural devices available, see *Cutler v. 65 Security Plan* (1993).

54 The rule was repeatedly reinforced and was reiterated as late as 1973 in *Zahn v. International Paper Co.* (1973). Also see *Snyder v. Harris* (1969). The rule remains good law (for example, *McCulloch v. Velez* 2004).

55 The doctrine of strict liability originated in a nineteenth-century British case, *Fletcher v. Rylands* (1865), holding that a defendant will be found liable when damages to another party are the result of the defendant's unusually dangerous or negligent action. In this case, Fletcher flooded his land to create a reservoir, but the water also flooded underground mines, operated by Rylands, on an adjacent parcel of property.

56 For example, third-party bystanders could recover for pain and suffering resulting from witnessing the injury of a family member (for example, *Dillon v. Legg* 1968); manufacturers' liability was extended beyond the purchaser to others (for example, *Henningsen v. Bloomfield Motors* 1960); and the notion of what constitutes a defective product was expanded beyond consideration of manufacturing defects to "design defects" (for example, *Barker v. Lull Engineering* 1978), to name only a few.

57 *Sherman Antitrust Act,* 15 U.S.C. §§ 1-7 (1890).

58 *Multi-District Litigation Act,* 28 U.S.C. §1407 at para. 1407c (1968). According to the statute, "[t]he judicial panel on multidistrict litigation shall consist of seven circuit and district judges designated from time to time by the Chief Justice of the United States, no two of whom shall be from the same circuit."

59 *Multi-Party, Multi-Forum Trial Jurisdiction Act of 2002,* 28 U.S.C. §1369.

60 Some have also argued that the procedure presents a range of ethical questions for attorneys representing the plaintiff class, ranging from conflict of interest to outright collusion (see, for example, Weinstein 1994; Coffee 1995).

61 Media markets, of course, are no longer confined to a local, or even national, reach, and the message about the US legal system has been heard globally. As we shall see (especially in Chapter 6), this has influenced the type of reforms considered and adopted as constitutional and institutional changes across the developed world in the past two decades.

Chapter 2: Mass Torts and Class Action

1 The Center for Disease Control and Prevention expects the number of deaths from asbestos exposure to rise over the next decade. The number of Americans who have died of asbestosis has increased dramatically over the years, from seventy-seven in 1968 to 1,493 in 2000 ("Asbestos Deaths" 2004).

2 North American Asbestos Corporation (1978), Johns-Manville (1982), Amatex Corporation (1982), UNR Industries (1982) (including Union Asbestos and Rubber), Waterman Steamship Corporation (1983), Wallace and Gale Company (1984), Forty-Eight Insulations (1985), Pacor, Incorporated (1986), Prudential Lines, Incorporated (1986), Standard Insulations, Incorporated (1986), Gatke Corporation (1987), Nicolet (1987), Delaware Insulations (1989), Hillborough Holdings (1989), Raytech Corporation (1989) (including Raymark Industries and Raymark Corporation), Celotex Corporation (1990) (including Carey Canada, Panacon,

Philip Carey Company, and Smith and Kanzler), National Gypsum (1990), Standard Asbestos Manufacturing and Insulation (1990), Eagle Pitcher Industries (1991), and H.K. Porter (1991) (including Southern Asbestos Company and Southern Textile). See Plevin and Kalish (2002, 18).

3 The following companies filed for bankruptcy in 2003: CE Thurston, Combustion Engineering, Congoleum, Flintkote, Kellogg Brown and Root/DII, and Muralo.

4 As we discuss in Chapter 3, much of the tobacco litigation was settled via a multi-state agreement.

5 In many hard hit jurisdictions, classes had been formed prior to the 1990s. For example, the eastern district of Texas was particularly overwhelmed by cases. There, District Judge Robert M. Parker, faced in the mid-1980s with over 900 asbestos-related personal injury cases, certified a large class. See *Jenkins v. Raymark Industries, Inc.* (1986).

6 At a press conference in December 2003, President Bush chided Congress, saying: "It was a mistake not to ... get asbestos reform" (Press Conference of the President 2003).

7 *Fairness in Asbestos Injury Resolution Act of 2006*, s. 3274. An analogous House of Representatives bill was sponsored by Chris Cannon (Republican, Utah) in 2005, along with fifty-nine mostly Republican co-sponsors.

8 In 2004, a federal judge certified the largest private civil rights class in history, a group of 1.6 million current and former Wal-Mart employees alleging sex discrimination on the part of the giant corporation (*Dukes v. Wal-Mart Stores* 2004). In February 2007, the Ninth Circuit Court upheld the certification (*Dukes v. Wal-Mart, Inc.* 2007).

9 Although the original diethylstilbestrol cases have largely been resolved, a new, "third generation" of plaintiffs (the granddaughters of women who took the drug), is now wending its way through courts (see Batt 1996).

10 For simplicity's sake, we use the name Merrell Dow or simply Merrell. In fact, Merrell has been sold numerous times over its history. For a good summary, see Sanders (1992, 311-12).

11 Judge Rubin, writing in *In re: Richardson-Merrell, Inc. "Bendectin" Products Liability Litigation* (1985, 1221, n. 6), estimated that were all the individual Bendectin cases to be tried separately, they "would require approximately 182 Judge years, i.e. 182 Judges for one entire year."

12 *Frye v. United States* (1923, 1014). *Frye* established the "general acceptance" test. That is, evidence from expert testimony "must be sufficiently established to have gained general acceptance in the particular field in which it belongs."

13 In 2000, a small Canadian firm gained permission to market Bendectin as Diclectin. See Kolata (2000).

14 Other diet-related suits involve Meridia (*In re: Meridia Products Liability Litigation* 2002); Phenylpropanolamine (*In re: Phenylpropanolamine (PPA) Products Liability Litigation* 2001); and Ephedra (*In re: Ephedra Products Liability Litigation* 2004).

15 See also *In re: Serzone Products Liability Litigation* (2002) and *In re: Zyprexa Products Liability Litigation* (2004).

16 In the first Vioxx case to go to trial, the widow of a former user was awarded $253.40 million in damages by a Texas jury. Since then, roughly 45,000 additional people have sued Merck. In 2004, Merck issued a voluntary worldwide recall of the drug. Merck, however, has seen more victories than losses. In May 2008, a Texas court of appeals reversed the jury verdict against Merck (*Merck v. Ernst* 2008). On the same day, a New Jersey court voided punitive damages in a separate Vioxx case (*McDarby v. Merck* 2008). In 2007, Merck and the Negotiating Plaintiffs' Counsel agreed to establish a nearly $5 billion pre-funded, structured private settlement program to resolve Vioxx claims involving heart attacks, ischemic strokes, and sudden cardiac deaths (*Vioxx Settlement Agreement 2007*, http://hosted.ap.org/specials/interactives/_documents/vioxx_settlement_agreement.pdf; also see *In re: Vioxx Marketing, Sales Practices and Products Liability Litigation* 2007).

17 Notably, however, Robins did not issue a general recall until 1980.

18 In what was called "the steal of the century," American Home Products (AHP) acquired Robins in 1989 in exchange for paying $2.3 billion into the Dalkon Shield Victims' Trust Fund and $900 million in stock for Robins' shareholders (Gladwell 1989). Notably, AHP

marketed Fenfluramine, which was widely used in conjunction with Phentermine as Fen-Phen. See AHP Diet Drug Settlement, http://www.settlementdietdrugs.com/.

19 The Department of Veterans Affairs does provide some care and compensation to Vietnam veterans with any health problems that may have resulted from Agent Orange exposure. In addition, the Department of Veterans Affairs manages the Agent Orange Registry Examination Program to identify and medically examine veterans concerned about Agent Orange exposure.

20 Additional money-based litigation fields include antitrust and sales practices.

21 *Private Securities Litigation Reform Act of 1995,* P.L. 104-67 (22 December 1995).

22 The "music publisher plaintiffs," as they were called, were part of a consolidated case, entitled *Lieber v. Consumer Empowerment BV* (2004).

23 In 2007, the Ninth Circuit Court affirmed the class.

24 Judge Jenkins refers in this quotation to *Molski v. Gleich* (2003, 947 and 950), which holds that (b)(2) class actions can include claims for monetary damages so long as such damages are not the "predominant" relief sought but, instead, are "secondary to the primary claim for injunctive or declaratory relief."

25 Formerly, the Association of Trial Lawyers of America.

26 See Chapter 4 in this text.

27 A case also may be filed in federal court based on the "diversity of citizenship" of the litigants, such as between citizens of different states or between United States citizens and those of another country.

28 Recent passage of the *Class Action Fairness Act,* P.L. 109-2 (18 February 2005), however, will presumably make such forum shopping much more difficult. See discussion later in this chapter.

29 See discussion in the introductory chapter.

30 Although they remain the exceptions, both Texas and Florida have relatively strong laws banning secret court agreements that would conceal health or safety hazards. For example, Florida's *Sunshine in Litigation Act,* Fla. Stat. § 69.081 (2003), reads in part: "Except pursuant to this section, no court shall enter an order or judgment which has the purpose or effect of concealing a public hazard or any information concerning a public hazard, nor shall the court enter an order or judgment which has the purpose or effect of concealing any information which may be useful to members of the public in protecting themselves from injury which may result from the public hazard." Moreover, although judges increasingly allow secret settlements, federal district judges in South Carolina voted unanimously in 2002 "to ban secret legal settlements, saying such agreements have made the courts complicit in hiding the truth about hazardous products, inept doctors and sexually abusive priests" (Liptak 2002, A1).

31 Analogously, the Bush administration has increasingly employed low-profile "deferred prosecution agreements" to settle alleged criminal wrongdoings on the part of corporations. Such deals "allow the government to collect fines and appoint an outside monitor to impose internal reforms without going through a trial. In many cases, the name of the monitor and the details of the agreement are kept secret" (Lichtblau 2008, 1).

32 For an excellent and thorough case study of this very effective strategy by defendant corporations, see Sobol (1991).

33 American Tort Reform Association (ATRA) offers a *partial* listing of its members at http://www.atra.org/about/members.php.

34 For just some of many, many such sites, see ATRA's "Looney Lawsuits," http://www.atra.org./display/13; Citizens against Lawsuit Abuse's "Lawsuit Horror Stories," http://www.tala.com/lawsuit.html; Power of Attorneys, "Stupid Lawsuits and Other Funny Stuff," http://www.power-of-attorneys.com/StupidLawsuit.htm; and Overlawyered.com, a Manhattan Institute site devoted entirely to what it considers silly suits, http://www.overlawyered.com/.

35 See, for example, the Law and Economics Center, George Mason University of Law, http://www.law.gmu.edu/lawecon/Programs.htm.

36 According to the *National Law Journal* poll, the percentage of people who said the profession of law was of "very great prestige" dropped from 36 percent in 1977 to 19 percent in 1997

(Klein 1997). Another indicator was the trial lawyers' association name change in 2006, which completely eliminated the phrase "trial lawyer!"

37 President Bill Clinton twice vetoed national tort limits during the 1990s. However, more recently, the *Class Action Fairness Act, supra* note 28, limiting jurisdiction in state courts, did pass in Congress (see discussion later in this text). In the Senate, former majority leader, Bill Frist (Republican, Tennessee), himself a physician, is a proponent of medical malpractice caps. In the House of Representatives, majority leader Tom DeLay (Republican, Texas) has long championed tort reform.

38 *Protection of Lawful Commerce in Firearms Act,* Public Law no. 109-092 (2005), s. 3(b). For more information, see the discussion in Chapter 4 in this text.

39 *Negligence: Limitation on Civil Liability Arising from Long-Term Consumption of Food and Non-alcoholic Beverages,* (2004) Fl. A.L.S. 88. See generally Chapter 5 in this text. See also, for example, the *Private Securities Litigation Reform Act,* Public Law No. 104-67 (1995).

40 *Class Action Fairness Act, supra* note 28. A rare exception would be when two-thirds of the plaintiffs are from the same state and the defendant is headquartered in that state.

41 See, for example, "ATRA Urges South Carolina High Court to Stem Forum Shopping" and "ATRA Urges Michigan High Court to Reject Claims by Uninjured Plaintiffs," American Tort Reform Association, http://www.atra.org./.

42 Robin Conrad is head of the National Chamber Litigation Center.

43 More recently, the Supreme Court of the United States overturned punitive damages against Philip Morris on grounds that jurors inappropriately calculated the figure to punish the cigarette manufacturer for the harm it caused to smokers other than the deceased for whom the suit was brought (*Philip Morris USA v. Williams* 2007b).

44 Immediately following the ruling, "Amar Sarwal, general litigation counsel for the US Chamber of Commerce, said the ruling gives an 'extraordinary amount of guidance' to courts beyond the Exxon Valdez case" (Yost 2008).

45 Codified as *Federal Rules of Evidence, Rules 701-3* (2000), cited in Legal Information Institute, "Federal Rules of Evidence," http://www.law.cornell.edu/rules/fre/.

46 Rosen (2008) quoting Thomas Goldstein, a long-time Supreme Court litigator.

47 "America's Best Graduate Schools 2006: Top 100 Law Schools," *US News and World Report,* http://www.usnews.com/usnews/edu/grad/rankings/law/brief/lawrank_brief.php. Our sample included 103 attorneys who had participated in more than one tobacco, gun, or implant litigation. Of the forty-six plaintiff attorneys, eight had attended a top-twenty law school. Of the fifty-seven defendant attorneys, twenty-five had.

48 Depending on the source, politics is the fight over "who gets what, when and how" (Lasswell 1950); over "leadership, structure, and policies" (Ginsberg, Lowi, and Weir 2005, A37); and over "the authoritative allocation of values" (Easton 1965, 50).

49 Litigation is "a contest authorized by law, in a court of justice"; and a "resort to the courts to determine a legal question" (Law.com Dictionary 2003).

Chapter 3: The Politics of Tobacco Litigation

1 *Federal Rules of Civil Procedure,* http://www.law.cornell.edu/rules/frcp/; *Multi-District Litigation Act,* 28 U.S.C. §1407 at §1407c (1968).

2 Ginsberg, Lowi, and Weir (2005, A34) define "iron triangle" as "the stable, cooperative relationships that often develop between a congressional committee, an administrative agency, and one or more supportive interest groups."

3 Industry-wide figures on growth are not readily available. Indicators of wealth, however, make the point. For example, Philip Morris reported revenues in excess of $4 billion in 1976, in excess of $6.6 billion in 1978, and in excess of $13 billion in 1983 (Altria Group 2005b). Philip Morris USA reported 2005 profits at $4.6 billion (Nocera 2006)! In 2006, the company's net revenues came in at a whopping $18.5 billion, an almost 2 percent increase over 2005 (Altria Group 2007). Cigarette companies spent a combined $68 billion in advertising alone between 1954 and 1997 (*United States v. Philip Morris* 2004a). Meanwhile, government tobacco subsidies totalled $531 million from 1995 to 2003 (Environmental Working Group 2005).

4 *Federal Cigarette Labeling and Advertising Act of 1965,* 15 U.S.C.S. 1331-40.
5 In *State Farm Insurance v. Preece* (2003), the Court found a jury's award, in a Utah court trial, of $145 million in punitive damages against an automobile insurer held to be excessive, in violation of the Fourteenth Amendment's due process clause, where full compensatory damages had been found to be only $1 million.
6 The Centers for Disease Control and Prevention (CDC) (2005f; 2005g) estimates productivity losses that are attributable to smoking total $98,340,790,000 in 2001. Total health care expenditures attributable to smoking were estimated to be in excess of $75,000,000,000 in 1998. According to the CDC, "during 1963-2002, per capita annual consumption of cigarettes among adults aged greater than eightenn years declined from 4,345 cigarettes to 1,979, the lowest figure recorded since 1941" (Centers for Disease Control and Prevention 2004a, para. 2). The CDC estimates that 22.5 percent of all adults smoked in 2004, down from 25.5 percent a decade earlier (Centers for Disease Control and Prevention 2004b; 1996).
7 Many states have passed smoke-free workplace laws. Twenty-two states as well as Washington, DC, and Puerto Rico have laws covering smoke-free restaurants and bars (Campaign for Tobacco-Free Kids 2007b).
8 Since 2002, forty-three states and the District of Columbia have increased cigarette taxes, "more than doubling the average state cigarette tax from 43.4 cents to $1.073 a pack" (Campaign for Tobacco-Free Kids 2007b, para. 1).
9 In law, subrogation means assuming the legal rights of one for whom expenses have been paid. Governments reckoned that public health and insurance programs such as Medicare and Medicaid have been forced to assume much of the cost of sick smokers. See generally Schuck (2001).
10 In a real twist, Steve Parrish, Philip Morris' senior vice president for corporate affairs, says that tobacco needs to be regulated by the Food and Drug Administration (FDA) (Nocera 2006; see also Philip Morris' endorsement of FDA regulation at http://www.philipmorrisusa.com/en/legislation_regulation/fda/regulation_tobacco_products.asp)! R.J. Reynolds USA and other industry participants continue to fight FDA regulation. In 2008, a bill giving the FDA broad regulatory authority over tobacco products was approved by the House of Representatives' Commerce Committee. Although the measure has broad support in both chambers of Congress, its fate remains very uncertain. Both President George Bush and Senate minority leader Mitch McConnell have voiced opposition (Saul 2008).
11 *Master Settlement Agreement,* National Association of Attorneys General, http://www.naag.org/tobac/index.html [*MSA*].
12 According to the CDC, "[t]he highest state estimates for cigarette smoking among men were in Kentucky (34.8 percent) and Mississippi (33.2 percent); [t]he highest estimates for cigarette smoking among women were in Kentucky (30.5 percent) and West Virginia (27.2 percent)" (Centers for Disease Control and Prevention 2004a, para. 4).
13 In Mississippi, the smoking-attributable death rate of 115 per 100,000 is far higher than the national average of 90 per 100,000 (Centers for Disease Control and Prevention 2005a).
14 According to the CDC, "Mississippi spent $204 per capita on smoking-attributable direct medical expenditures. In 1998, about 14 percent ($206,000,000 or $424.29 per recipient) of all Medicaid expenditures were spent on smoking-related illnesses and diseases" (Centers for Disease Control and Prevention 2005a).
15 Actually, the whole deal amounts to an extra tax on smokers. As Galanter (1999, 55) put it, "[t]he main difference from a tax is that legislators and governors are spared the dishonor of enacting it."
16 In 2004, states received a total appropriation of $14,095,507,000 (Kaiser Family Foundation 2005).
17 In 2007, bills were introduced in both chambers of Congress that would significantly increase the federal tax on cigarettes. A House bill proposes a 45-cent per pack increase and a Senate bill, a 61-cent increase. As of August 2007, the tobacco industry was claiming a catastrophic impact were Congress to raise the tax. President George Bush has threatened to veto any major increase ("Analyst: Tobacco Tax" 2007).

18 *MSA, supra* note 11, para. IX(d2E).
19 *Medical Care Recovery Act,* 42 U.S.C. §§ 2651-3; *Medicare Secondary Payer Provisions,* 42 U.S.C. §1395y); and *Racketeer Influenced and Corrupt Organizations Act,* 18 U.S.C. §§1961-8.
20 Government health spending is heavily implicated in the treatment of smoking-related diseases because there is a pronounced inverse relationship between socioeconomic status and tobacco consumption. The CDC reports: "Current smoking prevalence also was higher among adults living below the poverty level (32.9 percent) than among those at or above the poverty level (22.2 percent). During 1983-2002, the gap in smoking prevalence between those living below the poverty line and those living at or above it increased from 8.7 per-centage points to 10.7 percentage points. In addition, the percentage of smokers who had quit was higher for persons at or above the poverty level than for those below the poverty line. As with current smoking prevalence, this gap was larger in 2002 than in 1983 (20.0 percentage points versus 18.7 percentage points). Educational attainment has been associated consistently with adult smoking prevalence since 1983. By education level, smoking prevalence was highest among adults who had earned a General Educational Development diploma (42.3 percent) and lowest among those with graduate degrees (7.2 percent)" (Centers for Disease Control and Prevention 2004a, para. 5).
21 Notably, recall that the tobacco industry had not been particularly averse to the $520 bil-lion in long-term payments proposed in the failed 1998 congressional effort. Indeed, the industry had been ready to accept it. Thus, when it was able to settle with the states for a little over $200 billion, according to one analyst, "[t]his left a balance ... the industry would have been willing to pay ... In a sense, there is a $300 billion contingency fund, an 'account payable,' already contemplated by the industry for as yet unliquidated obligations which might be imposed by the federal government" (LaFrance 2000, 199).
22 Among its evidence, the government offered the industry's "Frank Statement to Smokers," which was published in hundreds of periodicals in 1954. In the advertisement, "defendants promised to safeguard the health of smokers, support disinterested research into smoking and health, and reveal to the public the results of research into the effects of smoking on smokers' health" (*United States v. Philip Morris* 2004b). On the contrary, the government maintains that tobacco companies "purposefully designed and sold products that delivered a pharmacologically effective dose of nicotine in order to create and sustain nicotine addic-tion in smokers" (*ibid.,* 47); that they marketed so-called "light" cigarettes as safe, knowing that they "do not actually deliver the low reported and advertised levels of tar and nicotine ... to human smokers" (*ibid.,* 51); that they "intentionally marketed cigarettes to youth under the legal smoking age while falsely denying that they have done and continue to do so" (*ibid.,* 53); and that they intentionally destroyed documents covering up illegal activities.
23 Harvard Business School professor Max H. Bazerman says he was pressured by Department of Justice lawyers to change his testimony. According to Bazerman, he was told to recom-mend a lesser penalty than he thought appropriate (Leonnig 2005).
24 The document is so huge that it has been divided into several parts by Lexis: parts 1-3 re-ported at 2006 U.S. Dist. LEXIS 61412; parts 4-6 reported at 2006 U.S. Dist. LEXIS 63477; parts 7-11 reported at 2006 U.S. Dist. LEXIS 61413; parts 12-16 reported at 2006 U.S. Dist. LEXIS 63478; parts 17-19 reported at 2006 U.S. Dist. LEXIS 61415; parts 20-22 reported at 2006 U.S. Dist. LEXIS 61416.
25 Moreover, tobacco stocks rallied following Kessler's announced judgment (Henderson 2006).
26 Defendants and the United States have filed notices of appeal. On 10 August 2007, joint defendants/appellants filed their opening brief. The defendant-appellant Altria Group, In-corporated, filed a separate brief. The defendant-appellant British American Tobacco (Invest-ments) Limited also filed a separate brief. The United States opening and responsive brief is due to be filed 19 November 2007 (see http://www.usdoj.gov/civil/cases/tobacco2/index. htm). In a parallel action, Philip Morris has requested and been granted *certiorari* by the Supreme Court of the United States in a case that will determine whether tobacco compan-ies can be sued under state law for falsely representing their products as "light" (*Altria Group v. Good* 2008).

ᵗ

27 *Barnes v. American Tobacco Co.* (1999); *Castano v. American Tobacco Co.* (1996); *Mahoney v. R.J. Reynolds Tobacco Co.* (2001); *Badillo v. American Tobacco Co.* (2001); *Guillory v. American Tobacco Co.* (2001); *Aksamit v. Brown and Williamson Tobacco Corp.* (2000); *Walls v. American Tobacco Co.* (2000); *Chamberlain v. American Tobacco Co.* (1999); *Hansen v. American Tobacco Co.* (1999); *Thompson v. American Tobacco Co.*; *Clay v. American Tobacco Co.* (1999); *Insolia v. Philip Morris, Inc.* (1998); *Emig v. American Tobacco Co.* (1998); *Barreras Ruiz v. American Tobacco Co.* (1998); *Smith v. Brown and Williamson Tobacco Corp.* (1997); *Tijerina v. Philip Morris Inc.* (1996); *Philip Morris, Inc. v. Angeletti* (2000); *Reed v. Philip Morris, Inc.* (1999); *Small v. Lorillard Tobacco Co.* (1999); *Geiger v. American Tobacco Co.* (2000).

28 Interestingly, two years later, in 1993, the Supreme Court of the United States ruled that a prison inmate exposed to environmental (second-hand) tobacco smoke had stated a proper basis of claim for relief under the US Constitution's 8th Amendment (*Helling v. McKinney* 1993).

29 Phase 1 of the trial was to hear all common issues, while Phase 2 would consider individual claims.

30 In 2004, the Florida Court of Appeals upheld an award to French of $500,000.

31 Members included: Daniel G. Abel, Attorney at Law, New Orleans, LA.; Alexander Firm, San Jose, CA.; Peter Angelos Firm, Towson, MD.; Baldwin and Baldwin, Marshall, TX.; Baggett, McCall and Burgess, Lake Charles, LA; Becnel, Landry and Becnel, Reserve, LA; Melvin Belli, Attorney at Law, San Francisco, CA; Branch Law Firm, Albuquerque, NM; Breazeale, Sachse and Wilson, New Orleans, LA; Brown Rudnick Berlack Israels, Boston, MA; Bruno and Bruno, New Orleans, LA; Carter and Cates, New Orleans, LA; Casey, Gerry, Reed and Schenk, San Diego, CA; Climaco, Lefkowitz, Peca, Wilcox and Garofoli, Cleveland, OH; Coale, Allen and Van Susteren, Washington, DC; Richard A. Daymard, Northeastern University School of Law, Boston, MA; Daughert, Hildre, Dudek and Haklard, San Diego, CA; Doffermyre, Shields et al., Atlanta, GA; Fayard and Honeycutt, Denham Springs, LA; Gauthier and Murphy, Metairie, LA; Herman, Herman, Katz and Cotlar, New Orleans, LA; Howarth and Smith, Los Angeles, CA; Johnson, Johnson, Barrios and Yacoubian, New Orleans, LA; Kohn, Nast and Graf, Philadelphia, PA; John B. Krental, Attorney at Law, Metairie, LA; Lieff, Cabraser, Heimann and Bernstein, San Francisco, CA; Levin, Fishbein et al., Philadelphia, PA; Loadholt, Richardson and Poole, Charleston, SC; Michaud, Hutton and Bradshaw, Wichita, KS; Moore, Walters, Shoenfelt and Thompson, Baton Rouge, LA; Murray and Associates, New Orleans, LA; Ness, Motley et al., Charleston, SC; Polack, Rosenberg, Endom and Riess, New Orleans, LA; Robinson, Calcagnie and Robinson, Newport Beach, CA; Roda and Nast, Lancaster, PA; Hugh Rodham, Fort Lauderdale, FL; Louie J. Roussel, III, Attorney at Law, Metairie, LA; St. Martin and Lirette, APLC, Houma, LA; Sheller, Ludwig and Badey, Philadephia, PA; Simon, Peragine, Smith and Redfearn, New Orleans, LA; Spohrer, Wilner, Maxwell and Matthews, Jacksonville, FL; Waite, Schneider, Bayless and Chesley, Cincinnati, OH; Weitz and Luxenberg, New York, NY; Williams and Troutwine, Portland, OR; and Zimmerman and Reed, Minneapolis, MN.

32 At the same time, the company agreed to settle suits with five states.

33 A jury awarded smokers $591 million. On appeal, the judgment was amended, reversed in part, and remanded (*Scott v. American Tobacco Company* 2007).

34 Supreme Court of Appeals of West Virginia upheld the jury verdict for defendant manufacturers.

35 See, for example, *Arch v. American Tobacco Company* (1997) and the Iowa case, *Wright v. Brooke Group, Ltd.* (2002) (cited at Sugarman 2001)

36 The award of attorneys' fees in these cases has itself become a point of considerable contention. For example, in the Davis/Ellis case, a mediation panel awarded the Castano Group members roughly 10 percent of California's share of the *MSA*, $1.25 billion (*In re: Application of Brown and Williamson Tobacco Corporation v. Stanley M. Chesley* (2004).

37 *Florida Rule of Civil Procedure*, No. 1.220.

38 See Chapter 1 in this text.

39 Upon word of the ruling, Altria Group shares hit a new fifty-two-week high of $79.10. R.J. Reynolds also saw its shares "hit a new high of $120.99" (Pye 2006, para. 2). As yet unresolved is $710 million sitting in escrow and promised by the tobacco companies to the

Florida smokers regardless of the outcome of the appeal. Of course, with no class, experts are doubtful whether this amount will ever paid. Surprisingly, it is not the subject of heated debate between the companies and attorneys (Haggman 2003).

40 *Consumer Fraud and Deceptive Business Practices Act,* 815 I.L.C.S. 505.

41 The defendant bar considers Madison County to be "one of the nation's 'judicial hellholes,' because of the number of high-dollar lawsuits filed and won there." Indeed, in January 2005, President George Bush made the county his first stop in pushing for his second-term lawsuit reform effort (VandeHei and Harris 2005, A3).

42 Much of the argument centred on the incidence of "titration" – virtually all smokers, according to expert testimony, will compensate in inhaling more to get the same levels of nicotine from lights as they did from regulars (Vock 2004).

43 The following were diseases listed in the judge's order: "lung cancer; laryngeal cancer; lip cancer; tongue cancer; mouth cancer; esophageal cancer; kidney cancer; pancreatic cancer; bladder cancer; ischemic heart disease; cerebrovascular heart disease; aortic aneurysm, peripheral vascular disease; emphysema; chronic bronchitis; or, chronic obstructive pulmonary disease" (*In re Simon II Litigation* 2002a, 108).

44 *Medicare as Secondary Payer Act,* 42 U.S.C., sec. 1395y(b)(5). This act is meant to click in after a "primary payer" (for example, a private insurance company) has met its responsibilities. The law creates a private cause of action (the private attorney general provision), allowing citizens to sue on behalf of Medicare.

45 In its annual tobacco settlement report, the Campaign for Tobacco-Free Kids finds that "most states fail to fund tobacco prevention programs at minimum levels recommended by the US Centers for Disease Control and Prevention (CDC), and altogether, the states are providing less than half what the CDC has recommended" (Campaign for Tobacco Free Kids 2007c, para. 2).

46 John Calfee (2002, 58) notes several other public health goals of the litigation, including laying "the basis for FDA regulation of tobacco products," advertising restrictions, adverse publicity for cigarette companies.

Chapter 4: The Politics of Gun Litigation

1 Like the tobacco industry, gun makers and distributors had long managed to lead charmed lives. Indeed, in some respects, the firearms industry out-charmed even the cigarette makers – individuals have been suing gun makers for injuries and death since the *early* twentieth century (Lytton 2000, 1255). And, with the exception of a few cases where guns literally malfunctioned, weapons makers managed until very recently to avoid any liability. See, for example, *Bender v. Colt Industries, Inc.* (1974), in which a gun discharged when it fell out of the buyer's pocket onto a concrete platform; *Sturm Ruger and Co. v. Day* (1979), in which a gun discharged when buyer grabbed the gun as it dropped out of his hand while unloading it; and *Cobb v. Insured Lloyds* (1980), in which a gun accidentally discharged while it was located underneath the seat of a moving car (Lytton 2000, 1255, n. 27).

2 However, see *Delahanty v. Hinckley* (1992), in which an officer wounded in the assassination attempt on President Ronald Reagan sought unsuccessfully to hold gun manufacturers liable under DC law for criminal use of a gun by John W. Hinckley, Jr.

3 That is, measuring the likelihood, based on a defendant company's share of its market, that this defendant would be responsible for the harm done (for example, Ausness 2002). See Chapter 2 in this text.

4 Included also in the suit were the family of Mary Caitrin Mahoney, who was murdered at a Georgetown Starbucks in 1997 and the families of two high school students killed in 2000 (Schoenberg 2002).

5 A straw purchase is one in which one buyer acts as a proxy for another who, under law, cannot legally purchase a firearm.

6 Notably, the agreement did generate a considerable amount of tit-for-tat litigation. Thus, suspecting other firearm companies of conspiring against Smith and Wesson for capitulating to government demands, the attorneys general of six states (Maryland, New York, Connecticut, California, Florida, and Massachusetts) joined in an antitrust investigation of the industry (Butterfield 2000). In response, the National Shooting Sports Foundation

and seven gun companies "sued Housing Secretary Andrew Cuomo, two state attorneys general and 19 municipal officials, alleging they violated the commerce clause of the U.S. Constitution by trying to force gun makers to adopt a safe-weapons 'code of conduct' or risk losing business" (Chebium 2000, para. 1).

7 Among others, Kairys has served on the legal teams representing Chicago, San Francisco, Los Angeles, Camden, New Jersey, and New York State. In addition, he was an advisor in *Ileto v. Glock* (2003). Resume of David Kairys (Spring 2004), http://www.pdfdownload.org/pdf2html/pdf2html.php?url=http%3A%2F%2Fwww.law.temple.edu%2Fpdfs%2FFaculty%2FResume%2FKairysResume.pdf&images=yes.

8 See Chapter 2 in this text.

9 No universally agreed upon statistics exist for the costs of gun violence. Nevertheless, data suggests that the costs are substantial and largely borne by the public. For example, in its complaint, Chicago estimated its costs in a single year to be $75,700,260 for police services, $1,282,047 for emergency communications, $605,461 for emergency medical services, and $526,773 for prosecuting violations of gun ordinances. Costs to Cook County included in excess of $50,000,000 over a four-year period to treat victims of gun violence and in excess of $25,000,000 in gun-related prosecutions and defence (*Chicago v. Beretta*, 1998, 76-77). Winett (1998, 500) reports "that acute medical care for patients with firearm-related injuries costs nearly $32,000 per hospital admission. It has also been estimated that 80 percent of the costs for treating firearm-inflicted injuries is paid for by taxpayers." Using mid-1990s data, Cook and Ludwig (2000, 156) find that the total lifetime medical cost per case for non-fatal gunshot injuries averages about $40,000. Again, most of this cost is absorbed by public institutions.

10 The following can be found on the Philip Morris USA website: "Philip Morris USA (PM USA) agrees with the overwhelming medical and scientific consensus that cigarette smoking causes lung cancer, heart disease, emphysema and other serious diseases in smokers. Smokers are far more likely to develop serious diseases, like lung cancer, than non-smokers. There is no safe cigarette" (Philip Morris USA 2008, para. 1).

11 40 La. R.S. 1799 (2004).

12 American Law Institute, *Restatement (Third) of Torts: Products Liability* (1998).

13 The city sought compensation for the costs of emergency medical services, law enforcement efforts, the prosecution of violations of gun control ordinances, and other related expenses. The county asked for compensation for the costs of treatment of victims of gun violence and the costs of prosecutions for criminal use of firearms, including the expenses associated with providing defence counsel to those accused of gun crimes.

14 "Illinois courts have adopted the *Restatement (Second) of Torts* definition of public nuisance. *Young v. Bryco Arms*, 327 Ill. App. 3d 948, 958, 765 N.E.2d 1, 262 Ill. Dec. 175 (2001), citing *Wheat v. Freeman Coal Mining Corp.*, 23 Ill. App. 3d 14, 18, 319 N.E.2d 290 (1974)" (*Chicago v. Beretta* 2002, 8).

15 Specific allegations included: (1) that gun manufacturers "know which federally licensed dealers are more likely to sell guns to straw buyers [resellers]"; (2) that manufacturers "marketing schemes are designed to appeal to criminals"; and (3) that "the gun industry advertises its guns as safe or beneficial for use in the home, while the presence of guns increases the risk of suicide and domestic violence involving firearms" (*ibid.*, 888).

16 *Uniform Firearms Act*, 18 Pa. C.S. §§6101-26.

17 The court found that the civic associations lacked standing because they failed to demonstrate that any alleged injury suffered by their members was "fairly traceable to the challenged action of the defendant[s]" (*Chicago v. Beretta* 2002, 896).

18 Pennsylvania adopted the definition of the *Restatement (Second) of Torts*: "It is negligence to permit a third person to use a thing or to engage in an activity which is under the control of the actor, if the actor knows or should know that such person intends or is likely to use the thing or to conduct himself in the activity in such a manner as to create an unreasonable risk of harm to others" (*ibid.*, 902-3).

19 Like the Supreme Court of Illinois, the US District Court rejected the plaintiffs' theory of damages as well, based on Pennsylvania's adoption of the "municipal cost recovery rule" (*ibid.*, 894-95).

20 *Sturm, Ruger and Company, Inc. v. Atlanta* (2002); *Ganin v. Smith and Wesson* (1999); *City of Camden v. Beretta U.S.A. Corp.* (2003); *Camden County Board of Chosen Freeholders v. Beretta U.S.A. Corp.* (2001); *Cincinnati v. Beretta* (2000) – in which the city council voted to drop the suit on 30 April 2003, while on 14 May 2003 an order was granted allowing the city to drop its suit without prejudice (see Brady Center, Legal Action Project, http://www.gunlaw-suits.org/docket/cities/cityview.php?RecordNo=11); *Detroit and Wayne County, MI v. Arms Technology, Inc.* (2003); *In re: Firearm Cases* (2005); *Penelas v. Arms Technology, Inc.* (1999); *James v. Arms Technology, Inc.* (2003); *New York v. Sturm, Ruger and Company, Inc.* (2003); *St. Louis v. Cernicek* (1999); and *Baker v. Smith and Wesson Corp.* (2002). In addition, in Washington, DC, a dismissal is currently on appeal: *District of Columbia v. Beretta* (2000). As it stands now, the city is limited to seeking subrogated damages for several named individual plaintiffs for whom it has incurred medical expenses (see *Lawson v. Beretta,* 2004, as noted earlier). And Boston dropped its suit in 2002, citing growing legal costs (Mishra 2002). *Boston v. Smith and Wesson Corp.* (2000).

21 Defendants, manufacturers, importers, and distributors of firearms sought dismissal on several counts. First, they argued that the city's case was essentially preempted by the Supreme Court of New York's ruling against the state (*New York v. Sturm, Ruger and Company, Inc.* 2003). Second, they maintained that the city failed to make a valid nuisance claim. And, finally, they asserted that "the injunctive relief demanded by the City places an impermissible burden on interstate commerce in violation of the Commerce Clause and Due Process Clause" (*New York City v. Beretta* 2004).

22 The Bureau of Alcohol, Tobacco, and Firearms (ATF) has the capability to "trace" or to determine a handgun's chain of sale by individual serial number. Traces are initiated in the main from requests by law enforcement agencies to the ATF based on the serial number of handguns recovered in connection with criminal investigations. The tracing process works essentially as follows. Upon receipt of a trace request from a law enforcement agency, the ATF contacts the manufacturer identified by the serial number. The manufacturer's records will point to the gun's distributor, who is then queried. That distributor's records will reveal the retail dealer. When asked to respond by the ATF, the retailer's records will indicate the consumer to whom the handgun was sold. The progress and results of the trace are recorded and retained by the ATF in a complex database called the Firearms Tracing System database. To aid it in its work, the ATF also maintains a second and independent database called the Firearms Licensing System, which contains records of Federal Firearms Licenses (FFLs) kept pursuant to the *Gun Control Act of 1968* and other controlling laws and includes, among other data, an FFL's name, number, and application history (*NAACP v. A.A. Arms* 2003).

23 *Consolidated Appropriations Act of 2005,* P.L. 109-108, 119 Stat. 2290 (2005) [emphasis added]. Section 630 reads: "(a) Tracing studies conducted by the Bureau of Alcohol, Tobacco, Firearms, and Explosives are released without adequate disclaimers regarding the limitations of the data. (b) The Bureau of Alcohol, Tobacco, Firearms, and Explosives shall include in all such data releases, language similar to the following that would make clear that trace data cannot be used to draw broad conclusions about firearms-related crime: (1) Firearm traces are designed to assist law enforcement authorities in conducting investigations by tracking the sale and possession of specific firearms. Law enforcement agencies may request firearms traces for any reason, and those reasons are not necessarily reported to the Federal Government. Not all firearms used in crime are traced and not all firearms traced are used in crime. (2) Firearms selected for tracing are not chosen for purposes of determining which types, makes or models of firearms are used for illicit purposes. The firearms selected do not constitute a random sample and should not be considered representative of the larger universe of all firearms used by criminals, or any subset of that universe. Firearms are normally traced to the first retail seller, and sources reported for firearms traced do not necessarily represent the sources or methods by which firearms in general are acquired for use in crime."

24 As examples, *Oklahoma Firearms Act,* 21 Okl. St. § 1289.24a (2004), states: "1. The State Legislature declares that the lawful design, marketing, manufacturing, or sale of firearms or ammunition to the public is not unreasonably dangerous activity and does not constitute a nuisance. 2. The authority to bring suit and right to recover against any firearms or

ammunition manufacturer, trade association, or dealer by or on behalf of any governmental unit created by or pursuant to an act of the Legislature or the Constitution, or any department, agency, or authority thereof, for damages, abatement, or injunctive relief resulting from or relating to the lawful design, manufacturing, marketing, or sale of firearms or ammunition to the public shall be reserved exclusively to the state." In Pennsylvania, the *Firearms and Ammunition Preemption Clause,* 18 Pa.C.S. § 6120 (2004), reads: "No political subdivision may bring or maintain an action at law or in equity against any firearms or ammunition manufacturer, trade association or dealer for damages, abatement, injunctive relief or any other relief or remedy resulting from or relating to either the lawful design or manufacture of firearms or ammunition or the lawful marketing or sale of firearms or ammunition to the public." And, Mississippi's statute, *Authority to Sue Traders in Firearms Reserved to State,* Miss. Code Ann. § 11-1-67 (2004), says: "The authority to bring an action against any firearms or ammunition manufacturer, distributor or dealer duly licensed under federal law on behalf of any governmental entity created by or pursuant to an act of the Mississippi Legislature or the Mississippi Constitution of 1890, or any department, agency or authority thereof, for damages, abatement, injunctive relief or any other relief or remedy resulting from or relating to the lawful design, manufacture, distribution or sale of firearms, firearm components, silencers, ammunition or ammunition components to the public, shall be exclusively reserved to the state."

25 *Protection of Lawful Commerce in Arms Act,* H.R. 1036 (2003).
26 According to one account, in an e-mail message sent to the senators, the National Rifle Association "warned it would remember those who defied it and voted for the bill" (Epstein 2004, A16).
27 *Protection of Commerce in Lawful Firearms Act of 2005,* Public Law No. 109-092.
28 *Ibid.,* s. 3(b).
29 In section 5(A), the act states that "[t]he term 'qualified civil liability action' ... shall not include – (i) an action brought against a transferor convicted under section 924(h) of title 19, United States Code, or a comparable or identical State felony law, by a party directly harmed by the conduct of which the transferee is so convicted; (ii) an action brought against a seller for negligent entrustment or negligence per se; (iii) an action in which a manufacturer or seller of a qualified product *knowingly violated a State* or *Federal statute applicable to the sale or marketing of the product, and the violation was a proximate cause of the harm for which relief is sought*" [emphasis added].
30 *New York Penal Law,* "Criminal Nuisance," s. 240.45.
31 As a second line of defence, the city had asked Weinstein to rule the *Protection of Commerce in Lawful Firearms Act, supra* note 25, unconstitutional on several grounds, something the judge refused to do.
32 *Consolidated Appropriations Act of 2005,* PL 108-447.
33 In 2007, the Court of Appeals of Indiana allowed Gary's suit to proceed despite passage of the federal legislation (*Smith and Wesson v. Gary* 2007).
34 *Crimes and Criminal Procedures: Firearms,* 18 U.S.C. § 922(g)(8).
35 *Protection of Lawful Commerce in Arms Act of 2005,* 109 P.L. 92.
36 Arms kept in the home for purposes of self-defence.
37 See especially the *Brady Handgun Control Act,* Public Law 103-159 (1990) and the *Assault Weapons Ban* as part of the *Violent Crime and Control Act of 1994,* Public Law 103-322.
38 The National Rifle Association was founded in 1871 but did not establish its legislative affairs division until 1934 (National Rifle Association 2005a).

Chapter 5: The Politics of Food Litigation
1 Even Cato, the elder, developed a method to determine whether wine had been watered down in approximately 234-149 BC (Burditt 1995).
2 *Food and Drugs Act,* 21 U.S.C. c. 9; *Meat Inspection Act,* 21 U.S.C. c. 12.
3 Major acts and amendments include the *Food, Drug, and Cosmetics Act of 1938,* 21 U.S.C. c. 9; the *Oleomargarine Act of 1950,* 21 U.S.C. c. 9, § 347; the *Miller Pesticides Amendment in 1954,* 21 U.S.C. c. 9, § 346A; the *Poultry Products Inspection Act of 1957,* 21 U.S.C. c. 10; the *Food Additives Amendment of 1958,* 21 U.S.C. c. 9, subchpt. IV, § 348; the *Color Additive*

Amendment of 1960, 21 U.S.C. c. 9, § 379E; the *Fair Packaging and Label Act of 1966,* 21 U.S.C.
c. 9, § 379S; the *Egg Product Inspection Act of 1970,* 21 U.S.C. c. 15 § 1033; the *Vitamin-Mineral Amendment of 1976,* 21 U.S.C. c. 5, § 350a; the *Infant Formula Act of 1980,* Pub. L. 96-359; the *Nutrition Labeling and Education Act of 1990,* Pub. L. 101-535; and the *Dietary Supplement Health and Education Act of 1994,* Pub. L. 103-417 (Burditt 1995).

4 Principal federal regulatory organizations responsible for providing consumer protection are the Department of Health and Human Services' (DHHS) Food and Drug Administration (FDA), the US Department of Agriculture's (USDA) Food Safety and Inspection Service and Animal and Plant Health Inspection Service, and the Environmental Protection Agency (EPA). The Department of Treasury's Customs Service assists the regulatory authorities by checking and occasionally detaining imports based on guidance provided. Many agencies and offices have food safety missions within their research, education, prevention, surveillance, standard-setting, and/or outbreak response activities, including the DHHS's Centers for Disease Control and Prevention and National Institutes of Health; the USDA's Agricultural Research Service; the Cooperative State Research, Education, and Extension Service; the Agricultural Marketing Service; the Economic Research Service; the Grain Inspection, Packers and Stockyard Administration; the US Codex office; and the Department of Commerce's National Marine Fisheries Service (Food and Drug Administration and Department of Agriculture 2000).

5 According to Robert Brackett, director of the FDA's Center for Food Safety and Applied Nutrition, "[n]ever before in history have we had the sort of system that we have now, meaning a globalization of the food supply." Indeed, "the average American eats about 260 pounds of imported foods [annually], including processed, ready-to-eat products and single ingredients. Imports account for about 13 percent of the annual diet." The FDA reportedly inspects just 1.3 percent of these imported foods (MSN Broadcast Company 2007, para. 8).

6 According to Buzby, Frenzen, and Rasco (2001, 7), in excess of forty food borne microbial pathogens are known to cause human illness, including bacteria, parasites, viruses, fungi, and their toxins."

7 The Centers for Disease Control and Prevention defines a food-borne disease outbreak "as the occurrence of two or more cases of a similar illness resulting from the ingestion of a common food" (Centers for Disease Control and Prevention 2006, unpaginated webpage).

8 See, for example, Food Poisoning Law Blog, http://foodpoisoning.pritzkerlaw.com/archives/cat-spinach-lawsuit.html; Marler Clark Attorneys at Law, http://www.marlerclark.com/news/spinach-ecoli002.htm.

9 Less traditionally, like asbestos, tobacco, and other modern mass-based litigation models, some law firms do specialize in seeking out potential food-injured clients. Particularly notable is the Seattle firm, Marler Clark. Marler Clark lists among its sponsored websites: OutBreak, Inc. – a not-for-profit business dedicated to explaining to companies why it is in their interest to avoid food-borne illness litigation; campylobacter – information on the most common form of food-borne bacterial illness, including symptoms, detection, and prevention of campylobacter infection; Campylobacter Blog – news updates on *campylobacter jejuni,* including research and outbreak cases; Cryptosporidium Blog – continually updated with news about cryptosporidium outbreaks and cryptosporidiosis; Cyclospora Blog – read continually updated news and information about cyclospora; E. coli O157:H7 – learn about E. coli O157:H7, a deadly pathogen as well as symptoms, risks, detection, and prevention of E. coli infection; E. coli litigation – keep current on the most recent litigation involving E. coli O157:H7; E. coli Blog – a great way to keep current on news and comments regarding all aspects of E. coli O157:H7; Food-borne Illness Resource Center – learn about the most common forms of food-borne illness – includes descriptions, resources, outbreaks, and more; Food Poisoning Blog – a blog that provides information about food poisoning and is continually updated with news about food-borne illness outbreaks; Hemolytic uremic syndrome (HUS) – a complication of E. coli O157:H7 infection that typically affects children and can lead to renal failure and central nervous system impairment; Hepatitis A – learn about symptoms and risks of hepatitis A infection and read news about recent hepatitis A outbreaks; Hepatitis A litigation – keep current on the most recent litigation involving Hepatitis A; Hepatitis A Blog – a great way to keep current on news and comments regarding

all aspects of Hepatitis A; Listeria monocytogenes – information on listeria bacterial infection: symptoms, risks, and prevention of listeriosis; Listeria Blog – a resource for recent news about listeria outbreaks, recalls, and research; Mad Cow Blog – a resource that is continually updated with news on mad cow disease; Norovirus – learn about the most common form of food-borne viral illness, including symptoms, detection, and prevention of norovirus (previously called Norwalk virus); Norvirus Blog – a great way to keep current on news and comments regarding all aspects of norovirus (Norwalk virus); Salmonella – information on symptoms, detection, and prevention of salmonella infection as well as news about salmonella outbreaks; Salmonella litigation – keep current on the most recent litigation involving salmonella; Salmonella Blog – a great way to keep current on news and comments regarding all aspects of salmonella; Shigella – information on shigellosis: symptoms, risks, detection, and prevention of shigella infection; Shigella Blog – keep up to date on shigella outbreaks, research, and lawsuits; Shigella litigation – dedicated to litigation resulting from shigella outbreaks; thrombotic thrombocytopenic purpura – a complication of E. coli O157: H7 infection, better known as adult HUS, which can lead to kidney failure and central nervous system and neurological impairment. See Marler Clark Attorneys at Law, http://www.marlerclark.com/sponsored-sites.htm.

10 *Introduction of Organisms and Products Altered or Produced through Genetic Engineering Which Are Plant Pests or Which There Is Reason to Believe Are Plant Pests,* 7 C.F.R. 340 at s. 340.1.

11 Currently, transgenic animals are primarily used as laboratory models and mainly are mice. However, "[t]ransgenic fish of various species of salmon, tilapia, channel catfish and others are being actively investigated worldwide as possible new food-producing varieties" (Food and Drug Administration, Center for Veterinary Medicine 2008, para. 11).

12 It has been only a decade since the first major planting of genetically modified (GM) crops (Friends of the Earth International 2006).

13 According to a Eurobarometer of 2005, public scepticism about GM remains high. Across all European Union member state populations, the largest percentage (37 percent) said they would *never* approve of developing GM crops in order to increase the variety of regionally grown food. Another 31 percent said they might approve them if the GM were crops "highly regulated and controlled." Moreover, in six of the countries surveyed a majority responded that they would never approve: Croatia (60 percent), Switzerland (58 percent), Cyprus (56 percent), Greece (54 percent), Slovenia (53 percent), and France (52 percent) (European Commission 2005). Major protests have also taken place in Europe. In France, Jose Bove has led other farmers in numerous protests including some in which GM corn and rice crops were destroyed. Though arrested frequently, Bove has maintained wide public support (see, for example, "French GM Corn Battle" 2004; Mulholland 2000). Protests against GM foods have also taken place in the United Kingdom and Germany, among other European Union countries. In 2002, a group of organic grain farmers in Saskatchewan filed a class action against Monsanto, claiming that their businesses were being damaged by the introduction of GM canola in the Canadian province. The provincial court ultimately denied certification to the class and dismissed the action (*Hoffman v. Monsanto Canada and Bayer Cropscience, Inc.* 2005).

14 A number of business cases, primarily patent infringement and misbranding issues, have come to court over the past decade. The majority have involved Monsanto as a plaintiff or defendant.

15 For information on the coalition, see generally Alliance for Bio-I, http://www.bio-integrity.org/FDADeception.html.

16 *National Environmental Protection Act,* Pub. L. 91-190, 42 U.S.C. 4321-47, 1 January 1970, as amended by Pub. L. 94-52, 3 July 1975, Pub. L. 94-83, 9 August 1975, and Pub. L. 97-258, § 4(b), 13 September 1982; and *Religious Freedom Restoration Act,* 42 U.S.C. § 2000bb. According to a since dismantled website of the Alliance for Bio-Integrity (now, Alliance for Bio-I), "[a]s a spiritual matter, millions of Americans feel obligated to refrain from some or all genetically altered foods on the basis of religious principle. Many Jews and Muslims want to avoid foods with substances from specific animals while devout vegetarians want to avoid substances from any animal. Additionally, a considerable portion of the population

is religiously motivated to avoid *all* genetically altered foods in order to separate themselves from an enterprise they view as irresponsibly and arrogantly disrupting the integrity of God's creation. Virtually all the religious plaintiffs share this motivation, even those who also must avoid foods with genes from particular species." See Alliance for Bio-I, http://www.bio-integrity.org/FDADeception.html. Seventeen plaintiffs objected to consuming genetically engineered foods on the basis of religious principle, including seven Christian clergy, three rabbis, a Buddhist priest, and a Hindu organization. Alliance for Bio-I, http://www.bio-integrity.org/FDADeception.html.

17 Aventis was later acquired by the German-based multinational Bayer. As part of the agreement, however, Aventis maintained its StarLink technology and all future liability (PR Newswire 2001).

18 A buffer grower raises crops designed, because of height or other characteristics, to capture any pollen escaping from a GM crop before it infects other crops.

19 Under Environment Protection Agency regulations, farmers growing StarLink crops had to plant, or contract with others to plant, buffer crops of non-modified plants, ostensibly to keep pollen from drifting into nearby fields and cross-breeding with unmodified crops (Kaufman 2001).

20 In 2003, the *Journal of Allergy and Clinical Immunology* reported that Dr. Finger, one of the named plaintiffs in the consumer suit was not allergic to StarLink corn after all (Pollack 2003).

21 For a more thorough discussion of nuisance, see Chapter 4 in this text. Indeed, in discussing private nuisance claims, Judge Moran cited some of the gun cases. A group of Canadian organic farmers (mostly located in Saskatchewan) also filed a class action (*Hoffman v. Monsanto Canada and Bayer Cropscience, Inc.* 2005). For a good discussion of the limitations of such litigation, compared to more explicitly administrative remedies, with special focus on the Canadian system, see McLeod-Kilmurray (2007).

22 Recently, scientists at the Pennington Biological Research Center in Baton Rouge have even suggested that some cases of obesity may be linked to a virus (Pennington Biological Research Center 2007).

23 Though not direct causes of litigation, three works have been particularly important in bringing the problems of fast food to the public consciousness. In 2001, to much critical acclaim, Eric Schlosser (2001) published *Fast Food Nation: The Dark Side of the All-American Meal*. The book painted a disturbing picture of the fast food industry, from ingredients to marketing practices to employment. In 2002, Marion Nestle (2002) published *Food Politics: How the Food Industry Influences Nutrition and Health*. Two years later, filmmaker Morgan Spurlock (2004) presented the award-winning documentary, *Super Size Me*, charting his own thirty days of a McDonald's-only diet – thirty days over which he gained substantial weight, saw his cholesterol level soar, and suffered a number of additional ill health effects.

24 Of course, fast food is both ubiquitous and generally cheap. Thus not surprisingly, the poorest state in the nation according to the 2006 census, Mississippi, is also the fattest state (Centers for Disease Control and Prevention 2007).

25 Wendy's International reported 2004 revenues well in excess of $3 billion (Cable News Network 2005); Yum! Brands, which owns Kentucky Fried Chicken, Long John Silver's, Pizza Hut, and Taco Bell generated more than $9 billion in revenues in 2004 (Yum! Brands 2006). And Burger King claims to serve approximately 11.8 million customers daily worldwide (Burger King 2006).

26 In *Staron v. McDonald's Corp.* (1995, 356), three children with asthma and a woman with lupus sued McDonald's and Burger King restaurants, alleging discrimination under the *Americans with Disabilities Act*, 42 U.S.C. § 12101 et seq. Plaintiffs sought a complete smoking ban at all of the defendants' restaurants. The trial court dismissed the case, finding that a complete smoking ban was not a reasonable modification, as a matter of law. The Second Circuit Court reversed the trial court's decision and remanded the case. The court asserted that whether an action is a reasonable modification is to be decided by the facts on a case-by-case basis "that considers, among other factors, the effectiveness of the modification in light of the nature of the disability in question and the cost to the organization that would

implement it" (*ibid.*, 356). On the day the district court dismissed the case, McDonald's announced a complete no-smoking policy in all of its corporate owned-and-operated restaurants.

27   McDonald's sincerely apologizes to Hindus, vegetarians and others for failing to provide the kind of information they needed to make informed dietary decisions at our US restaurants.
     We acknowledge that, upon our switch to vegetable oil in the early 1990's for the purpose of reducing cholesterol, mistakes were made in communicating to the public and customers about the ingredients in our French fries and hash browns. Those mistakes included instances in which French fries and hash browns sold at US restaurants were improperly identified as 'vegetarian.'
     We regret we did not provide these customers with complete information, and we sincerely apologize for any hardship that these miscommunications have caused among Hindus, vegetarians and others. We should have done a better job in these areas, and we're committed to doing a better job in the future. As a direct result of these events, McDonald's has enhanced its disclosures concerning the source of ingredients in its food products. This information is available at McDonald's website, www.mcdonalds.com, and will be available at each store. McDonald's has created a Dietary Practice/Vegetarian Advisory Panel consisting of experts in consumer dietary practices that will advise McDonald's on relevant dietary restrictions and guidelines, which McDonald's and others can use for marketing to persons who follow those restrictions. As part of this settlement, McDonald's is donating $10 million to Hindu, vegetarian and other groups whose charitable and educational activities are closely linked to the concerns of these consumers.
     McDonald's Apology, http://hbharti.com/h_bharti_mcd/mc_d_apology.htm.
28   An earlier obesity lawsuit was filed in 1978 by a District of Columbia police officer seeking extra retirement benefits on the basis that odd hours and stressful conditions caused him to smoke and eat junk food to excess. His case was dismissed (*Liberty v. District of Columbia Police and Firemen's Retirement and Relief Board* 1982).
29   According to *Fortune Magazine,* Hirsch had "never heard of Banzhaf or Daynard" when he launched the litigation. However, Banzhaf quickly became an advisor to the case (Parloff 2003, para. 13.).
30   Jay Leno hypothesized future fast food employees who, upon seeing a Barber-like customer, would say, "I'm sorry sir, but you've had enough. Now back away from the Whopper." Pacific Research Institute [on file with author]. Also see Haltom and McCann (2004a, 179-81).
31   Plaintiffs had initially filed in state court and had wished to remain there. McDonald's, however, argued for and won on diversity jurisdiction (*Pelman v. McDonald's* 2003b, 521-23).
32   *Pelman II* was a petition by an adult, Rivka Robbin Freeman, to intervene as a third named party. The petition was denied (*Pelman v. McDonald's* 2003a).
33   According to section 12(e) of the *Federal Rules of Civil Procedure* (Motion for More Definite Statement), "[i]f a pleading to which a responsive pleading is permitted is so vague or ambiguous that a party cannot reasonably be required to frame a responsive pleading, the party may move for a more definite statement before interposing a responsive pleading. The motion shall point out the defects complained of and the details desired. If the motion is granted and the order of the court is not obeyed within 10 days after notice of the order or within such other time as the court may fix, the court may strike the pleading to which the motion was directed or make such order as it deems just."
34   See McDonald's, http://www.mcdonalds.com/usa/eat/features/salads.html. Among others joining the salad bandwagon are Arby's "Market-Fresh® Salads," http://www.arbys.com/nutrition/ and Wendy's "Garden Sensation® Salads," http://www.wendys.com/.
35   Although in 2007, McDonald's introduced "Hugo" sized (forty-two ounce) drinks in some markets (Marco 2007)!
36   See McDonald's Happy Meal Choices, http://www.mcdonalds.com/usa/ronald/newchoices.html.

37 For example, we now know that a Quarter Pounder® with cheese, large fries with ketchup and salt, washed down with a McFlurry® with M and Ms® candies adds up to 1,720 calories, 75 grams of fat, 30 grams of saturated fat, 11 grams of trans fat, 150 milligrams of cholesterol, 2,040 grams of sodium, 212 grams of carbohydrates, 11 grams of fiber, and 49 grams of protein. "Get the Nutrition Facts for a McDonald's Menu Item," http://nutrition. mcdonalds.com/bagamcmeal/chooseCustomize.do.

38 *Personal Responsibility in Food Consumption Act of 2005,* H.R. 554.

39 *Ibid.* at preamble. Exceptions include "breach of express contract or express warranty, provided that the grounds for recovery being alleged in such action are unrelated to a person's weight gain, obesity, or a health condition associated with a person's weight gain or obesity" and "marketing, advertisement, or labeling" deception in violation of federal or state law *(ibid.).*

40 *Commonsense Consumption Act of 2005,* H.R. 2183, s. 1323.

41 The industry's interest in defending against lawsuits is reflected in part by a substantial spike in political action committee contributions in congressional elections. Between the 2004 and 2006 cycles, when passage of the *Commonsense Consumption Act, supra* note 40, seemed possible, the National Restaurant Association's spending increased by more than half a million dollars (OpenSecrets.org 2008a).

42 A 64-ounce 7-11 Double Gulp features not only a lot of liquid but also over 600 calories to boot (Lillien 2007).

43 Massachusetts is one of only a few states where plaintiffs do not have to demonstrate actual damage in a consumer-protection case. They only need to show that a violation has occurred (Mayer 2005). Moreover, "unlike most state consumer protection laws, a Massachusetts statute – General Law Chapter 93A, *Regulation of Business Practices for Consumers Protection,* 15 M.G.L. 93A – appears to permit plaintiffs to bring a claim as a class action without first establishing several of the requirements of a traditional Rule 23 class" (Fennell et al. 2006).

44 The guidelines recommend the following:

Elementary School

- bottled water
- up to 8 ounce servings of milk and 100 percent juice
- low-fat and non-fat regular and flavoured milk with up to 150 calories / 8 ounces
- 100 percent juice with no added sweeteners and up to 120 calories / 8 ounces

Middle School

- same as elementary school, except juice and milk may be sold in 10 ounce servings

High School

- bottled water
- no or low-calorie beverages with up to 10 calories / 8 ounces
- up to 12 ounce servings of milk, 100 percent juice, light juice, and sports drinks
- low-fat and non-fat regular and flavoured milk with up to 150 calories / 8 ounces
- 100 percent juice with no added sweeteners and up to 120 calories / 8 ounces
- light juices and sports drinks with no more than 66 calories / 8 ounces
- at least 50 percent of beverages must be water and no or low-calorie options

The William J. Clinton Foundation is a non-profit developed by President Bill Clinton to promote among other things, economic opportunity, health, sustainable development in Africa, and treatment of HIV/AIDS and malaria.William J. Clinton Foundation, http://www. clintonfoundation.org/what-we-do/.

45 In reality, if recent cases involving the liquor industry are any indication, the attractive nuisance argument would not be terribly successful. In February 2006, US district court judge Donald C. Nugent dismissed a class action against Anheuser-Busch that accused the beer manufacturer of "deliberate and reckless targeting of underage consumers in their advertising and marketing of certain alcoholic beverages" (*Eisenberg v. Anheuser-Busch, Inc.* 2006). And a Wisconsin state court recently dismissed a nearly identical lawsuit for failure

to adequately plead a legal injury (*Tomberlin v. Adolph Coors Co., et al.* 2006; cited in Jackson 2006, para. 2).

46 From the SpongeBob theme song: "Oh! Who lives in a pineapple under the sea? SpongeBob SquarePants!" http://www.spongebobworld.com/themesong.htm.

47 See footnote 44 in this chapter to understand the significance of Massachusetts as the state of choice.

48 According to the "Letter of Intent to Sue," "'advertisement' and 'advertise' include all forms of marketing in all forms of media and venues, including without limitation print advertisements, television and radio commercials, product labels, magazines, use of licensed characters, use of celebrities, viral marketing, websites, contests, premiums, incentives, toys and other merchandise, games, advergaming, sponsorships, school-based marketing (such as book covers and sponsored educational material), and kids clubs" (Center for Science in the Public Interest 2006b).

49 General Law Chapter 93A, *Regulation of Business Practices for Consumers Protection, supra* note 43.

50 Joseph is the founder of the advocacy group Ban Trans Fats, http://www.bantransfats.com/.

51 *California Civil Code,* § 1714.45).

52 Kraft's official announcement of change came in July 2003. When Joseph announced plans to drop his suit, a company spokesperson claimed that the suit's "legal premise was weak" and that Kraft was already "exploring how to eliminate *trans* fats from their products" (Severson 2003).

53 The district court ruled that Center for Science in the Public Interest (CSPI) had no standing in federal court and has remanded the case to the Superior Court of the District of Columbia.

54 See, for example, Burger King "Big Book of Nutrition Facts," http://www.bk.com/#menu=3,-1,-1; McDonald's "Bag a Meal," http://nutrition.mcdonalds.com/bagacmeal/choose Customize.do; KFC "Nutrition Calculator," http://www.yum.com/nutrition/menu. asp?brandID_Abbr=2_KFC; Taco Bell "Nutrition Calculator," http://www.yum.com/ nutrition/menu.asp?brandID_Abbr=5_TB; Wendy's "Nutrition Facts," http://www.yum. com/nutrition/menu.asp?brandID_Abbr=5_TB; Chipotle "Nutrition Calculator 2.0," http:// www.chipotlefan.com/index.php?id=nutrition_calculator.

55 In August 2004, CSPI "visited 29 of 33 (88 percent) of the McDonald's outlets in Washington, DC, and visually inspected the premises, as well as asked cashiers or restaurant managers whether they had nutrition information available in the restaurant." The researchers found that "59 percent of McDonald's outlets provided in-store nutrition information for the majority of their standard menu items. In 62 percent of the restaurants, it was necessary to ask two or more employees in order to obtain a copy of that information" (National Institute of Health 2006).

56 See McDonald's, http://www.mcdonalds.com/usa/eat.html.

57 From October to December 2002, McDonald's posted its first quarterly loss in its forty-seven-year history (Herzog 2003). The corporation has since rebounded very nicely.

58 Recent actions by the tobacco industry (flavoured cigarettes, smokeless tobacco, clever advertising, and so on) suggest that they will contrive strategies to achieve their desired ends regardless.

Chapter 6: International Developments in the Politics of Litigation

1 Also see, for example, *Knight v. Florida* (1999, 995) (Breyer, J., dissenting from denial of *certiori*).

2 Justice Gérard La Forest of the Supreme Court of Canada recently noted:

> Until the enactment of the Canadian Charter of Rights and Freedoms 1 in 1982, our courts resolved the disputes that came before them almost solely by reference to the statutes and case law of Canada and England. Only the most limited reliance was placed on other Commonwealth or American sources, and virtually never did our courts stray further than this. The Charter changed all this. In the last six years the Supreme Court of Canada has become one of, if not the most, cosmopolitan of national

courts in terms of the sources to which we have turned in dealing with the appeals that come before us. (La Forest 1988, 230; also see, for example, Manfredi 1990; MacIntyre 1966)

Brian Opeskin (2001) reports that the High Court of Australia has also referenced case law from a range of foreign sources, particularly in constitutional litigation since the 1990s (also see Goldsworthy 2006).

3 More recent evidence, perhaps tied to increased political and legal integration accompanying development of the European Union (EU), suggests that American style adversarial legalism is on the rise across Europe (for example, Keleman 2006).

4 The province of Québec was among the first to adopt a class action reform, relying heavily upon *Rule 23* of the US *Federal Rules of Civil Procedure,* http://www.law.cornell.edu/rules/frcp/ (*Code of Civil Procedure,* R.S.Q., c. C-25; first enacted as S.Q. 1978, c. 8, s. 3). Part IVA of the *Federal Court of Australia Act 1976,* Commonwealth of Australia Law, No. 156, allow multi-party actions to proceed in the federal courts, again using *Rule 23* as a primary model. Also see the Australian Law Reform Commission's report of 1979 and the Ontario Law Reform Commission's exhaustive report and recommendations issued in 1982. Although its legal system is quite different, Brazil was also influenced by class action developments in the United States in working through a model in 1985 (see, for example, Gidi 2003, 326ff).

5 For example, law reform commissions issued reports, often leading to draft legislation in Manitoba (1999) (Law Reform Commission, http://www.gov.mb.ca/justice/mlrc/pubs/classproc.html); British Columbia (2000) (Law Society of British Columbia, http://www.lawsociety.bc.ca/index.html); Ireland (2003) (http://www.lawreform.ie/lawunderreview/lawreview.htm); Australia (2000) "Second Programme of Law Reform"; Scotland (1996) (http://www.scotlawcom.gov.uk/downloads/rep154.pdf); South Africa (1995) "The Recognition of a Class Action in South African Law," Working Paper no. 57 (1995); South African Law Commission, *The Recognition of Class Actions and Public Interest Actions in South African Law* (1998), http://www.saflii.org/za/other/zalc/report/1998/5/; Japan (1996 *Code of Civil Procedure of Japan,* http://www.japanlaw.co.jp/procedure/civilcode.html, Article 30); and Italy (1996) (see Taruffo 2001). The People's Republic of China adopted a representative litigation model in 1991 (Liebman 1998).

6 Indeed, Lord Johan Steyn of the British upper chamber notes "marked cultural differences," between the United States and the United Kingdom and asserts: "There is also an unarticulated but nevertheless real conviction among judges that we must not allow our social welfare state to become a society bent on litigation. The introduction of United States style class actions cannot but contribute to such unwelcome developments in our system" (cited in Hodges 2001, foreword, iii).

7 As Sherman (2002, 403) observes, "[h]orror stories about an overly litigious society, entrepreneurial plaintiff attorneys, runaway jury verdicts, abusive class action practices, and legal blackmail through meritless suits that drive up business costs are well-known abroad. Whether or not such stories convey an accurate picture, most other countries view American class actions as a Pandora's box that they want to avoid opening. Thus, a good deal of attention is being devoted these days to studying and experimenting with procedures for aggregation of cases that can avoid the perceived excesses of the American experience." Also see, for example, Burke 2002; Taruffo 2001, 414-15.

8 See, for example, Boggio (2003), comparing the experience of European systems in dealing with asbestos claims, especially in the United Kingdom, Belgium, and Italy. Also see Best (2003) comparing activities in Germany and the United Kingdom.

9 Although there are signals of movement (see, for example, Gotanda 2007), the general sentiment outside the United States has been that the American punitive damage system is excessive (Gotanda 2004).

10 There are, of course, exceptions. Both the United Kingdom and Australia were slow in adopting adequate compensation schemes to address the vast asbestos problems, especially associated with exposed workers, and the corporate record is too often one of repeated attempts to evade liability. Only after significant multi-party court actions successfully ran their course, did the British and Australian governments construct more serious worker compensation programs. The Canadian government was more aggressive in addressing the

problem earlier on, and litigation has not been as necessary a tool in that country. We discuss the asbestos questions specific to each system later in this chapter.

11 This is not always true with regard to product liability and other personal injury tort claims. Under the British scheme, for example, public assistance is available only if the claim is found to have "wider public interest" (see, for example, *Lubbe v. Cape PLC* 2000a (filed on behalf of a group of South African asbestos miners).

12 EC Directive 2003/8 to Improve Access to Justice in Cross-Border Disputes by Establishing Minimum Common Rules Relating to Legal Aid for Such Disputes, O.J. L26/41, 31 January 2003, http://eur-lex.europa.eu/LexUriServ/LexUriServ.do?uri=CELEX:32003L0008:EN: HTML.

13 Kritzer (2002) notes that even prior to the issuance of this policy directive, the prohibitions against contingency fee arrangements was beginning to soften, especially in France, Italy, Portugal, and Greece. Also see Willett (2005).

14 EC Directive 98/27 on Injunctions for the Protection of Consumers' Interests, O.J. L166, 51, 1998. Also see Taruffo (2001).

15 In *Adair v. New River Co.* (1805), Lord Eldon allowed a case to proceed even though all of the relevant parties could not be identified and whose prior consent to be represented and bound by the outcome, obviously, could not be obtained.

16 Lord Cottenham's words were quoted soon thereafter by the Supreme Court of the United States in *Bacon v. Robertson* (1855, 485) and much more recently by the Supreme Court of Canada in *Western Canadian Shopping Centres Inc. v. Dutton* (2001, para. 23).

17 *Supreme Court of Judicature Act of 1873*, 36 and 37 Vict. c. 66; *Rule 10* of the *Federal Rules of Civil Procedure, supra* note 4, stated: "Where there are numerous parties having the same interest in one action, one or more of such parties may sue or be sued, or may be authorised by the Court to defend in such action, on behalf or for the benefit of all parties so interested."

18 For example, *Bedford v. Ellis* (1901); and *Taff Vale Railway Co. v. Amalgamated Society of Railway Servants* (1901).

19 We noted a few of those cases in Chapter 1 as being of some relevance to nineteenth-century American judges as they grappled with approaches to group litigation.

20 By creating a collective fund, the court avoided the two-stage process employed in *Prudential Assurance v. Newman* Industries (1981). Also see *M. Michael Furriers Ltd v. Askew* (1983).

21 *European Convention on Human Rights*, 1950, http://conventions.coe.int/treaty/en/ Treaties/Html/005.htm.

22 For example, *Loveday v. Renton* (1990) (pertussis vaccine); *Davies v. Eli Lilly* (1987) (Opren); and *Foster v. Roussel Laboratories Ltd.* (1997) (Norplant contraceptive device).

23 For example, *Griffiths and Others v. British Coal* (1998).

24 For example, *Hodgson v. Imperial Tobacco Ltd.* (1999b).

25 See, for example, Howells (1998) for a discussion of this connection and related litigation.

26 *Civil Procedure Rules, Parties and Group Litigation*, Part 19.6, http://www.justice.gov.uk/civil/ procrules_fin/contents/parts/part19.htm.

27 Solicitors wishing to be a part of the process are expected to form a solicitor's group, and the group then selects one solicitor to represent them all in submitting the application and pursing other aspects of the case. The initiative for clustering similar claims under a single group litigation order (GLOs) can also come from the court as a case management tool.

28 *Courts and Legal Services Act 1990*, c. 41.

29 The *Conditional Fee Agreements Order 1995*, S.I. 1995/1674; the *Conditional Fee Agreements Regulation 1995*, S.I. 1995/1675; the *Conditional Fee Agreements Order 1998*, S.I. 1998/1860. Currently, conditional fee arrangements are allowable in all civil matters, except family law, and are not permitted in criminal cases. See, for example, Boon (2001).

30 See *Hodgson v. Imperial Tobacco Ltd.* (1999b); Action on Smoking and Health – The Law Courts: UK Tobacco Litigation, http://old.ash.org.uk/html/litigation/uktobal.html. Also see Albright (1997); Rogers (1998).

31 One closely watched Scottish case, *McTear's Executrix v. Imperial Tobacco Ltd.* (1997), finally went to trial in 2005, resulting in a decision for the defendant.

32 Her Majesty's Court Service maintains a full list of all GLOs in chronological order at http://www.hmcourts-service.gov.uk/cms/150.htm.

33 The *Constitutional Reform Act 2005*, c. 4, http://www.opsi.gov.uk/acts/acts2005/ukpga_20050004_en_1, among other changes, creates a new high court that will assume most of the important judicial functions historically performed by the Law Lords of the upper parliamentary chamber.

34 *Hunting Act 2004*, c. 37.

35 Members of the Countryside Alliance, which collectively owned and operated land traditionally devoted to fox hunting in addition to ancillary activities.

36 The *Hunting Act 2004, supra* note 34, became law after passage in the House of Commons in two successive sessions but without a vote by the House of Lords, according to little-used provisions in the *Parliament Act 1911*, c. 13 and amended in the *Parliament Act 1949*, c. 103, as a measure to strengthen the governing position of the lower chamber.

37 For a more thorough assessment of the decision and implications, see Twomey (2007).

38 *Constitution Act*, 1982, http://laws.justice.gc.ca/en/const/annex_e.html; *Australia Act*, 1986, http://www.austlii.edu.au/au/legis/cth/consol_act/aa1986114/.

39 *Supreme Court of Judicature Act 1873*, 36 and 37 Vict. c. 66, which consolidates the chancery courts, with equity jurisdiction and the common law courts, and adopting *Rule 10*.

40 *An Act Respecting the Class Action*, S.Q. 1978, c. 8.

41 See, for example, *Nault v. Canadian Consumer Co. Ltd.* (1981), in which the plaintiff attempted to launch a class action on behalf of all purchasers who ordered a $16.88 set of cutlery that was never delivered. The Court found that contractual relations are, by their nature, individually specific and not suitable for combined treatment. Also see *Comité de citoyens et d'action municipale de St-Césaire Inc. v. Ville de St-Césaire* (1985) (filed by citizens of a township against their local government over water treatment). The Court found that although all similarly situated parties might not want the same remedy, all would be bound by the result. Thus, the class action formula was not deemed appropriate.

42 Robins had argued that the case should not go forward as a group action because the class members presented circumstances and legal issues that varied considerably. The court reaffirmed its view of class actions in *Syndicat National des Employés de l'Hôpital St-Ferdinand c. Québec (Curateur Public)* (1994).

43 *Rule 75* of the *Rules of Practice*, cited in *G.M. (Canada) v. Naken* (1983) of the Supreme Court of Ontario stated succinctly: "Where there are numerous persons having the same interest, one or more may sue or be sued or may be authorized by the Court to defend on behalf of or for the benefit of all."

44 The Court was also heavily criticized (see, for example, Bogart 1994).

45 *Class Proceedings Act*, S.O. 1992, c. 6. In 1995, British Columbia followed Québec and Ontario with legislation in 1996. *Class Proceedings Act*, R.S.B.C. 1996, c. 50. The other provinces were slower to act but have more recently done so: Saskatchewan in 2001(*Class Actions Act*, R.S.S. 2001, c. C-12.01); Newfoundland and Labrador in 2001 (*Class Actions Act*, S.N.L. 2001, c. C-18.1); Manitoba in 2002 (*Class Proceedings Act*, S.M. 2002, c. 14); and Alberta in 2003 (*Class Proceedings Act*, S.A. 2003, c. C-16.5). Nationally, federal rules went into effect in 2002 (*Federal Court Rules*, S.O.R. 98-106, R. 299.1-299.42 (1998)).

46 There have been a few big ones. See, for example, *Serwaczek v. Medical Engineering Corp.* (1996) (the largest of several breast implant class actions with CDN $50 million-plus recovery); *Dabbs v. Sun Life Assurance Co. of Canada* (1998); *McKrow v. Manufacturers Life Ins. Co.* (1998) (the so-called vanishing insurance premium cases, resulting in settlements valued at CDN $140 million); and *Parsons v. Canadian Red Cross Society* (1999) (CDN $1.5 billion award in the Hepatitis C litigation).

47 *Canadian Charter of Rights and Freedoms*, Part 1 of the *Constitution Act 1982*, being Schedule B to the *Canada Act, 1982* (U.K.), 1982, c. 11.

48 Some have argued, however, that the Court had signaled a more liberal approach to class actions in the period since *Naken v. General Motors of Canada Ltd.* (1983). See, for example, McGillivray and McLennan (2002).

49 It also followed that neither judicial economy nor behaviour modification would likely be furthered in this case.

50 In jurisdictions without legislation, the courts are expected to accommodate class actions under the *Western Canadian Shopping Centres Inc. v. Dutton* rationale.

51 British Columbia (*Bouchanskaia v. Bayer Inc.* 2003); Saskatchewan (*Lamb v. Bayer Inc.* 2003); Manitoba (*Walls v. Bayer Inc.* 2005); Ontario (*Coleman v. Bayer Inc.* 2004), Québec (*Dufour c. Bayer Inc.* 2004); and Newfoundland (*Wheadon v. Bayer Inc.* 2004; *Pardy v. Bayer Inc.* 2003).

52 The first national class was certified in 1995 in Ontario courts (*Nantais v. Telectronics Proprietary Ltd.* 1995). The case involved allegedly defective heart pacemaker implants and was eventually settled for CDN \$23.1 million (Watson 2001, 276). A number of other national class actions followed, as judges sought to satisfy the three primary rationales: judicial efficiency, enhanced access to justice among the population, and behaviour modification of wrongdoers. Also see, for example, *Carom v. Bre-x Minerals Ltd.* (1999) (fraudulent misrepresentation of gold deposits). *Carom* also had cross-border implications, as the original litigation in Canada included American citizens among the class members. See, for example, *McNamara v. Bre-X Minerals Ltd.* (1999). And in an important case involving parallel transnational class actions, see *Parsons v. McDonalds* 2005) (alleging that promotional contests had been rigged), in which the Supreme Court of Ontario indicated a willingness to enforce judgments reached in US courts involving Canadians, assuming no problematic jurisdictional and due process issues.

53 For example, *Ragoonanan v. Imperial Tobacco* (2000) (product liability regarding so-called fire-safe cigarettes, in which the case has dragged on for six years without a decision; *Knight v. Imperial Tobacco* (2005) (alleging deception in marketing of "lite" cigarettes, class finally certified after three years of procedural wrangling).

54 *Tobacco Damages Recovery Act,* S.B.C. 1997, c. 41.

55 *Tobacco Damages and Health Care Costs Recovery Act,* S.B.C. 2000, c. 30.

56 The decision will likely have a significant impact, as the governments in Ontario, Newfoundland, and Labrador had also already enacted similar legislation using the same formulas, allowing recovery of smoking-related health care costs to the public.

57 The decision was appealed, to no avail, and the Supreme Court of the United States declined to hear it. *Service Employees Int'l Union Health and Welfare Fund v. Philip Morris Incorporated* (1999).

58 *Environmental Assessment Act 1979-80,* http://www.qp.gov.sk.ca/documents/English/Statutes/Statutes/E10-1.pdf; and the *Environmental Management and Protection Act 2002,* http://www.qp.gov.sk.ca/documents/English/Statutes/Statutes/E10-21.pdf.

59 Using as precedent *Anns v. Merton London Borough Council* (1978).

60 The task force, co-chaired by Health Canada and the Heart and Stroke Foundation of Canada, was created following an action by the House of Commons in 2004. The final report, titled "Transforming the Food Supply," represents an extensive review of current research and contains sweeping recommendations for regulation. The report is available online at Health Canada, http://www.hc-sc.gc.ca/fn-an/nutrition/gras-trans-fats/tf-ge/tf-gt_rep-rap-eng.php.

61 Both countries also have a federal system, which exerts a decentralizing influence and multiplies the number of judicial access points.

62 A distinction can be made based upon whether a claim is filed by one plaintiff representing others (under the *Markt* precedent) or a number of parties whose claims are aggregated as a class. Actions in Victoria state courts are called "group proceedings."

63 *Federal Court of Australia Act of 1976, supra* note 4.

64 The Australian regime replaces the oversight involved in certification with active judicial scrutiny in various case phases, such as the process by which group members are notified in order to make an opt-out decision, approval of settlement terms, approval of a representative party's withdrawal, and/or insertion of a more appropriate representative party.

65 For example, Part 8 r.13(1) of the *Rules of the Supreme Court of New South Wales,* 1970, http://www.austlii.edu.au/au/legis/nsw/consol_reg/scr1970232/ provide: "Where numerous persons have the same interest in any proceedings the proceedings may be commenced, and, unless the Court otherwise orders, continued, by or against any one or more of them as representing all or as representing all except one or more of them."

66 The fees were calculated individually and separately, and, although the claims were substantially similar, the Court determined that the transactions amounted to separate contracts and could not be understood as a series.

67 *Supreme Court Act,* W.A. 1984, s. 62 (1C).

68 The legislation applied only to cases originating in the federal courts but not to procedures in the states.

69 Indeed, legal advocates and commentators in Australia have avoided using the term "class action," because it is so closely associated with the American practice, which has been much maligned in the press as leading to aggressive lawyering by unscrupulous entrepreneurial attorneys who have little regard for the public interest and whose tactics leave corporate financial ruin in their wake (see, for example, Sherman 2002, 403).

70 *Federal Court of Australia Amendment Act 1991,* (Vic) Commonwealth of Australia Law.

71 *Credit Act 1984* (NSW).

72 This is the description offered by the High Court of Australia in responding to the inevitable appeal (*Carnie v. Esanda* 1995).

73 In his concurrence, Justice McHugh applauded the liberalization of the rules: "In the Age of Consumerism, it is proper that this should be so. The cost of litigation often makes it economically irrational for an individual to attempt to enforce legal rights arising out of a consumer contract. Consumers should not be denied the opportunity to have their legal rights determined when it can be done efficiently and effectively on their behalf by one person with the same community of interest as other consumers. Nor should the courts' lists be cluttered by numerous actions when one action can effectively determine the rights of many" (*ibid.,* 429-30 [McHugh, J., concurring]).

74 This "opt-in" requirement was essentially the same as that enacted by the Victorian Parliament in 1986 – *Supreme Court Act 1986* (Vic.), para. 35(2)(a) – but which had been heavily criticized by the courts as likely to victimize those least likely to be able to protect their interests. See, for example, *Zentahope Pty. Ltd. v. Bellotti* (1992); and *A and J Partitions Pty. Ltd. v. Jolly* (1993). Such criticism ultimately produced further legislative reform in Victoria and in the federal courts.

75 *Supreme Court Act 1986, supra* note 74; and *Rule IVA,* http://www.austlii.edu.au/au/legis/vic/consol_act/sca1986183.

76 The situation in the Wittenoom area, adjacent to a mine operated by a subsidiary of CSR Limited, was particularly serious. Residue "tailings" cast off from the mining operations were used extensively in the 1950s and 1960s throughout Wittenoom as an inexpensive gravel and sand substitute, for streets, walkways, landscaping, playgrounds, and the like. The result, by the 1970s and 1980s, was a major health and safety problem, as the townspeople suffered extraordinarily high rates of mesothelioma and other related diseases. The residents and their survivors sued, and the courts found CSR responsible (*CSR Ltd. v. Young* 1998).

77 *Pilmer v. McPherson's Limited* (1985) [unreported].

78 *Asbestos-related Claims (Management of Commonwealth Liabilities) (Consequential and Transitional Provisions) Bill 2005,* Bills Digest No. 176, 2004-05, Parliament of Australia, http://www.aph.gov.au/LIBRARY/Pubs/bd/2004-05/05bd176.htm). CSR, the larger of two Australian corporations engaged in asbestos mining since the early nineteenth century, was a major supplier to US markets. In its 2005 financial report, the company indicates that it had settled some 128,000 claims in the United States and 1,577 in Australia, with another 684 domestic claims pending (as of March 2005) (CSR Limited 2001, 65).

79 For an in-depth analysis of this case, see Everingham and Woodward (1991).

80 For a thorough analysis of this case, see Cameron and Liberman (2003). There have also been a number of cases regarding the effects of second-hand smoke. See, for example, *Sharp v. Port Kembla RSL Club* (2001).

81 At about the same time another case was commenced by an organization established for the purpose of engaging in class action litigation on behalf of Australian smokers and to establish a fund through which compensation might be paid to tobacco users who subsequently developed health problems. This case also was ultimately dismissed by the Federal Court of Australia (*Tobacco Control Coalition Inc. v. Philip Morris (Australia) Ltd.* 2000).

82   For example, in July 2005, the University of Sydney Law School announced that Peter Cashman was joining the faculty (Gawler 2005). According to the university press release, Cashman has been a class action "pioneer" in Australia and has appeared before many US courts in major product liability cases and class actions including Dalkon Shield inter-uterine litigation, the Bjork-Shiley heart valve, and breast implants. In addition, he served as national president of the Australian Plaintiff Lawyers Association and was a member of the Board of Governors of the Association of Trial Lawyers of America. Indeed, Cashman is a senior partner of a prominent Melbourne law firm, whose webpage presents a long list of class action activities, Maurice Blackburn Lawyers, http://www.mauriceblackburncashman.com.au/areas/class_actions/. Also see for example, Mullenix (2001).

83   The McMullins brought suit on behalf of other ranchers, agents, slaughterhouse operators and meat processors, pasture protection boards, and feed lot operators *(McMullin v. ICI Australia Operations Pty Ltd.* (1997).

84   Subsequently, Knipsel Fruit sued Peter and Theo Constas, independent orange growers. In 2003, the Federal Court of Australia deemed the Constas brothers ultimately liable for losses suffered by the fruit juice company, ordering them to pay in excess of AUS \$3 million (Fewster and Anderson 2003).

85   The symposium, titled "Obesity: Should There be a Law against It?" attracted a range of health law and policy academics and practitioners. The proceedings were subsequently published in the *Australia and New Zealand Health Policy Journal* (Magnusson 2008).

86   For example, Murphy (2005, 5, n. 33) quotes an Australian observer as saying: "We are getting more and more laboured with these cases ... and unless we get some negative rulings from the courts, we will see an explosion." This negative view of American-style class action is not uncommon (see, for example, Taruffo 2001, 414-15).

87   Stevens (2001) observes that the Law Lords signaled a willingness to assert their independence a few years earlier in the 1998 extradition case involving General Augusto Pinochet (reported as *In re: Pinochet* (1998); *R. v. Bow Street Metropolitan Stipendiary Magistrate, Ex parte Pinochet Ugarte (1999).*

88   For a more general assessment of the High Court of Australia's emerging profile, see Pierce (2006).

89   *Universal Declaration of Human Rights,* 1948, http://www.un.org/Overview/rights.html.

Conclusions

1   Shapiro (1981) demonstrates that, although the logic of the triad often collapses, the form is quite consistent across time and cultures.

2   The revised model (group litigation orders) put into place in 2000 has a more flexible grouping formula, but it requires individual litigants to "opt in" in order to become part of the larger package.

3   It was not uncommon, especially before the nineteenth century, to see defendant "class" litigation. See our discussion of this case in Chapter 1. Father Martin was able to enforce a burial tax upon his entire constituency with a single action, thus accomplishing a public policy through the process of litigation. *Martin, Rector of Barkway v. Parishioners of Nuthamstead* (1199), discussed in Yeazell (1997, 688).

4   *Master Settlement Agreement,* National Association of Attorneys General, http://www.naag.org/tobac/index.html [*MSA*].

5   In March 2008, the Altria Group completed its spin-off of Philip Morris International.

6   Recent major regulatory failures in the United Kingdom, involving asbestos and food safety issues, are suggestive of similar relationships there.

7   All figures from Open Secrets, Lobbying Database, http://www.opensecrets.org/lobbyists/index.asp.

8   *Class Action Fairness Act of 2005,* Pub. L. No. 109-2, 119 Stat. 4 (2005). The vast majority of the trial lawyers' money has gone to Democratic candidates.

9   For example, as recently as 2003, the Supreme Court of Connecticut recited the same quote in upholding a class certification (*Collins v. Anthem Health Plans, Inc.* 2003, 19, n. 3). Moreover, in 1999, Justice Souter, writing for the majority in *Ortiz v. Fibreboard Corporation* (1999,

831), quoted Story's *Randall* opinion, even while striking down a massive asbestos settlement class).

10 See, for example, Sawer (1968), Bzdera (1993), and Pierce (2006) on the conservative tradition and strength of the rule of precedent on the High Court of Australia and see Epp (1998, ch. 7) on the historical conservative bent of the British House of Lords. Moreover, Harlow and Rawlings (1992, 5-7) observe that the UK legal culture has been very much apolitical, adhering to a strict separation between the political policy-making process and the judicial process (also see Le Sueur 2004). However, these traditions are very much in flux, and the judiciary in all three countries has recently taken counter-traditionally assertive actions (for example, Dickson 2007).

11 The Carnie litigation against the Esanda Finance Corporation in Australia followed a very similar scenario (*Carnie v. Esanda* 1995). Moreover, the Opren litigation, which attributes brain damage among young children who were given the pertussin vaccine in the United Kingdom, could also be placed in this category (*Davies v. Eli Lilly* 1987). See Harlow and Rawlings (1992, 129-35) for an interesting discussion of this and related cases.

12 Leading the defence team was Douglas K. Laidlaw, one of Canada's premier trial and appellate attorneys. He was a member of the Advocates' Society of Ontario and recipient (post-humously) of the organization's highest honor (Advocates' Society, http://www.advocates.ca).

13 On the other hand, activities that extended beyond US borders, if they occurred, were not detected. Admittedly, we did not give this question a thoroughgoing assessment.

14 There is a growing literature on these and related movements as well as "cause lawyering" in domestic and international venues (see, for example, Sarat and Scheingold 1998; 2001; 2005; 2006; Scheingold and Sarat 2004; Scheingold 2004; Epp 1998; Harlow and Rawlings 1992).

15 See, for example, Justice Scalia's dissent in *Roper v. Simmons* (2005), joined by Justice Thomas and Chief Justice Rehnquist.

General References

"44 Claim Illness Was Caused by Biotech Corn in Food." 2000. *Washington Post*. 29 November.

Administrative Office of the US Courts. 2003. "Judge Charles Weiner: Record Matched by Few." 35 *Third Branch* 7 (July).

Ahmed, Azam. 2008. "NRA Sues Chicago, Three Suburbs to Repeal Their Firearms Bans." *Chicago Tribune*. 27 June.

Albert, Tanya. 2003. "Measure Stalls in Senate: 'We'll Be Back,' Say Tort Reformers." American Medical Association, Amednews.com, http://www.ama-assn.org/amednews/2003/07/28/gvl10728.htm.

Albright, Audra A. 1997. "Could This Be the Last Gasp? England's First Case against the British Tobacco Industry." 11 *Temple International and Comparative Law Journal* 363.

Alemanno, Alberto. 2007. *Trade in Food: Regulatory and Judicial Approaches in the EC and the WTO*. London: Cameron May.

Algero, Mary Garvey. 1999. "In Defense of Forum Shopping: A Realistic Look at Selecting a Venue." 78 *Nebraska Law Review* 79.

Alliance for Bio-I. 2008, http://www.bio-integrity.org/FDADeception.html.

Alston, Phlip. 1997. "The Myopia of the Handmaidens: International Lawyers and Globalization." 8 *European Journal of International Law* 435.

Altria Group. 2005a. 2004 Fourth-Quarter and Full-Year Result. 26 January, http://www.altria.com/download/pdf/investors_2004_Q4AltriaRelease.pdf.

–. 2005b. "The Philip Morris USA Story," http://www.altria.com/about_altria/1_6_2_philipmorrisusastory.asp.

–. 2007. 2007 Annual Report, http://www.altria.com/AnnualReport/ar2007/2007ar_01_0100.aspx.

American Association for Justice. 2004. "Biased 'Tort Reform' Polls and Surveys: What They Really Show," http://www.justice.org/cps/rde/xchg/justice/hs.xsl/default.htm.

American Bar Association, Standing Committee on Pro Bono and Public Service. 2008. http://www.abanet.org/legalservices/probono/lawschools/77.html.

American Judicature Society. 2004. "Judicial Selection in Alabama," http://www.judicialselection.us/judicial_selection/methods/selection_of_judges.cfm?state=AL.

American Tort Reform Association. 2002. "Regulation through Litigation," http://www.atra.org/issues.

–. 2003. "Voters Say 'Too Many Lawsuits,' According to New National Poll on Tort Reform." 27 February, http://www.atra.org/show/7525.

–. 2004a. "2004 State Tort Reform Enactments," http://www.atra.org/files.cgi/7797_2004Enactments.pdf.

–. 2004b. *Bringing Justice to Judicial Hellholes*, http://www.atra.org./reports/hellholes/.

"Analyst: Tobacco Tax Could Hurt Reynolds, Lorillard Earnings." 2007. *Business Journal of the Greater Triad Area*. 7 August.

Andrews, Neil. 2001. "Multi-Party Proceedings in England: Representative and Group Actions." 11 *Duke Journal of Comparative and International Law* 249.

Asbestos Alliance. 2004. *The Scope of the Asbestos Litigation Problem*, http://www.asbestossolution.org/scope.html.

"Asbestos Deaths Expected to Continue to Increase." 2004. *Washington Post*. 23 July, http://www.washingtonpost.com/wp-dyn/articles/A7535-2004Jul22.html.

Ashton, Bronwyn, Heather Morton, and Johanna Mithen. 2003. "Children's Health or Corporate Wealth? The Case for Banning Television Food Advertising to Children." A Briefing Paper by the Coalition on Food Advertising to Children, Adelaide, South Australia, http://www.chdf.org.au/i-cms_file?page=664/BriefingPaperFinalCopy.pdf.

Association of Trial Lawyers of America. 2004a. "All about ATLA Litigation Groups," http://www.atlanet.org/Networking/Tier3/LitigationGroups.aspx.

–. 2004b. "Legal Research Exchange," http://www.atlanet.org/LegalResearchServices/Tier3/Exchange.aspx.

Ausness, Richard C. 2002. "Tort Liability for the Sale of Non-Defective Products: An Analysis and Critique of the Concept of Negligent Marketing." 53 *South Carolina Law Review* 907.

Australian Law Reform Commission. 1979. *Access to the Courts II – Class Actions*. Discussion Paper no. 11. Canberra: Australian Government Publishing Service.

–. 2000. "Managing Justice: A Review of the Federal Civil Justice System." Report no. 89. Canberra: Australian Government Publishing Service.

Badinter, Robert, and Stephen Breyer, eds. 2004. *Judges in Contemporary Democracy: An International Conversation*. New York: New York University Press.

Bagaric, Mirko, and Sharon Erbacher. 2005. "Fat and the Law: Who Should Take the Blame?" 12 *Journal of Law and Medicine* 323.

Bailey, Brandon. 2007. "Lawsuit Targets Chinese Supplier in Tainted Pet Food Case." *San Jose Mercury News*. 8 August.

Ban Trans Fats. 2006. "The Oreo Case," http://www.bantransfats.com/theoreocase.html.

Banzhaf, John. 2004. Legal Activism, Course no. 637. George Washington Univesity Law School, http://banzhaf.net/.

Batt, Tracy L. 1996. "Note: DES Third-Generation Liability: A Proximate Cause." 18 *Cardozo Law Review* 1217.

Bechamps, Anne-Therese. 1990. "Sealed Out-of-Court Settlements: When Does the Public Have a Right to Know?" 66 *Notre Dame Law Review* 117.

Beck, Susan. 2004. "Webb's Way." *American Lawyer*. 12 October.

Bentley, Arthur F. 1908. *The Process of Government*. Chicago: University of Chicago Press.

Berenson, Alex. 2007. "Plaintiffs Find Payday Elusive in Vioxx Cases." *New York Times*. 21 August.

Bernstein, David E. 2002. "Disinterested in Daubert: State Courts Lag Behind in Opposing 'Junk' Science." Legal Opinion Letter. *Washington Legal Foundation*, http://www.wlf.org/upload/6-21-02Bernstein.pdf.

Best, Richard. 2003. "Private Law Liability for Asbestos-Related Disease in England and Germany." 4 *German Law Journal* 661.

Betts, Jason. 2006. "Are We Becoming More American? Class Action Litigation: Australia versus the US." *Lawyers Weekly*. 9 June, http://www.lawyersweekly.com.au/articles/DD/0C0251DD.asp?Type=55andCategory=1120.

Biggs, Mandy. 2006. "Overweight and Obesity in Australia." E-brief prepared for the Parliamentary Library, Parliament of Australia. 5 October, http://www.aph.gov.au/library/INTGUIDE/sp/obesity.htm.

Birnbaum, Jeffrey H. 2005. "A Quiet Revolution in Business Lobbying." *Washington Post*. 5 February.

Blake, Tony. 2007. "Trans-Fats." British Broadcasting Corporation: Food Matters, July, http://www.bbc.co.uk/food/food_matters/transfats.shtml.

Bloomberg, Mayor Michael. 2007. "Two More Gun Dealers Enter into Settlements Consistent with Prior Agreements." PR-302-07, 17 August, http://167.153.130.51/portal/site/nycgov/menuitem.c0935b9a57bb4ef3daf2f1c701c789a0/index.jsp?pageID=mayor_press_ release&catID=1194&doc_name=http%3A%2F%2F167.153.130.51%2Fhtml%2Fom %2Fhtml%2F2007b%2Fpr302-07.html&cc=unused1978&rc=1194&ndi=1.

Bogart, W.A. 1994. *Courts and Country: The Limits of Litigation and the Social and Political Life of Canada*. Oxford: Oxford University Press.

Boggio, Andrea. 2003. *The Puzzle of Mass Torts : A Comparative Study of Asbestos Litigation*. J.S.D. dissertation, Stanford University [unpublished].

Boon, Andrew. 2001. "Cause Lawyers in a Cold Climate: The Impact(s) of Globalization on the United Kingdom." In Austin Sarat and Stuart Scheingold, eds., *Cause Lawyering and the State in a Global Era*, 143. New York: Oxford University Press.

Borrud, Lori, Cecilia Wilkinson Enns, and Sharon Mickle. 1996. "What We Eat in America: USDA Surveys Food Consumption Changes." 19 *Food Review* 14.

Breyer, Stephen. 2003. "The Supreme Court and the New International Law." Remarks delivered to the annual meeting of the American Society of International Law, Washington, DC, 4 April, http://www.supremecourtus.gov/publicinfo/speeches/sp_04-04-03.html.

British Broadcasting Company. 2003. "Why Fast Food Makes You Get Fat." 22 October, http://news.bbc.co.uk/1/hi/health/3210750.stm.

–. 2007. "Mattel Recalls Millions More Toys." 14 August, http://news.bbc.co.uk/2/hi/business/6946425.stm.

Brodeur, Paul. 1985. *The Dusting of America: A Story of Asbestos – Carnage, Cover-Up, and Litigation*. New York: Pantheon Books.

Brown, David. 2006. "Nicotine Up Sharply in Many Cigarettes; Some Brands More Than 30 percent Stronger. *Washington Post*. 31 August.

Browning, Ron. 2004. "Gary Gun Suit Moves Forward." *Indiana Lawyer*. 15 December.

Buckley, Neil. 2004. "Fifty Years of Fraud: Washington Sues Big Tobacco for Dollars 280bn of Alleged Ill-Gotten Gains." *Financial Times*. 8 September.

Burditt, George M. 1995. "The History of Food Law." 50 *Food and Drug Law Journal* 197.

Bureau of Justice Statistics. U.S. Department of Justice. 2004. "Homicide Trends in the U.S: Trends by City Size," http://www.ojp.usdoj.gov/bjs/homicide/city.htm.

Burger King. 2006. Global Fact Sheet, http://www.bk.com/CompanyInfo/bk_corporation/fact_sheets/global_facts.aspx.

Burke, Thomas Frederick. 2002. *Lawyers, Lawsuits, and Legal Rights: The Battle over Litigation in American Society*. Berkeley: University of California Press.

Bush, President George W. 2004. Interview with Wayne LaPierre and Chris Cox. 18 October, http://www.nraila.org/Issues/Articles/Read.aspx?ID=147.

–. 2005. State of the Union Address, CBSNews.com, http://www.cbsnews.com/stories/2005/02/02/politics/main671254.shtml.

Butterfield, Fox. 2000. "Three More States Join an Investigation of Gun Industry." *New York Times*. 6 April.

Buxbaum, Hannah L. 2004. "From Empire to Globalization ... and Back? A Post-Colonial View of Transjudicialism." 11 *Indiana Journal of Global Legal Studies* 183.

Buzby, Jean C., Paul D. Frenzen, and Barbara Rasco. 2001. "Product Liability and Microbial Foodborne Illness." Agricultural Economic Report no. AER799, US Department of Agriculture, http://www.ers.usda.gov/publications/aer799/.

Bzdera, André. 1993. "Comparative Analysis of Federal High Courts: A Political Theory of Judicial Review." 26 *Canadian Journal of Political Science* 3.

Cable News Network. 2003. "TV, Lots of Fast Food Triple Obesity Risk." 10 March, http://www.cnn.com/2003/HEALTH/diet.fitness/03/10/fastfood.tv.ap/.

–. 2005. CNN Money: Fortune 500 – 2005: Wendy's International, http://money.cnn.com/magazines/fortune/fortune500/snapshots/1562.html.

Cahn, Robert A. 1976. "A Look at the Judicial Panel on Multidistrict Litigation." 72 *Federal Rules Decisions* 211.

Caldeira, Gregory A. 1985. "The Transmission of Legal Precedent: A Study of State Supreme Courts." 79 *American Political Science Review* 178.

Calfee, John E. 2002. "Comment." In W. Kip Viscusi, ed., *Regulation through Litigation*, 52. Washington, DC: Brookings.

Cameron, Camille, and Jonathan Liberman. 2003. "Destruction of Documents before Proceedings Commence: What Is a Court to Do?" 27 *Melbourne University Law Review* 273.

Campaign for a Commercial-Free Childhood. 2006. "Frequently Asked Questions about the Lawsuit against Viacom and Kellogg," http://www.commercialexploitation.org/pressreleases/lawsuitfaq.htm.

Campaign for Tobacco-Free Kids. 2005. "State Cigarette Excise Tax Rates and Rankings," http://tobaccofreekids.org/research/factsheets/pdf/0097.pdf.

–. 2007a. "Warning: Big Tobacco Targets Women and Girls," http://tobaccofreekids.org/reports/women/.

–. 2007b. State Initiatives, http://tobaccofreekids.org/campaign/state/.

– 2007c. "A Broken Promise to Our Children," http://www.tobaccofreekids.org/reports/settlements/2008/fullreport.pdf.

Canadian Broadcasting Corporation. 2007. "Calgary Moves against Trans Fats." CBCNews. ca. 29 December, http://www.cbc.ca/canada/story/2007/12/29/calgary-fats.html.

–. 2008. "Trans Fats: The Move Away from Bad Fats." News Report. 21 July, http://www.cbc.ca/health/story/2008/07/21/f-transfats.html.

Cape PLC. 2008. "Our History," http://www.capeplc.com/.

Cardinale, Carin. 2004. "The Long Island Breast Cancer Study: Results of an Epidemiological Study Cause Considerable Barriers to Legal Relief." 9 *Albany Law Environmental Outlook* 147.

Cardwell, Diane. 2006. "New York City Sues Fifteen Gun Dealers in Five States, Charging Illegal Sales." *New York Times*. 16 May.

Carroll, Jill. 2002. "Judge Will Approve a Settlement on Use of StarLink Corn Products." *Wall Street Journal*. 7 March.

Carroll, Stephen, J., Deborah R. Hensler, Allan Abrahamse, Jennifer Gross, J. Scott Ashwood, Elizabeth M. Sloss, and Michelle White. 2002. *Asbestos Litigation Costs and Compensation: An Interim Report*. Rand Institute for Civil Justice, http://www.rand.org/pubs/documented_briefings/2005/DB397.pdf.

Carter, Owen B.J. 2006. "The Weighty Issue of Australian Television Food Advertising and Childhood Obesity." 17 *Health Promotion Journal of Australia* 5.

Castleman, Barry I. 1996. *Asbestos: Medical and Legal Aspects,* 4th edition. Englewood Cliffs, NJ: Aspen Law and Business.

Cates, Cynthia L., and Wayne McIntosh. 2001. *Law and the Web of Society*. Washington, DC: Georgetown University Press.

Cauvin, Henri E. 2006. "Federal Law Negates D.C.'s Suit against Gunmakers, Judge Rules." *Washington Post*. 23 May.

Cavadini, Claude, Anna Maria Siega-Riz, and Barry M Popkin. 2000. "US Adolescent Food Intake Trends from 1965 to 1996." 83 *Archives of Disease in Childhood* 18.

Center for Science in the Public Interest (CSPI). 2006a. "CSPI Applauds Agreement to Get High-Calorie Drinks Out of Schools; Drops Planned Litigation." Statement of CSPI Executive Director Michael F. Jacobson. 3 May, http://www.cspinet.org/new/200605031.html.

–. 2006b. "Letter of Intent to Sue Viacom Inc., Viacom International Inc., and Kellogg Company." 18 January.

–. 2006c. "Parents and Advocates Will Sue Viacom and Kelloggs," http://www.cspinet.org/new/200601181.html.

–. 2007a. "Burger King Hit with Trans Fat Lawsuit." CSPI Newsroom, http://www.cspinet.org/new/200705161.html.

–. 2007b. "Kellogg Makes Historic Settlement Agreement." CSPI Newsroom, http://www.cspinet.org/new/200706141.html.

–. 2008. "Menu Labeling," http://www.cspinet.org/menulabeling/.

Centers for Disease Control and Prevention. 1996. "Cigarette Smoking among Adults – United States, 1994," http://www.cdc.gov/mmwr/preview/mmwrhtml/00042976.htm.

–. 2001. "Investigation of Human Health Effects Associated with Potential Exposure to Genetically Modified Corn." A Report to the US Food and Drug Administration from the Centers for Disease Control and Prevention, http://www.cdc.gov/nceh/ehhe/Cry9cReport/pdfs/cry9creport.pdf.

–. 2004a. "Fortieth Anniversary of the First Surgeon General's Report on Smoking and Health," http://www.cdc.gov/mmwr/preview/mmwrhtml/mm5303a1.htm.

–. 2004b. "Adult Cigarette Smoking in the United States: Current Estimates," http://www.cdc.gov/TOBACCO/data_statistics/fact_sheets/adult_data/adult_cig_smoking.htm.

–. 2005a. "State Tobacco Highlights: Mississippi," http://apps.nccd.cdc.gov/statesystem/statehilite.aspx?dir=epi_report&ucName=UCProfileRpt&state=MS&year=2005&outputtype=htmlreport508.

–. 2005b. "Preemptive State Smoke-Free Indoor Air Laws – United States, 1999-2004," http://www.cdc.gov/mmwr/preview/mmwrhtml/mm5410a4.htm#tab.

–. 2005c. "Foodborne Illness," http://www.cdc.gov/ncidod/dbmd/reportfi.htm.

–. 2005d. "2004 Summary Statistics." Food Borne Outbreak Response and Surveillance Unit, http://www.cdc.gov/foodborneoutbreaks/documents/fbsurvsumm2004.pdf.

–. 2005e. Investigation of Human Health Effects Associated with Potential Exposure to Genetically Modified Corn. National Center for Environmental Health, http://www.cdc.gov/nceh/ehhe/Cry9cReport/background.htm.

–. 2005f. "Smoking-Attributable Medical Expenses, 1998," http://apps.nccd.cdc.gov/sammec/show_same_data.asp.

–. 2005g. "Smoking-Attributable Productivity Losses, United States, 2001," http://apps.nccd.cdc.gov/sammec/earn_reports.asp.

–. 2006. "Surveillance for Foodborne-Disease Outbreaks – United States, 1998–2002," http://www.cdc.gov/MMWR/preview/mmwrhtml/ss5510a1.htm.

–. 2007. "U.S. Obesity Trends 1985-2006," http://www.cdc.gov/nccdphp/dnpa/obesity/trend/maps/index.htm.

–. 2008. "U.S. Obesity Trends 1985–2007," http://www.cdc.gov/nccdphp/dnpa/obesity/trend/maps/.

Chafee, Zechariah, Jr. 1932. "Bills of Peace with Multiple Parties." 45 *Harvard Law Review* 1297.

"Chairman Markey Responds to Kellogg Decision to Pull Ads Targeting Children." 2007. *States News Service*. 14 June.

Chebium, Raju. 2000. "Gun Industry Sues Public Officials over Firearms 'Code of Conduct,'" *Cnn.com*. 26 April, http://archives.cnn.com/2000/LAW/04/26/gunlawsuit/index.html.

Cheng, Edward K., and Albert H. Yoon. 2005. "Does Frye or Daubert Matter? A Study of Scientific Admissibility Standards." 91 *Virginia Law Review* 471.

Choe, Howard. 2003. "The Smoke around Big Tobacco Clears." *Business Week Online*. 22 May, http://www.businessweek.com/.

Clinton, President William J. 1999a. Address before a Joint Session of the Congress on the State of the Union. 19 January. American Presidency Project, http://www.presidency.ucsb.edu/ws/index.php?pid=57577.

–. 1999b. Press Conference by the President. 8 December. GlobalSecurity.org, http://www.globalsecurity.org/military/library/news/1999/12/991208-wh1.htm.

–. 2004. *My Life*. New York: Alfred A. Knopf.

Clinton Foundation. 2008. http://www.clintonfoundation.org/what-we-do/.

Coffee, Jr., John C. 1995. "Class Wars: Dilemma of the Mass Tort Class Action." 95 *Columbia Law Review* 1343.

Cole, Marcus. 2002. "Corporate Bankruptcy in the New Millennium: Limiting Liability through Bankruptcy." Fifteenth Annual Corporate Law Symposium. 70 *University of Cincinnati Law Review* 1245.

Columbia Broadcasting System News. 2006. "Soda Fueling Obesity Epidemic." Early Show. 6 June, http://www.cbsnews.com/stories/2004/09/21/earlyshow/contributors/emilysenay/main644824.shtml.

Compassionate Spirit. 2008. "McDonald's Lawsuit, http://www.compassionatespirit.com/McDonalds-Lawsuit-article.htm.

Contrubis, John. 1997. *Attorneys' Fees in the State Tobacco Litigation Cases*. Congressional Research Service, http://www.law.umaryland.edu/marshall/crsreports/crsdocuments/97-883_A.pdf.

Cook, Philip J., and Jens Ludwig. 2002. "Litigation as Regulation: Firearms." In W. Kip Viscusi, ed., *Regulation through Litigation*, 67. Lanham, MD: AEI Press.

–, and Jen Ludwig. 2000. *Gun Violence: The Real Costs*. New York: Oxford University Press.

Cornerstone Research Group. 2008. "Securities Class Action Case Filings: 2007: A Year in Review." Stanford Law School Securities Class Action Clearinghouse, http://securities.stanford.edu/clearinghouse_research/2007_YIR/20080103-01.pdf.

Craig, Tim. 2007. "VA Tells NYC to Stop Gun Stings." *Washington Post*. 10 May.

Cramton, Roger C. 1995. "Individualized Justice, Mass Torts, and 'Settlement Class Actions': An Introduction." 95 *Columbia Law Review* 811.

Cranston, Ross. 1997. *Making Commercial Law: Essays in Honour of Roy Goode*. Oxford: Clarendon Press.

CSR Limited. 2001. *Annual Report to Securities and Exchange Commission*, 31 March, http://www.csr.com.au/investorcentre/files/report20050331/csr_ar05_financials.pdf.

Curriden, Mark. 1995. "Tobacco Companies Are under Siege." *Chattanooga Times*. 12 April.

Davies, Paul. 2006. "Plaintiffs' Lawsuits against Companies Sharply Decline Court Rulings, Legislators Curb Asbestos, Silicosis Claims; Indicted Firm Cuts Filings; Questioning 'Jackpot Justice.'" *Wall Street Journal*. 26 August.

Dean, Doug, and Mike Feeley. 2000. "One-Step Program Works." *Denver Post*. 3 April.

Deer, Brian. 2005. "Vioxx Death Toll May Hit 2,000 in UK." *Times Online*. 21 August, http://www.timesonline.co.uk/tol/news/uk/article557471.ece.

Delacourt, Susan, and Les Whittington. 2005. "Ottawa May Sue U.S. Gun Makers." *Toronto Star*. 22 October.

Delaney, Kevin J. 1992. *Strategic Bankruptcy: How Corporations and Creditors Use Chapter 11 to Their Advantage*. Berkeley, CA: University of California Press.

Deligiannis, Amalia. 2004. "Congress Attempts the Impossible: An Asbestos Bill." *Corporate Legal Times*. 24 May.

Derthick, Martha. 2002. *Up in Smoke*. Washington, DC: CQ Press.

Dezalay, Yves, and Bryant G. Garth. 2001. "Constructing Law Out of Power: Investing in Human Rights as an Alternative Political Strategy." In Austin Sarat and Stuart Scheingold, eds., *Cause Lawyering and the State in a Global Era*, 354. New York: Oxford University Press.

Dickson, Brice, ed. 2007. *Judicial Activism in Common Law Supreme Courts*. Oxford: Oxford University Press.

Dingel, Dorthe Dahlgaard. 1999. *Public Procurement: A Harmonization of the National Judicial Review of the Application of European Community Law*. London: Kluwer Law International.

Discovery Communications. 2007. "Discovery Kids Makes Healthy Food Pledge." Press Release. 13 August, http://corporate.discovery.com/discovery-news/discovery-kids-makes-healthy-food-pledge/.

Division of Cancer Epidemiology and Genetics. 2004. "Cancer Mortality Maps and Graphs: Maps for Cancer of the Lung, Trachea, Bronchus, and Pleura." National Cancer Institute, http://www.dceg2.cancer.gov/cgi-bin/atlas/avail-maps?site=lun.

Dobner, Jennifer. 2007. "Polygamist Leader Sentenced to Prison." *Associated Press*, 21 November, http://abcnews.go.com/us/wireStory?id=3894251.

Easton, David. 1965. *A Systems Analysis of Political Life*. New York: Wiley.

Ecomall. 2008. "Ten Years of Genetically Modified Crops Failed to Deliver," http://ecomall.com/greenshopping/foegmo.htm.

Edsall, Thomas B., and James V. Grimaldi. 2004. "New Routes for Money to Sway Voters." *Washington Post*. 27 September.

Eggen, Jean Macchiaroli, and John G. Culhane. 2002. "Gun Torts: Defining a Cause of Action for Victims in Suits against Gun Manufacturers." 81 *North Carolina Law Review* 115.

Eilperin, Juliet. 2003. "Daschle Joins Move to Shoot Down Some Liability of Gun Merchants." *Washington Post*, 20 October.

Elliott, Stuart. 2007. "A New Camel Brand Is Dressed to the Nines." *AOL Money and Finance*. 15 February, http://money.aol.com/news/articles/_a/a-new-camel-brand-is-dressed-to-the/20070215105409990001.

Environmental Working Group. 2005. "Farm Subsidy Database," http://www.ewg.org/farm/progdetail.php?fips=00000andprogcode=tobacco.

Epp, Charles R. 1998. *The Rights Revolution: Lawyers, Activists and Supreme Courts in Comparative Perspective*. Chicago: University of Chicago Press.

Epstein, Lee. 1991. "Courts and Interest Groups." In John B. Gates and Charles A. Johnson, eds., *The American Courts: A Critical Assessment*. Washington, DC: CQ Press.

Epstein, Edward. 2004. "Gun-Liability Bill Dies in Senate." *San Francisco Chronicle*. 3 March.

Erbacher, Sharon, and Mirko Bagaric. 2006. "Obesity and the Right to Sue: Would You Like Fries with That?" 80 *Law Institute Journal* 62.

Erichson, Howard M. 2000a. "Coattail Class Actions: Reflections on Microsoft, Tobacco, and the Mixing of Public and Private Lawyering in Mass Litigation." 34 *University of California Davis Law Review* 1.

–. 2000b. "Informal Aggregation: Procedural and Ethical Implications of Coordination among Counsel in Related Lawsuits." 50 *Duke Law Journal* 381.

–. 2005. "Private Lawyers, Public Lawsuits: Plaintiffs' Attorneys in Municipal Gun Litigation." In Timothy D. Lytton, ed., *Suing the Gun Industry: A Battle at the Crossroads of Gun Control and Mass Torts*, 129. Ann Arbor: University of Michigan Press.

European Commission. 2003. EC Regulation no. 1829/2003 on Genetically Modified Food and Feed, http://europa.eu.int/eur-lex/pri/en/oj/dat/2003/l_268/l_26820031018en00010023.pdf.

–. 2005. "Social Values, Science, and Technology." Special Eurobarometer, http://europa.eu.int/comm/public_opinion/archives/ebs/ebs_225_report_en.pdf.

European Economic Commission. 2008. "Economic Impacts of Genetically Modified Crops on the Agri-Food Sector: Glossary," http://ec.europa.eu/agriculture/publi/gmo/fullrep/gloss.htm.

Everingham, Roland, and Stephen Woodward. 1991. *Tobacco Litigation, the Case against Passive Smoking: AFCO v. TIA, An Historic Australian Judgement*. Sydney, Australia: Legal Books.

Falkner, Gerda, Oliver Treib, Miriam Hartlapp, and Simone Leiber. 2005. *Complying with Europe: EU Harmonization and Soft Law in the Member States*. New York: Cambridge University Press.

Fauber, John, and Mark Johnson. 2004. "Downsizing Supersizing: Will Chain's Move Change Our Eating – Again?" *Milwaukee Journal Sentinel*. 4 March.

Fennell, Thomas E., Jones Day, Carol A. Hogan, and Charles H. Moellenberg, Jr. 2006. "Product Liability Update: Attacks on Food Industry Escalate." *Metropolitan Corporate Counsel*, Northeast Edition. April.

Ferguson, Andrew. 2002. "Tobacco Lesson for McDonald's in Fat War." Bloomberg.com. 10 September, http://banzhaf.net/docs/bloomb.html.

Fewster, Sean, and Anderson, Laura. 2003. *The Law as It Could Be*. New York: New York University Press.

Fiss, Owen M. 1996. "The Political Theory of the Class Action." 53 *Washington and Lee Law Review* 21.

Flemming, John G. 1994. "Mass Torts." 42 *American Journal of Comparative Law* 507.

Food and Drug Administration. 1999. "Milestones in U.S. Food and Drug Law History." FDA Backgrounder, http://www.fda.gov/opacom/backgrounders/miles.html.

–. 2000. *Enforcement Report for November 2000: Recalls and Field Corrections: Foods – Class 2*, http://www.fda.gov/bbs/topics/ENFORCE/ENF00666.html.

–. 2004. "Revealing *Trans* Fat." Pub no. FDA04-1329C, http://www.fda.gov/FDAC/features/2003/503_fats.html.

–. 2007. "FDA Finalizes Report on 2006 Spinach Outbreak." FDA News. 23 March, http://www.fda.gov/bbs/topics/NEWS/2007/NEW01593.html.

–. 2008. "Salmonellosis Outbreak in Certain Types of Tomatoes." 8 July, http://www.fda.gov/oc/opacom/hottopics/tomatoes.html#outbreak.

Food and Drug Administration, Center for Veterinary Medicine. 2008. "Questions and Answers about Transgenic Fish," http://www.fda.gov/cvm/transgen.htm.

Food and Drug Administration, and Department of Agriculture. 2000. "United States Food Safety System," http://www.foodsafety.gov/~fsg/fssyst2.html.

Food Standards Agency. 2007. "Board Recommends Voluntary Approach for Trans Fats." UK Food Standards Agency, 13 December, http://www.food.gov.uk/news/newsarchive/2007/dec/trans.

"French GM Corn Battle." 2004. *The Mercury.* 27 September 2004, chapter 5.

Friedman, Lawrence M. 1973. *A History of American Law.* New York: Touchstone.

–. 1987. *Total Justice.* Boston: Beacon Press.

Friendly, Henry J. 1973. *Federal Jurisdiction: A General View.* New York: Columbia University Press.

Friends of the Earth International. 2006. "Ten Years of Genetically Modified Crops Failed to Deliver the Promises Made By Biotech Giants." Press Release, http://www.foe.org/new/releases/January2006/gmcrops011006.html.

Fuller, Lon. 1978. "The Forms and Limits of Adjudication." 92 *Harvard Law Review* 364.

Galanter, Marc. 1966. "The Modernization of Law." In Myron Weiner, ed., *Modernization,* 153. New York: Basic Books.

–. 1974. "Why the 'Haves' Come Out Ahead: Speculations on the Limits of Legal Change." 9 *Law and Society Review* 950.

–. 1992. "Law Abounding." 55 *Modern Law Review* 1.

–. 1999. "Big Tobacco: Winning by Losing." *American Lawyer* 55.

–. 2004. "The Vanishing Trial: An Examination of Trials and Related Matters in Federal and State Courts." 1 *Journal of Empirical Legal Studies* 459.

Garofoli, Joe. 2005. "$7 Million for Suit on Trans Fats." *San Francisco Chronicle.* 12 February.

Garth, Bryant G. 1982. "Conflict and Dissent in Class Actions: A Suggested Perspective." 77 *Northwestern University Law Review* 492.

–, Ilene H. Nagel, and S. Jay Plager. 1988. "The Institution of the Private Attorney General: Perspectives from an Empirical Study of Class Action Litigation." 61 *Southern California Law Review* 353.

Gawler, Virginia. 2005. "Class Action Expert Joins Sydney Law School" *University of Sydney News.* 12 July, http://www.usyd.edu.au/news/84.html?newsstoryid=601.

Gee, David, and Morris Greenberg. 2001. "Asbestos: From 'Magic' to Malevolent Mineral." European Union, European Environmental Agency, http://reports.eea.eu.int/environmental_issue_report_2001_22/en/issue-22-part-05.pdf.

Gibson, Elizabeth S. 2000. "Case Studies of Mass Tort Limited Fund Class Action Settlements and Bankruptcy Reorganizations." Federal Judicial Center, http://www.fjc.gov.

Gidi, Antonio. 2003. "Class Actions in Brazil – A Model for Civil Law Countries." 51 *American Journal of Comparative Law* 311.

Ginsberg, B., Theodore J. Lowi, and Margaret Weir. 2005. *We the People: An Introduction to American Politics,* 5th edition. New York: W.W. Norton.

Glaberson, William H. 2004. "U.S. Court Considers a Once-and-for-All Tobacco Lawsuit." *New York Times.* 14 September.

Gladwell, Malcolm. 1989. "American Home's 'Steal' of a Deal for A.H. Robins." *Washington Post.* 15 December.

Gleason, Phil, and Carol Suitor. 2001. *Children's Diets in the Mid-1990s: Dietary Intake and Its Relationship with School Meal Participation.* Alexandria, VA: US Department of Agriculture, Food and Nutrition Service, Office of Analysis, Nutrition and Evaluation.

Goldsworthy, Jeffrey. 2006. "Australia: Devoted to Legalism." In Jeffrey Goldsworthy, ed., *Interpreting Constitutions: A Comparative Study,* 106. Oxford: Oxford University Press.

Goodstein, Laura. 2001. "Beef Flavor in Fries Prompts Hindus to Sue McDonald's." *New York Times.* 20 May.

Goodwyn, Wade. 2006. "Silicosis Ruling Could Revamp Legal Landscape." *National Public Radio.* 6 March.

Gotanda, John Y. 2004. "Punitive Damages: A Comparative Analysis." 42 *Columbia Journal of Transnational Law* 391.

–. 2007. "Charting Developments Concerning Punitive Damages: Is the Tide Changing?" 45 *Columbia Journal of Transnational Law* 507.

Gottlieb, Henry. 2007. "U.K. Vioxx Users Denied Recourse to New Jersey's Plaintiff-Friendly Forum." Law.com. 1 August, http://www.law.com/jsp/article.jsp?id=1185883306082.

Grady, Denise, and Gardiner Harris. 2004. "Overprescribing Prompted Warning on Antidepressants." *New York Times.* March.

Grant, Susannah. 2002. *Erin Brockovich.* Hollywood, CA: Universal/MCA.

Green, Michael D. 1996. *Bendectin and Birth Defects*. Philadelphia, PA: University of Pennsylvania Press.

Grundfest, Joseph A., and Michael A. Perino. 1997. "Ten Things We Know and Ten Things We Don't Know about the Private Securities Litigation Reform Act of 1995." Joint Written Testimony of the Subcommittee on Securities of the Committee on Banking, Housing, and Urban Affairs, United States Senate. 24 July.

Gumbel, Andrew. 2002. "The Man Who Is Taking Fat to Court." *Sydney Herald*. 14 July.

Guthrie, Joanne F., and Joan F. Morton. 2000. "Food Sources of Added Sweeteners in the Diets of Americans." 100 *Journal of the American Dietary Association* 43.

Haddad, Charles. 2000. "Why Big Tobacco Can't Be Killed." *Business Week*. 24 April, http://www.businessweek.com/archives/2000/b3678128.arc.htm.

Haggman, Matthew. 2003. "Decertification of Florida Smokers Raises Questions." *Legal Intelligencer*. 20 June.

Hall, Ben, and Michael Peel. 2006. "Law Change to Speed up Asbestos Cases Compensation Claims." *Financial Times*. 21 June.

Haltom, William, and Michael McCann. 2004a. *Distorting the Law: Politics, Media, and the Litigation Crisis*. Chicago: University of Chicago Press.

–. 2004b. "Framing the Food Fights: How Mass Media Construct and Constrict Public Interest Litigation." Prepared for delivery at the annual meetings of the Western Political Science Association, Portland, Oregon, 2004.

Hansen, Mark. 1996. "Crack in Tobacco Armor." 82 *American Bar Association Journal* 22.

Harlow, Carol. 2005. "Law and Public Administration: Convergence and Symbiosis." 71 *International Review of Administrative Sciences* 279.

–, and Richard Rawlings. 1992. *Pressure through Law*. London: Routledge.

Harper, Prime Minister Stephen. 2008. "PM Offers Full Apology on Behalf of Canadians for the Indian Residential Schools System." 11 June, http://www.pm.gc.ca/eng/media.asp?id=2146.

Harr, Jonathan. 1996. *A Civil Action*. New York: Vintage Books.

Harris, Charles J. 2001. "State Tobacco Settlement: A Windfall of Problems." Note. 17 *Journal of Law and Politics* 167.

Harris, John F. 2005. "Victory for Bush on Suits: New Law to Limit Class-Action Cases." *Washington Post*. 18 February.

Harvard School of Public Health. 2005. "Internal Documents Show Cigarette Manufacturers Developed Candy-Flavored Brands Specifically to Target Youth Market Despite Promises." 10 November, http://www.hsph.harvard.edu/news/press-releases/2005-releases/press11102005.html.

Hays, Tom. 2006. "Judge Allows Class Action Tobacco Suit." *Washington Post*. 25 September.

Hazard, Geoffrey C., Jr. 1961. "Indispensable Party: The Historical Origin of a Procedural Phantom." 61 *Columbia Law Review* 1254.

–, John L. Gedid, and Stephen Sowle. 1998. "An Historical Analysis of the Binding Effect of Class Suits." 146 *University of Pennsylvania Law Review* 1849.

Heaps, John, and Simon Jackson. 2007. "US-Style Litigation and the Spread of the Class Action." 1 *Law and Financial Markets Review* 135.

Heinz, John P., and Edward O. Laumann. 1994. *Chicago Lawyers: The Social Structure of the Bar*, revised edition. Evanston, IL: Northwestern University Press.

–, Edward O. Laumann, Ethan Michelson, and Robert L. Nelson. 1998. "The Changing Character of Lawyers' Work: Chicago in 1975 and 1995." 32 *Law and Society Review* 751.

Heller, Keith E., Brian A. Burt, and Stephen A. Eklund. 2001. "Sugared Soda Consumption and Dental Caries in the United States." 80 *Journal of Dental Research* 1949.

Henderson, Nell. 2006. "Tobacco Ruling Seen as a Win for Shareholders." *Washington Post*. 19 August.

Hensler, Deborah R. 2001. "Revisiting the Monster: New Myths and Realities of Class Action and Other Large-Scale Litigation." 11 *Duke Journal of Comparative and International Law* 179.

Hensler, Deborah R., Nicholas M. Pace, Bonnie Dombey-Moore, Elizabeth Giddens, Jennifer Gross, and Erik Moller. 2000. *Class Action Dilemmas: Pursuing Public Goals for*

Private Gain. Santa Monica, CA: RAND Institute for Civil Justice, http://www.rand.
 org/publications/MR/MR969/.
Herman, Eric. 2006. "Restaurant Sues over Lost Spinach." *Chicago Sun Times*. 19 September.
Herzog, Boaz. 2003. "McDonald's Franchise Owners Adjust to Leaner Times." *The Oregonian*.
 1 May.
Hirsch, Jerry. 2006. "Health Risks Spur Suit against KFC over Trans Fats." *Los Angeles Times*.
 14 June.
Hirschl, Ran. 2004. *Towards Juristocracy: The Origins and Consequences of the New Constitu-
 tionalism*. Cambridge: Harvard University Press.
Hodges, Christopher. 2001. *Multi-Party Actions*. Oxford: Oxford University Press.
Holland, Debra, and Helen Pope. 2003. *EU Food Law and Policy*. The Hague: Kluwer Law
 International.
Horovitz, Bruce. 2003. "Under Fire, Food Giants Switch to Healthier Fare." *USA Today*. 1
 July.
Howe, Paul, and Peter H. Russell, eds. 2001. *Judicial Power and Canadian Democracy*. Montreal
 and Kingston: McGill-Queen's University Press.
Howells, Geraint. 1998. "Tobacco Litigation in the U.S.: Its Impact in the United Kingdom."
 22 *Southern Illinois University Law Journal* 693.
Human Genome Project. 2008. "Genetically Modified Foods and Organisms," http://www.
 ornl.gov/sci/techresources/Human_Genome/elsi/gmfood.shtml.
International Obesity Task Force. 2008. "The Global Epidemic," http://www.iotf.org/
 globalepidemic.asp.
Jackson, J. Russell. 2006. "Federal and State Courts Reject 'Attractive Advertising' Claims."
 Legal Backgrounder. 10 March.
Jackson, Robert H. 1941. *The Struggle for Judicial Supremacy*. New York: Alfred A. Knopf.
Jacobson, Douglas N. 1989. "After *Cipollone v. Liggett Group, Inc.*: How Wide Will the Flood-
 gates of Cigarette Litigation Open?" Note. 38 *American University Law Review* 1021.
Jacobson, Richard, and Jeffery R. White. 2004. *David v. Goliath: American Trial Lawyers of
 America and the Fight for Everyday Justice*. Washington, DC: Association of Trial Lawyers of
 America.
Jensen, Bryce A. 2001. "From Tobacco to Health Care and Beyond – A Critique of Lawsuits
 Targeting Unpopular Industries." 86 *Cornell Law Review* 1334.
"John Coale's Next Case." 1999. *The Economist*. 27 February.
Johnson, David C. 2004. "The Attack on Trial Lawyers and Tort Law." Commonweal
 Institute Report. 1 October, http://www.commonwealinstitute.org/category/tags/
 the-attack-on-trial-lawyers-and-tort-law.
Judicial Panel on Multi-District Litigation. 2005. "Statistical Analysis of Multidistrict Litiga-
 tion, Cumulative from September 1968 through 30 September 2005," http://www.jpml.
 uscourts.gov/General_Info/Statistics/Statistical-Analysis-2005.pdf.
–. 2008. "Docket Information," http://www.jpml.uscourts.gov/Resources/resources.html.
Kagan, Robert A. 1996. "American Lawyers, Legal Culture, and Adversarial Legalism." In
 Lawrence M. Friedman and Harry N. Scheiber, eds., *Legal Culture and the Legal Profession*,
 7. Boulder, CO: Westview Press.
–. 2001. *Adversarial Legalism: The American Way of Law*. Cambridge, MA: Harvard University
 Press.
–, and Lee Axelrad, eds. 2000. *Regulatory Encounters: Multinational Corporations and American
 Adversarial Legalism*. Berkeley, CA: University of California Press.
Kairys, David. 1998. "Taking Aim at the Gun Makers: An Interview with David Kairys." *All
 Business*. 1 June, http://www.allbusiness.com/legal/law-firms-attorneys/695775-1.html.
Kaiser Family Foundation. 2005. "United States: Allocation of Annual Appropriation of
 Tobacco Settlement Funds, SFY2004," http://statehealthfacts.org/cgi-bin/healthfacts.cgi?
 action=profileandcategory=Health+Costs+ percent26+Budgetsandsubcategory=
 Tobacco+Settlement+Fundsandtopic=Allocation+of+Annual+Appropriationandlink_
 category=andlink_subcategory=andlink_topic=andwelcome=0andarea=United+States.
Kalven, Harry, Jr., and Maurice Rosenfield. 1941. "The Contemporary Function of the Class
 Suit." 8 *University of Chicago Law Review* 684.

Kamp, Allen R. 1987. "The History behind *Hansberry v. Lee.*" 20 *University of California Davis Law Review* 481.

Kasperowicz, Pete. 2007. "Cigar Tax Proposal Threatens US Retailers, Latin American Countries." Forbes.com. 30 July, http://www.forbes.com/home/feeds/afx/2007/07/30/afx3966264.html.

Kaufman, Marc. 1999. "Health Advocates Sound Alarm as Schools Strike Deals with Coke and Pepsi." *Washington Post.* 23 March.

–. 2001. "Engineered Corn Turns Up in Seed." *Washington Post.* 1 March.

Kazanjian, John A. 1973. "Class Actions in Canada." 11 *Osgoode Hall Law Journal* 397.

Keeling, David T. 2004. *Intellectual Property Rights in EU Law: Free Movement and Competition Law.* Oxford: Oxford University Press.

Keeton, W. Page, and William Lloyd Prosser, eds. 1984. *Prosser and Keeton on Torts,* 5th edition. Eagan, MN: West Group.

Kelder, Graham, and Patricia Davidson. 1999. "The Multistate Master Settlement Agreement and the Future of State and Local Tobacco Control: An Analysis of Selected Topics and Provisions of the Multi-State Master Settlement Agreement of November 23, 1998." Tobacco Control Resource Center, Northeastern University School of Law. 24 March, http://www.tobacco.neu.edu/tobacco_control/resources/msa/.

Kelemen, R. Daniel. 2006. "Suing for Europe: Adversarial Legalism and European Governance." 39 *Comparative Political Studies* 101.

–, and Eric Sibbitt. 2004. "The Globalization of American Law." 58 *International Organization* 103.

Kennedy, David. 2004. *The Dark Sides of Virtue: Reassessing International Humanitarianism.* Princeton: Princeton University Press.

Kibble, Emma. 2000. "Nippy's Clears Way for Damages." *The Advertiser.* 2 May.

Klarman, Michael J. 2004. *From Jim Crow to Civil Rights: The Supreme Court and the Struggle for Racial Equality.* New York: Oxford University Press.

Klein, Chris. 1997. "Poll: Lawyers Not Liked." *National Law Journal.* 25 August.

Kluger, Richard. 1976. *Simple Justice: The History of Brown V. Board of Education and Black America's Struggle for Equality.* New York: Alfred A. Knopf.

Koch, Harald. 2001. "Non-Class Group Litigation under EU and German Law." 11 *Duke Journal of Comparative and International Law* 355.

Koch, Wendy. 2007. "As Cigarette Sales Dip, New Products Raise Concerns." *USA Today.* 7 August.

Kolata, Gina. 2000. "Controversial Drug Makes a Comeback." *New York Times.* 26 September.

Kondro, Wayne. 2004. "Lawsuits Mount in Wake of Rofecoxib (Vioxx) Withdrawal." 171 *Canadian Medical Association Journal* 1335.

Kritzer, Herbert M. 2002. "Seven Dogged Myths Concerning Contingency Fees." 80 *Washington University Law Quarterly* 739.

–, and Susan Silbey, eds. 2003. *In Litigation Do The "Haves" Still Come Out Ahead?* Stanford, CA: Stanford University Press.

La Forest, Gérard. 1988. "The Use of International and Foreign Material in the Supreme Court of Canada." 17 *Canadian Council on International Law Proceedings* 230.

LaFrance, Arthur B. 2000. "Tobacco Litigation: Smoke, Mirrors and Public Policy." 26 *American Journal of Law and Medicine* 187.

Laidlaw, Stuart. 2001. "Starlink Fallout Could Cost Billions Future of Modified Crops Thrown in Doubt, Report Says." *Toronto Star.* 9 January, http://www.mindfully.org/GE/StarLink-Fallout-Cost-Billions.htm.

Landay, Jerry. 2000. "The Federalist Society: The Conservative Cabal That Is Transforming American Law." *Washington Monthly.* March, http://www.washingtonmonthly.com/features/2000/0003.landay.html.

Landes, William M., Lawrence Lessig, and Michael E. Solimine. 1998. "Judicial Influence: A Citation Analysis of Federal Courts of Appeal Judges." 27 *Journal of Legal Studies* 271.

Lasswell, H.D. 1950. *Politics: Who Gets What, When and How.* New York: Peter Smith.

Lauter, David. 1984. "Bendectin Pact Creating Furor; Revolt in the Plaintiffs' Bar." *National Law Journal*. 30 July.

Law.com Dictionary. 2003. http://dictionary.law.com/.

Law Reform Commission of Ireland. 2003. *Consultation Paper on Multi-Party Litigation*. LRC CP 25-2003, http://www.lawreform.ie/files/Consultation%20Paper%20Multi%20Party%20Litigation%20_Class%20Actions_.pdf.

The Lawyer.com. 2005. "UK Firms Line Up for Vioxx Litigation." 23 August, http://www.thelawyer.com/cgi-bin/item.cgi?id=116508andd=11andh=24andf=23.

Le Sueur, Andrew, ed. 2004. *Building the UK's New Supreme Court: National and Comparative Perspectives*. New York: Oxford University Press.

Leach, Richard. H. 1963. "The Uniform Law Movement in Australia." 12 *American Journal of Comparative Law* 206.

Lee, Trymaine. 2007. "Metro Briefing." *New York Times*. 17 August.

Legrand, Pierre. 1996. "European Legal Systems Are Not Converging." 45 *International and Comparative Law Quarterly* 52.

Leonnig, Carol D. 2005. "Expert Says He Was Told to Soften Tobacco Testimony." *Washington Post*. 20 June.

Levi, Edward Hirsh, and James W. Moore. 1937. "Bankruptcy and Reorganization: A Survey of Changes." 5 *University of Chicago Law Review* 1.

Levin, Myron. 2003. "Judge Slashes Philip Morris' Appeal Bond." *Los Angeles Times*. 15 April.

–. 2005. "U.S. Can't Go after Tobacco's Past Profits." *Los Angeles Times*. 5 February.

Lichtblau, Eric. 2008. "In Justice Shift, Corporate Deals Replace Trials." *New York Times*. 9 April.

Lieberman, Jethro K. 1981. *The Litigious Society*. New York: Basic Books.

Liebman, Benjamin L. 1998. "Class Action Litigation in China." 111 *Harvard Law Review* 1523.

Lillien, Lisa. 2007. "Hungry Girl: How Convenient!" *New York Daily News: Food and Dining*. 23 August, http://www.nydailynews.com/lifestyle/food/2007/08/23/2007-08-23_hungry_girl_how_convenient.html.

Lindblom, Per Henrik. 1996. "Group Actions and the Role of the Courts: A European Perspective." 23 *Forum Internationale* 1.

–. 1997. "Individual Litigation and Mass Justice: A Swedish Perspective and Proposal on Group Actions in Civil Procedure." 45 *American Journal of Comparative Law* 805.

Liptak, Adam. 2002. "Judges Seek to Ban Secret Settlements in South Carolina." *New York Times*. 2 September.

Lowery, David, and Virginia Gray. 1998. "The Dominance of Institutions in Interest Representation." 42 *American Journal of Political Science* 231.

Ludwig, David S., Karen E. Peterson, and Steven L. Gortmaker. 2001. "Relation between Consumption of Sugar-Sweetened Drinks and Childhood Obesity: A Prospective Observational Analysis." 357 *Lancet* 505.

Luke, Susan. 2003. Philip Morris' Bond Halved." *Associated Press*. 15 April, http://agpolicy.ky.gov/Documents/article_030415_philipmorris2_CJ.pdf.

Lyons, Jeffery. 1998. "Open Forum: Coordinated Food Systems and Accountability Mechanisms for Food Safety: A Law and Economics Approach." 53 *Food and Drug Law Journal* 729.

Lytle, Leslie A., Sara Seifert, Jessica Greenstein, and Paul McGovern. 2000. "How Do Children's Eating Patterns and Food Choices Change over Time? Results from a Cohort Study." 14 *American Journal of Health Promotion* 222.

Lytton, Timothy D. 2000. "Lawsuits against the Gun Industry: A Comparative Institutional Analysis." 32 *Connecticut Law Review* 1247.

MacIntyre, J.M. 1966. "The Use of American Cases in Canadian Courts." 2 *University of British Columbia Law Review* 478.

Maclachlan, Claudia. 1995. "Fifth Circuit Next for Tobacco Suit." *National Law Journal*. 6 March.

–, and Andrew Blum. 1996. "Tobacco Foes Dealt Blow." *National Law Journal.* 3 June [on file with author].

MacMaoláin, Caoimhín. 2007. *EU Food Law: Protecting Consumers and Health in a Common Market.* Portland, OR: Hart.

Magnusson, Roger, ed. 2008. "Obesity: Should There Be a Law against it? Introduction to a Symposium." 5 *Australia and New Zealand Health Policy Journal* 9.

Manfredi, Christopher. 1990. "The Use of United States Decisions by the Supreme Court of Canada under the Charter of Rights and Freedoms." 23 *Canadian Journal of Political Science* 499.

–. 2001. *Judicial Power and the Charter: Canada and the Paradox of Liberal Constitutionalism.* New York: Oxford University Press.

Marcin, Raymond B. 1974. "Searching for the Origin of the Class Action." 23 *Catholic University Law Review* 515.

Marco, Meg. 2007. "Introducing the 42 oz McDonald's 'Hugo' Drink." *The Consumerist,* http://consumerist.com/consumer/410-calories-without-taking-a-bite/introducing-the-42-oz-mcdonalds-hugo-drink-281188.php.

Martin, Andrew. 2007. "Kellogg Phases Out Some Food Ads to Children." *New York Times.* 14 June.

Martin, Robert Ivan. 2005. *The Most Dangerous Branch: How the Supreme Court Of Canada Has Undermined Our Law and Our Democracy.* Montreal and Kingstom: McGill-Queen's University Press.

"Mass Tort Litigation and Bankruptcy." 2003. Third Circuit Judicial Conference, 10 November, http://www.ca3.uscourts.gov/conf2003/3rdCircuit.manuscript.pdf.

Mauro, Tony. 2003. "Despite Personal Tragedy, Solicitor General Triumphs." *Texas Lawyer.* 8 July.

Mayer, Caroline. 2005. "Lawyers Ready Suit over Soda." *Washington Post.* 2 December.

McDermott, John T. 1973. "The Judicial Panel on Multidistrict Litigation." 57 *Federal Rules Decisions* 215.

McDonald's Corporation. 2007. Annual Report, http://www.mcdonalds.com/corp/invest/pub/2007_annual_report.html.

–. 2008a. Frequently Asked Questions about McDonald's USA Food and Nutrition, http://www.mcdonalds.com/usa/eat/nutrition_info/nutrition_faq/tfa.html.

–. 2008b. *Bag A Meal.* http://nutrition.mcdonalds.com/bagamcmeal/chooseCustomize.do.

"McDonald's USA Announces Significant Reduction of Trans Fatty Acids with Improved Cooking Oil." 3 September, Regulations.gov, http://www.regulations.gov/search/redirect.jsp?objectId=09000064804fefb9&disposition=attachment&contentType=pdf.

McGillivray, Douglas A., and Graham McLennan. 2002. "Shattering the Myth behind Western Canadian Shopping Centres Inc. v. Dutton." In J.J. Camp and Douglas A. McGillivray, eds., *Litigating Class Actions: The Roadmap for Bringing and Defending Class Actions in Western Canada,* 55. Toronto: Canadian Institute.

McGreevy, Patrick. 2008. "Schwarzenegger Signs Law Banning Trans Fats in Restaurants." *Los Angeles Times.* 26 July.

McHugh, Michael. 2006. "Compensation Boost for Asbestos Victims." *Belfast Telegraph.* 28 July.

McLeod-Kilmurray, Heather. 2007. "'Hoffman v. Monsanto': Courts, Class Actions, and Perceptions of the Problem of GM Drift." 27 *Bulletin of Science, Technology and Society* 188.

Melnick, Katie, 2008. "In Defense of the Class Action Lawsuit: An Examination of the Implicit Advantages and a Response to Common Criticisms." 22 *St. John's Journal of Legal Commentary* 755.

Merck Frosst. 2008. "Statement: Merck to Seek Appellate Review of Class Certification Decision in Vioxx Proceedings in Ontario." 28 July, http://www.merck.com/newsroom/vioxx/pdf/Ontario_Class_FINAL_29_July_2008.pdf.

Mesothelioma Legal Information Center. 2004. "Asbestos Bankruptcies – The New Wave," http://www.mesothelioma.net/AsbestosBankruptcies.html.

Mickle, Sharon J., Alvin B. Nowverl, and Katherine S. Tippett. 1998. *Eating Out in America: Impact on Food Choices and Nutrient Profiles*. Beltsville, MD: Food Surveys Research Group, US Department of Agriculture.

Miller, Arthur R. 1979. "Of Frankenstein Monsters and Shining Knights: Myth, Reality and the 'Class Action Problem.'" 92 *Harvard Law Review* 664.

Miller, Bill. 2000. "Judge Carves a Chunk Out of Tobacco Suit." *Washington Post*. 28 September, A1.

Mishra, Raja. 2002. "Boston Drops Lawsuit on Guns." *Boston Globe*. 28 March.

Misko, Fred, Jr., Frank E. Goodrich, and Alba Conte. 1996. "Managing Complex Litigation: Class Actions and Mass Torts." 48 *Baylor Law Review* 1001.

Monsanto. 2008. "Benefits of Our Products," http://www.monsanto.com/products/benefits.asp.

Moore, Mike. 1998. "Interview: Inside the Tobacco Deal." Frontline Online, http://www.pbs.org/wgbh/pages/frontline/shows/settlement/interviews/moore.html.

–. 2002. *Bowling for Columbine*. United Artists, Alliance Atlantis, and Dog Eat Dog Films.

–. 2003. "Tobacco: States' Use of Settlement Funds." Testimony before the US Senate Committee on Commerce, Science, and Transportation. 12 November.

Morabito, Vince. 2007. "Group Litigation in Australia – 'Desperately Seeking' Effective Class Action Regimes." National Report for Australia prepared for the Globalisation of Class Actions Conference, Oxford University, December.

Morain, Dan. 2004. "State May Let Casinos Pay to Grow." *Los Angeles Times*. 1 April.

Morton, F.L., and Rainer Knopff. 2000. *The Charter Revolution and the Court Party*. Peterborough, ON: Broadview Press.

MSN Broadcast Company. 2006. "Farmers Given Sharp Warning before Outbreak." 19 September, http://www.msnbc.msn.com/id/14841731/.

–. 2007. "U.S. Food Imports Rarely Inspected: FDA Lacks Resources to Assure Safety of Fish and Other Products, Experts Say." 16 April, http://www.msnbc.msn.com/id/18132087/.

Mueller, Erica. 2001. "A Structure That Does Not Function: An Examination of the History and Current Regulatory Status of Dietary Supplements and Their Label Claims." Legal Electronic Document Archive, http://leda.law.harvard.edu/leda/data/378/Mueller.pdf.

Mulheron, Rachael. 2004. *The Class Action in Common Law Legal Systems: A Comparative Perspective*. Oxford: Hart Publishing.

Mulholland, Rory. 2000. "The Roquefort Revolutionary." *The Independent*. 20 February.

Mullenix, Linda S. 2001. "Lessons from Abroad: Complexity and Convergence." 46 *Villanova Law Review* 1.

Muñoz, Kathryn A., Susan M. Krebs-Smith, Rachel Ballard-Barbash, and Linda E. Cleveland. 1997. "Food Intakes of US Children and Adolescents Compared with Recommendations." 100 *Pediatrics* 323.

Murphy, Bernard. 2005. "Current Trends and Issues in Australian Class Actions." Paper presented to the International Class Actions Conference, Melbourne, Australia, 1-2 December.

Mydans, Seth. 2003. "Researchers Raise Estimate on Defoliant Use in Vietnam War." *New York Times*, 16 April.

Nader, Ralph. 1965. *Unsafe at Any Speed*. New York: Grossman Publishers.

National Association of Attorneys General. 1998. "Tobacco Settlement Announcement." Press Release, http://www.naag.org/tobac/npr.htm.

National Center for State Courts. 2004. "State Caseload Highlights," http://www.ncsconline.org/D_Research/csp/Highlights/Highlights_Main_Page.html.

National Conference of State Legislatures. 2004. "Tobacco Prevention and the Master Settlement Act: An Update on Trends in the States," Spring Forum. 30 April, http://www.ncsl.org/programs/health/tobaccoslides.htm.

National Governors Association. 2005. "Tobacco Prevention and Control," http://www.nga.org/cda/files/TOBACCOPREVENTION.pdf.

National Institute of Environmental Health Sciences. 2002. National Institutes of Health. 18 November, http://www.niehs.nih.gov/oc/factsheets/dioxin.htm.

National Institute of Health. 2004. "Eating at Fast-Food Restaurants More Than Twice Per Week Is Associated with More Weight Gain and Insulin Resistance in Otherwise Healthy Young Adults." National Institute of Health News. 30 December, http://www.nhlbi.nih.gov/new/press/04-12-30.htm.

–. 2006. "Availability of Point-Of-Purchase Nutrition Information at a Fast-Food Restaurant." U.S. National Library of Medicine. Pubmed, http://www.ncbi.nlm.nih.gov/pubmed/16934863.

National Restaurant Association. 2008. "Policy Issue Briefs: Menu Labeling," http://www.restaurant.org/government/issues/issue.cfm?Issue=menulabel.

National Rifle Association. 2005a. "A Brief History of the NRA," http://www.nrahq.org/history.asp.

–. 2005b. "Reckless Lawsuit Preemption Bills Introduced." 16 February, http://www.newsbull.com/forum/topic.asp?TOPIC_ID=22026.

Nemitz, Bill. 1998. "Tobacco Deal Just Smoke and Mirrors." *Portland Press Herald*. 22 November.

Nestle, Marion. 2002. *Food Politics: How the Food Industry Influences Nutrition and Health*. Berkeley, CA: University of California Press.

"New Jersey Judge Rules That Health Plans Can Sue as a Class over Vioxx Spending." 2005. *New York Times*. Business Digest. 30 July.

New York City Department of Health and Mental Hygiene. 2007. "Board of Health Approves Regulation to Phase Out Artificial Trans Fat: FAQ," http://www.nyc.gov/html/doh/html/cardio/cardio-transfat-healthcode-faq.shtml#8.

New York City Law Department. 2008. "Federal Court Upholds New York City Health Code Provision Requiring Certain Restaurants To Post Calorie Information on Menu and Menu Boards." Press Release of the Office of Corporation Counsel. 16 April, http://www.nyc.gov/html/law/downloads/pdf/pr041608.pdf.

Nocera, Joe. 2006. "If It's Good for Philip Morris, Can It Also Be Good for Public Health?" *New York Times Sunday Magazine*. 18 June.

O'Beirne, Kate. 2001. "Cash Bar – How Trial Lawyers Bankroll the Democratic Party." *National Review*. 20 August.

O'Leary, Shannon. 2004. "Non-Profit Takes a Bite Out of Fast-Food Maker." *Corporate Legal Times*. October.

Oliver, Peter C. 2005. *The Constitution of Independence: The Development of Constitutional Theory in Australia, Canada and New Zealand*. Oxford: Oxford University Press.

O'Malley, Christopher J. 2008. "Breaking Asbestos Litigation's Chokehold on the American Judiciary." 2008 *University of Illinois Law Review* 1101.

Olson, Walter. 1999. "The Florida Tobacco Jurors: Anything but Typical." *Wall Street Journal*. 12 July, http://www.manhattan-institute.org/html/_wsj-fla_tobacco_jurors.htm.

Ontario Law Reform Commission. 1982. *Report on Class Actions*, 3 volumes. Toronto: Ministry of the Attorney General.

OpenSecrets.org. 2008a. "Data Available for National Restaurant Association," http://www.opensecrets.org/orgs/summary.php?id=D000000150.

–. 2008b. "Heavy Hitters: American Association for Justice," http://opensecrets.org/orgs/summary.php?id=D000000065.

Opeskin, Brian. 2001. "Australian Constitutional Law in a Global Era." Conference of the Australian Association of Constitutional Law – A Celebration of a Federation: The Australian Constitution in Retrospect and Prospect, Perth, 21-23 September, http://www.alrc.gov.au/events/speeches/BRO/20010921.pdf.

Page, Susan. 2001. "The Changing Politics of Guns – Democrats Back Off on Firearms." *USAToday*. 13 August.

Park, Michael Y. 2002. "Lawyers See Fat Payoffs in Junk Food Lawsuits." *Fox News*. 23 January, http://www.foxnews.com/story/0,2933,43735,00.html.

Parloff, Roger. 2003. "Is Fat the Next Tobacco? For Big Food, the Supersizing of America Is Becoming a Big Headache." *Fortune Magazine*. 3 February, http://money.cnn.com/magazines/fortune/fortune_archive/2003/02/03/336442/index.htm.

Pennington Biological Research Center. 2007. "Can a Virus Cause Obesity?" News Release. August, http://www.pbrc.edu/News/Featured_Stories/Story.asp?id=9.

Pfennigstorf, Werner. 1984. "The European Experience with Attorney Fee Shifting." 47 *Law and Contemporary Problems* 37.

Philip Morris USA. 2008. Smoking and Health Issues," http://www.philipmorrisusa.com/en/cms/Products/Cigarettes/Health_Issues/default.aspx?src=search.

Pierce, Jason L. 2006. *Inside the Mason Court Revolution: The High Court of Australia Transformed.* Durham, NC: Carolina Academic Press.

Plevin, Mark D., and Paul W. Kalish. 2002. "Where Are They Now? A History of the Companies That Have Sought Bankruptcy Protection Due to Asbestos Claims." 18 *Mealey's Litigation Report: Asbestos* 17.

Plevin, Mark D., Victor E. Schwartz, and Paul W. Kalish. 2001. "Don't Bankrupt Asbestos." *Legal Times.* 19 March.

Pollack, Andrew. 2003. "Study Raises Doubt about Allergy to Genetic Corn." *New York Times.* 10 November.

Poncibò, Cristina. 2005. "Regulation and Private Litigation: A Debate over the European Perspective." Working Paper, http://ssrn.com/abstract=1028527.

Powell, Michael. 2000. "Call to Arms" *Washington Post Sunday Magazine.* 6 August.

PR Newswire. 2001. "Bayer Acquires Aventis CropScience." 2 October, http://www.prnewswire.com/cgi-bin/stories.pl?ACCT=105&STORY=/www/story/10-02-2001/0001583226.

Prakash, Snigdha, and Vikki Valentine. 2008. "Timeline: The Rise and Fall of Vioxx." *National Public Radio.* 31 July, http://www.npr.org/templates/story/story.php?storyId=5470430.

Press Conference of the President. 2003. The White House. 15 December, http://www.whitehouse.gov/news/releases/2003/12/20031215-3.html.

Pringle, Peter. 1999. "The Chronicles of Tobacco: An Account of the Forces That Brought the Tobacco Industry to the Negotiating Table." 25 *William Mitchell Law Review* 387.

Public Broadcasting Service. 1999. "Breast Implants on Trial." Frontline, http://www.pbs.org/wgbh/pages/frontline/implants/cron.html.

Public Health Advocacy Institute. 2006. E-mail correspondence with Richard Daynard [on file with author].

Pye, John. 2006. "Florida Ruling Keeps Tobacco Industry Alive." *Financial Wire.* 7 July.

Ranii, David. 1984. "How the Plaintiffs' Bar Shares Its Information." *National Law Journal.* 23 July.

Rashke, Richard L. 2000. *The Killing of Karen Silkwood: The Story behind the Kerr-McGee Plutonium Case.* Ithaca, NY: Cornell University Press.

Ratzan, Scott C. 1997. *The Mad Cow Crisis: Health and the Public Good.* London: Routledge.

Raustiala, Kal. 2002. "The Architecture of International Cooperation: Transgovernmental Network and the Future of International Law." 43 *Virginia Journal of International Law* 1.

Reich, Robert. 1999. "Regulation Is Out, Litigation Is In." *USA Today.* 11 February.

Resnik, Judith, Dennish E. Curtis, and Deborah R. Hensler. 1996. "Individuals within the Aggregate: Relationships, Representation, and Fees." 71 *New York University Law Review* 296.

Rheingold, Paul. 1968. "The MER/29 Story: An Instance of Successful Mass Disaster Litigation." 56 *California Law Review* 116.

Rogers, Kristen Gartman. 1998. "'Mad Plaintiff Disease?' Tobacco Litigation and the British Debate over Adoption of U.S.-Style Tort Litigation Methods." 27 *Georgia Journal of International and Comparative Law* 199.

Rosen, Jeffrey. 2008. "Supreme Court, Inc." *New York Times Sunday Magazine.* 16 March.

Rosenbaum, Dávid E. 1998. "Cigarette Makers Quit Negotiations on Tobacco Bill." *New York Times.* 9 April.

Rosenberg, Gerald N. 1991. *The Hollow Hope: Can Courts Bring about Social Change?* Chicago: University of Chicago Press.

Russell, Peter H. 2005. *Recognizing Indigenous Title: The Mabo Case and Indigenous Resistance to English-Settler Colonialism.* Toronto: University of Toronto Press.

–, and David M. O'Brien, eds. 2001. *Judicial Independence in the Age of Democracy: Critical Perspectives from around the World*. Charlottesville: University Press of Virginia.

Rustad, Michael L., and Thomas H. Koenig. 2002. "Taming the Tort Monster: The American Civil Justice System as a Battleground of Social Theory." 68 *Brooklyn Law Review* 1.

Ryan, Antony L. 2000. "Principles of Forum Selection." 103 *West Virginia Law Review* 167.

Saad, Lydia. 2008. "U.S. Smoking Rate Still Coming Down." Gallup. 24 July. http://www.gallup.com/poll/109048/US-Smoking-Rate-Still-Coming-Down.aspx.

Salisbury, Robert. 1984. "Interest Representation: The Dominance of Institutions." 78 *American Political Science Review* 64.

Sanders, Joseph. 1992. "The Bendectin Litigation: A Case Study in the Life Cycle of Mass Torts." 43 *Hastings Law Journal* 301.

Sarat, Austin, and Stuart A. Scheingold, eds. 1998. *Cause Lawyering: Political Commitments and Professional Responsibilities*. New York: Oxford University Press.

–. 2001. *Cause Lawyering and the State in a Global Era*. New York: Oxford University Press.

–. 2005. *The Worlds Cause Lawyers Make: Structure and Agency in Legal Practice*. Stanford, CA: Stanford University Press.

–. 2006. *Cause Lawyering and Social Movements*. Stanford, CA: Stanford University Press.

Saul, Stephanie. 2008. "Bill to Regulate Tobacco Moves Forward." *New York Times*. 3 April.

Saumier, Genevieve. 2005. "USA-Canada Class Actions: Trading in Procedural Fairness." 5(2) *Global Jurist Advances* 1.

Saunders, Cheryl. 2006. "The Use and Misuse of Comparative Constitutional Law." 13 *Indiana Journal of Global Legal Studies* 37.

Sawer, Geoffrey. 1968. *Australian Federalism in the Courts*. Melbourne: Melbourne University Press.

Sayles, Marnie L., and James R. Lambden. 2001. "Stop Shooting Down Tort Liability: It Is Time to Resuscitate the Abnormally Dangerous Activity Doctrine against Handgun Manufacturers." 12 *Stanford Law and Policy Review* 143.

Schattschneider, E.E. 1960. *The Semisovereign People: A Realist's View of Democracy in America*. New York: Holt, Rinehart and Winston.

Scheingold, Stuart A. 2004. *The Politics of Rights: Lawyers, Public Policy, and Political Change*, 2nd edition. Ann Arbor: University of Michigan Press.

–, and Austin Sarat. 2004. *Something to Believe In: Politics, Professionalism, and Cause Lawyering*. Stanford, CA: Stanford University Press.

Schlosser, Eric. 2001. *Fast Food Nation: The Dark Side of the All-American Meal*. Boston: Houghton Mifflin.

Schlozman, Kay Lehman, and John T. Tierney. 1986. *Organized Interests and American Democracy*. New York: Harper and Row.

Schoenberg, Tom. 2002. "D.C. Judge Holds Fire: Still No Ruling in City's Novel Suit over Gun Violence." *Legal Times*. 20 May.

Schroth, Tracy. 1992. "Poking the Ashes of Tobacco Liability: Why Five Suits against the Industry Were Dropped in a Single Week." *New Jersey Law Journal*. 16 November.

Schuck, Peter H. 1986. *Agent Orange on Trial: Mass Toxic Disasters in the Courts*. New Haven, CT: Yale University Press.

–. 1995. "Mass Torts: An Institutional Evolutionist Perspective." 80 *Cornell Law Review* 941.

–. 2001. "Smoking Gun Lawsuits." *American Lawyer*. September.

Schulte, Constanze. 2004. *Compliance with Decisions of the International Court of Justice*. New York: Oxford University Press.

Schwartz, John. 1994. "Internal Papers Fuel Tobacco Debate." *Washington Post*. 14 May.

–. 2001. "Smoking Gun Lawsuits." *American Lawyer*. September.

Segal, David. 1999. "After Tobacco Success, Lawyers Pick Gun Fight; Same Tactics Aimed at Firearms Industry." *Washington Post*. 5 January.

Segarra, Alejandro E., and Jean M. Rawson. 2001. "StarLink Corn Controversy: Background." Congressional Research Service Report, Order Code RS20732, http://ncseonline.org/nle/crsreports/agriculture/ag-101.cfm.

Severson, Kim. 2003. "S.F. Lawyer Plans to Drop Oreo Suit." *San Francisco Chronicle.* 15 May.

–. 2006. "New York Gets Ready to Count Calories." *New York Times.* 13 December.

Shapiro, Martin. 1981. *Courts: A Comparative and Political Analysis.* Chicago: University of Chicago Press.

–. 1993. "The Globalization of Law." 1 *Indiana Journal of Global Legal Studies* 37.

Sherman, Edward F. 2002. "Group Litigation under Foreign Legal Systems: Variations and Alternatives to American Class Actions." 52 *DePaul Law Review* 401.

Siebel, Brian J. 1999. "City Lawsuits against the Gun Industry: A Roadmap for Reforming Gun Industry Misconduct." 18 *St. Louis University Public Law Review* 248.

Sinclair, Upton. 1906. *The Jungle.* New York: Grosset and Dunlap.

Sixty Minutes, Australia. 2002. "Transcript: Food Fight." 15 September, http://sixtyminutes. ninemsn.com.au/article.aspx?id=258966.

Skeel, David. 2001. *Debt's Dominion: A History of Bankruptcy Law in America.* Princeton, NJ: Princeton University.

Slaughter, Anne-Marie. 1994. "A Typology of Transjudicial Communication." 29 *University of Richmond Law Review* 99.

–. 2003. "A Global Community of Courts." 44 *Harvard International Law Journal* 191.

–. 2004. *A New World Order.* Princeton, NJ: Princeton University Press.

Smith, Jillian. 2004. "Settlements: What You Don't Know Can Kill You!" *Michigan State Law Review* 237.

Smith, Stephen E. 2002. "Counterblastes to Tobacco: Five Decades of North American Tobacco Litigation." 14 *Windsor Review of Legal and Social Issues* 1.

Smith and Wesson. 2005. Financial report filed with the US Securities and Exchange Commission, http://www.secinfo.com/dsVs6.z2az.c.htm.

Smyth, Julie Carr. 2006. "Smokers' Lawsuits over Light Cigarettes Cannot Carry Class Action Status, Court Rules." *Seattle Times.* 14 June.

Sobol, Richard B. 1991. *Bending the Law: The Story of the Dalkon Shield Bankruptcy.* Chicago: University of Chicago Press.

Songer, Donald R. 2009. *The Transformation of the Supreme Court of Canada: An Empirical Examination.* Toronto: University of Toronto Press [forthcoming].

Sparshott, Jeffrey. 2004. "European Union Allows Sale of Genetically Modified Corn." *Washington Times.* 20 May.

Spender, Peta. 2003. "Blue Asbestos and Golden Eggs: Evaluating Bankruptcy and Class Actions as Just Responses to Mass Tort Liability." 25 *Sydney Law Review* 223.

Spurlock, Morgan. 2004. *Super Size Me.* Morgan Spurlock, director. New York, NY: Hart Sharp Video.

Starky, Sheena. 2005. "The Obesity Epidemic in Canada." Paper prepared for the Parliamentary Information and Research Service, Library of Parliament. 15 July, http://www.parl. gc.ca/information/library/prbpubs/prb0511-e.htm.

Steele, Jonathan. 2001. "Blue Death." *The Guardian.* 15 September.

Stevens, Robert. 2001. "Judicial Independence in England: A Loss of Innocence." In Peter H. Russell and David M. O'Brien, eds., *Judicial Independence in the Age of Democracy: Critical Perspectives from around the World,* 155. Charlottesville: University Press of Virginia.

Stone Sweet, Alec. 2000. *Governing with Judges: Constitutional Politics in Europe.* Oxford: Oxford University Press.

Story, Joseph. 1836. *Commentaries on Equity Jurisprudence, as Administered in England and America.* 2 vols. Boston: Hilliard, Gray and Company.

–. 1838. *Commentaries on Equity Pleadings, and the Incidents Thereto, According to the Practice of the Courts of Equity of England and America.* Boston: Little Brown.

Stout, David. 1999. "Housing Agencies to Sue Gun Makers." *New York Times.* 8 December.

Stout, Stolberg D., and Sheryl Gay. 2004. "Bill to Limit Lawsuits Falls Victim to Politics." *New York Times.* 9 July.

Street, Thomas Atkins. 1909. *Federal Equity Practice: A Treatise on the Pleadings Used and Practice Followed in Courts of the United States in the Exercise of Their Equity Jurisdiction.* New York: Edward Thompson.

Sturm, Roland et al. 2004. *Obesity and Disability: The Shape of Things to Come.* RAND Corporation, http://www.rand.org/pubs/research_briefs/RB9043-1/.

Subar, Amy F., Susan M. Krebs-Smith, Annetta Cook, and Lisa L. Kahle. 1998. "Dietary Sources of Nutrients among US Children, 1989-1991." 102 *Pediatrics* 913.

Sugarman, Stephen D.. 2001. "Tobacco Litigation Update Prepared for the Robert Wood Johnson Foundation's Substance Abuse Policy Research Program Conference." 14 November, http://www.law.berkeley.edu/faculty/sugarmans.

"Support Down in Poll on Gun Restrictions." 2000. *New York Times*. 12 May.

Symposium. 2003. "Judge Jack B. Weinstein, Tort Litigation, and the Public Good: A Roundtable Discussion to Honor One of America's Great Trial Judges on the Occasion of His Eightieth Birthday." 12 *Journal of Law and Policy* 149.

Szaller, Jim. 1999. "One Lawyer's Twenty-Five Year Journey: The Dalkon Shield Saga." 9 *Ohio Trial* 4.

Szymanczyk, Mike. 2007. "Written Statement of Mike Szymanczyk, Chairman and Chief Executive Officer, Philip Morris USA." Submitted to the Senate Health, Education, Labor and Pensions Committee. 27 February, http://www.philipmorrisusa.com/en/our_initiatives/downloads/pdf/Health_Education_Labor_Pensions_Written_Testimony.pdf.

Tait, Nikki. 2003. "Cape Settles Asbestos Claims." *Financial Times* [London]. 28 June.

Taruffo, Michele. 2001. "Some Remarks on Group Litigation in Comparative Perspective." 11 *Duke Journal of International and Comparative Law* 405.

Tate, C. Neal, and Torbjorn Vallinder, eds. 1995. *The Global Expansion of Judicial Power*. New York: New York University Press.

Teubner, Gunther, ed. 1997. *Global Law without a State*. Aldershot, UK: Dartmouth Publishing Company.

"Tobacco Cases Master Settlement Agreement: A.D. Bedell Wholesale Co. v. Philip Morris Inc." 1999. 7 *Antitrust Litigation Reporter* 2.

"Tobacco Company Wins Individual Case in Mississippi." 2000. 14 *Mealey's Litigation Report* 2.

Tobacco.org. 2000. "R.J. Reynolds Tobacco Company Pleased with Nunnally Verdict." 12 July, http://www.tobacco.org/news/46117.html.

de Tocqueville, Alexis. 1969. *Democracy in America,* edited by J.P. Maier, translated by George Lawrence. Garden City, NY: Anchor Books.

Tomatis, Lorenzo. 2004. "Asbestos and International Organizations." 112 *Environmental Health Perspectives* 6, National Institute of Environmental Health Sciences, http://ehp.niehs.nih.gov/docs/2004/112-6/correspondence.html.

Toner, Robin. 2000. "Mothers Rally to Assail Gun Violence." *New York Times*. 15 May.

Tong, Vinnee. 2007. "Eleven Food, Drink Firms Restrict Child Ads." *USAToday.com*. 18 July, http://www.usatoday.com/money/economy/2007-07-18-756954327_x.htm.

"Top Cases of 2003." 2004. *New York Law Journal*. 23 February.

Trans Fat Task Force. 2006. "Transforming the Food Supply." Health Canada, http://www.hc-sc.gc.ca/fn-an/nutrition/gras-trans-fats/tf-ge/tf-gt_rep-rap-eng.php.

"Trial Likely in Class Action." 1999. *The Advertiser*. 20 November.

Truman, David B. 1951. *The Governmental Process*. New York: Knopf.

Tucker, Jill. 2008. "Restaurants Sue over Nutrition Posting Law." *San Francisco Chronicle*. 8 July, http://www.sfgate.com/cgi-bin/article.cgi?f=/c/a/2008/07/08/BA5P11LAT9.DTL.

Tushnet, Mark V. 1987. *The NAACP's Legal Strategy against Segregated Education, 1925-1950*. Chapel Hill: University of North Carolina Press.

Tweedale, Geoffrey. 2000. *Magic Mineral to Killer Dust: Turner and Newall and the Asbestos Hazard*. Oxford: Oxford University Press.

Twomey, Anne. 2007. "Implied Limitations on Legislative Power in the United Kingdom." Legal Studies Research Paper no. 07/59. Social Science Research Network Electronic Library, http://ssrn.com/abstract=1007343.

Unah, Isaac. 1998. *The Courts of International Trade: Judicial Specialization, Expertise and Bureaucratic Policy-Making*. Ann Arbor, MI: University of Michigan Press.

Uniform Law Conference of Canada. 2005. *Report on the National Class and Related Interjurisdictional Issues: Background, Analysis, and Recommendations*. Vancouver, BC: Uniform Law Conference of Canada.

United Kingdom, Department of Health. 2008. "Obesity." 20 February, http://www.dh.gov.uk/en/Publichealth/Healthimprovement/Obesity/DH_078098.

United Press International. 2007. "Nickelodeon Cuts Character Junk Food Ties," 22 August, http://www.upi.com/Business_News/2007/08/22/Nickelodeon_cuts_character_junk-food_ties/UPI-12131187790729/.

United States, Department of Agriculture, Food Safety and Inspection Service. 2006. "The Federal Meat Inspection Act," http://www.fsis.usda.gov/Regulations_and_Policies/Federal_Meat_Inspection_Act/index.asp.

United States, Department of Health and Human Services. 1964. "Smoking and Health: Report of the Advisory Committee to the Surgeon General of the Public Health Service," http://profiles.nlm.nih.gov/NN/B/C/X/B/.

–. 2006. "Overweight and Obesity at a Glance," http://www.surgeongeneral.gov/topics/obesity/calltoaction/fact_glance.htm.

United States, Department of Health and Human Services, and US Department of Agriculture. 2005. *Dietary Guidelines for Americans*, http://www.health.gov/dietaryguidelines/.

United States, Department of Justice. 2004. "Whether the Second Amendment Secures an Individual Right." *Memorandum Opinion for the Attorney General*. 24 August, http://www.usdoj.gov/olc/secondamendment2.pdf.

–. 2005. *Litigation against Tobacco Companies*, http://www.usdoj.gov/civil/cases/tobacco2/.

United States, Department of Labor, Occupational Safety and Health Administration. 2008. "Safety and Health Topics: Silica, Crystalline," http://www.osha.gov/SLTC/silicacrystalline/index.html.

United States, Department of Treasury. 2000. "Clinton Administration and State and Local Governments Reach Breakthrough Gun Safety Agreement with Smith & Wesson," http://www.treasury.gov/press/releases/ls474.htm.

United States, Environmental Protection Agency. 1999. "EPA Asbestos Materials Bans: Clarification," http://www.epa.gov/asbestos/pubs/asbbans2.

United States, House of Representatives, Judiciary Committee. 2000. "Dissenting Views to H.R. 1283, the 'Asbestos Compensation Act of 2000,'" http://www.house.gov/judiciary_democrats/dissentinghr1283.htm.

Uren, Kate. 2001. "Some Nippy's Payouts May Top $100,000." *The Advertiser*. 23 March.

"US Judge Rules Tobacco Ad Ban Also Applies to Foreign Sales." 2007. *Financial Wire*. 19 March.

"U.S. Taco Bell Franchisees to Get $60 Million." 2001. *Business First*. 8 June, http://www.bizjournals.com/louisville/stories/2001/06/04/daily40.html.

Van Voris, Bob. 1999. "Lawyers Debate Who Won Gun Suit." *National Law Journal*, 1 March.

VandeHei, Jim, and John F. Harris. 2005. "Bush to Seek Limits on Lawsuits." *Washington Post*. 5 January.

Vaver, David, and Lionel Bently, eds. 2004. *Intellectual Property in the New Millennium: Essays in Honour of Willam R. Cornish*. New York: Cambridge University Press.

Violence Policy Center. 2000. *"Smith & Wesson 'Clarification' of Agreement between Government and Gunmaker Exposes 'Landmark' Settlement to Be a Sham."* 12 April, http://www.vpc.org/press/0004smit.htm.

Vioxx Lawyer Australia. 2005. Solicitoradvice.com, http://www.solicitoradvice.com/vioxx_lawyers.htm.

Viscusi, W. Kip, ed. 2002. *Regulation through Litigation*. Washington, DC: Brookings.

Vock, Daniel C. 2004. "Tobacco Case Takes on Star-Studded Life of Its Own." *Chicago Lawyer*. November.

Vose, Clement E. 1959. *Caucasians Only: The Supreme Court, The NAACP, and the Restrictive Covenant Cases*. Berkeley, CA: University of California Press.

Walker, Jack L., Jr. 1991. *Mobilizing Interest Groups in America*. Ann Arbor: University of Michigan Press.

Wardell, Jane. 2008. "Recession? Eat, Drink, Smoke, and Be Merry." *Associated Press State and Local Wire*. 12 August.

Warner, Melanie. 2005a. "McDonald's to Add Facts on Nutrition to Packaging." *New York Times*. 26 October.

–. 2005b. "The Food Industry Empire Strikes Back." *New York Times*. 7 July.

Waters, Meghan. 2006. "All US Spinach Banned as E. Coli Outbreak Grows." *Toronto Star*. 23 September.

Watson, Garry D. 2001. "Class Actions: The Canadian Experience." 11 *Duke Journal of Comparative and International Law* 269.

Weinstein, Jack B. 1994. "Ethical Dilemmas in Mass Tort Litigation." 88 *Northwestern University Law Review* 469.

–. 1995. *Individual Justice in Mass Tort Litigation: The Effect of Class Actions, Consolidations and Other Multiparty Devices*. Evanston, IL: Northwestern University Press.

Wheeler, Fiona, and John Williams. 2007. "'Restrained Activism' in the High Court of Australia." In Brice Dickson, ed., *Judicial Activism in Common Law Supreme Courts*, 19. Oxford: Oxford University Press.

White, Michelle J. 2004. "Asbestos and the Future of Mass Torts." 18 *Journal of Economic Perspectives* 183.

Wilcox, Clyde. 1998. "The Dynamics of Lobbying the Hill." In Paul S. Herrnson et al., eds. *The Interest Group Connection*, 89. New Jersey: Chatham House.

Will, George. 2004. "Liberals Who Lament Voter Apathy Should Be Careful What They Wish For." *Chicago Sun-Times*. 14 October.

Willett, Linda A. 2005. *U.S.-Style Class Actions in Europe: A Growing Threat?* Washington, DC: National Legal Center for the Public Interest.

Williams, John M. 2001. "Judicial Independence in Australia." In Peter H. Russell and David M. O'Brien, eds. *Judicial Independence in the Age of Democracy: Critical Perspectives from around the World*, 173. Charlottesville: University Press of Virginia.

Wilson, Catherine. 2000. "Tobacco Industry Told to Pay $145B." *Associated Press Online*. 14 July.

Wilson, Thomas. 2002. "Adulteration and Misbranding." Food Law: Lecture 3. Michigan State University, https://www.msu.edu/course/fsc/421/Powerpoints/Introduction%20Course%20Basics.ppt.

Winett, Liana B. 1998. US Department of Health and Human Services. "Constructing Violence as a Public Health Problem." 113 *Public Health Reports* 498.

Wood, James M. 1999. "The Judicial Coordination of Drug and Device Litigation: A Review and Critique." 54 *Food and Drug Law Journal* 325.

Woodyard, Chris. 1997. "Deal Pleases Advocate Widow Plans to Continue Tobacco-Education Fight." *USA TODAY*. 2 July.

Woolf, Lord Harry K. 1996. *Access to Justice: Final Report to the Lord Chancellor on the Civil Justice System in England and Wales*. London: Department for Constitutional Affairs, http://www.dca.gov.uk/civil/final/contents.htm.

Yeazell, Stephen C. 1987. *From Medieval Group Litigation to the Modern Class Action*. New Haven, CT: Yale University Press.

–. 1989. "Collective Litigation as Collective Action." *University of Illinois Law Review* 43.

–. 1997. "The Past and Future of Defendant and Settlement Classes in Collective Litigation." 39 *Arizona Law Review* 687.

Yost, Pete. 2008. "Court Slashes Damages Award in '89 Exxon Oil Spill." *Washington Post*. 26 June.

Yum! Brands. 2006. *About Yum! Brands*, http://www.yum.com/about/default.asp.

Zaring, David T. 2006. "The Use of Foreign Decisions by Federal Courts: An Empirical Analysis." 3 *Journal of Empirical Legal Studies* 297.

Case References

Australia

A. and J. Partitions Pty. Ltd. v. Jolly, [1993] BC 9300648 (Vict.).
Australian Federation of Consumer Organizations Inc. v. Tobacco Institute of Australia Ltd., [1991] 100 A.L.R. 568 (F.C.A., NSW Dist.).
Bright v. Femcare, [1999] FCA 1377, 166 A.L.R. 743.
Bright v. Femcare Ltd., [2002] 195 A.L.R. 574.
Butler v. Kraft Foods Ltd. [settled in 1997].
Carnie v. Esanda, [1995] 182 C.L.R. 398.
Carnie v. Esanda, [1996] 38 N.S.W.L.R. 465.
Courtney v. Medtel, [2003] FCA 36.
CSR Ltd. v. Young, [1998] CA 40037/95, 1998 N.S.W. 393 (LEXIS) (N.S.W.S.C.).
Darcy v. Medtel, [2001] FCA 1369.
Dowdell v. Knispel Fruit Juices Pty Ltd., [2003] FCA 851.
Esanda Finance Corporation Ltd v. Carnie, [1992] 29 N.S.W.L.R. 382.
Femcare Ltd. v. Bright, [2000] 172 A.L.R. 713.
Graham Barclay Oysters v. Ryan, [2000] FCA 1099.
Mabo v. Queensland (No. 2), [1992] 175 C.L.R. 1.
Marino v. Esanda Ltd., [1986] V.R. 735.
McCabe v. British American Tobacco Australia Services Ltd., [2002] VSC 73, [2002] VSCA 197 (overturned by Supreme Court of Victoria, *British American Tobacco Australia Services Limited v. Cowell* [as representing the estate of Rolah Ann McCabe, deceased]).
McMullin v. ICI Australia Operations Pty Ltd., [1996] FCA 1511.
McMullin v. ICI Australia Operations Pty Ltd., [1997] FCA 541.
Mobil Oil Australia Pty. Ltd. v. Victoria, [2002] 21 C.L.R. 1.
Nixon v. Philip Morris (Australia) Ltd., [1999] FCA 1107.
Payne v. Young, [1981] 145 C.L.R. 609.
Philip Morris (Australia) v. Nixon, [2000] 170 A.L.R. 487.
Pilmer v. McPherson's Limited, 1985 (Vic. S.C.) [unreported], http://vsc.sirsi.net.au/ Judgments/Civil/239906.pdf.
Sharp v. Port Kembla RSL Club, [2001] NSWSC 336.
Tobacco Control Coalition Inc. v. Philip Morris (Australia) Ltd., [2000] FCA 1004.
Wong v. Silkfield Pty. Ltd., [1999] 199 C.L.R. 255.
Zentahope Pty. Ltd. v. Bellotti, [1992] BC 9203164 (Vict.).

Canada

Blais v. Imperial Tobacco, Quebec Superior Court, 21 February 2005 (unpublished order); petition to dismiss denied Quebec Court of Appeal, 2007 QCTA 694.
Bouchanskaia v. Bayer Inc., 2003 BCSC 1306, [2003] B.C.J. No. 1969 (Prov. Ct.) (QL).
British Columbia v. Imperial Tobacco, 2003 BCSC 877, [2003] 227 D.L.R. (4th) 323.

British Columbia v. Imperial Tobacco Canada Ltd., 2005 SCC 49, [2005] 2 S.C.R. 473.
Caputo v. Imperial Tobacco Ltd., [1997] 148 D.L.R. (4th) 566; [1999] 44 O.R. (3d) 554; [2004] Carswell Ont. 423.
Carom v. Bre-x Minerals Ltd., [1999] 46 B.L.R. (2d) 247, 35 C.P.C. (4th) 43, 44 O.R. (3d) 173 (S.C.J.).
Coleman v. Bayer Inc., [2004] O.J. No. 1974 (QL).
Comité de citoyens et d'action municipale de St-Césaire Inc. v. Ville de St-Césaire, [1985] C.S. 35, aff'd [1986] R.J.Q. 1061 (C.A.).
Dabbs v. Sun Life Assurance Co. of Canada, [1998] 40 O.R. (3d) 776 (Gen. Div.).
Dufour c. Bayer Inc., [2004] J.Q. No. 11125 (QL).
G.M. (Canada) v. Naken, [1983] 1 S.C.R. 72.
Hoffman v. Monsanto, [2005] S.J. No. 304 (QL).
Hoffman v. Monsanto, [2006] S.J. No. 723 (QL).
Hoffman v. Monsanto, [2007] C.S.C.R. 347.
Hoffman v. Monsanto Canada and Bayer Cropscience, Inc., 2005 SKQB 225.
Hollick v. Toronto (City), 2001 SCC 68.
JTI-Macdonald Corp. v. British Columbia, 2000 BCSC 312, [2000] 184 D.L.R. (4th) 335.
Knight v. Imperial Tobacco, 2005 BCSC 172.
Lamb v. Bayer Inc., 2003 SKQB 442, [2003] S.J. No. 692 (QL).
Létourneau v. Imperial Tobacco, Quebec Superior Court, 21 February 2005 (unpublished order); petition to dismiss denied Quebec Court of Appeal, 2007 QCTA 694.
McKrow v. Manufacturers Life Ins. Co., [1998] O.J. No. 4692 (Ont. Gen. Div.) (QL).
Naken v. General Motors of Canada Ltd., [1979] 92 D.L.R. (3d) 100 (Ont. C.A.).
Naken v. General Motors of Canada Ltd., [1983] 1 S.C.R. 72, 144 D.L.R. (3d) 385 (S.C.C.).
Nantais v. Telectronics Proprietary Ltd., [1995] 25 O.R. (3d) 331 (Gen. Div.).
Nault v. Canadian Consumer Co. Ltd., [1981] 1 S.C.R. 553.
Pardy v. Bayer Inc. [2003] N.J. No. 1982 (QL).
Parsons v. Canadian Red Cross Society, [1999] 40 C.P.C. (4th) 151 (Ont. Sup. Ct.), 101 A.C.W.S. (3d) 694.
Parsons v. McDonalds, [2005] O.J. No. 506 (C.A.) (QL).
Ragoonanan v. Imperial Tobacco, [2000] O.J. No. 4597 (QL).
Rumley v. British Columbia, 2001 SCC 69.
Serwaczek v. Medical Engineering Corp., [1996] 3 C.P.C. (4th) 386 (Gen. Div.).
Syndicat National des Employés de l'Hôpital St-Ferdinand c. Québec (Curateur Public), [1994] R.J.Q. 2761 (QC C.A.).
Tremaine v. A.H. Robins Canada Inc., [1990] R.D.J. 500.
Walls v. Bayer Inc., 2005 MBQB 3, [2005] M.J. No. 4 (QL).
Western Canadian Shopping Centres Inc. v. Dutton, 2001 SCC 46.
Wheadon v. Bayer Inc, [2004] N.J. No. 147 (QL).

United Kingdom
AB v. John Wyeth and Brothers Ltd, [1993] 4 Med L.R. 1.
Adair v. New River Co., [1805] 11 Ves. 429.
Adams v. Cape Industries P/C, [1990] 1 Ch. 433.
Adams and Others v. Cape Industries PLC and Anor, [1991] 1 All E.R. 929.
Anns v. Merton London Borough Council, [1978] A.C. 728 (H.L.).
Bank of America National Trust and Savings Association v. Taylor, [1992] 1 Lloyd's Rep. 484 (Q.B.).
Barker v. Corus, [2006] UKHL 20.
Bedford v. Ellis, [1901] A.C. 1.
Bogle v. McDonalds Restaurants Limited, [2002] EWHC 490 (Q.B.).
Brown v. Vermuden, [1676] 1 Ch. Ca. 272, 22 E.R. 796.
Chancey v. May, [1722] 24 E.R. 265 (Ch.).
Cockburn v. Thompson, [1809] 16 Ves. 328.
Davies v. Eli Lilly, [1987] 1W.L.R. 1136 (C.A.).
Discart v. Otes, [1914] 30 Seldon Society 137 (No. 158, P.C. 1309).

E.M.I. Records v. Riley, [1981] 1 W.L.R. 923 (Ch.).

Fairchild v. Glenhaven Funeral Services Ltd., [2002a] UKHL 22.

Fairchild v. Glenhaven Funeral Services Ltd., [2002b] 3 W.L.R. 89, 3 All E.R. 305 (H.L.).

Fletcher v. Rylands, [1865] 159 E.R. 737, rev'd [1866] L.R. 1 Ex. 265, aff'd as *Rylands v. Fletcher*, [1868] 3 L.R. 330 (H.L.).

Foster v. Roussel Laboratories Ltd. (unreported, Q.B., 30 June 1997).

Griffiths and Others v. British Coal Corporation (British Coal Respiratory Disease Litigation) (unpublished order, Q.B., 23 January 1998); reviewed and upheld, [2004] E.W.C.H. 1372 (Q.B.).

Hitchens v. Congreve, [1828] 38 E.R. 917 (Ch.).

Hodgson v. Imperial Tobacco Ltd., [1998] 1 W.L.R. 1056.

Hodgson and Ors v. Imperial Tobacco Ltd. and Gallaher Group PLC, [1999a] P.I.Q.R. Q1.

Hodgson and Ors v. Imperial Tobacco Ltd., [1999b] C.L.Y. 459 (Q.B.D.).

Irish Shipping Ltd. v. Commercial Union Assurance Co. (The Irish Rowan), [1991] 2 QB 206.

Jackson v. Attorney General, [2005] UKHL 56.

Loveday v. Renton, [1990] 1 Med L.R. 117 (Q.B.).

Lubbe v. Cape PLC, [2000a] 4 All E.R. 268.

Lubbe v. Cape PLC., [2000b] UKHL 41.

M. Michael Furriers Ltd v. Askew, [1983] 127 S.J. 597.

Markt and Co. v. Knight Steamship Co., [1910] 2 K.B. 1021 (C.A.).

Martin, Rector of Barkway v. Parishioners of Nuthamstead (1199). Reported in Norma Adams and Charles Donahue, Jr., eds. *Select Cases from the Ecclesiastical Courts of the Province of Canterbury, c. 1200-1301*. London: Selden Society, 1981.

McTear's Executrix v. Imperial Tobacco Ltd., [2005] CSOH 69, [1997] S.L.T. 53.

National Bank of Greece SA v. RM Outhwaite, [2001] 317 Syndicate at Lloyds (Q.B.).

In re: Pinochet, [1998] H.L.J. No. 52 (Q.L.).

Prudential Assurance v. Newman Industries, [1981] Ch. 229.

R. v. Bow Street Metropolitan Stipendiary Magistrate, Ex parte Pinochet Ugarte (No. 2), [1999] 1 All E.R. 577 (H.L.).

Roswell v. Vaughn, [1606] 79 E.R. 171 (K.B.).

Smith Kline and French Lab. Ltd. v. Bloch, [1983] 2 All E.R. 72 (C.A.).

Taff Vale Railway Co. v. Amalgamated Society of Railway Servants, [1901] A.C. 426.

Wallworth v. Holt, [1841] 4 My. and Cr. 619, 41 E.R. 238.

Ward v. Newalls Insulation Co. and Cape Contracts Ltd., [1998] 1 W.L.R. 1722.

United States

A.D. Bedell Wholesale Company, Inc. v. Philip Morris, Inc., 104 F. Supp. 2d 501 (W. Dist. Pa. 2000)).

In re: "Agent Orange" Product Liability Litigation, 100 F.R.D. 718 (E. Dist. N.Y. 1983) (certifying the class), aff'd, 818 F.2d 145 (2nd Cir. 1987).

In re: "Agent Orange" Product Liability Litigation, 597 F. Supp. 740 (E. Dist. N.Y. 1984).

In re: A.H. Robins Company, Inc., 89 B.R. 555 (E. Dist. Va. 1988).

In re: A.H. Robins Company, Inc., 880 F.2d 709 4 (Cal. 1989).

Aksamit v. Brown and Williamson Tobacco Corp., [2000] U.S. Dist. No. 18880 (D.S.C. 2000) (LEXIS).

Allen v. R.J. Reynolds Tobacco Company, Case No. 01-4319 (S. Dist. Fla., Miami Division 2003).

Alliance for Bio-Integrity v. Shalala, 116 F. Supp. 2d 166 (D. 2000).

Altria Group v. Good, Docket No. 07-562 (Sup. Ct. 2008).

Alyeska Pipeline Co. v. Wilderness Society, 421 U.S. 240 (1975).

Ambrosio v. Carter's Country, Case No. 99,669 (Dist. Ct. Tex., Fort Bend County, 1998), aff'd, Case No. 14-99-00105-CV (Ct. App. Tex. 2000).

Amchem Products v. Windsor, 521 U.S. 591 (1997).

American Steel and Wire Co. v. Wire Drawers' and Die Makers' Unions, 90 F. 598 (Cir. Ct. N. Dist. Ohio 1898).

Anderson v. Bryco Arms Corp., Case No. 00L 007476 (Cir. Ct. Ill., Cook County 2000) (complaint filed).

Anderson v. Fortune Brands Inc., Case No. 4281/97 (Super. Ct. N.Y., Kings County 2000).

In re: Application of Brown and Williamson Tobacco Corporation v. Stanley M. Chesley, 7 A.D.3d 368 (Sup. Ct. N.Y., App. Div., 1st Dept. 2004).

Arcambel v. Wiseman, 3 U.S. 306 (1796).

Arch v. American Tobacco Company, 175 F.R.D. 469 (E. Dist. Pa. 1997).

In re: Asbestos Litigation, 134 F.3d 668 (5th Cir. 1998).

Bacon v. Robertson, 59 U.S. 480 (1855).

Badillo v. American Tobacco Co., 202 F.R.D. 261 (D. Nev. 2001).

Baker v. Smith and Wesson Corp., [2002] No. 3174152 (Super. Ct. Del.) (WL).

Barber v. McDonald's, Index No. 23145/2003 (Sup. Ct. N.Y., New York County 2002) (summons and complaint).

Barker v. Lull Engineering, 20 Cal. 3d 413 (1978).

Barnes v. American Tobacco Co., 161 F.3d 127 (3rd Cir. 1998), cert. denied, 526 U.S. 1114, 143 L. Ed. 2d 791, 119 S. Ct. 1760 (1999).

Barreras Ruiz v. American Tobacco Co., 180 F.R.D. 194 (D.P.R. 1998).

Baskins v. United Mine Workers, 150 Ark. 398 (1921).

Bates v. State Bar of Arizona, 433 U.S. 350 (1977).

In re: Baycol Products Liability Litigation, US Courts' Multidistrict Litigation Action No. 1431, (D. Minn. 2004).

Beatty v. Kurtz, 27 U.S. 566 (1829).

In re: Bendectin Products Liability Litigation, 749 F.2d 300 (1984).

Bender v. Colt Industries, Inc., 517 S.W.2d 705 (Ct. App. Mo. 1974).

Bichler v. Eli Lilly and Company, 436 N.E.2d 182 (Ct. App. N.Y. 1982).

Block v. McDonald's, Case No. 01 CH 9137 (Cir. Ct. Ill., Cook County 2002).

Blum v. Merrell Dow Pharmaceutical, Inc., [1997] Pac. Super. No. 3861 (Super. Ct. Pa. 1997) (LEXIS).

BMW of North America v. Gore, 517 U.S. 559 (1996).

Bogle v. McDonalds Restaurants Limited, [2002] E.W.H.C. 490 (Q.B.).

Bolling v. Sharpe, 347 U.S. 497 (1954).

Borel v. Fibreboard Paper Products Corporation, 493 F.2d 1076 (5th Cir. 1973).

Boston v. Smith and Wesson Corp., Civil Action No. 99–2590C (Super. Ct., Mass, Suffolk County 1999).

Boston v. Smith and Wesson, Case No. 1999-02590 (Super. Ct., Mass, Suffolk County 2000), petition for interlocutory appeal denied, Case No. 2000-J-0483 (Ct. App. Mass. 2002).

Bowling v. Pfizer, Inc., 922 F. Supp. 1261 (S. Dist. Ohio 1996).

Broin v. Philip Morris, 641 So. 2d 888 (Ct. App. Fla., 3rd Dist. 1994).

Brown v. Board of Education, 347 U.S. 483 (1954).

Brown and Williamson v. U.S. FDA, 153 F. 3d 155 (4th Cir. 1998).

Bullock v. Philip Morris, Case No. BC 249171 (Super. Ct., Cal., Los Angeles County 2002).

Burke v. Kleiman, 277 Ill. App. 519 (App. Ct. Ill. 1934).

Camden v. Beretta, Superior Court of New Jersey, Law Division, Camden County, Docket No. L-451099 (1999).

Camden County Board of Chosen Freeholders v. Beretta U.S.A. Corp., 123 F. Supp.2d 245 (Dist. Ct. N.J. 2000), aff'd, 273 F.3d 536 (3rd Cir. 2001).

Castano v. American Tobacco Company, Civil Action No. 94-1044, section "S"(5), 160 F.R.D. 544 (E. Dist. La. 1995).

Castano v. American Tobacco Company, 84 F.3d 734 (5th Cir. 1996).

Central Railroad and Banking Co. v. Pettus, 113 U.S. 116 (1885).

Chamberlain v. American Tobacco Co., 70 F. Supp. 2d 788 (N. Dist. Ohio 1999).

Chicago v. Beretta, Case No. 98 CH 01559 (Cir. Ct. Ill., Cook County, Ch. Div. 1998) (first amended complaint).

Chicago v. Beretta, Case No. 98 CH 15596 (Cir. Ct. Ill., Cook County, Ch. Div. 2000) (report of proceedings).

Chicago v. Beretta, 337 Ill. App. 3d 1 (App. Ct. Ill., 1st Dist., 1st Div. 2002).

Chicago v. Beretta U.S.A., [2004] Ill. No. 1665 (Sup. Ct. Ill. 2004) (LEXIS).

Cincinnati v. Beretta, Case No. A9902369, Court of Common Pleas (Civ. Div. Ohio, Hamilton County 1999).
Cincinnati v. Beretta USA Corp, Case Nos. C-990729, C-990814, C-990815, [2000] No. 3601 (Ct. App. Ohio, Hamilton County, 1st App. Dist. 2000), 95 Ohio St. 3d 416, [2002] No. 2480 (Sup. Ct. Ohio 2002).
Cipollone v. Liggett Group, Inc., 693 F. Supp. 208 (Dist. Ct. N.J. 1988).
Cipollone v. Liggett Group, 505 U.S. 504 (1992).
City of Atlanta v. Smith & Wesson, Corp. et al., 99VS0149217J, aff'd, 543 S.E.2d 16 (Ga. 2001), rev'd, Sturm, Ruger & Company, Inc. et al. v. City of Atlanta, 560 S.E.2d 525(Ga. Ct. App. 13 February 2002).
City of Camden v. Beretta U.S.A. Corp., Case No. CAM-L-4510-99 (Sup. Ct. N.J., Camden County, Law Div. 2003).
City of New York v. Beretta USA, 524 F.3d 384 (U.S. Ct. App., 2nd Cir, 2008).
Clark v. Paul Gray, Inc., 306 U.S. 583 (1939).
Clay v. American Tobacco Co., 188 F.R.D. 483 (S. Dist. Ill. 1999).
Cobb v. Insured Lloyds, 387 So. 2d 13 (App. Ct. La. 1980).
Collins v. Anthem Health Plans, Inc., 266 Conn. 12 (2003).
Conrad Johnson et al. v. Bull's Eye Shooter Supply, Case No. 03-2-03932-8 (Sup. Ct. Wash., Pierce County 2003).
CSPI v. Burger King Corp., 534 F. Supp. 2d 141 (D. 2008).
Cutler v. 65 Security Plan, 831 F. Supp. 1008 (E. Dist. N.Y. 1993).
Daubert v. Merrell Dow Pharmaceuticals, Inc., 727 F. Supp. 570 (S. Dist. Ct. App. 1989).
Daubert v. Merrell Dow Pharmaceuticals, Inc., 509 U.S. 579 (1993).
Daubert v. Merrell Dow Pharmaceuticals, Inc., 43 F.3d 1311 (Ct. App. 1995).
Delahanty v. Hinckley, 799 F. Supp. 184 (D. 1992).
DeLoach v. Philip Morris, Case No. 00-CV-294 (Dist. Ct. N.C. 2003).
Detroit and Wayne County, MI v. Arms Technology, Inc., 258 Mich. App. 48, 669 N.W.2d 845 (Ct. App. Mich. 2003).
In re: Diet Drugs, US Courts' Multidistrict Litigation Action No. 1203 (E. Dist. Pa. 2004).
Dillon v. Legg, 68 Cal. 2d 728 (1968).
District of Columbia v. Beretta, Case No. 00-0000428 (Sup. Ct. D.C. 2000), 847 A.2d 1127 (Ct. App. D.C. 2004).
District of Columbia v. Heller, 128 S. Ct. 2783 (2008).
Dix v. Beretta U.S.A. Corp., Case No. 750681-9 (Sup. Ct. Alameda County 1998), on appeal, Case No. A086018 (Ct. App. Cal., 1st Dist., Div. 1, 2000).
Dothard v. Rawlinson, 433 U.S. 321 (1977).
Dukes v. Wal-Mart Stores, Inc., Case No. C 01-2252 MJJ, 222 F.R.D. 137 (N. Dist. Cal. 2004).
Dukes v. Wal-Mart, Inc., Case No. 04-16720 (9th Cir. 2007), http://www.walmartclass.com/walmartclass_casedevelopments.html.
Eisen v. Carlisle and Jacquelin, 417 U.S. 156 (1974).
Eisenberg v. Anheuser-Busch, Inc., Case No. 1:04 CV 1081, [2006] No. 290308 (N. Dist. Ohio) (WL).
Eiser v. Brown and Williamson, Case No. EM 2007 (E. Dist. Pa. 2003).
Emig v. American Tobacco Co., 184 F.R.D. 379 (Dist. Ct. Kan. 1998).
Engle v. Liggett Group, Case No. SC03-1856 (Sup. Ct. Fla. 2006).
Engle v. R.J. Reynolds Tobacco Co., 672 So.2d 39 (Dist. Ct. App. Fla., 3d Dist. 1996).
In re: Ephedra Products Liability Litigation, US Courts' Multidistrict Litigation Action No. 1598 (S. Dist. N.Y. 2004).
Escola v. Coca Cola Bottling Company, 24 Cal. 2d 453 (Sup. Ct. Cal. 1944).
Estate of Pascal Charlot v. Bushmaster Firearms, Inc., Case No. 03-2501 (D. 2003).
Exxon Shipping Company v. Baker, 2008 U.S. No. 5263 (2008) (LEXIS).
In re: "Factor VIII or IX Concentrate Blood Products" Products Liability Litigation, US Courts' Multidistrict Litigation Action No. 986 (N. Dist. Ill. 1993).
FDA v. Brown and Williamson, 529 U.S. 120 (2000).
Ferens v. John Deere Co., 494 U.S. 516 (1990).

Fettke v. McDonald's Corp., Case No. CV 044109 (Super. Ct. Cal. 2004).

In re: Firearm Cases, 2005 Cal. App. No. 211 (Ct. App. Cal., 1st App. Dist, Div. 1 2005) (LEXIS).

Fischer v. Johns-Manville, 103 N.J. 643, 512 A.2d 466 (Sup. Ct. N.J. 1986).

Fleischmann Distilling Corp. v. Maier Brewing Co., 386 U.S. 714 (1967).

Friend v. Childs Dining Hall Co., 231 Mass. 65 (Sup. Jud. Ct. Mass., Suffolk County 1918).

Frye v. United States, 293 F.2d 1013 (Cir. Ct. D.C. 1923).

Galpin v. Page, 85 U.S. 350 (1873).

Ganin v. Smith and Wesson, 258 Conn. 313 (Super. Ct. Farfield, Conn. 1999), 780 A.2d 98 (Sup. Ct. Conn. 2001).

Gary v. Smith and Wesson, Case No. 45D02-9908-CT-0355 (Super. Ct. Lake County 1999), 801 N.E.2d 1222 (Sup. Ct. Ind. 2003).

Geiger v. American Tobacco Co., 181 Misc. 2d 875, 696 N.Y.S.2d 345 (Sup. Ct. N.Y. 1999), aff'd, 277 A.D.2d 420, 716 N.Y.S.2d 108 (App. Div. N.Y. 2000).

General Electric v. Joiner, 522 U.S. 136 (1997).

Georgine v. Amchem Products, Inc., 878 F. Supp. 716 (E. Dist. Pa. 1994); 83 F.3d 610 (3rd Cir. 1996).

Graham v. Richardson, 403 U.S. 365 (1971).

Gratz v. Bollinger, 539 U.S. 244 (2003).

Green v. American Tobacco Company, 304 F2d 70 (Ct. App. Fla, 5th Dist. 1962).

Grunow v. Valor Corp. of Florida, Case No. 00-9657 (Cir. Ct. Fla., Palm Beach County 2000).

Guffanti v. National Surety Co., 196 N.Y. 452 (1909).

Guillory v. American Tobacco Co., [2001] U.S. Dist. No. 3353 (N. Dist. Ill. 2001) (LEXIS).

Haines v. Liggett Group, Inc., Civil Action No. 84-678, 814 F. Supp. 414 (Dist. Ct. N.J. 1993) (memorandum from J. Michael Jordan to unspecified smoking and health attorneys, 29 April 1988).

Hale v. Hale, 146 Ill. 227 (1893).

Hall v. Cole, 412 U.S. 1 (1973).

Hamilton v. Accu-tek, Case No. CV-95-0049 (E. Dist. N.Y. 1999).

Hamilton v. Beretta, 264 F.3d 21 (2nd Cir. 2001a).

Hamilton v. Beretta, 96 N.Y.2d 222 (Ct. App. N.Y. 2001b).

Haney v. United States, 264 F.3d 1161 (10th Cir. 2002) (cert. denied).

Hansberry v. Lee, 311 U.S. 32 (1940).

Hansen v. American Tobacco Co., 1999 U.S. Dist. No. 11277 (E. Dist. Ark. 1999) (LEXIS).

Harrison v. Perea, 168 U.S. 311 (1897).

Hartford Life Ins. Co. v. Ibs, 237 U.S. 662 (1915).

Helling v. McKinney, 509 U.S. 25 (1993).

Henley v. Philip Morris, Inc., Case No. 995172 (Super. Ct. Cal., San Francisco County 1999).

Henningsen v. Bloomfield Motors, 32 N.J. 358 (1960).

Hicks v. TandM Jewelry, Inc., Case No. 97-Ci 2617 (Circ. Ct. Ky., Fayette County 1999).

Hopper v. Wal-Mart Stores, Inc., Civic Action No. 98-C-1496-NE (N. Dist. Ala. 1999).

Hoyte v. Yum! Brands d/b/a KFC, Civil Action No. 06-1127 (Sup. Ct. D.C. 2006).

Hymowitz v. Eli Lilly, 539 N.E.2d 1069 (Ct. App. N.Y. 1989).

Ileto v. Glock, 194 F. Supp. 2d 1040 (2002).

Ileto v. Glock, 349 F.3d 1191 (9th Cir. 2003), cert. denied, 125 S. Ct. 865 (2005).

Ileto v. Glock, 421 F. Supp. 2d 1274 (C. Dist. Cal. 2006).

Insolia v. Philip Morris, Inc., 186 F.R.D. 535 (W. Dist. Wis. 1998).

James v. Arms Technology, Inc., 820 A.2d 27 (Super. Ct. N.J., App. Div. 2003).

Jenkins v. Raymark Industries, Inc., 782 F.2d 468 (5th Cir. 1986).

Johns-Manville Sales Corp. v. Janssens, 463 So. 2d 242 (Ct. App. Fla., 1st Dist. 1984).

Karges Furniture Co. v. Amalgamated Woodworkers Local Union, 165 Ind. 421 (1905).

Kitchen v. K-Mart Corp., 697 So.2d 1200 (Sup. Ct. Fla. 1997).

Knight v. Florida, 528 U.S. 990 (1999).

Kumho Tire Company v. Carmichael, 526 U.S. 137 (1999).

Kurtz v. Beatty, 14 F.Cas. 881 (1826).

In re: Latex Gloves Products Liability Litigation, US Courts' Multidistrict Litigation Action No. 1148 (E. Dist. Pa. 1997).

Lawrence v. Texas, 539 US 558 (2003).

Lawson v. Beretta, 847 A.2d 1127 (Ct. App. D.C. 2004).

Lee v. Hansberry, 372 Ill. 369 (1939).

Lemongello and McGuire v. Will Jewelry and Loan, [2003] No. 21488208 (Cir. Ct. W.Va. 2003) (WL) [unpublished].

Lexecon Inc. v. Milberg Weiss Bershad Hynes and Lerach, 523 U.S. 26 (1998).

Liberty v. District of Columbia Police and Firemen's Retirement and Relief Board, 452 A.2d 1187 (Cir. Ct. D.C. 1982).

Liebeck v. McDonald's Restaurants, P.T.S., Inc., Case No. D-202 CV-93-02419, [1995] no. 360309 (Dist. Ct. N.Mex., Bernalillo County 1994) (WL).

Lieber v. Consumer Empowerment BV, Case No. CV 01-9923 (2004).

Liggett Group, Inc. v. Engle, 853 So. 2d 434 (Ct. App. Fla., 3rd Dist. 2003).

Lightle v. Kirby, 194 Ark. 535 (1937).

Linn v. Radio Center Delicatessen, Inc., 169 Misc. 879 (Mun. Ct. N.Y., Borough of Manhattan, 1st Dist. 1939).

Loe v. Lenhardt, 227 Or. 242 (1961).

Lucier v. Philip Morris, Case No. 02AS01909 (Super. Ct. Cal., Sacramento County 2003).

Lowe v. R.J. Reynolds Tobacco Company, Case No. 9871 (E. Dist. Mo. 1954).

Lyon v. Premo Pharmaceutical Labs, Inc., 406 A.2d 185 (Super. Ct. N.J. App. Div. 1979).

Mahoney v. R.J. Reynolds Tobacco Co., 204 F.R.D. 150 (S. Dist. Iowa 2001).

Mathieu v. Fabrica D'Armi Pietro Beretta SPA and Beretta U.S.A., Case No. 97-CV-12818-NG (Dist. Ct. Mass. 2000).

Maxfield v. Bryco Arms, [2005] No. 419595 (Super. Ct. Cal., Alameda County 2005) (WL)

Mayhew v. Mattel, Inc., Case No. CV07-05126 (C. Dist. Cal. 2007).

McCulloch v. Velez, 364 F.3d 1 (1st Cir. 2004).

McDarby v. Merck, Case Nos. A-0076-07T1 and A-0077-07T1 (Super. Ct. N.J., App. Div. 2008).

McLaughlin v. American Company, 522 F.3d 215 (2nd Cir. 2008).

McNamara v. Bre-X Minerals Ltd. 68 F. Supp. 2d 759 (E. Dist. Tex. 1999) [unpublished].

Mekdeci v. Merrell National Laboratories, 711 F.2d 1510 (Ct. App. 1983).

Merck v. Ernst, Case No. 14-06-00835-CV (Ct. App. Tex. 2008).

In re: Meridia Products Liability Litigation, US Courts' Multidistrict Litigation Action No. 1481 (N. Dist. Ohio 2002).

Merrill v. Navegar, Inc. (In re: 101 California Street Litigation), 75 Cal. App. 4th 500 (Ct. App. Cal., 1st Dist., Div. 2 1999), reversed Case No. A079863 (Sup. Ct. Cal.), 89 Cal. R. 2d 146 (Ct. App. Cal. 1999), review granted, 92 Cal. R. 2d 256 (Ct. App. Cal. 2000).

Merrill v. Navegar, Inc., 26 Cal. 4th 465 (Sup. Ct. Cal. 2001).

MGM Studios, Inc. v. Grokster, 125 S. Ct. 2764 (2005).

Mills v. Electric Auto-Lite Co., 396 U.S. 375 (1970).

Missouri ex. rel. Gaines v. Canada, 305 U.S. 337 (1938).

Molski v. Gleich, 318 F.3d 937 (9th Cir. 2003).

Monroe ex. rel. Monroe, Case No. 07cv3410 (E. Dist. Pa. 2007).

Moore v. American Tobacco Company, Case No. 94-1429 (Ch. Ct., Miss., Jackson County 1994).

Morial v. Smith and Wesson Corp., Case No. 98-18578 (Civ. Dist. Ct., Parish of Orleans 1998), http://www.gunlawsuits.com/pdf/docket/neworleans.pdf.

NAACP v. A.A. Arms, 271 F.Supp. 435 (E. Dist. N.Y. 2003).

NAACP v. Alabama, 357 U.S. 449 (1958).

New York v. Sturm, Ruger & Co., Inc., No. 402586/00 (Sup. Ct. N.Y. County 2001).

New York v. Sturm, Ruger and Company, Inc., 309 A.D.2d 91, 761 N.Y.S.2d 192 (Sup. Ct. N.Y., App. Div., 1st Dep. 2003).

New York City v. A-1 Jewelry and Pawn, Inc, 501 F. Supp. 2d 369 (E. Dist. N.Y. 2007).

New York City v. Beretta, 315 F. Supp. 2d 256 (E. Dist. N.Y. 2004).

New York City v. Beretta, 401 F. Supp. 2d 244 (2005).

New York City v. Beretta, 429 F. Supp. 2d 517 (2006).

New York City v. Beretta USA, 524 F.3d 384 (2nd Cir. 2008).

New York City v. Bob Moates' Sport Shop, Inc., 06 CV 6504 (E. Dist. N.Y. 2008).

New York State Restaurant Association v. New York City Board of Health, 509 F. Supp. 2d 351 (S. Dist. N.Y. 2007a).

New York State Restaurant Association v. New York City Board of Health, 2008 U.S. Dist. No. 31451 (S. Dist. N.Y. 2007b) (LEXIS).

In re: Northern District of California Dalkon Shield IUD Products Liability Litigation, 526 F. Supp. 887 (Ct. App. 1981).

In re: Northern District of California Dalkon Shield IUD Products Liability Litigation, 693 F.2d 847 (Ct. App. 1982).

Nunnally v. R.J. Reynolds, Case No. 92-270-CD (Cir, Ct. Miss., Desoto County 2000).

Ontario, The Minister of Health and Long Term Care v. Imperial Tobacco, Ltd., Case No. 00CIV1593 (S. Dist. N.Y. 2000).

Ortiz v. Fibreboard Corporation, 527 U.S. 815 (1999).

Parker v. District of Columbia, 311 F. Supp. 2d 103 (2004).

Parker v. District of Columbia, 478 F.3d 370 (2007).

In re: Paxil Products Liability Litigation, US Courts' Multidistrict Litigation Action No. 1574 (C. Dist. Cal. 2003).

Pelman v. McDonald's, 215 F.R.D. 96 (S. Dist. N.Y. 2003a).

Pelman v. McDonald's, 237 F. Supp. 2d 512 (S. Dist. N.Y. 2003b).

Pelman v. McDonald's, Case No. 02 CV 7821 (RWS) (S. Dist. N.Y. 2003c).

Pelman v. McDonald's, 396 F.3d 508 (2nd Cir. 2005a).

Pelman v. McDonald's, 396 F. Supp. 2d 439 (S. Dist. N.Y. 2005b).

Penelas v. Arms Technology, Case No. 99-01941 (Cir. Ct. Fla., Dade County 1999), 778 So. 2d 1042 (Ct. App. Fla., 3rd Dist. 2001), petition for review denied, [2001] Fla. No. 2245 (LEXIS).

In re: Phenylpropanolamine (PPA) Products Liability Litigation, US Courts' Multidistrict Litigation Action No. 1407 (W. Dist. Wash. 2001).

Philadelphia v. Beretta, 126 F. Supp. 2d 882 (E. Dist. Pa. 2000).

Philadelphia v. Beretta, 277 F.3d 415 (3rd Cir. 2002).

Philip Morris, Inc. v. Angeletti, 752 A.2d 200 (Ct. App.Md. 2000).

Philip Morris v. French, 2004 Fla. App. No. 19630, 5 Fla. 3d (Dist. Ct. App. 2004) (LEXIS).

Philip Morris USA Inc. v. Williams, 540 U.S. 801 (2004).

Philip Morris USA v. Williams, 549 U.S. 346 (2007a).

Philip Morris USA v. Williams, 127 S. Ct. 1057 (2007b).

Phillips Petroleum Co. v. Shutts, 472 U.S. 797 (1985).

Pickett v. Walsh, 192 Mass. 572 (Sup. Ct. Mass. 1906).

Price v. Philip Morris, Case No. 00-L-112 (Cir. Ct. Ill., Madison County 2003a).

Price v. Philip Morris, 793 N.E.2d 942 (App. Ct. Ill. 5th Dist. 2003b).

Price v. Philip Morris, 219 Ill. 2d 182, 848 N.E.2d 1 (Sup. Ct. 2005).

In re: Propulsid Products Liability Litigation, US Courts' Multidistrict Litigation Action No. 1355 (E. Dist. La. 2000).

Reed v. Philip Morris, Inc., [1997] No. 538921 (Super. Ct. D.C. 1997), on second motion, Case No. 96-5070 (Super. Ct. D.C. 1999) (WL).

In re: Rezulin Products Liability Litigation, US Courts' Multidistrict Litigation Action No. 1348 (S. Dist. N.Y. 2000).

In re: Rhone-Poulenc Rorer, Inc., 51 F.3d 1293 (7th Cir. 1995).

In re: Richardson-Merrell, Inc. "Bendectin" Products Liability Litigation, 624 F. Supp. 1212 (S. Dist. Ohio 1985).

Rissman v. Target Sports, Inc., (Cir. Ct. Mich., Oakland County 2000), cited at http://www.gunlawsuits.org/docket/casestatus.php?RecordNo=46.

Roe v. Wade, 410 U.S. 113 (1973).

Roper v. Simmons, 543 U.S. 551 (2005), 125 S.Ct. 1183 (2005).

Rosado v. Wyman, 397 U.S. 397 (1970).

Rosenfeld v. A.H. Robins Co., Inc., 63 A.D.2d 11 (Sup. Ct. N.Y., App. Div., 2nd Dept. 1978).

Santa Clara County v. Southern Pacific Railroad Company, 118 U.S. 394 (1886).

Sarjent v. Fisher-Price, Inc., Case No. 1:07-CV-1060-JDT-TAB (S. Dist. Ind. 2007).

Schuehle v. Reiman, 86 N.Y. 270 (Ct. App. N.Y. 1881).

Schwab v. Philip Morris USA, Inc., 449 F. Supp. 2d 992, 2006 U.S. Dist. No. 73196 (E. Dist. N.Y. 2006) (LEXIS).

Scott v. American Tobacco Company, Civil Case No. 96-8461 (Dist. Ct. La., Orleans Parish 2004).

Scott v. American Tobacco Company, Case No. 2004-CA-2095 (Ct. App. La., 4th Cir. 2007).

Service Employees Int'l Union Health and Welfare Fund v. Philip Morris Incorporated, 83 F. Supp. 2d 70 (D. 1999), 249 F.3d 1068 (Cir. Ct. D.C. 2001), cert. denied sub nom. *Republic of Guatemala v. Tobacco Institute, Inc.,* 122 S. Ct. 463 (2001).

In re: Serzone Products Liability Litigation, US Courts' Multidistrict Litigation Action No. 1477 (S. Dist. W. Va. 2002).

Shelley v. Kramer, 334 U.S. 1 (1948).

Shoukry v. Fisher-Price, Inc., Case No. 07 CV 7182 (S. Dist. N.Y. 2007).

In re: Silica Products Liability Litigation, US Courts' Multidistrict Litigation Action No. 1553 (S. Dist. Tex., Corpus Chirti Div. 2005), 398 F. Supp. 2d 563 (2005).

In re: Silicone Gel Breast Implants Products Liability Litigation, US Courts' Multidistrict Litigation Action No. 926 (N. Dist. Ala. 1992).

Silkwood v. Kerr-McGee, 464 U.S. 238 (1984).

In re: Simon II Litigation, 211 F.R.D. 86 (2002a).

In re: Simon II Litigation, [2002b] U.S. Dist. No. 25632 (LEXIS) (expanded memorandum and order).

In re: Simon II Litigation, 407 F.3d 125 (2nd Cir. 2005).

In re: Simon II Litigation, 233 F.R.D. 123 (E. Dist. N.Y. 2006).

Sindell v. Abbott Laboratories, 607 P.2d 924 (Sup. Ct. App. 1980).

Small v. Lorillard Tobacco Co., 252 A.D.2d 1, 679 N.Y.S.2d 593 (App. Div. 1998), aff'd, 94 N.Y.2d 43, 720 N.E.2d 892, 698 N.Y.S.2d 615 (Sup. Ct. N.Y., App. Div., 1st Dep. 1999).

Smith v. Allwright, 321 U.S. 649 (1944).

Smith v. Brown and Williamson Tobacco Corp., 174 F.R.D. 90 (W. Dist. Mo. 1997).

Smith v. Bryco Arms, 131 N.M. 87 (Ct. App. N. Mex. 2001).

Smith v. Lockheed Propulsion Co., 56 Cal.R. 128 (1967).

Smith v. Swormstedt, 57 U.S. 288 (1854).

Smith and Wesson v. Gary, 875 N.E.2d 422 (Ct. App. Ind. 2007).

Snyder v. Harris, 394 U.S. 332 (1969).

Sprague v. Ticonic National Bank, 307 U.S. 161 (1939).

In re: St. Jude Medical, Inc., Silzone Heart Valves Products Liability Litigation, US Courts' Multidistrict Litigation Action No. 1396 (Dist. Ct. Minn. 2001).

St. Louis v. Cernicek, Case No. 992-01209 (Cir. Ct. Miss., St. Louis 1999), 145 S.W.3d 37 (Ct. App. Miss., E. Dist., 1st Div. 2004).

In re: Starlink Corn Products Liability Litigation, US Courts' Multidistrict Litigation Action No. 1403, Case No. 01 C 4928 and all other related cases, 212 F. Supp. 2d 828 (N.D Ill. 2002).

In re: Starlink Corn Products Liability Litigation: US Courts' Multidistrict Litigation Action No. 1403 (N. Dist. Ill. 2003) (notice of pendency of class action, settlement class certification, proposed settlement and fairness hearing).

Staron v. McDonald's, 51 F.3d 353 (2nd Cir. 1995).

State Farm Fire and Casualty Co. v. Tashire, 386 U.S. 523 (1967).

State Farm Insurance v. Preece, 538 U.S. 408 (2004), 123 S. Ct. 1513 (2003).

State Farm Mutual Automobile Insurance Company v. Campbell, 538 U.S. 408 (2003).

Strawbridge v. Curtiss, 7 U.S. 267 (1806).

Sturm, Ruger and Company, Inc. v. Atlanta, 253 Ga. App. 713, 560 S.E.2d 525 (Ct. App. Ga., 2nd Div. 2002).

Sturm Ruger and Company v. Day, 594 P.2d 38 (Sup. Ct. Alaska 1979).

In re: Sulzer Orthopedics, Inc., Hip Prosthesis and Knee Prosthesis Products Liability Litigation, US Courts' Multidistrict Litigation Action No. 1401 (N. Dist. Ohio 2001).

Supreme Council of the Royal Arcanum v. Green, 237 U.S. 531 (1915).

Supreme Tribe of Ben-Hur v. Cauble, 255 U.S. 356 (1921).

Sutowski v. Eli Lilly and Company, 696 N.E.2d 187 (Sup. Ct. Ohio 1998).

Sweatt v. Painter, 339 U.S. 629 (1950).

Tellabs v. Makor, 127 S. Ct. 2499 (2007).

Thompson v. American Tobacco Co., 189 F.R.D. 544 (Dist. Ct. Minn. 1999).

Tijerina v. Philip Morris Inc., [1996] U.S. Dist. No. 20915 (LEXIS), [1996] No. 885617 (N. Dist. Tex. 1996) (WL).

Tilley v. TJX Companies, 212 F.R.D. 43 (Dist. Ct. Mass. 2003a).

Tilley v. TJX Companies, 345 F.3d 34 (1st Cir. 2003b).

In re: Tobacco/Governmental Health Care Costs Litigation, US Courts' Multidistrict Litigation Action No. 1279, Misc. No. 99-213 (Dist. Ct. Pa. 2000).

In re: Tobacco Litigation (Medical Monitoring Cases), 215 W. Va. 476 (Sup. Ct. App. W. Va. 2004).

Tomberlin v. Adolph Coors Co., et al., Case No. 05 CV 545, slip opinion (Cir. Ct. Wisc., Dane County 2006).

Tomplait v. Combustion Engineering, Inc., Civil Case No. 5402 (E. Dist. Tex. 1968).

Toole v. Richardson-Merrell, 251 Cal. App. 2d 689 (Ct. App. Cal., 1st App. Dist., 3rd Div. 1967).

Trustees v. Greenough, 105 U.S. 527 (1881).

United Mine Workers v. Coronado Coal, 259 U.S. 344 (1922).

United Seniors Association v. Philip Morris, Case No. 06-2447 (1st Cir. 2007).

United States v. Carolene Products, 304 U.S. 144 (1938).

United States v. Emerson, Case No. 6:98-CR-103-C (N. Dist. Tex. 1999).

United States v. Emerson, 270 F.3d 203 (5th Cir. 2001) (cert. denied).

United States v. Equitable Trust Co., 283 U.S. 738 (1931).

United States v. Kilgus, 571 F.2d 508 (9th Cir. 1978).

United States v. Philip Morris, Civil Action No. 99-2496 (GK) (D. 2000) (memorandum opinion).

United States v. Philip Morris, Civil Action No. 99-2496 (GK) (D. 2004a) (first amended complaint for damages and injunctive and declaratory relief), http://www.tobacco.org/resources/documents/040224DOJvMO.html.

United States v. Philip Morris, Civil Action No. 99-2496 [GK] (D. 2004b) (final proposed findings of fact).

United States v. Philip Morris, U.S. App. No. 1824 (Cir. Ct. D.C. 2005) (LEXIS).

United States v. Philip Morris, Civil Action No. 99-2496 (GK) (2006a), Parts 1-3 reported at [2006] U.S. Dist. No. 61412; Parts 4-6 reported at [2006] U.S. Dist. No. 63477; Parts 7-11 reported at [2006] U.S. Dist. No. 61413; Parts 12-16 reported at [2006] U.S. Dist. No. 63478; Parts 17-19 reported at [2006] U.S. Dist. No. 61415; Parts 20-22 reported at [2006] U.S. Dist. No. 61416 (LEXIS).

United States v. Philip Morris, Civil Action No. 99-2496 (GK), [2006b] U.S. Dist. No. 57759 (LEXIS) (final judgment and remedial order).

Van Dusen v. Barrack, 376 U.S. 612 (1964).

In re: Vioxx Marketing, Sales Practices and Products Liability Litigation, US Courts' Multidistrict Litigation Action No. 1657 (E. Dist. La. 2007).

In re: Vioxx Products Litigation, US Courts' Multidistrict Litigation Action No. 1657 (E. Dist. La. 2005), http://vioxx.laed.uscourts.gov/.

Walls v. American Tobacco Co., [2000] U.S. Dist. No. 16040 (N. Dist. Okla. 2000) (LEXIS).

In re: Welding Rod Products Liability Litigation, Case No. 1:03-CV-17000, US Courts' Multidistrict Litigation Action no. 1535 (N. Dist. Ohio 2004).

West v. Randall, 29 F.Cas. 718 (1820).

White v. Smith and Wesson, 97 F. Supp. 2d 816 (N. Dist. Ohio 2000).

White et al. v. Mattel Inc., Case No. 07-05366 (C. Dist. Cal. 2007).

Whiteley v. Raybestos-Manhattan Inc., Case No. 303184 (Super. Ct. Cal., San Francisco County 2000).

Williams-Branch ex rel. Estate of Williams v. Philip Morris, Inc., Case No. 9705-03957 (Cir. Ct. Or., Multnomah County 1999).

Wolff v. McDonnell, 418 U.S. 539 (1974).

Wood River Area Dev. Corp. v. Germania Fed. Sav. and Loan Ass'n, 555 N.E.2d 1150 (Ill. App. Ct. 1990).

Wright v. Brooke Group, Ltd., 652 N.W.2d 159 (Sup. Ct. Iowa 2002).

Zahn v. International Paper Co., 414 U.S. 291 (1973).

In re: Zyprexa Products Liability Litigation, US Courts' Multidistrict Litigation Action No. 1596 (E. Div. N.Y. 2004).

General Index

Note: All entries refer to the United States unless indicated as referring to Australia (Aus), Canada (Can), or the United Kingdom (UK)

abatement: definition of, 108-9; problems with, 109-10, 111, 112
aboriginal land rights (Aus), 8, 177, 205n19
absent parties, 14, 30; binding of, 26-27, 29, 31; in litigations, 23, 24, 25
abuse of class action, 68, 84, 113, 155, 187, 212n34
access to justice, 6, 173, 183, 187, 198, 203
Access to the Courts II (Aus), 178
Action on Smoking and Health, 133
activism, judicial, 152, 177; in Australia, 177; in Canada, 2, 187, 188
adjudication, 6, 41, 88, 154, 209n50
adversarial legalism, 7, 153, 157, 199, 227n3
advertising by attorneys, 37
Agent Orange, 39, 50, 55, 212n19
aggregation, 4, 14, 15, 33; in Australia, 183; multi-district, 36; practicality of, 25, 172; procedures for, 227n7
Alabama Supreme Court, 69
Alito, Samuel, 70
Alliance for a Healthier Generation, 138
Alliance for Bio-Integrity, 127-28, 147, 222n16
American Association for Justice (AAJ), 59, 60, 64, 196, 200
American Bar Foundation, 197
American Beverage Association, 138, 149
American Cancer Society, 91
American Chemistry Council, 195
American Heart Association, 138, 141, 149
American Tort Reform Association (ATRA), 64-66, 69-70, 194, 195, 204n1, 212nn33-34, 213n41

American Trial Lawyers Association (ATLA), 60, 91, 200
amici, 9, 10, 81, 195, 209n49
antitrust, 35, 37, 39, 82, 217n6; *Sherman Antitrust Act,* 37
asbestos, 91, 95, 156, 157; in Australia, 181-82, 227n10; in Canada, 45, 174; health issues, 40, 46, 56, 210n1, 211n5; litigation, 38, 39, 41, 42, 63; manufacturer's cover-up, 45; and need for reform, 66; overview of, 44-49; secret settlements and, 63; in South Africa, 169; timeline of, 72-73; in the UK, 164-66
Asbestos Alliance, 48
"attractive nuisance," 137-38, 225n45
Australia: aboriginal land rights, 177; asbestos, 181-82, 227n10; *Access to Courts II,* 178; Australian Law Reform Commission (ALRC), 178, 185; bankruptcy, 182; British influence, 152, 176, 177; class action, defined, 177; common law, 176, 179; constitutional reform, 2, 188; *Credit Act,* 178; due process, 188; *Federal Court of Australia Act (1976),* 177; *Federal Court of Australia Amendment Act (1991),* 178; Federal Court Rules, 4; federal structure, 177; genetically modified foods in, 184; High Court, 8, 177, 178, 179, 180; identical claims, 177; judicial changes, 177; judicial independence, 192; juries, not empanelled, 177; legal reform, 176, 177, 178; legislative reform, 177, 187; loser pays, 177, 180, 188; obesity, 131, 184; opt-in, opt-out, 177, 180, 184, 188; representative litigation, 180, 182-83; rewards, limits

on, 188; Rule IVA, 178, 180; rules of procedure, 199; tobacco litigation, 2, 191; US influence, 177

bankruptcy, 40, 47, 84, 156, 210n51; asbestos and, 63-64; in Australia, 182; Chapter 11 filings, 44, 54; debtor in possession financing and, 64; firearms and, 104
Bankruptcy Code, 63
Banzhaf, John F., III, 130, 133, 135, 193
Barber, Steven, 134-35, 143, 148, 193
Bendectin, 39, 49-53, 211n11
Bernstein, David, 69
"bill of peace," 19, 20
Bill of Rights, Canada, 5
bill of rights issues, 6, 15
blackmail, legal, 156, 159, 168, 227n7
Bloomberg, Michael, 114, 115, 193
Boggio, Andrea, 227n8
Brennan, William, 8, 33, 205n19
Breyer, Stephen, 70, 153, 205n2
British American Tobacco Australia, 182
British High Court, 25
British influence, 152, 170, 176, 177, 182
Brodeur, Paul, 45-46
Bureau of Alcohol, Tobacco and Firearms (ATF), 111-12, 219nn22-23
Bush, George W., 66, 70, 113, 122, 214n10, 214n17, 217n41
Bush, Jeb, 66
Bush Administration: deferred prosecution agreements and, 212n31; firearms and, 105, 115-16, 121; tobacco and, 83, 214n17
Business Roundtable, 195
Buzby, Jean, 125, 221n6

Campaign for a Commercial-Free Childhood, 139
Campaign for Tobacco-Free Kids, 94, 100, 214nn7-8, 217n45
Canada: asbestos, 45, 174; Bill of Rights, 5, 204n14; British influence, 152, 170; Charter of Rights and Freedoms, 2, 171; class action advantages, 173; common law, 175-76; compared to US, 171; constitutional reform, 174, 188; Dalkon Shield and, 170; due process, 188; fees, 171; firearms and, 60, 106, 119, 173; food industry litigation, 175, 176; history of class action, 171, 172; Indian Residential Schools Settlement Agreement, 205; judicial activism, 2, 187, 188; judicial changes, 171, 188; legal reform, 170, 173, 174, 176; leverage, creating, 202;

loser pays, 171; national class action, 4; nuisance and negligence action, 173; Ontario Law Reform Commission (OLRC), 171, 227n4; opt-in, opt-out, 171, 188; Parliamentary Information and Research Service, 131; provincial variations, 171; punitive damages in, 171; *RICO* suit with US, 175; rules of procedure, 199; Supreme Court, 171, 173, 188, 192, 200; tobacco and, 59, 92, 96, 97, 174, 191; Uniform Law Conference, 173
Castano Group, 59, 60, 96, 195; and firearms, 106, 119; and tobacco, 85-87, 92, 216n36
Cato Institute, 64, 195
Center for Claims Resolution (CCR), 47
Center for Disease Control (CDC): food and, 125, 129, 131; tobacco and, 100, 214n6, 214n12, 214n14, 215n20
Center for Indoor Air Research (CIAR), 84
Center for Public Integrity, 205n18
Center for Science in the Public Interest (CSPI), 138-39, 140, 142-43, 146, 196, 226n48, 226n53
Center for Tobacco Research (CTR), 84
Chamber of Commerce (US), 67, 74, 194, 195
Citizens Against Lawsuit Abuse, 64, 212n34
Civil Procedure Rules, 151, 167
Civil Rights Act, 35, 48
civil rights issues, 39, 48, 58; in Canada, 174; development of, 15, 34; legislation, 211n8; litigation, 33, 35, 209n49; organizations, 31
Civil Rules Advisory Committee, 35, 36
class action: abuse of, 155, advantages of, 173; advertising on children's television, 139; as American invention, 154; asbestos and, 47, 63; in Australia, 182-85; in Canada, 4, 171-73, 175, 176, 230n53; as challenge to large institutions, 13; civil rights and, 58; community interests, rather than necessary parties, 26; comparison of US, Canada, Australia, and UK, 159, 188; contemporary, 48; as cost-saving measure, 18; defined, 4, 29, 209n50; development of, 20, 43; employment and, 58; environmental contaminants and, 55-57; in European Union, 154-55, 157; globalization of, 172, 190; growth, 154-55, 198-99, 200; individual rights and, 6; institutional reform and, 48; intellectual property and, 57-58; medical products and,

53-55; monetary damage and, 212n24; multi-district litigation, 173; national class action, 4; pharmaceuticals and, 49-53; political process and policy, 42; regulation of, 187; revised rule 23, 31-32; tobacco and, 59, 85-90, 224n26; unions and, 24-25; winners and losers, 95, 118, 143, 193

Class Action Fairness Act, 66-67, 196, 212n28, 213n37, 213n40

Clinton administration, 104, 119

Clinton, Bill, 11, 82, 104, 108, 118, 138. *See also* William J. Clinton Foundation

Code of Federal Regulations (US), 10

collective litigation, 9, 15, 19, 154, 200, 203; in Australia, 177, 183; in Canada, 188; due process and, 14; in Europe, 158; expenses and, 41; procedural rules and, 39; public policy and, 3, 13, 155; purpose of, 28, 32, 33; in UK, 186

collective rights, 16, 54

Commentaries on Equity Jurisprudence, 20

commercially sponsored litigation, 9

common fund doctrine, 23, 27-28, 163

common law: of associations, 27; in Australia, 176, 179; in Canada, 175-76; damages and due process, 65, 68; discrimination, 8; doctrine, 65; international law and, 205n19; limits on damages and, 68; market and, 179; nuisance and, 109, 111, 130; on product liability, 124, 134, 135; as tradition, 147, 160, 169, 186, 199; in UK, 160, 169, 186

Commonsense Consumption Act, 137

community of interests, 23, 25, 26, 29

comparison of countries, 152, 157, 159. *See also* individual countries

Consolidation Appropriations Act of 2005, 112, 114, 219n23

constitutional reform, worldwide, 147, 152

Constitutional Reform Act (2005) (UK), 169, 204n3, 229n33

Consumer Fraud and Deceptive Business Practice Act, 88, 89

Consumer Product Safety Commission, 125

Consumer Protection Act (UK), 5

Coordinating Committee for Multi-District Litigation, 37

corporate misconduct, global implications, 165

Council for Tobacco Research, 82, 98

Courts and Legal Services Act, 168

Credit Act (1984) (Aus), 178

Dalkon Shield, 39, 53, 54, 55, 59; in Canada, 170

Daynard, Richard, 133, 138, 224n29

defendant classes, 57

defendants' bar, 53, 64, 70, 200, 202

defensive legislation, 64

deferred prosecution agreements, 212n31

degree of reprehensibility, 68

Department of Agriculture, 128, 129

Department of Housing and Urban Development (HUD), 104, 119, 120

Department of Justice: Canada, 10; US, 78, 83, 92, 99, 115, 215n23

Department of Labor, 48, 56

desegregation litigation, 38, 48, 208n41

Dickerson, Earl B., 31

Dickson, Brice, 2, 3, 6, 152, 169, 199, 233n10

dietary guidelines in schools, 138, 149, 225n44

diethylstilbestrol (DES), 39, 49, 165, 211n9

Douglas, William O., 32, 33, 34

due process, 3, 5, 188, 190, 191; basic to US law, 71; conflict with group leverage, 13; constitutional provision, 34, 48; defined, 5, 19; fairness, 5; Fourteenth Amendment, 34; group rights vs, 3, 13, 54, 156, 205n2; individual and collective rights, 16, 17, 30-31, 32, 54, 188; issues with, 41, 203; modern analysis, 18; punitive damages, 68, 100, 214n5; tradition, 205n2. *See also* equity; opt-in, opt-out; *Rule 23* of the *Federal Rules of Civil Procedure*

Eisen controversy, 34, 35, 36

employment litigation, 58

England, medieval, 155, 160

English Court of Appeals, 162

entrepreneurial lawyering, 1, 159, 168, 203

Environmental Assessment Act (CAN), 175

environmental contaminants litigation, 35, 55-57

Environmental Management and Protection Act (CAN), 175

Environmental Protection Agency (EPA), 35, 46, 73, 128, 147, 221n4

Epp, Charles, 168, 203, 233n10, 233n14

Epstein, Lee, 9, 113, 220n26

equity, 20-22; chancery courts (UK), 19, 160, 163; court of, 24; Federal Rule 23, 25-26, 48

Erichson, Howard, 28, 59, 106, 118

Europe: asbestos issues, 164, consumer protection legislation, 159; contrasted to US and Canada, 159; entrepreneurial lawyering, 159; injunctive relief, 159

European Commission, 158, 159
European Convention of Human Rights, 166
European Court of Human Rights, 153
European Parliament and Council, 158
European Union (EU), 154, 157, 159-60, 197
Evidence Rule 403, 52
excessive awards, 68, 90

factionalism, as political concern, 15
Fairness in Asbestos Injury Resolution Act (2006) (FAIR Act), 48, 73
fast food litigation, 123, 129, 131, 132
Federal Cigarette Labeling and Advertising Act of 1965, 75
Federal Communications Commission (FCC), 140
Federal Court of Australia Act (1976), 177
Federal Court of Australia Amendment Act (1991), 178
Federal Court Rules (Aus), 4
Federal Equity Rule 48, 23, 24, 25, 26
Federal Rules of Civil Procedure, 15, 68, 74. *See also Rule 23* of the *Federal Rules of Civil Procedure*
Federal Rules of Evidence (FRE), 52, 68
federal structure, 154; of Australia, 177, 197; of Canada, 197; of the UK, 160
Federal Trade Commission (FTC), 89
fees: comparable rules in the UK, Australia, and Canada, 1-2; contingency, 168; court-awarded, 171; flexible, 1; loser pays, 28, 163; system of, 157
Fifth Amendment, takings clause, 15
firearms: industry relief acts, 66, 113; litigation timeline, 119-22; manufacturers and litigation, 60, 62, 101-3; manufacturers pressured by government, 104-5; sellers and litigation, 104; tracing, 23, 219n22; violence, 106, 117
food: inspection, 125; law firms dealing with, 221n9; litigation history, 123, 124; litigation timeline, 147-50; regulatory acts and agencies, 124, 221n4; safety, 157
Food and Drug Act, 123
Food and Drug Administration (FDA), 49-51, 78, 126, 129, 147
forum non conveniens, 166
forum shopping, 61-62, 67, 111; international, 202
Fourteenth Amendment, due process clause, 29, 30, 34, 68
"free rider," 28, 41
Friedman, Lawrence, 37, 197
Friends of the Earth International, 127, 201, 222n12

Fuller, Lon, 6

Galanter, Marc, 9, 62, 64, 71, 146, 192
Garth, Bryant, 15, 41, 157
Gauthier, Wendell, 59, 85, 97, 106, 118, 193
Gedid, John, 22, 24, 26, 29
genetically engineered foods (GE), 126, 127, 128-29
genetically modified foods (GM), 126-27, 128, 158, 175-76; in Australia, 184; buffer crops and, 223nn18-19; politics and, 222n13; religion and, 222n16
Ginsburg, Ruth Bader, 47, 70, 73, 153
Giuliani, Rudy, 110, 120, 193
global: economy, 187, 190; legal reform, 155, 200; legal system, 152, 202, 203; markets, growth of, 53, 125, 160; misconduct issues, 165; trends, 60, 126, 154, 160
globalization: class action and, 172, 190; constitutional change and, 147; defined, 152; early litigation and, 190; expansion of legal authority and, 3; food and, 125, 160, 221n5; human rights and, 152, 153, 205; information technology and, 152; intellectual property and, 152; judicial, 147, 152-53; law and, 152, 202, 203; litigation of, 5; need for legal reform, 152; political economy and, 4, 155, 197-99; risk and retribution, 4; transnational network of legal advocates and, 147; transportation and, 152
Goldsworthy, Jeffrey, 153, 227n2
group: development, 14, 17; dynamics, 33-34; leverage and due process, 31; litigation reform, 190; politics, 7; rights, 3; trends, 160. *See also* class action; mass tort
Group Litigation Order (GLO) (UK), 167-68, 169, 186, 188
guns. *See* firearms

Haltom, William, 42, 49, 64, 85, 204n1, 205n20, 206n7, 224n30
Hansberry, Lorraine, 31, 33
Harlan, John Marshall, 28, 34
Harper, Stephen, 205n19
"haves and have-nots," 9, 42, 62, 181, 189, 192, 200. *See also* repeat players; winners and losers
Hazard, Geoffrey, 22, 24, 26, 29, 31, 207n17
Health Survey for England, 131
Heinz, John P., 60, 70
Hensler, Deborah R., 3, 4, 10, 28, 35, 49, 62
Hirsch, Samuel, 135, 193

Hirschl, Ran, 3, 5, 15, 152, 187, 199
historical litigation, 13, 42, 185, 188,
    207n31, 208n42; Australia, 177; UK,
    160, 198
Hodges, Christopher, 158, 168, 227n6
House of Lords (UK), 27
Houston, Charles, 33
human rights, 152, 153, 201, 202, 205n19
"hybrid" class, 29, 33

"identical interest" (UK), 163
individual and collective justice or
    conflict, 42
individual justice, 188; sacrificed for
    regulatory and policy issues, 41. *See also*
    due process
individual rights, 15, 41, 42, 43, 49; class
    action and, 6, 190; constitutional change
    and, 192; as foundation of social action
    and legal thought, 16; as law, 5
individualism, as political concern, 15
information technology and globalization,
    152
injunctive relief, 107-8, 119, 159, 219n21,
    219n24
intellectual property: globalization, 152;
    litigation, 57-58
interest groups and politics, 3, 209n49
international: defence groups, 202; law,
    152, 205; litigation, 169, 175; Obesity
    Task Force, 131; organizations, 27, 61,
    127, 201; political development, 151-60,
    197; publicity, 141, 145
iron triangles, 74, 213n2

Jackson, Robert, 7
Johns-Manville, 45, 63, 72, 210n2
judges, 4, 7, 8, 11, 16, 26; in Australia,
    177, 182, 187; in Canada, 186, 187;
    comparison of, 153, 185, 187, 189, 199,
    200; decision-making latitude of, 167,
    168, 169, 172; as gatekeepers, 52, 68;
    globalization and, 147, 152, 202, 203;
    issues facing, 13, 23, 37, 39, 43, 191;
    reform and, 64, 153, 154; in UK, 18,
    152, 169, 186, 190
judicial: activism, 2, 152, 177, 187, 188;
    authority in governing regime, 2; black-
    mail, 156; ethics, 8; institutions, 192;
    power from constitutional reform, 3. *See
    also* individual countries
Judicial Panel on Multi-District Litigation
    (JPML), 4, 37
justice, individual and collective, 41-43

Kagan, Robert, 7, 153, 154, 157, 199

Kairys, David, 101, 105, 106, 107, 218n7
Kalven, Harry, 29, 31, 33, 35, 60, 155, 191
Kennedy, Anthony, 153
Kerr-McGee, 1
Kessler, Gladys, 83-84
"kidnapped rider" problem, 41
Kritzer, Herbert, 34, 228n13

labour legislation, 29
Laumann, Edward O., 60, 70
Law Reform Commission of Ireland, 156
lawsuits, classes of, 29-32, 33, 35-37
legal aid: public, 89, 168; European, 158
Legal Defense and Education Fund (LDEF),
    33, 34
legal fees: and class litigation, 27;
    distribution of, 28
legal reform, 66, 151, 181; in Australia,
    176, 177, 178; in Canada, 170, 172-73,
    174, 176; demand for, globally, 152; in
    UK, 163-64, 168, 187
legal research exchange, fee based, 60
legal system, criticism of, 156-57
legislature and interest groups, 3, 8
liability: as cause for change, 10; shield
    laws, 116, 144, 196
litigation: as adjustment of power, 7;
    categories of class, 26; Chamber of
    Commerce, 67; civil rights, 29-34;
    coalitions, 10, 194; collective, 33-34;
    comparison, 133, 144; co-operative,
    199-202; as court-centred strategy, 2;
    de-emphasized, 154; defined, 213n49; as
    demand for definition of policies, 7; as
    enforcement of activity, 7; environment-
    al, 35; 55-57; fast food, 123; future of
    multi-party, 148, 167; impact on health,
    93; individual compared to group, 23;
    intellectual property, 57-58; as legal and
    political, 2, 3, 7, 8, 92-95, 151, 193;
    medical products, 53-55; mimics
    legislative process, 71; pharmaceutical,
    49-53, 198; as regulation, 11, 92, 93, 117,
    118, 144, 159, 195; securities, 57; tobacco,
    59, 74-77, 167, 193, 198; workplace
    safety, 167, 198
lobbying: alternative routes of, 8; groups,
    118; for specific justices, 70
lobbyists, prohibited from direct encoun-
    ters with judges, 8
"loser pays," 171, 158, 163, 188, 208n32

Macnaghten, Lord, 25, 161-62
Madison, James, 15
"market share" of liability, 49
Marshall, Thurgood, 33, 208

mass tort, 38, 39, 44; benefits of, 46; class action, 49; defined, 3: demands on US legal system, 36; environmental, 55-57; history of, 11; medical, 53-55; as power, 6; securities actions, 57; subrogation, 78, 104. *See also* strategy and politics of mass torts

Master Settlement Agreement (MSA): as agreement between big tobacco and states, 78-80; benefits to big tobacco, 80, 81, 82; cases leading to, 87; costs to big tobacco, 194, 195, 196; payoffs to big tobacco, 146; as success of big tobacco, 92-93; terms of, 98

McCann, Michael, 42, 64, 85, 143, 146, 204n1, 206n7, 224n30

McDonald's, 132-34, 135-37, 139, 141-42; apology, 224n27; coffee lady, 9, 204n1, 205n20

Meat Inspection Act, 123

media, 5, 42, 82, 194, 204n1; focus of, 8, 9, 69-70, 153; food industry and, 139, 141, 145

medical: mass screenings to demonstrate injury, 56; products litigation, 38, 53-55

Medical Care Recovery Act (MCRA), 82-83

Medicare Secondary Payer Provisions (MSP), 82-83, 91, 92

Memorandum Opinion of the Attorney General, 115

Merrell Dow, 50-53, 68, 211n10

Methodist Episcopal Church, 23-24

misconduct, sanctions for, 68

misuse of lawful products, 109, 110

monetary rewards compared to harm done, 68

Moore, Mike, 76, 79, 92, 93, 97

moot-court arguments, 67

'movement' politics, theory of, 92

multi-district aggregation, 36

Multi-District Litigation (MDL), 4, 5, 36-39; *Act of 1968,* 37, 74; asbestos, 47; Canada, 173; current issues, 48-49; as law, 74; pharmaceuticals, 51; social issues and, 40-41

multi-party actions: demand for, 155; as means of creating change, 151

Nader, Ralph, 35, 130

National Association for the Advancement of Colored People (NAACP), 7, 31, 33, 62, 111-12, 120, 121; Legal Defense and Education Fund, 31; "necessary party" rule, 18-19, 20

National Association of Manufacturers, 195

national class action, Canada, 4

National Environmental Policy Act, 35, 128, 209n49

National Obesity Task Force (Aus), 184, 198

National Restaurant Association, 131, 137, 141, 225n41

National Rifle Association (NRA): lawsuits challenging gun laws, 117; money and membership of, 107, 195; as powerful interest group, 118, 194; protective legislation efforts, 66, 113, 193

National Shooting Sports Foundation, 113

National Spinal Cord Injury Association, 105

negligence, 37, 54, 86, 98, 99; defined, 218n18, 220n29; in firearm sales, 103, 105, 108, 109, 110; in marketing, 102, 108, 110

Nelson, Samuel, 24

New England Journal of Medicine, 4

New York Penal Law, 114

non-opt-out, 51, 90

North American Asbestos Corporation (NAAC), 166

notification process, 19, 36, 86, 156, 175, 184

nuisance: abatement and negligence, 105, 108, 109, 110; attractive, 137-38, 225n45; defined, 114; private, 109, 223n21; public, 22, 108-9, 111, 130, 148

nutrition labeling, 142-43

obesity, 130, 140, 184-85; fast food and, 132-34; worldwide statistics, 131

O'Brien, David, 3, 6, 152, 199

Occupational Health and Safety Administration (OSHA), 46, 72

one-shotters. *See* repeat players

online legal outreach, 61, 126

Ontario Law Reform Commission (OLRC), 171, 227n4

opt-in, opt-out: in Australia, 177, 180, 184, 188; in Canada, 171, 188; choices for individuals and organizations, 14, 17; class concerns and, 32, 36; fairness and, 191; limitations on, 51, 210n51; merits, 156; protection provided, 40, 49; rules, old and new, 49; universal declaration of human rights and, 188

personal responsibility, 144, 146

Personal Responsibility in Food Consumption Act, 137

Pharmaceutical Research and Manufacturers of America, 195

pharmaceuticals, 49-53, 167
Philip Morris, 88-92, 98-100, 144, 145,
   197; in Australia, 182-83; earnings of,
   106, 194; growth strategy of, 94-95;
   litigation, 68, 76, 77, 81-85, lobbying,
   195; product liability laws, 107
Pierce, Jason, 177, 187, 199, 232n88,
   233n10
plaintiffs' bar, 39, 59, 60, 70, 146, 156,
   189, 192
politics: advocacy, 64; changed by
   litigation, 3; culture, 154, 155; expectations of judicial institutions, 192;
   expediency, 6; in gun control, 219n24;
   issues and torts, 38; legal dynamics and,
   8; litigation compared with, 6; as policy,
   10; as power, 6, 71
pre-trial issues, 37-38
prison reform, class action, 48
"private attorneys general," 32, 60, 159,
   191
product liability, 37, 49, 107, 108-9,
   124-25
Protection of Lawful Commerce in Arms Act
   (PLCAA), 113, 114, 122
public policy, 203; influenced by Hansberry, 3
punitive damage assessment, 68

*R*acketeer Influenced and Corrupt Organizations Act (RICO), 82, 83, 175
ratio between harm done and monetary
   award, 68
reform, 11, 66; demand for, 152, 156;
   institutional, 48; legislation, as access to
   justice, 6, 146, 152, 158; prison, 48; tort,
   44, 64-65, 67, 68-69, 71; in welfare, 48
regulatory: activity following Great
   Depression, 31; effectiveness, 10;
   failures, 157; influence, 155; intent of
   food litigation, 144; litigation, 32, 159
Rehnquist, William, 206, 233
repeat players, 9, 10, 75, 77, 80, 189. *See
   also* "haves and have-nots"; winners and
   losers
representative litigation, 15, 17, 19, 159; in
   UK, 163, 177; in Australia, 180, 182-83
res judicata, 29, 30
Restatement (Second) of Torts, 108, 109,
   218n14
Roberts, John, 70
Rosenberg, Gerald, 1, 11, 42, 191, 192
Rosenfield, Maurice, 29, 31, 33, 35, 60,
   151, 155, 191
Rule 48. *See* Federal Equity Rule 48
Rule IVA (Aus), 178, 180, 181

Rule 10 (1873 England), 170
Rule 23 of the *Federal Rules of Civil
   Procedure:* as adopted and readopted, 15,
   28-29, 36, 42; amended, 35; asbestos
   litigation and, 47; as basis for mass tort
   action, 39-40; criticism and confusion
   about, 33; damages and settlements, 41,
   58; defendant classes, 57, 58; foreign
   interest in, 170, 171, 180, 197, 227n4;
   group action categories, 28-29, 33, 35;
   race and, 29-32, 33, 35; tobacco litigation
   and, 85. *See also* equity; opt-in, opt-out
Russell, Peter, 3, 6, 8, 152, 177, 199

sanctions for comparable misconduct, 68
Sawer, Geoffrey, 233n10
Scalia, Antonin, 116, 233n15
Schattschneider, E.E., 8
Scheingold, Stuart, 60, 233n14
Schlosser, Eric, 136
school desegregation, class action, 38, 48
Schuck, Peter, 39, 42, 55, 156
Second Amendment, 114, 115-17
second-hand smoke litigations, 85
secret: court decisions, 212n30; deferred
   prosecution agreements, 212n31;
   settlements, 45, 63
securities litigation, 39
Selikoff, Irving, 46
separation of powers doctrine, 11
Shapiro, Martin, 152, 190, 191, 232n1
Sherman Antitrust Act, 37
shield laws, 116, 144, 146, 196
Skeel, David, 63
Slaughter, Anne-Marie, 147, 152, 153, 202
Smith and Wesson, 104-7
social: expectations of judicial institutions,
   192; reform, 11
sociological issues and tort cases, 38
Souter, David, 44, 205n2, 232n9
Sowle, Stephen, 22, 24, 26, 29
Specter, Arlen, 48, 73
"spurious" class, 29, 31, 32
Spurlock, Morgan, 136
StarLink, 128, 129, 147, 148
Stone, Harlan, 30, 209n43
Stone Sweet, Alec, 6, 7, 152, 199
Story, Joseph, 20-23, 24, 25, 41, 199
strategy and politics of mass torts:
   bankruptcy, 63, 64; choose defendants,
   62, 63; form groups and exchange
   information, 59-60; forum shopping,
   61-62; judge selection, 69-70; legal
   precedents and judicial placement, 67;
   lobby for protective legislation, 64;
   outreach and advertising, 60-61;

population and prestige, 70-71; secret
settlements, 63
subject-specific websites, 61
subrogation: defined, 214n9; in mass
torts, 78, 104
Supreme Court Act (Aus), 178, 180
Supreme Court of Canada, 171, 173, 176,
187, 192, 200
Supreme Court of India, 153
Supreme Court of Judicature Act (Can), 170
Supreme Court of the United Kingdom, 2,
169, 186
Supreme Court of the United States, 34,
37, 38, 116, 153; and asbestos, 41, 47,
91; Constitution and, 115, 116; on
expert scientific data, 52; fee structure
and, 27, 28, 199; history of, 21, 34, 67,
186, 208n42; procedures of, 23, 26;
punitive damages and, 90, 194, 213n43;
on tobacco, 75, 77
Sweet, Robert, 135-36

Taco Bell, 128-30, 142
Taft, William Howard, 27
Tate, C. Neal, 3, 6, 152, 199
taxpayer litigation, 26
theory of movement politics, 92
theory of tort law, 37
Thomas, Clarence, 233n15
tobacco: foreign suits with American
companies, 175; industry capitulations,
79-80; interest groups (Aus), 74, 77,
82, 84, 98, 182; legislation, 174; light
cigarettes, 81, 84, 88, 89, 215n22;
litigation, 59, 75-78, 167, 193, 194;
litigation timeline, 96-100; partnering
with government, 80
Tocqueville, Alexis de, 11, 15
tort law, theory of, 37
tort reform, 64, 65, 67, 69, 71
trace data, 111, 112, 122
Trans Fat Task Force (Can), 176
trans fats, 140-42, 176
transgenic plants and animals, 126, 127
transnational: issues, 160; litigation, 202
tripartite division, 33; eliminated, 35
"true" actions, 29

Uniform Firearms Act, 110
unions, 24, 27
United Kingdom: asbestos, 164-66;
chancery courts, 19, 160, 163; *Civil
Procedures Rule,* 151, 167; class action

rules, 163; common law, 160, 169, 186;
compared to US, 158; conditional fee
agreement, 158; constitutional reform,
188; *Constitutional Reform Act,* 169;
Consumer Protection Act, 5; due process,
188; early development of group
litigation, 17-20; fees in, 28, 158, 168,
186; firearm litigation, 169; food
industry changes, 158; group litigation
order (GLO), 167-68, 169, 186, 188;
history of group-based litigation, 160;
House of Commons, 158, 165, 229n36;
House of Lords, 27, 160, 161, 165;
interests and grievances, 162, 163;
judicial independence, 192; Law Society
of England and Wales, 168; legal aid,
158; legal reform, 163-64, 168, 187;
limitations of multi-party actions, 151;
loser pays, 158, 163; mad cow disease,
157; medieval courts, 155, 160; obesity
statistics, 131; opt-in, 168, 186, 188;
regulatory system, 164, 186; representative action, 161, 162, 163, 177; rules of
procedure, 199; same interest clause,
151; tobacco litigation, 167, 168, 191
United Seniors Association, 91
Universal Declaration of Human Rights, 15,
188

Vallinder, Torbjorn, 3, 6, 152, 199
Viscusi, W. Kip, 93

Warren, Earl, 33, 35, 37, 207
Washington Legal Foundation, 185
Weinstein, Jack, 13, 20, 36, 38; firearm
litigation and, 62, 111, 112, 114, 115;
food litigation and, 102; tobacco
litigation and, 90-91, 99
welfare reform, class action, 48
whistle-blowers, 2
White, Byron, 28
William J. Clinton Foundation, 138,
225n44
winners and losers, 3, 6, 7-10, 95-96,
143-44, 193-94. *See also* "haves and
have-nots"; repeat players
women's rights, class action, 48
workplace safety litigation, 167

Yeazell, Stephen, 13, 34, 205n1; and Anglo-
American law, 16, 17; scope of litigation,
27; on Justice Story, 23, 207n17
Yum! Brands, 142, 149, 223n25, 226n54

Case Index

Australia

A. and J. Partitions Pty. Ltd. v. Jolly (1993), 231n34

Australian Federation of Consumer Organizations Inc. v. Tobacco Institute of Australia Ltd. (1991), 182

Bright v. Femcare (1999), 183

Bright v. Femcare Ltd. (2002), 181

Butler v. Kraft Foods Ltd. (1997), 183, 184

Carnie v. Esanda (1995), 179, 231n72, 233n11

Carnie v. Esanda (1996), 180

Courtney v. Medtel (2003), 183

CSR Ltd. v. Young (1998), 231n76

Darcy v. Medtel (2001), 183

Dowdell v. Knispel Fruit Juices Pty Ltd. (2003), 183, 184

Esanda Finance Corporation Ltd v. Carnie (1992), 178

Femcare Ltd. v. Bright (2000), 180

Graham Barclay Oysters v. Ryan (2000), 183

Mabo v. Queensland (No. 2) (1992), 8, 177

Marino v. Esanda Ltd. (1986), 178

McCabe v. British American Tobacco Australia Services Ltd. (2002), 182

McMullin v. ICI Australia Operations Pty Ltd. (1996), 183

McMullin v. ICI Australia Operations Pty Ltd. (1997), 183-84, 232n87

Mobil Oil Australia Pty. Ltd. v. Victoria (2002), 180

Nixon v. Philip Morris (Australia) Ltd. (1999), 182, 183

Payne v. Young (1981), 178

Philip Morris (Australia) v. Nixon (2000), 182

Pilmer v. McPherson's Limited (1985), 231n77

Sharp v. Port Kembla RSL Club (2001), 231n80

Tobacco Control Coalition Inc. v. Philip Morris (Australia) Ltd. (2000), 231n81

Wong v. Silkfield Pty. Ltd. (1999), 180

Zentahope Pty. Ltd. v. Bellotti (1992), 231n74

Canada

Blais v. Imperial Tobacco (2005), 174

Bouchanskaia v. Bayer Inc. (2003), 230n51

British Columbia v. Imperial Tobacco (2003), 174

British Columbia v. Imperial Tobacco Canada Ltd. (2005), 174

Caputo v. Imperial Tobacco Ltd. (1997), 174

Carom v. Bre-x Minerals Ltd. (1999), 230n52

Coleman v. Bayer Inc. (2004), 230n51

Comité de citoyens et d'action municipale de St-Césaire Inc. v. Ville de St-Césaire (1985), 229n41

Dabbs v. Sun Life Assurance Co. of Canada (1998), 229n46

Dufour v. Bayer Inc. (2004), 230

G.M. (Canada) v. Naken (1983), 229n43

Hoffman v. Monsanto (2005), 175-76

Hoffman v. Monsanto (2006), 176

Hoffman v. Monsanto (2007), 176

Hoffman v. Monsanto Canada and Bayer Cropscience, Inc. (2005), 222n13, 223n21

Hollick v. Toronto (City) (2001), 172, 173

JTI-Macdonald Corp. v. British Columbia (2000), 174

Knight v. Imperial Tobacco (2005), 230n53

Lamb v. Bayer Inc. (2003), 230n51

Létourneau v. Imperial Tobacco (2005), 174

McKrow v. Manufacturers Life Ins. Co. (1998), 229n46

Naken v. General Motors of Canada Ltd.
(1979), 170
Naken v. General Motors of Canada Ltd.
(1983), 170, 172, 178, 200, 229n48
Nantais v. Telectronics Proprietary Ltd.
(1995), 230n52
Nault v. Canadian Consumer Co. Ltd.
(1981), 229n41
Pardy v. Bayer Inc. (2003), 230n51
Parsons v. Canadian Red Cross Society
(1999), 171
Parsons v. McDonalds (2005), 230n52,
229n46
Ragoonanan v. Imperial Tobacco (2000),
230n53
Rumley v. British Columbia (2001), 172
Serwaczek v. Medical Engineering Corp.
(1996), 229n46
*Syndicat National des Employés de l'Hôpital
St-Ferdinand c. Québec (Curateur Public)*
(1994), 229n42
Tremaine v. A.H. Robins Canada Inc. (1990),
170
Walls v. Bayer Inc. (2005), 230n51
*Western Canadian Shopping Centres Inc. v.
Dutton* (2001), 172, 198, 208n40,
228n16, 230n50
Wheadon v. Bayer Inc. (2004), 230n51

United Kingdom
AB v. John Wyeth and Brothers Ltd (1993),
167
Adair v. New River Co. (1805), 161, 228n15
Adams v. Cape Industries PLC (1990), 166
*Adams and Others v. Cape Industries PLC
and Anor* (1991), 166
Anns v. Merton London Borough Council
(1978), 230n59
*Bank of America National Trust and Savings
Association v. Taylor* (1992), 164
Barker v. Corus (2006), 165
Bedford v. Ellis (1901), 25, 161, 162, 179,
228n18
Bogle v. McDonalds Restaurants Limited
(2002), 205n2
Brown v. Vermuden (1676), 206n15
Chancey v. May (1722), 207n16
Cockburn v. Thompson (1809), 161
Davies v. Eli Lilly (1987), 228n22, 233n11
Discart v. Otes (1914), 18
E.M.I. Records v. Riley (1981), 164
Fairchild v. Glenhaven Funeral Services Ltd.
(2002a), 165
Fairchild v. Glenhaven Funeral Services Ltd.
(2002b), 165

Fletcher v. Rylands (1865), 210n55
Foster v. Roussel Laboratories Ltd. (1997),
228n22
*Griffiths and Others v. British Coal Corpora-
tion* (1998), 228n23
Hitchens v. Congreve (1828), 207n16
Hodgson v. Imperial Tobacco Ltd. (1998), 8,
167, 168, 228n24, 228n30
*Hodgson and Ors v. Imperial Tobacco Ltd.
and Gallaher Group PLC* (1999a), 168
Hodgson and Ors v. Imperial Tobacco Ltd.
(1999b), 228n30
*Irish Shipping Ltd. v. Commercial Union
Assurance Co. (The Irish Rowan)* (1991),
164
Jackson v. Attorney General (2005), 169, 186
Loveday v. Renton (1990), 228n22
Lubbe v. Cape PLC (2000a), 165-66, 228n11
Lubbe v. Cape PLC. (2000b), 166, 167
M. Michael Furriers Ltd v. Askew (1983),
228n20
Markt and Co. v. Knight Steamship Co.
(1910), 25, 151, 177, 179, 186, 191,
207n24
*Martin, Rector of Barkway v. Parishioners of
Nuthamstead* (1199), 17, 206n12, 232n3
McTear's Executrix v. Imperial Tobacco Ltd.
(2005), 228n31
National Bank of Greece SA v. RM Outhwaite
(2001), 164
In re: Pinochet (1998), 232n87
Prudential Assurance v. Newman Industries
(1981), 163, 228n20
*R. v. Bow Street Metropolitan Stipendiary
Magistrate, Ex parte Pinochet Ugarte
(No. 2)* (1999), 232n87
Roswell v. Vaughn (1606), 124
Smith Kline and French Lab. Ltd. v. Bloch
(1983), 157
*Taff Vale Railway Co. v. Amalgamated
Society of Railway Servants* (1901), 27,
207n29, 228n18
Wallworth v. Holt (1841), 160
*Ward v. Newalls Insulation Co. and Cape
Contracts Ltd.* (1998), 157

United States
*A.D. Bedell Wholesale Company, Inc. v.
Philip Morris, Inc.* (2000), 82
*In re: "Agent Orange" Product Liability
Litigation* (1983), 55
*In re: "Agent Orange" Product Liability
Litigation* (1984), 50
In re: A.H. Robins Company, Inc. (1988), 54
In re: A.H. Robins Company, Inc. (1989), 53

Aksamit v. Brown and Williamson Tobacco Corp. (2000), 216n27

Allen v. R.J. Reynolds Tobacco Company (2003), 77, 99

Alliance for Bio-Integrity v. Shalala (2000), 128, 147

Altria Group v. Good (2008), 215

Alyeska Pipeline Co. v. Wilderness Society (1975), 28

Ambrosio v. Carter's Country (2000), 103

Amchem Products v. Windsor (1997), 41, 47, 73

American Steel and Wire Co. v. Wire Drawers' and Die Makers' Unions (1898), 24, 208n34

Anderson v. Bryco Arms Corp. (2000), 102

Anderson v. Fortune Brands Inc. (2000), 76, 98

In re: Application of Brown and Williamson Tobacco Corporation v. Stanley M. Chesley (2004), 87, 98

Arcambel v. Wiseman (1796), 28, 199

Arch v. American Tobacco Company (1997), 216n35

In re: Asbestos Litigation (1998), 73

Bacon v. Robertson (1855), 228n16

Badillo v. American Tobacco Co. (2001), 216n27

Baker v. Smith and Wesson Corp. (2002), 219n20

Barber v. McDonald's (2002), 135, 148, 195, 197

Barker v. Lull Engineering (1978), 210n56

Barnes v. American Tobacco Co. (1999), 216n27

Barreras Ruiz v. American Tobacco Co. (1998), 216n27

Baskins v. United Mine Workers (1921), 207n28

Bates v. State Bar of Arizona (1977), 37, 60

In re: Baycol Products Liability Litigation (2004), 53

Beatty v. Kurtz (1829), 21, 207nn18-19

Bender v. Colt Industries, Inc. (1974), 217n1

Bichler v. Eli Lilly and Company (1982), 49, 50

Block v. McDonald's (2002), 134, 148

Blum v. Merrell Dow Pharmaceutical, Inc. (1997), 53

BMW of North America v. Gore (1996), 68, 90

Bogle v. McDonalds Restaurants Limited (2002), 205n20

Bolling v. Sharpe (1954), 209n45

Borel v. Fibreboard Paper Products Corporation (1973), 45, 72

Boston v. Smith & Wesson Corp. (1999), 120

Boston v. Smith and Wesson (2000), 219n20

Bowling v. Pfizer, Inc. (1996), 55

Broin v. Philip Morris (1994), 85

Brown v. Board of Education (1954), 7, 34, 48, 208n41, 209n45

Brown and Williamson v. U.S. FDA (1998), 78

Bullock v. Philip Morris (2002), 76, 99, 100

Burke v. Kleiman (1934), 30, 208n36

Camden v. Beretta (1999), 120

Camden County Board of Chosen Freeholders v. Beretta U.S.A. Corp. (2001), 120, 219n20

Castano v. American Tobacco Company (1995), 86

Castano v. American Tobacco Company (1996), 86, 87, 97, 156, 216n27

Central Railroad and Banking Co. v. Pettus (1885), 28

Chamberlain v. American Tobacco Co. (1999), 216n27

Chicago v. Beretta (1998), 106, 108, 119, 218n9

Chicago v. Beretta (2000), 108

Chicago v. Beretta (2002), 109, 218n14, 218n17

Chicago v. Beretta U.S.A. (2004), 108, 121

Cincinnati v. Beretta (1999), 120

Cincinnati v. Beretta USA Corp (2000), 219n20

Cipollone v. Liggett Group, Inc. (1988), 75

Cipollone v. Liggett Group (1992), 8, 75, 97, 167

City of Atlanta v. Smith & Wesson Corp. (2001), 120

City of Camden v. Beretta U.S.A. Corp (2003), 219n20

City of New York v. Beretta USA (2008), 122

Clark v. Paul Gray, Inc. (1939), 36

Clay v. American Tobacco Co. (1999), 216n27

Cobb v. Insured Lloyds (1980), 217n1

Collins v. Anthem Health Plans, Inc. (2003), 232n9

Conrad Johnson et al. v. Bull's Eye Shooter Supply (2003), 103

CSPI v. Burger King Corp. (2008), 142, 150

Cutler v. 65 Security Plan (1993), 210n53

Daubert v. Merrell Dow Pharmaceuticals, Inc. (1989), 52

Daubert v. Merrell Dow Pharmaceuticals, Inc. (1993), 52, 68

Daubert v. Merrell Dow Pharmaceuticals, Inc. (1995), 53

Delahanty v. Hinckley (1992), 217n2

DeLoach v. Philip Morris (2003), 82

Detroit and Wayne County, MI v. Arms Technology, Inc. (2003), 219n20
In re: Diet Drugs (2004), 53
Dillon v. Legg (1968), 210
District of Columbia v. Beretta (2004), 111, 120, 219n20
District of Columbia v. Heller (2008), 116, 122
Dix v. Beretta U.S.A. Corp. (2000), 102, 119
Dothard v. Rawlinson (1977), 48
Dukes v. Wal-Mart Stores, Inc. (2004), 58, 211n8
Dukes v. Wal-Mart, Inc. (2007), 211n8
Eisen v. Carlisle and Jacquelin (1974), 33, 34, 35, 36, 42
Eisenberg v. Anheuser-Busch, Inc. (2006), 225n45
Eiser v. Brown and Williamson (2003), 77, 99
Emig v. American Tobacco Co. (1998), 216n45
Engle v. Liggett Group (2006), 88, 99
Engle v. R.J. Reynolds Tobacco Co. (1996), 97
In re: Ephedra Products Liability Litigation (2004), 211n14
Escola v. Coca Cola Bottling Company (1944), 125
Estate of Pascal Charlot v. Bushmaster Firearms, Inc. (2003), 103
Exxon Shipping Company v. Baker (2008), 68
In re: "Factor VIII or IX Concentrate Blood Products" Products Liability Litigation (1993), 55
FDA v. Brown and Williamson (2000), 98
Ferens v. John Deere Co. (1990), 62
Fettke v. McDonald's Corp. (2004), 141, 149
In re: Firearm Cases (2005), 219n20
Fischer v. Johns-Manville (1986), 45, 63
Fleischmann Distilling Corp. v. Maier Brewing Co. (1967), 207n31
Friend v. Childs Dining Hall Co. (1918), 124
Frye v. United States (1923), 211n12
Galpin v. Page (1873), 206n3
Ganin v. Smith and Wesson (2001), 120, 121, 219n20
Gary v. Smith and Wesson (2003), 111, 120
Geiger v. American Tobacco Co. (2000), 216n27
General Electric v. Joiner (1997), 68
Georgine v. Amchen Products, Inc. (1994), 73
Georgine v. Amchen Products, Inc. (1996), 73
Graham v. Richardson (1971), 48
Gratz v. Bollinger (2003), 153
Green v. American Tobacco Company (1962), 96
Grunow v. Valor Corp. of Florida (2000), 103

Guffanti v. National Surety Co. (1909), 26
Guillory v. American Tobacco Co. (2001), 216
Haines v. Liggett Group, Inc. (1993), 76
Hale v. Hale (1893), 26
Hall v. Cole (1973), 207n30
Hamilton v. Accu-tek (1999), 101, 119
Hamilton v. Beretta (2001), 62, 101, 102, 111, 121
Haney v. United States (2002), 115
Hansberry v. Lee (1940), 29, 30, 31, 33
Hansen v. American Tobacco Co. (1999), 216n27
Harrison v. Perea (1897), 207n30
Hartford Life Ins. Co. v. Ibs (1915), 207n27
Helling v. McKkinney (1993), 216n28
Henley v. Philip Morris, Inc. (1999), 76, 98
Henningsen v. Bloomfield Motors (1960), 210n56
Hicks v. TandM Jewelry, Inc. (1999), 103, 108
Hopper v. Wal-Mart Stores, Inc. (1999), 103
Hoyte v. Yum! Brands d/b/a KFC (2006), 142, 149
Hymowitz v. Eli Lilly (1989), 50
Ileto v. Glock (2002), 120, 121
Ileto v. Glock (2005), 102, 218n7
Ileto v. Glock (2006), 103
Insolia v. Philip Morris, Inc. (1998), 216n27
James v. Arms Technology, Inc. (2003), 219
Janssens v. Johns-Manville (1984), 63
Jenkins v. Raymark Industries, Inc. (1986), 211n5
Johns-Manville Sales Corp. v. Janssens (1984), 45, 72
Karges Furniture Co. v. Amalgamated Woodworkers Local Union (1905), 207n28
Kitchen v. K-Mart Corp. (1997), 103, 104
Knight v. Florida (1999), 226n1
Kumho Tire Company v. Carmichael (1999), 69
Kurtz v. Beatty (1826), 21
In re: Latex Gloves Products Liability Litigation (1997), 55
Lawrence v. Texas (2003), 153
Lawson v. Beretta (2004), 102, 219n20
Lee v. Hansberry (1939), 29, 3
Lemongello and McGuire v. Will Jewelry and Loan (2003), 103
Lexecon Inc. v. Milberg Weiss Bershad Hynes and Lerach (1998), 38
Liberty v. District of Columbia Police and Firemen's Retirement and Relief Board (1982), 224n28
Liebeck v. McDonald's Restaurants, P.T.S., Inc. (1995), 205n20
Lieber v. Consumer Empowerment BV (2004), 212n22

Liggett Group, Inc. v. Engle (2003), 87

Lightle v. Kirby (1937), 26

Linn v. Radio Center Delicatessen, Inc. (1939), 124

Loe v. Lenhardt (1961), 37

Lowe v. R.J. Reynolds Tobacco Company (1954), 96

Lucier v. Philip Morris (2003), 79, 99

Lyon v. Premo Pharmaceutical Labs, Inc. (1979), 50

Mahoney v. R.J. Reynolds Tobacco Co. (2001), 216n27

Mathieu v. Fabrica D'Armi Pietro Beretta SPA and Beretta U.S.A. (2000), 102, 119

Mayhew v. Mattel, Inc. (2007), 204n7

McCulloch v. Velez (2004), 210n54

McDarby v. Merck (2008), 211n16

McLaughlin v. American Company (2008), 90, 100

Mekdeci v. Merrell National Laboratories (1983), 51

Merck v. Ernst (2008), 5, 204n8, 211n16

In re: Meridia Products Liability Litigation (2002), 211n14

Merrill v. Navegar, Inc. (2001), 102, 121

MGM Studios, Inc. v. Grokster (2005), 57

Mills v. Electric Auto-Lite Co. (1970), 207n30

Missouri ex. rel. Gaines v. Canada (1938), 208n41

Molski v. Gleich (2003), 212n24

Monroe ex. rel. Monroe (2007), 204n7

Moore v. American Tobacco Company (1994), 79, 97

Morial v. Smith and Wesson Corp. (1998), 106, 107, 119

NAACP v. A.A. Arms (2003), 111, 112, 120, 121

NAACP v. Alabama (1958), 34

New York v. Sturm, Ruger and Co., Inc. (2001), 120

New York v. Sturm, Ruger and Company, Inc. (2003), 219n20

New York City v. A-1 Jewelry and Pawn, Inc. (2007), 122

New York City v. Beretta (2004), 111, 120, 219n21

New York City v. Beretta (2005), 114

New York City v. Beretta (2006), 114

New York City v. Beretta USA (2008), 114, 122

New York City v. Bob Moates' Sport Shop, Inc. (2008), 115, 122

New York State Restaurant Association v. New York City Board of Health (2007a), 143

New York State Restaurant Association v. New York City Board of Health (2007b), 143

In re: Northern District of California Dalkon Shield IUD Products Liability Litigation (1981), 54

In re: Northern District of California Dalkon Shield IUD Products Liability Litigation (1982), 54

Nunnally v. R.J. Reynolds (2000), 76, 98

Ontario, The Minister of Health and Long Term Care v. Imperial Tobacco, Ltd. (2000), 175

Ortiz v. Fibreboard Corporation (1999), 42, 44, 47, 73, 91, 205n2, 232n9

Parker v. District of Columbia (2004), 116

Parker v. District of Columbia (2007), 116

In re: Paxil Products Liability Litigation (2003), 53

Pelman v. McDonald's (2003a), 224n32

Pelman v. McDonald's (2003b), 135, 148, 224

Pelman v. McDonald's (2003c), 134, 136

Pelman v. McDonald's (2005a), 136, 149

Pelman v. McDonald's (2005b), 136, 195

Penelas v. Arms Technology (2001), 219

In re: Phenylpropanolamine (PPA) Products Liability Litigation (2001), 211n14

Philadelphia v. Beretta (2000), 110, 120

Philadelphia v. Beretta (2002), 110, 121

Philip Morris, Inc. v. Angeletti (2000), 216n27

Philip Morris v. French (2004), 85

Philip Morris USA Inc. v. Williams (2004), 77

Philip Morris USA v. Williams (2007a), 68, 100

Philip Morris USA v. Williams (2007b), 77, 213n43

Phillips Petroleum Co. v. Shutts (1985), 206n3

Pickett v. Walsh (1906), 207n28

Price v. Philip Morris (2003a), 88, 99

Price v. Philip Morris (2003b), 81

Price v. Philip Morris (2005), 90, 99

In re: Propulsid Products Liability Litigation (2000), 53

Reed v. Philip Morris, Inc. (1999), 216n27

In re: Rezulin Products Liability Litigation (2000), 53

In re: Rhone-Poulenc Rorer, Inc. (1995), 156

In re: Richardson-Merrell, Inc. "Bendectin" Products Liability Litigation (1985), 51, 211n11

Rissman v. Target Sports, Inc. (2000), 103

Roe v. Wade (1973), 48

Roper v. Simmons (2005), 153, 233n15

Rosado v. Wyman (1970), 48

Rosenfeld v. A.H. Robins Co., Inc. (1978), 54

Santa Clara County v. Southern Pacific Railroad Company (1886), 208n42

Sarjent v. Fisher-Price, Inc. (2007), 204n7

Schuehle v. Reiman (1881), 26

Schwab v. Philip Morris USA, Inc. (2006), 100

Scott v. American Tobacco Company (2004), 87

Scott v. American Tobacco Company (2007), 216n33

Service Employees Int'l Union Health and Welfare Fund v. Philip Morris Incorporated (1990), 230n57

In re: Serzone Products Liability Litigation (2002), 211n15

Shelley v. Kramer (1948), 33, 208n37, 208n41

Shoukry v. Fisher-Price, Inc. (2007), 204n7

In re: Silica Products Liability Litigation (2005), 56

In re: Silicone Gel Breast Implants Products Liability Litigation (1992), 55

In re: Simon II Litigation (2002a), 90, 217n43

In re: Simon II Litigation (2002b), 91

In re: Simon II Litigation (2005), 91

In re: Simon II Litigation (2006), 91

Sindell v. Abbott Laboratories (1980), 50

Small v. Lorillard Tobacco Co. (1998), 216n27

Smith v. Allwright (1944), 208n41

Smith v. Brown and Williamson Tobacco Corp (1997), 216n27

Smith v. Bryco Arms (2001), 102, 119, 121

Smith v. Lockheed Propulsion Co. (1967), 37

Smith v. Swormstedt (1854), 23, 24, 25, 207n23, 207n27

Smith and Wesson v. Gary (2007), 122, 220n33

Snyder v. Harris (1969), 210n54

Sprague v. Ticonic National Bank (1939), 207n54

In re: St. Jude Medical, Inc., Silzone Heart Valves Products Liability Litigation (2001), 55

St. Louis v. Cernicek (2004), 219n20

In re: Starlink Corn Products Liability Litigation (2002), 129, 130, 148

In re: Starlink Corn Products Liability Litigation (2003), 130, 148

Staron v. McDonald's (1995), 223

State Farm Fire and Casualty Co. v. Tashire (1967), 37

State Farm Insurance v. Preece (2003), 214n5

State Farm Insurance v. Preece (2004), 77

State Farm Mutual Automobile Insurance Company v. Campbell (2003), 68

Strawbridge v. Curtiss (1806), 62

Sturm, Ruger and Company v. Day (1979), 217n1

Sturm, Ruger and Company, Inc. v. Atlanta (2002), 121, 219n20

In re: Sulzer Orthopedics, Inc., Hip Prosthesis and Knee Prosthesis Products Liability Litigation (2001), 55

Supreme Council of the Royal Arcanum v. Green (1915), 207n27

Supreme Tribe of Ben-Hur v. Cauble (1921), 27, 207n27

Sutowski v. Eli Lilly and Company (1998), 50

Sweatt v. Painter (1950), 208n41

Tellabs v. Makor (2007), 57

Thompson v. American Tobacco Co. (1999), 216n27

Tijerina v. Philip Morris Inc. (1996), 216n27

Tilley v. TJX Companies (2003a), 58

Tilley v. TJX Companies (2003b), 57, 58

In re: Tobacco Litigation (Medical Monitoring Cases) (2004), 87

Tomberlin v. Adolph Coors Co., et al. (2006), 226n45

Tomplait v. Combustion Engineering, Inc. (1968), 45, 72

Toole v. Richardson-Merrell (1967), 59

Trustees v. Greenough (1881), 27

United Mine Workers v. Coronado Coal (1922), 27, 207n27

United Seniors Association v. Philip Morris (2007), 92, 100

United States v. Carolene Products (1938), 209n43

United States v. Emerson (1999), 115

United States v. Emerson (2001), 115

United States v. Equitable Trust Co. (1931), 207n30

United States v. Kilgus (1978), 52

United States v. Philip Morris (2000), 83

United States v. Philip Morris (2004a), 83, 213n3

United States v. Philip Morris (2004b), 215n22

United States v. Philip Morris (2005), 83

United States v. Philip Morris (2006a), 84, 99

United States v. Philip Morris (2006b), 84

Van Dusen v. Barrack (1964), 37

In re: Vioxx Marketing, Sales Practices and Products Liability Litigation (2007), 53

In re: Vioxx Products Litigation (2005), 53

Walls v. American Tobacco Co. (2000),
    216n27
*In re: Welding Rod Products Liability
    Litigation* (2004), 56
West v. Randall (1820), 20, 21, 199
White v. Smith and Wesson (2000), 111
White et al. v. Mattel Inc. (2007), 204n7
Whiteley v. Raybestos-Manhattan Inc.
    (2000), 76, 98

*Williams-Branch ex rel. Estate of Williams v.
    Philip Morris, Inc.* (1999), 76, 98, 195
Wolff v. McDonnell (1974), 48
*Wood River Area Dev. Corp. v. Germania Fed.
    Sav. and Loan Ass'n* (1990), 208n40
Wright v. Brooke Group, Ltd. (2002), 216n35
Zahn v. International Paper Co. (1973),
    210n54
In re: Zyprexa Products (2004), 211n15

Renisa Mawani
Colonial Proximities: Crossracial Encounters and Juridical Truths in British Columbia, 1871-1921 (2009)

Catherine E. Bell and Robert K. Paterson (eds.)
Protection of First Nations Cultural Heritage: Laws, Policy, and Reform (2008)

Hamar Foster, Benjamin L. Berger, and A.R. Buck (eds.)
The Grand Experiment: Law and Legal Culture in British Settler Societies (2008)

Richard J. Moon (ed.)
Law and Religious Pluralism in Canada (2008)

Catherine E. Bell and Val Napoleon (eds.)
First Nations Cultural Heritage and Law: Case Studies, Voices, and Perspectives (2008)

Douglas C. Harris
Landing Native Fisheries: Indian Reserves and Fishing Rights in British Columbia, 1849-1925 (2008)

Peggy J. Blair
Lament for a First Nation: The Williams Treaties in Southern Ontario (2008)

Lori G. Beaman
Defining Harm: Religious Freedom and the Limits of the Law (2007)

Stephen Tierney (ed.)
Multiculturalism and the Canadian Constitution (2007)

Julie Macfarlane
The New Lawyer: How Settlement Is Transforming the Practice of Law (2007)

Kimberley White
Negotiating Responsibility: Law, Murder, and States of Mind (2007)

Dawn Moore
Criminal Artefacts: Governing Drugs and Users (2007)

Hamar Foster, Heather Raven, and Jeremy Webber (eds.)
Let Right Be Done: Aboriginal Title, the Calder Case, and the Future of Indigenous Rights (2007)

Dorothy E. Chunn, Susan B. Boyd, and Hester Lessard (eds.)
Reaction and Resistance: Feminism, Law, and Social Change (2007)

Margot Young, Susan B. Boyd, Gwen Brodsky, and Shelagh Day (eds.)
Poverty: Rights, Social Citizenship, and Legal Activism (2007)

Rosanna L. Langer
Defining Rights and Wrongs: Bureaucracy, Human Rights, and Public Accountability (2007)

C.L. Ostberg and Matthew E. Wetstein
Attitudinal Decision Making in the Supreme Court of Canada (2007)

Chris Clarkson
Domestic Reforms: Political Visions and Family Regulation in British Columbia, 1862-1940 (2007)

Jean McKenzie Leiper
Bar Codes: Women in the Legal Profession (2006)

Gerald Baier
Courts and Federalism: Judicial Doctrine in the United States, Australia, and Canada (2006)

Avigail Eisenberg (ed.)
Diversity and Equality: The Changing Framework of Freedom in Canada (2006)

Randy K. Lippert
Sanctuary, Sovereignty, Sacrifice: Canadian Sanctuary Incidents, Power, and Law (2005)

James B. Kelly
Governing with the Charter: Legislative and Judicial Activism and Framers' Intent (2005)

Dianne Pothier and Richard Devlin (eds.)
Critical Disability Theory: Essays in Philosophy, Politics, Policy, and Law (2005)

Susan G. Drummond
Mapping Marriage Law in Spanish Gitano Communities (2005)

Louis A. Knafla and Jonathan Swainger (eds.)
Laws and Societies in the Canadian Prairie West, 1670-1940 (2005)

Ikechi Mgbeoji
Global Biopiracy: Patents, Plants, and Indigenous Knowledge (2005)

Florian Sauvageau, David Schneiderman, and David Taras,
with Ruth Klinkhammer and Pierre Trudel
The Last Word: Media Coverage of the Supreme Court of Canada (2005)

Gerald Kernerman
Multicultural Nationalism: Civilizing Difference, Constituting Community (2005)

Pamela A. Jordan
Defending Rights in Russia: Lawyers, the State, and Legal Reform in the Post-Soviet Era (2005)

Anna Pratt
Securing Borders: Detention and Deportation in Canada (2005)

Kirsten Johnson Kramar
Unwilling Mothers, Unwanted Babies: Infanticide in Canada (2005)

W.A. Bogart
Good Government? Good Citizens? Courts, Politics, and Markets in a Changing Canada (2005)

Catherine Dauvergne
Humanitarianism, Identity, and Nation: Migration Laws in Canada and Australia (2005)

Michael Lee Ross
First Nations Sacred Sites in Canada's Courts (2005)

Andrew Woolford
Between Justice and Certainty: Treaty Making in British Columbia (2005)

John McLaren, Andrew Buck, and Nancy Wright (eds.)
Despotic Dominion: Property Rights in British Settler Societies (2004)

Georges Campeau
From UI to EI: Waging War on the Welfare State (2004)

Alvin J. Esau
The Courts and the Colonies: The Litigation of Hutterite Church Disputes (2004)

Christopher N. Kendall
Gay Male Pornography: An Issue of Sex Discrimination (2004)

Roy B. Flemming
Tournament of Appeals: Granting Judicial Review in Canada (2004)

Constance Backhouse and Nancy L. Backhouse
The Heiress vs the Establishment: Mrs. Campbell's Campaign for Legal Justice (2004)

Christopher P. Manfredi
Feminist Activism in the Supreme Court: Legal Mobilization and the Women's Legal Education and Action Fund (2004)

Annalise Acorn
Compulsory Compassion: A Critique of Restorative Justice (2004)

Jonathan Swainger and Constance Backhouse (eds.)
People and Place: Historical Influences on Legal Culture (2003)

Jim Phillips and Rosemary Gartner
Murdering Holiness: The Trials of Franz Creffield and George Mitchell (2003)

David R. Boyd
Unnatural Law: Rethinking Canadian Environmental Law and Policy (2003)

Ikechi Mgbeoji
Collective Insecurity: The Liberian Crisis, Unilateralism, and Global Order (2003)

Rebecca Johnson
Taxing Choices: The Intersection of Class, Gender, Parenthood, and the Law (2002)

John McLaren, Robert Menzies, and Dorothy E. Chunn (eds.)
Regulating Lives: Historical Essays on the State, Society, the Individual, and the Law (2002)

Joan Brockman
Gender in the Legal Profession: Fitting or Breaking the Mould (2001)

Printed and bound in Canada by Friesens

Set in Stone by Artegraphica Design Co. Ltd.

Copy editor and proofreader: Stacy Belden

ENVIRONMENTAL BENEFITS STATEMENT

UBC Press saved the following resources by printing the pages of this book on chlorine free paper made with 100% post-consumer waste.

TREES	WATER	ENERGY	SOLID WASTE	GREENHOUSE GASES
9	**3,238**	**6**	**416**	**780**
FULLY GROWN	GALLONS	MILLION BTUs	POUNDS	POUNDS

Calculations based on research by Environmental Defense and the Paper Task Force.
Manufactured at Friesens Corporation